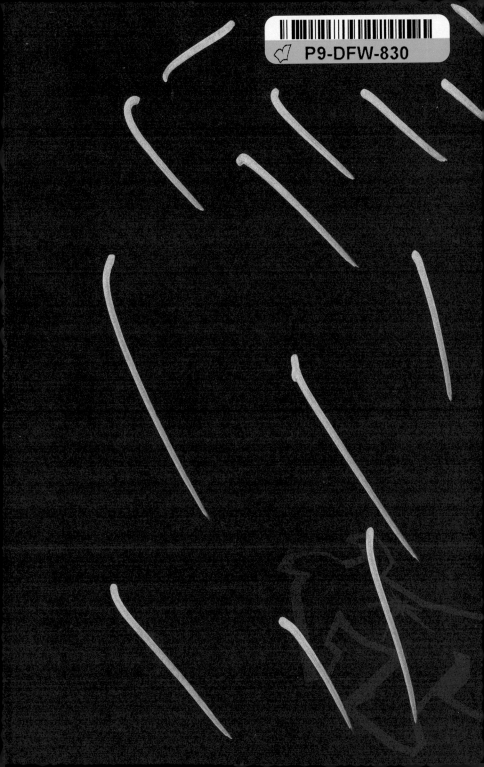

THE EXECUTOR

VERTIGO CRIME

WRITER
JON EVANS

ART
ANDREA MUTTI

LETTERS
CLEM ROBINS

THE
EXECUTOR

Karen Berger SVP – Executive Editor
Will Dennis Editor
Mark Doyle Associate Editor
Robbin Brosterman Design Director – Books
Louis Prandi Art Director

DC COMICS
Paul Levitz President & Publisher
Richard Bruning SVP – Creative Director
Patrick Caldon EVP – Finance & Operations
Amy Genkins SVP – Business & Legal Affairs
Jim Lee Editorial Director – WildStorm
Gregory Noveck SVP – Creative Affairs
Steve Rotterdam SVP – Sales & Marketing
Cheryl Rubin SVP – Brand Management

**THE EXECUTOR
VERTIGO CRIME**

HC ISBN: 978-1-4012-1385-5 SC ISBN: 978-1-4012-2621-7

SUSTAINABLE
FORESTRY
INITIATIVE

Certified Chain of Custody
60% Certified Fiber Sourcing and
40% Post-Consumer Recycled
www.sfiprogram.org

NSF-SFICOC-C0001801

This label applies to the text stock.

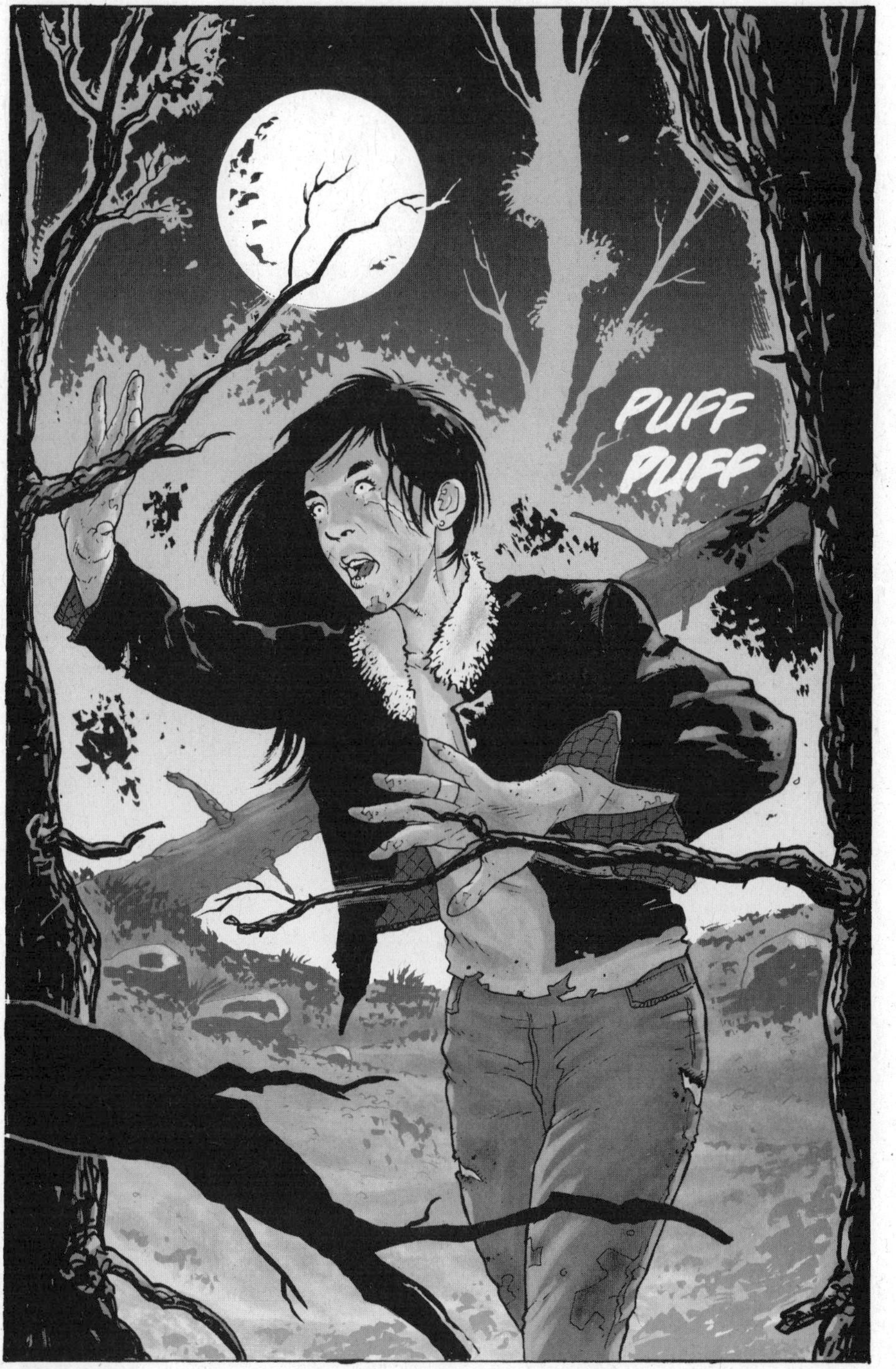
PUFF
PUFF

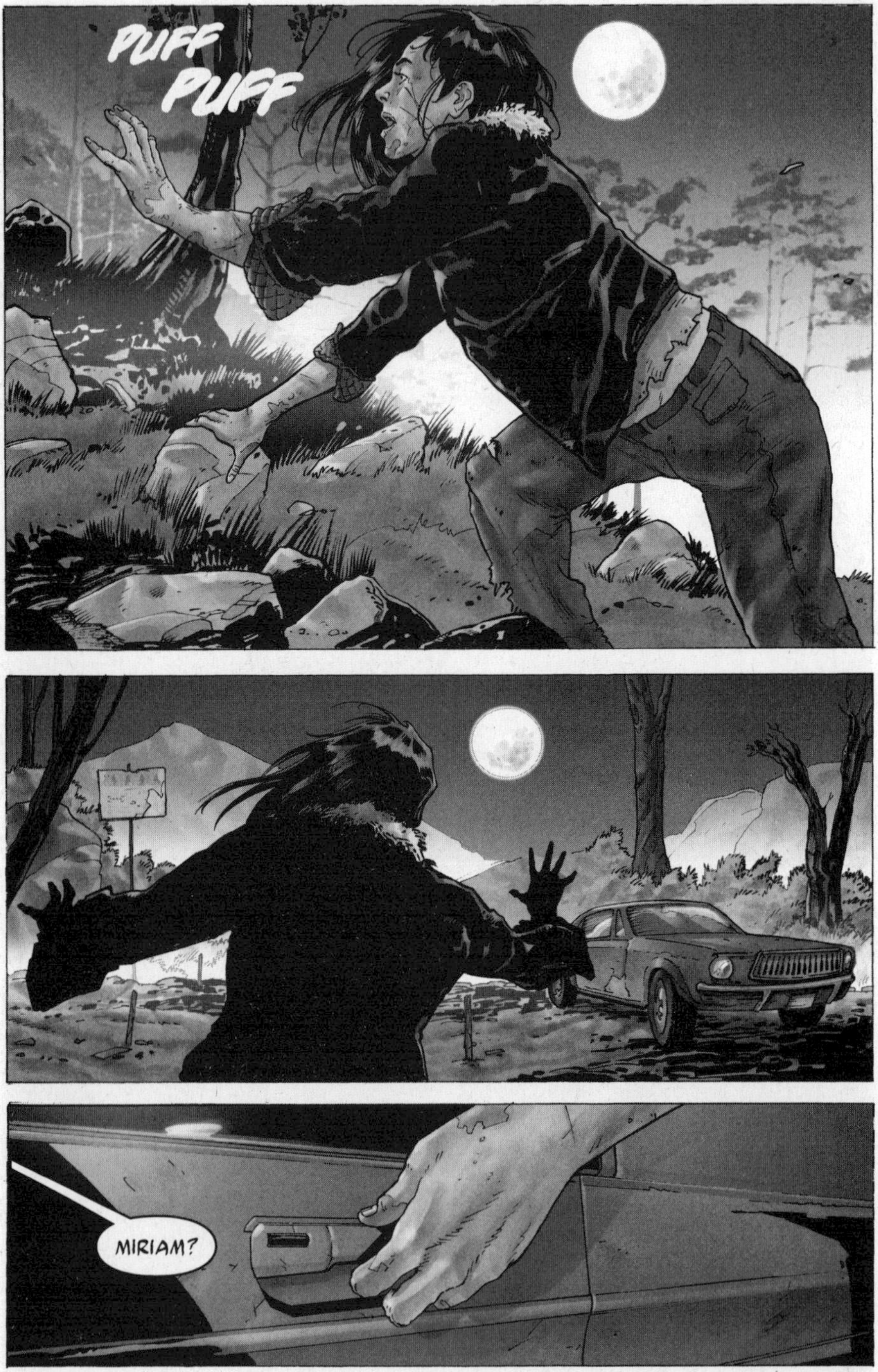
PUFF
PUFF
MIRIAM?

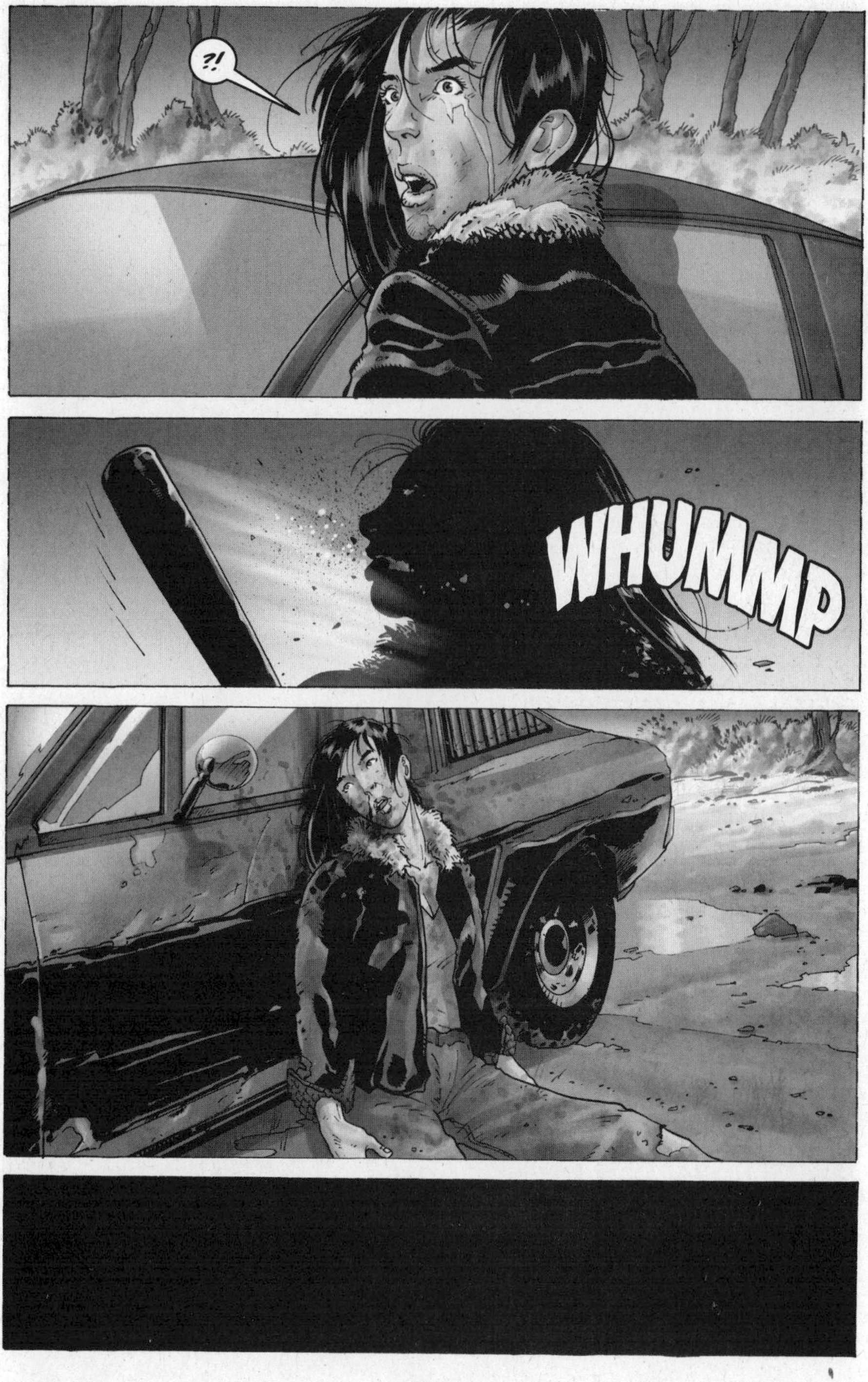
?!
WHUMMP

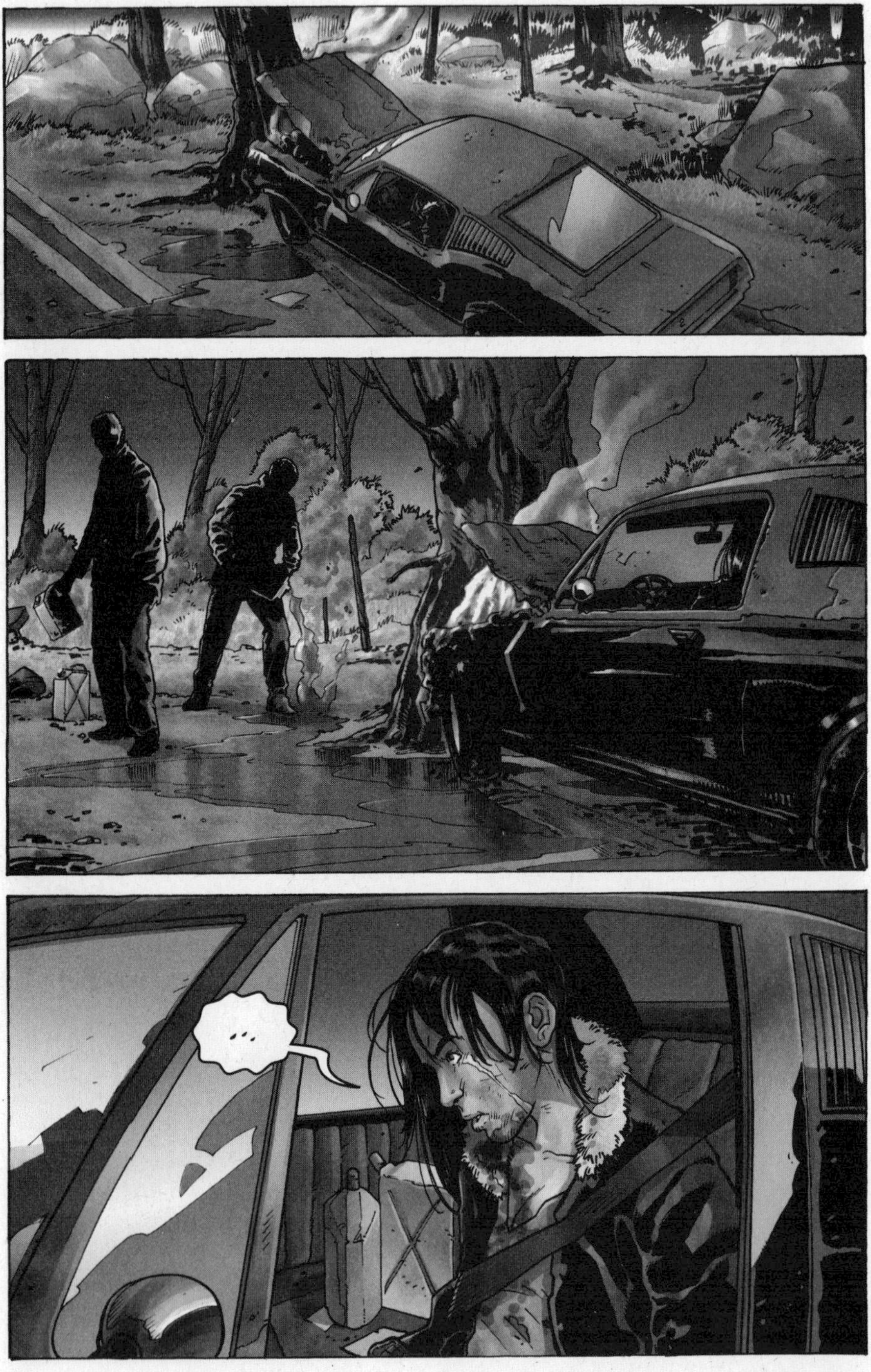
...

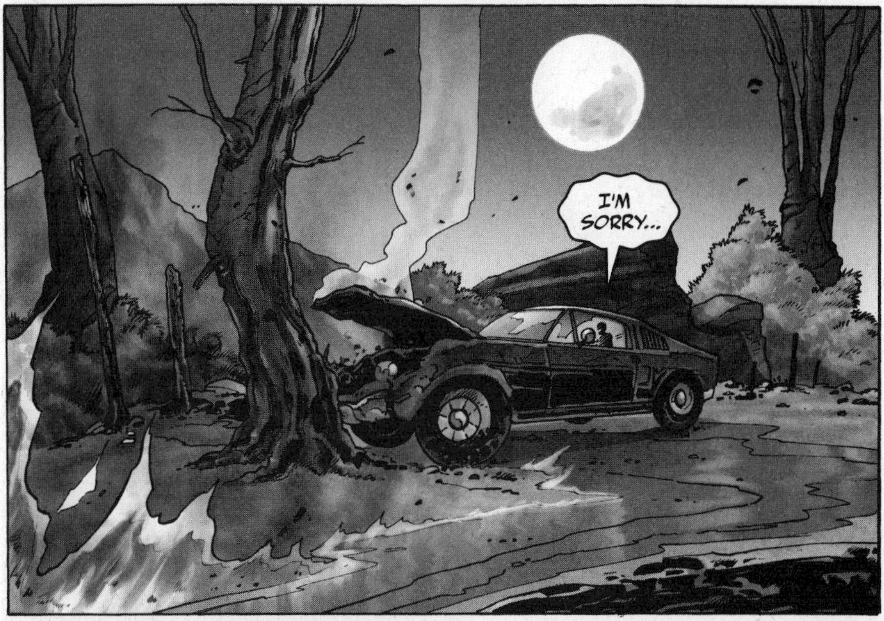
I'M SORRY...

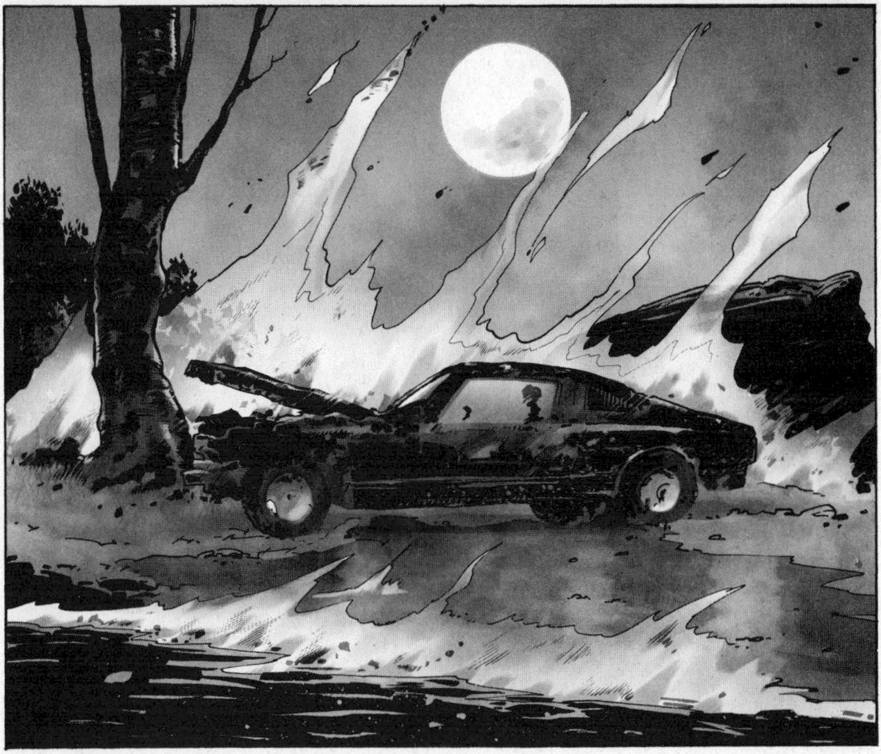

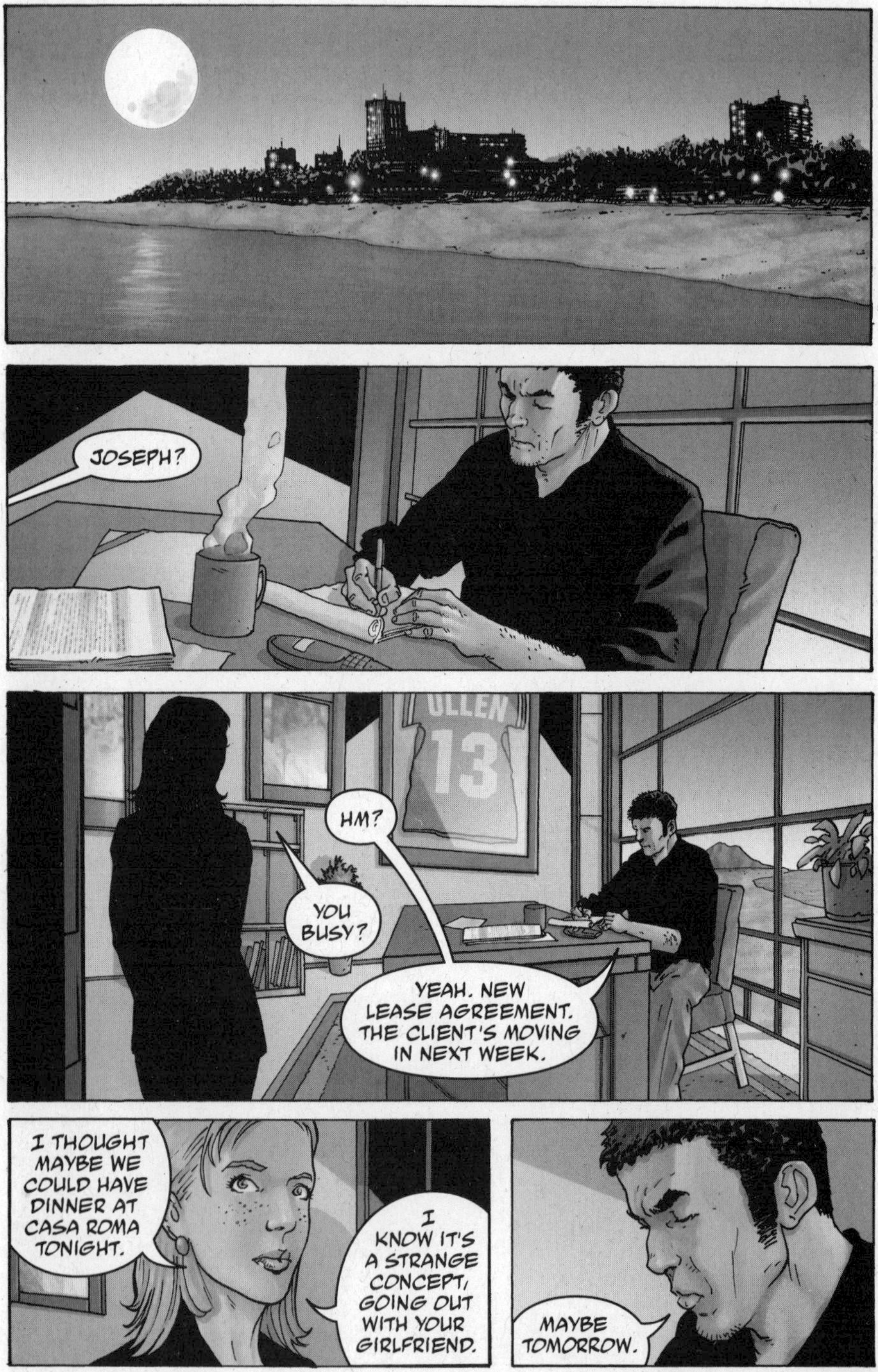
JOSEPH?
ULLEN
13
YOU BUSY?
HM?
YEAH. NEW LEASE AGREEMENT. THE CLIENT'S MOVING IN NEXT WEEK.
I THOUGHT MAYBE WE COULD HAVE DINNER AT CASA ROMA TONIGHT.
I KNOW IT'S A STRANGE CONCEPT, GOING OUT WITH YOUR GIRLFRIEND.
MAYBE TOMORROW.

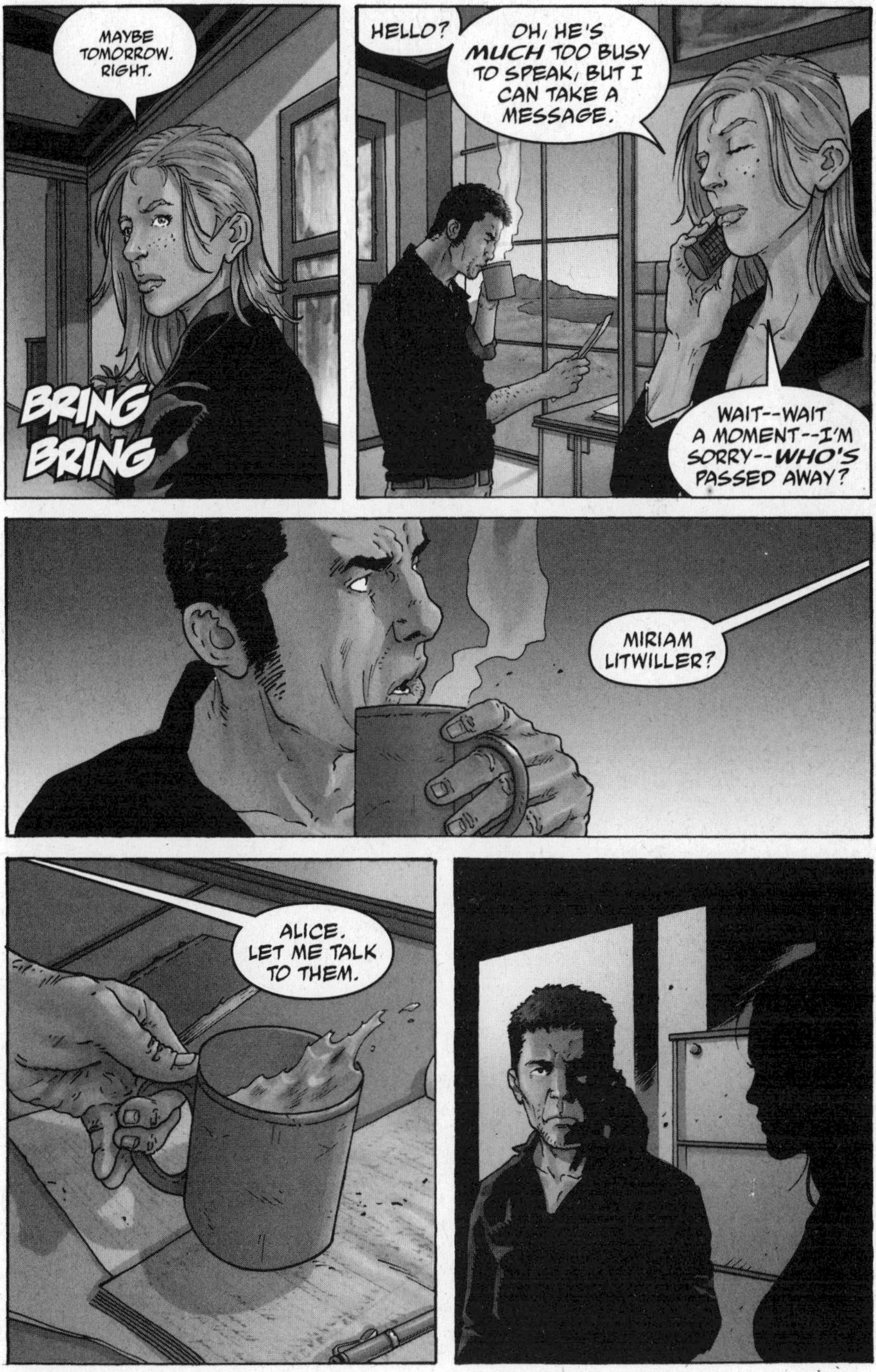
MAYBE TOMORROW. RIGHT.
BRING BRING
HELLO?
OH, HE'S MUCH TOO BUSY TO SPEAK, BUT I CAN TAKE A MESSAGE.
WAIT--WAIT A MOMENT--I'M SORRY--WHO'S PASSED AWAY?
MIRIAM LITWILLER?
ALICE. LET ME TALK TO THEM.

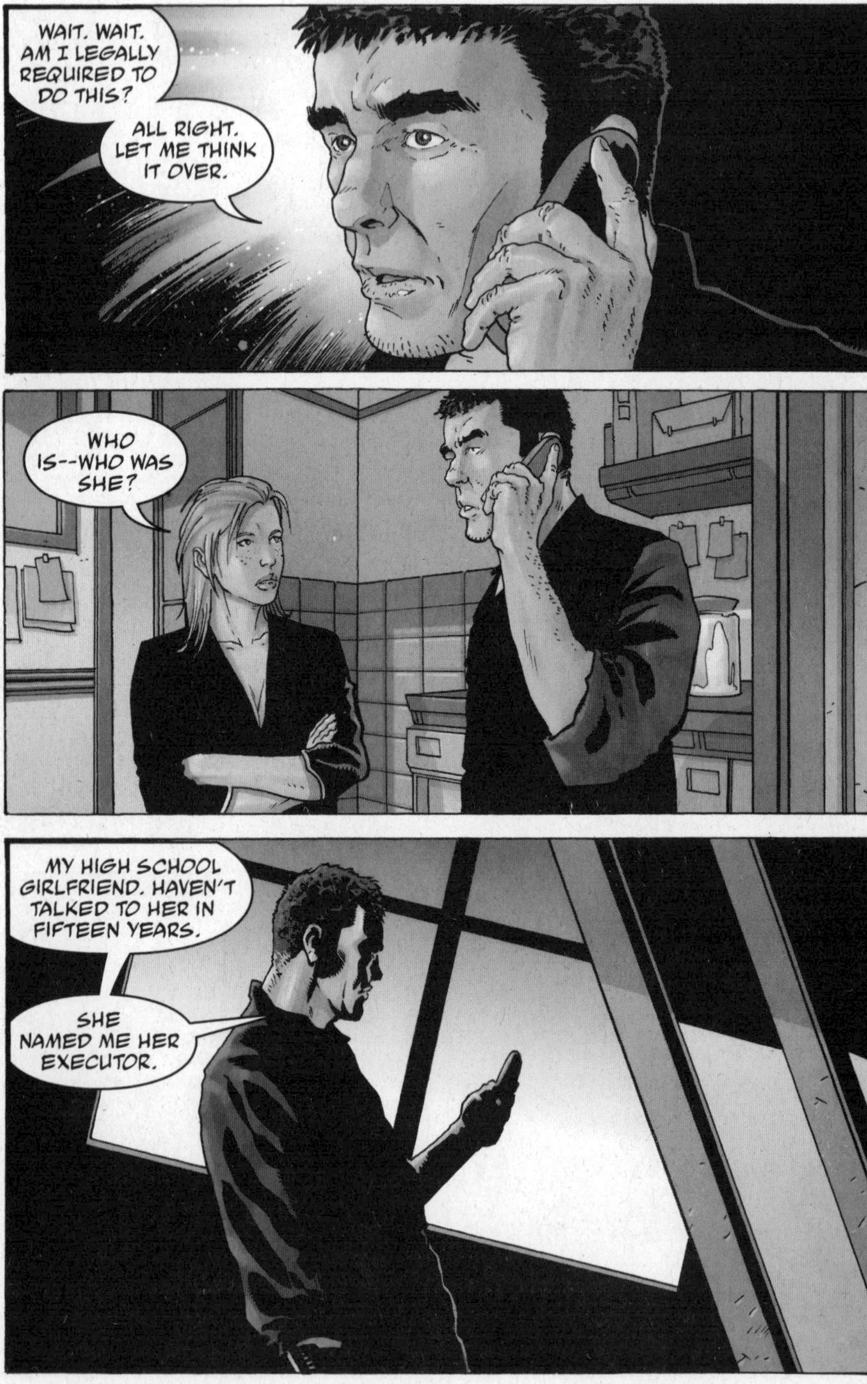
WAIT. WAIT. AM I LEGALLY REQUIRED TO DO THIS?
ALL RIGHT. LET ME THINK IT OVER.
WHO IS--WHO WAS SHE?
MY HIGH SCHOOL GIRLFRIEND. HAVEN'T TALKED TO HER IN FIFTEEN YEARS.
SHE NAMED ME HER EXECUTOR.

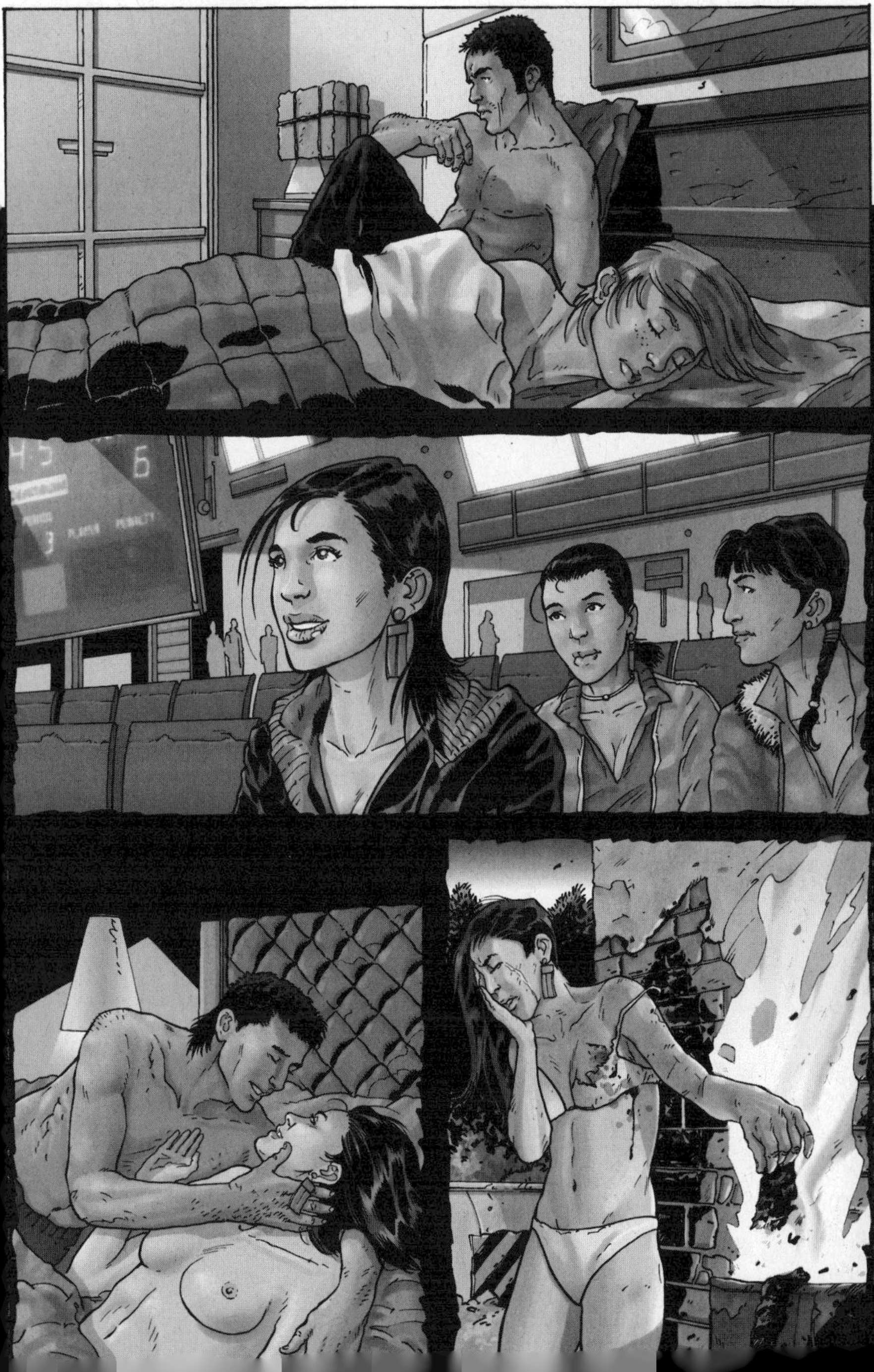

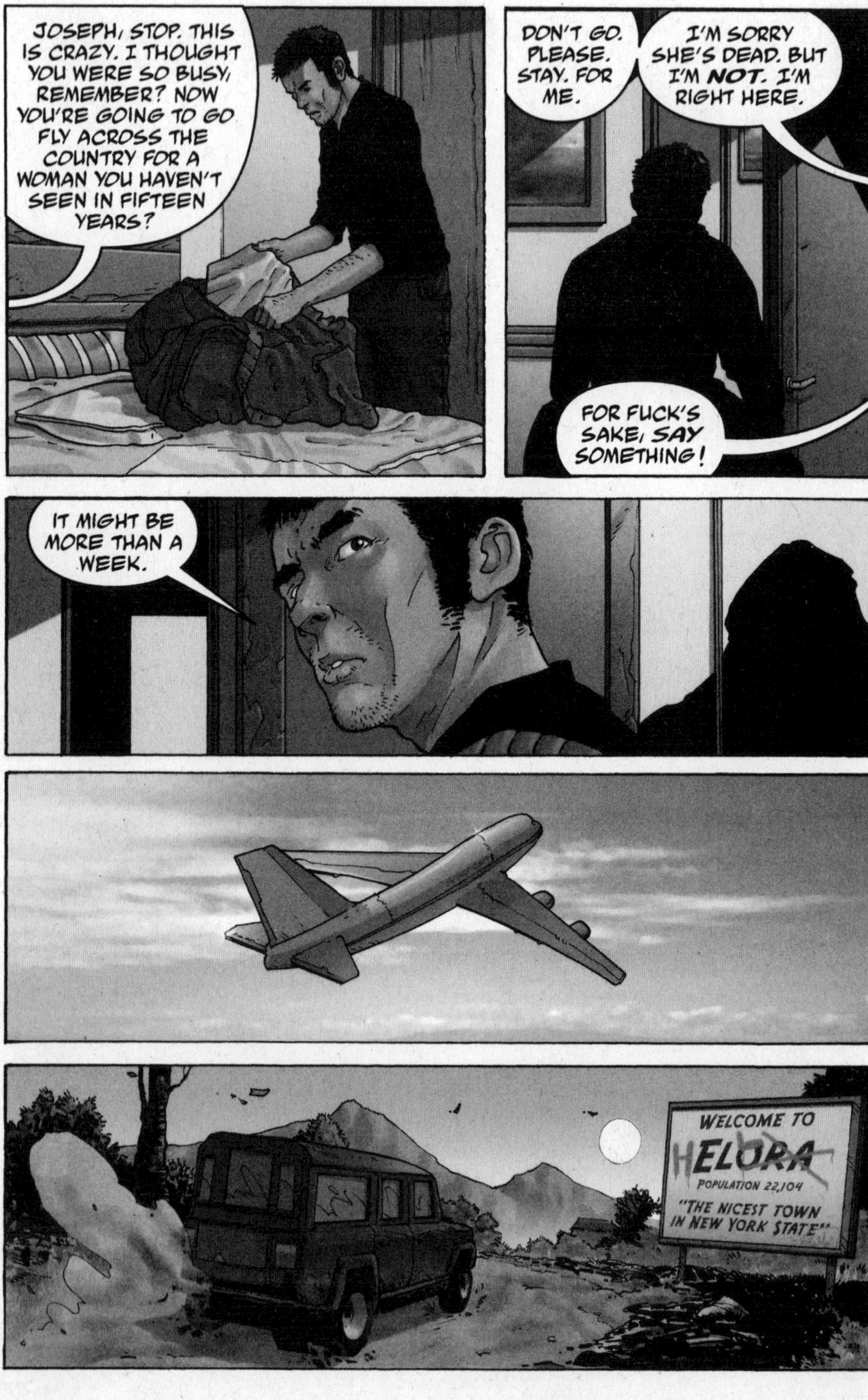
JOSEPH, STOP. THIS IS CRAZY. I THOUGHT YOU WERE SO BUSY, REMEMBER? NOW YOU'RE GOING TO GO FLY ACROSS THE COUNTRY FOR A WOMAN YOU HAVEN'T SEEN IN FIFTEEN YEARS?
DON'T GO. PLEASE. STAY. FOR ME.
I'M SORRY SHE'S DEAD. BUT I'M NOT. I'M RIGHT HERE.
FOR FUCK'S SAKE, SAY SOMETHING!
IT MIGHT BE MORE THAN A WEEK.
WELCOME TO
HELORA
POPULATION 22,104
"THE NICEST TOWN IN NEW YORK STATE"

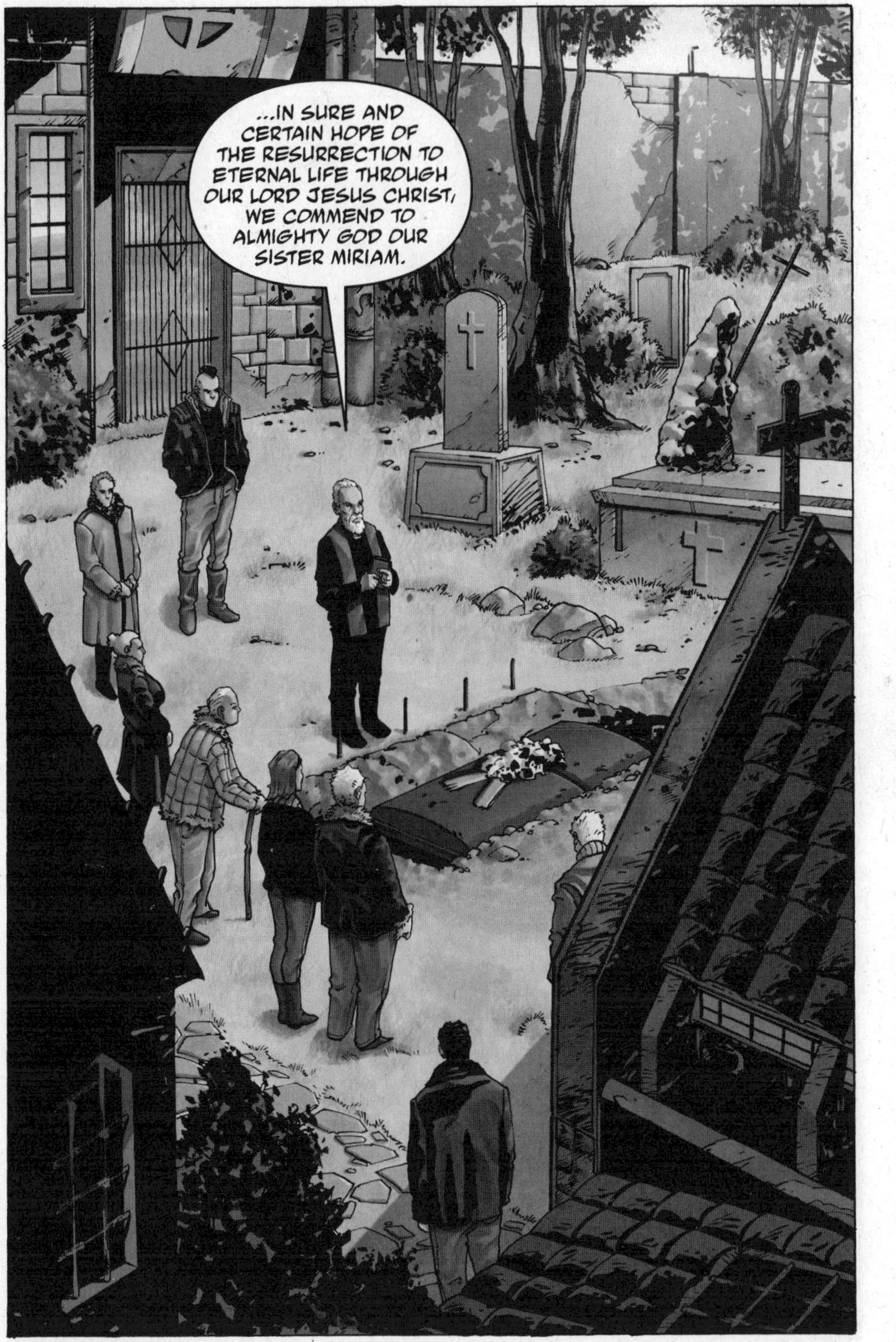
...IN SURE AND CERTAIN HOPE OF THE RESURRECTION TO ETERNAL LIFE THROUGH OUR LORD JESUS CHRIST, WE COMMEND TO ALMIGHTY GOD OUR SISTER MIRIAM.

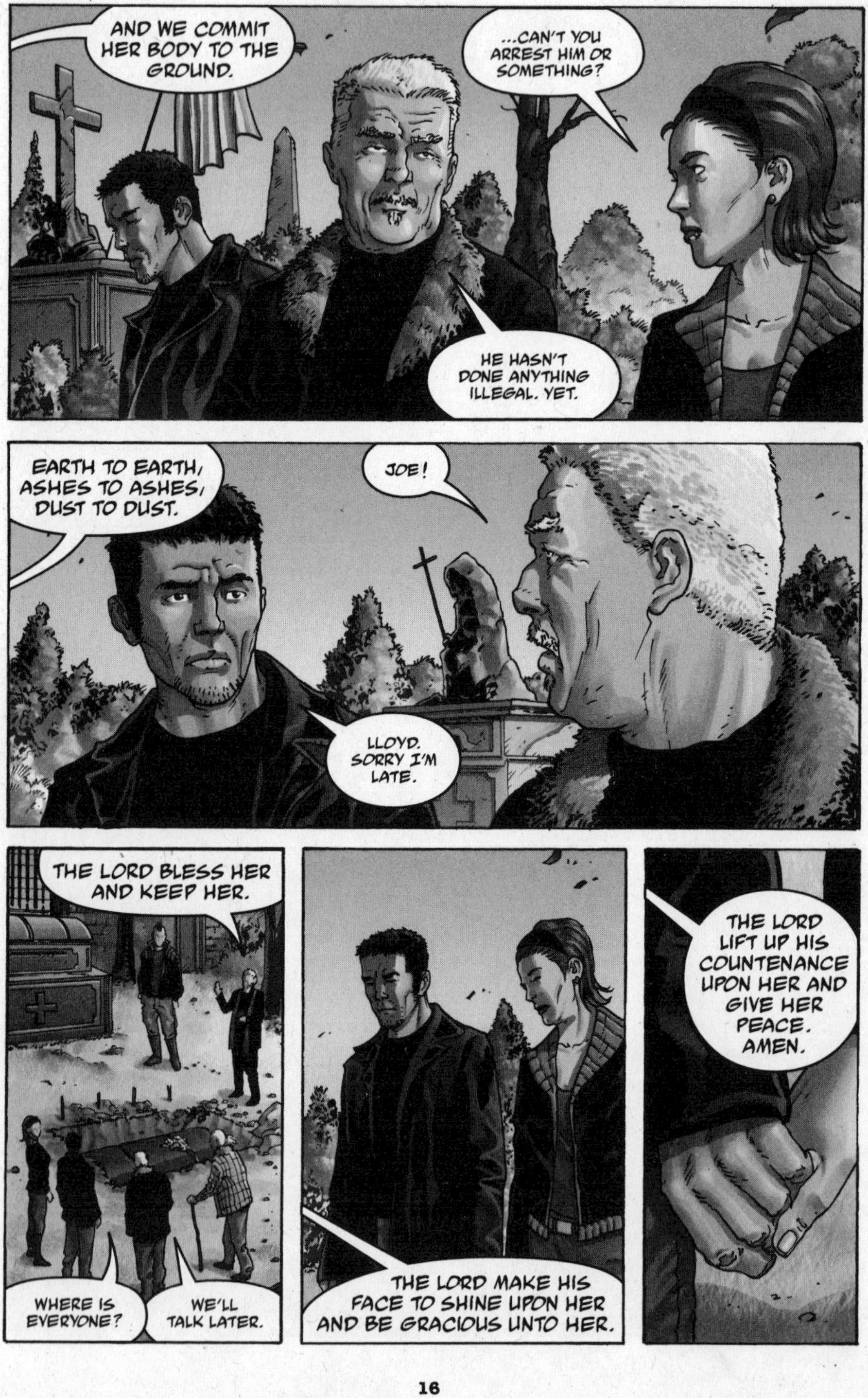
AND WE COMMIT HER BODY TO THE GROUND.
...CAN'T YOU ARREST HIM OR SOMETHING?
HE HASN'T DONE ANYTHING ILLEGAL. YET.
EARTH TO EARTH, ASHES TO ASHES, DUST TO DUST.
JOE!
LLOYD. SORRY I'M LATE.
THE LORD BLESS HER AND KEEP HER.
WHERE IS EVERYONE?
WE'LL TALK LATER.
THE LORD MAKE HIS FACE TO SHINE UPON HER AND BE GRACIOUS UNTO HER.
THE LORD LIFT UP HIS COUNTENANCE UPON HER AND GIVE HER PEACE. AMEN.

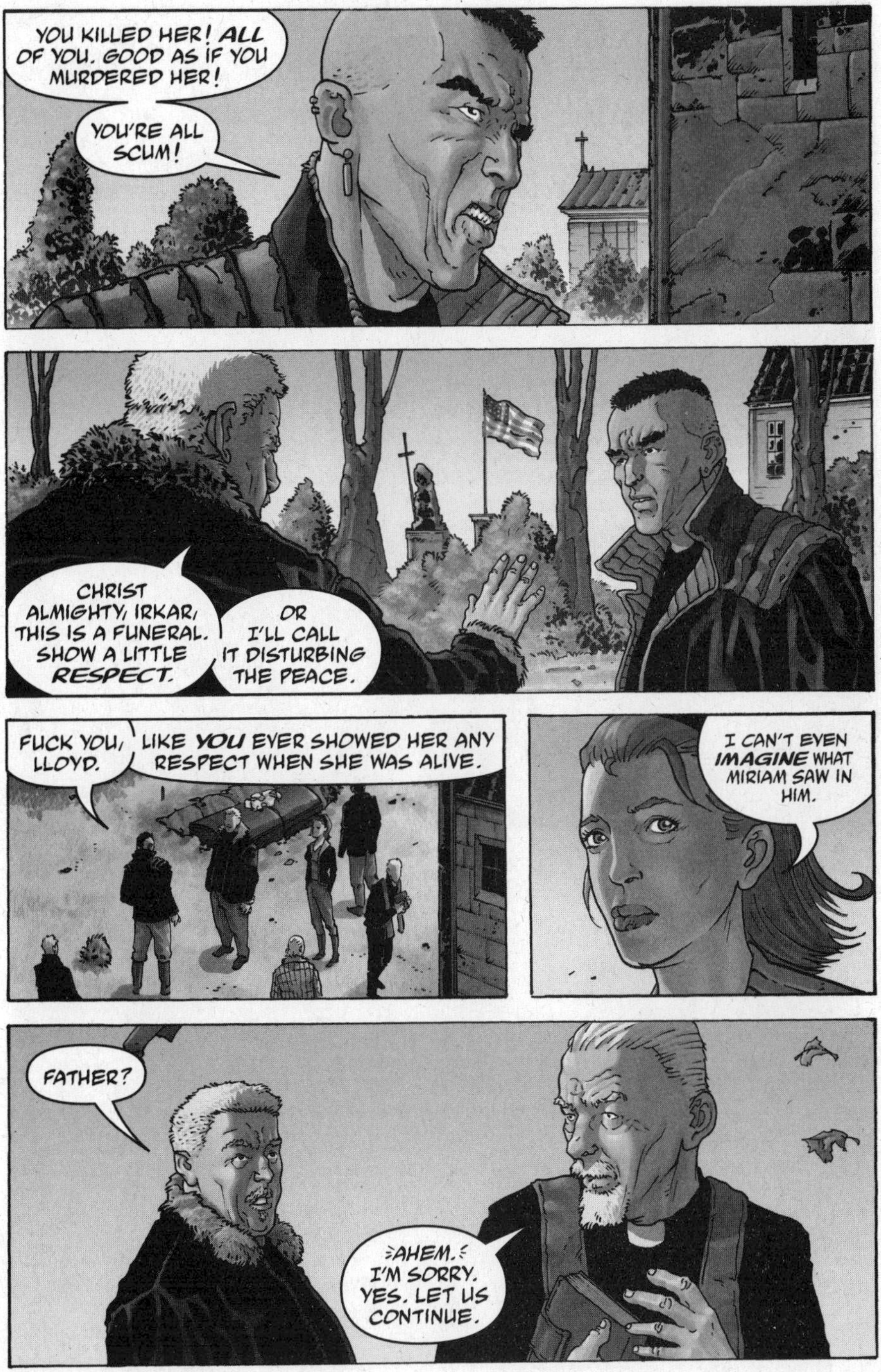
YOU KILLED HER! ALL OF YOU. GOOD AS IF YOU MURDERED HER!
YOU'RE ALL SCUM!
CHRIST ALMIGHTY, IRKAR, THIS IS A FUNERAL. SHOW A LITTLE RESPECT.
OR I'LL CALL IT DISTURBING THE PEACE.
FUCK YOU, LLOYD.
LIKE YOU EVER SHOWED HER ANY RESPECT WHEN SHE WAS ALIVE.
I CAN'T EVEN IMAGINE WHAT MIRIAM SAW IN HIM.
FATHER?
AHEM. I'M SORRY. YES. LET US CONTINUE.

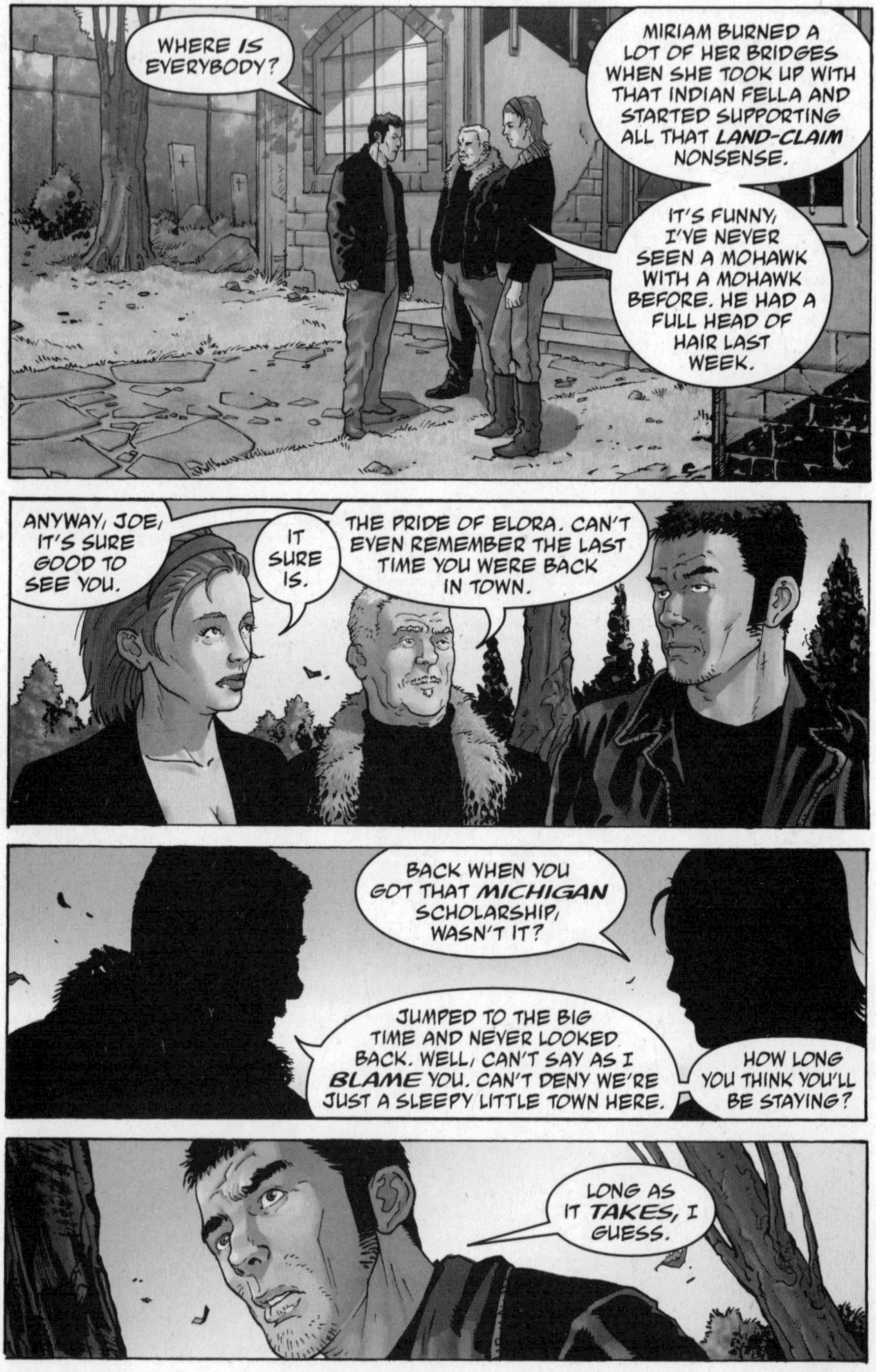
WHERE IS EVERYBODY?
MIRIAM BURNED A LOT OF HER BRIDGES WHEN SHE TOOK UP WITH THAT INDIAN FELLA AND STARTED SUPPORTING ALL THAT LAND-CLAIM NONSENSE.
IT'S FUNNY, I'VE NEVER SEEN A MOHAWK WITH A MOHAWK BEFORE. HE HAD A FULL HEAD OF HAIR LAST WEEK.
ANYWAY, JOE, IT'S SURE GOOD TO SEE YOU.
IT SURE IS.
THE PRIDE OF ELORA. CAN'T EVEN REMEMBER THE LAST TIME YOU WERE BACK IN TOWN.
BACK WHEN YOU GOT THAT MICHIGAN SCHOLARSHIP, WASN'T IT?
JUMPED TO THE BIG TIME AND NEVER LOOKED BACK. WELL, CAN'T SAY AS I BLAME YOU. CAN'T DENY WE'RE JUST A SLEEPY LITTLE TOWN HERE.
HOW LONG YOU THINK YOU'LL BE STAYING?
LONG AS IT TAKES, I GUESS.

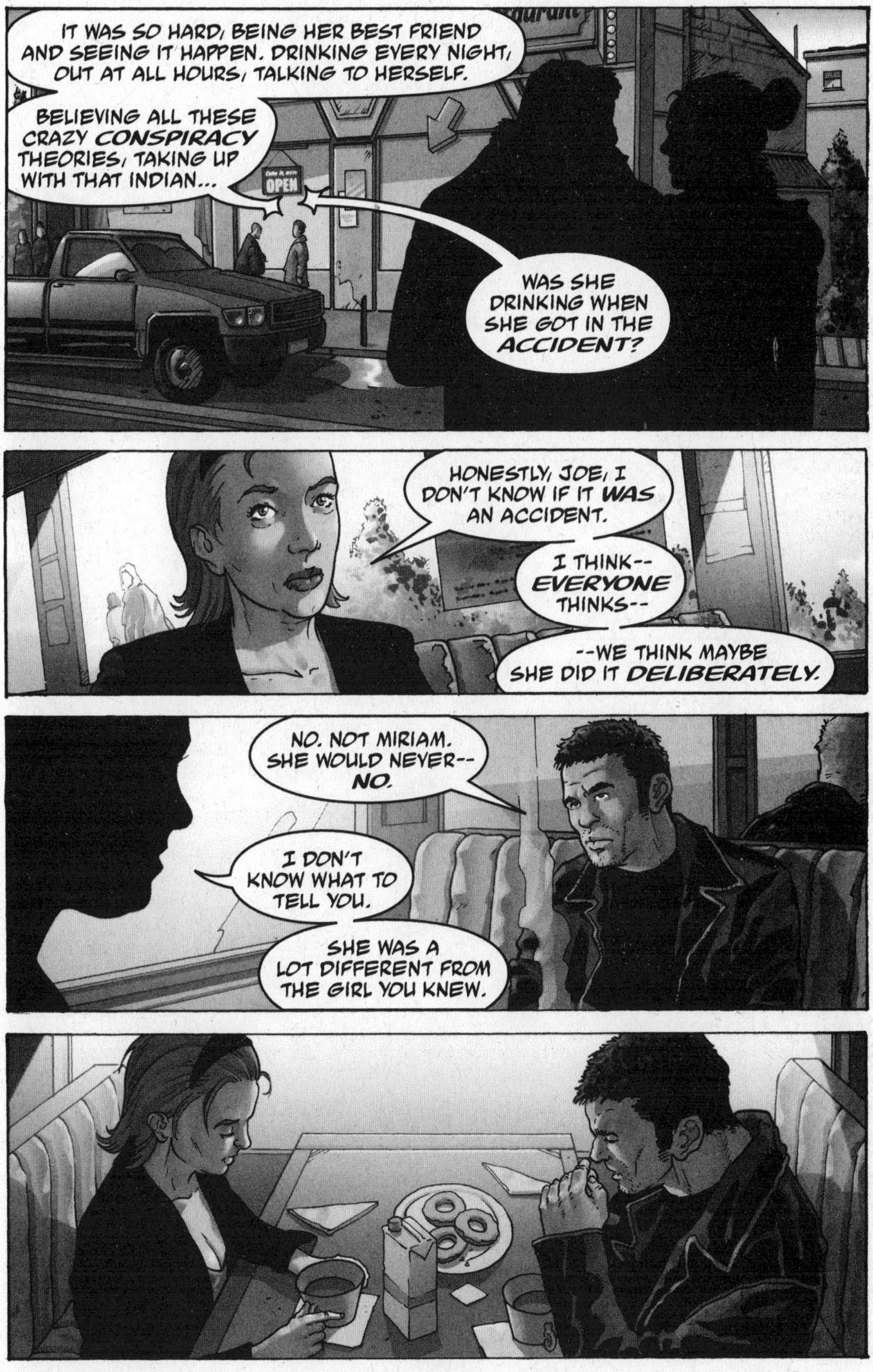
IT WAS SO HARD, BEING HER BEST FRIEND AND SEEING IT HAPPEN. DRINKING EVERY NIGHT, OUT AT ALL HOURS, TALKING TO HERSELF.
BELIEVING ALL THESE CRAZY CONSPIRACY THEORIES, TAKING UP WITH THAT INDIAN...
OPEN
WAS SHE DRINKING WHEN SHE GOT IN THE ACCIDENT?
HONESTLY, JOE, I DON'T KNOW IF IT WAS AN ACCIDENT.
I THINK-- EVERYONE THINKS--
--WE THINK MAYBE SHE DID IT DELIBERATELY.
NO. NOT MIRIAM. SHE WOULD NEVER-- NO.
I DON'T KNOW WHAT TO TELL YOU.
SHE WAS A LOT DIFFERENT FROM THE GIRL YOU KNEW.

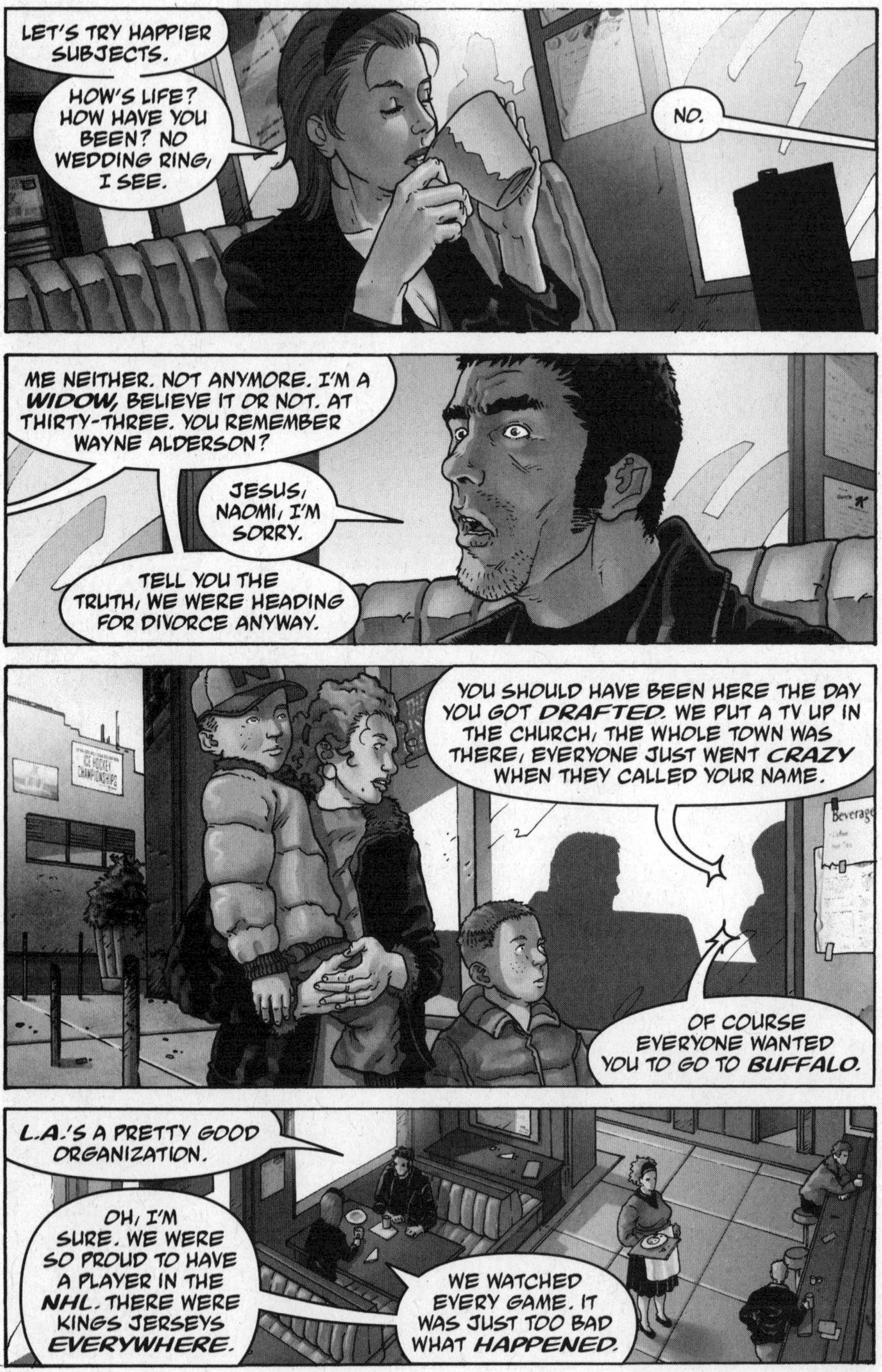
LET'S TRY HAPPIER SUBJECTS.
HOW'S LIFE? HOW HAVE YOU BEEN? NO WEDDING RING, I SEE.
NO.
ME NEITHER. NOT ANYMORE. I'M A *WIDOW*, BELIEVE IT OR NOT. AT THIRTY-THREE. YOU REMEMBER WAYNE ALDERSON?
JESUS, NAOMI, I'M SORRY.
TELL YOU THE TRUTH, WE WERE HEADING FOR DIVORCE ANYWAY.
ICE HOCKEY CHAMPIONSHIPS
YOU SHOULD HAVE BEEN HERE THE DAY YOU GOT *DRAFTED*. WE PUT A TV UP IN THE CHURCH, THE WHOLE TOWN WAS THERE, EVERYONE JUST WENT *CRAZY* WHEN THEY CALLED YOUR NAME.
OF COURSE EVERYONE WANTED YOU TO GO TO *BUFFALO*.
L.A.'S A PRETTY GOOD ORGANIZATION.
OH, I'M SURE. WE WERE SO PROUD TO HAVE A PLAYER IN THE *NHL*. THERE WERE KINGS JERSEYS *EVERYWHERE*.
WE WATCHED EVERY GAME. IT WAS JUST TOO BAD WHAT *HAPPENED*.

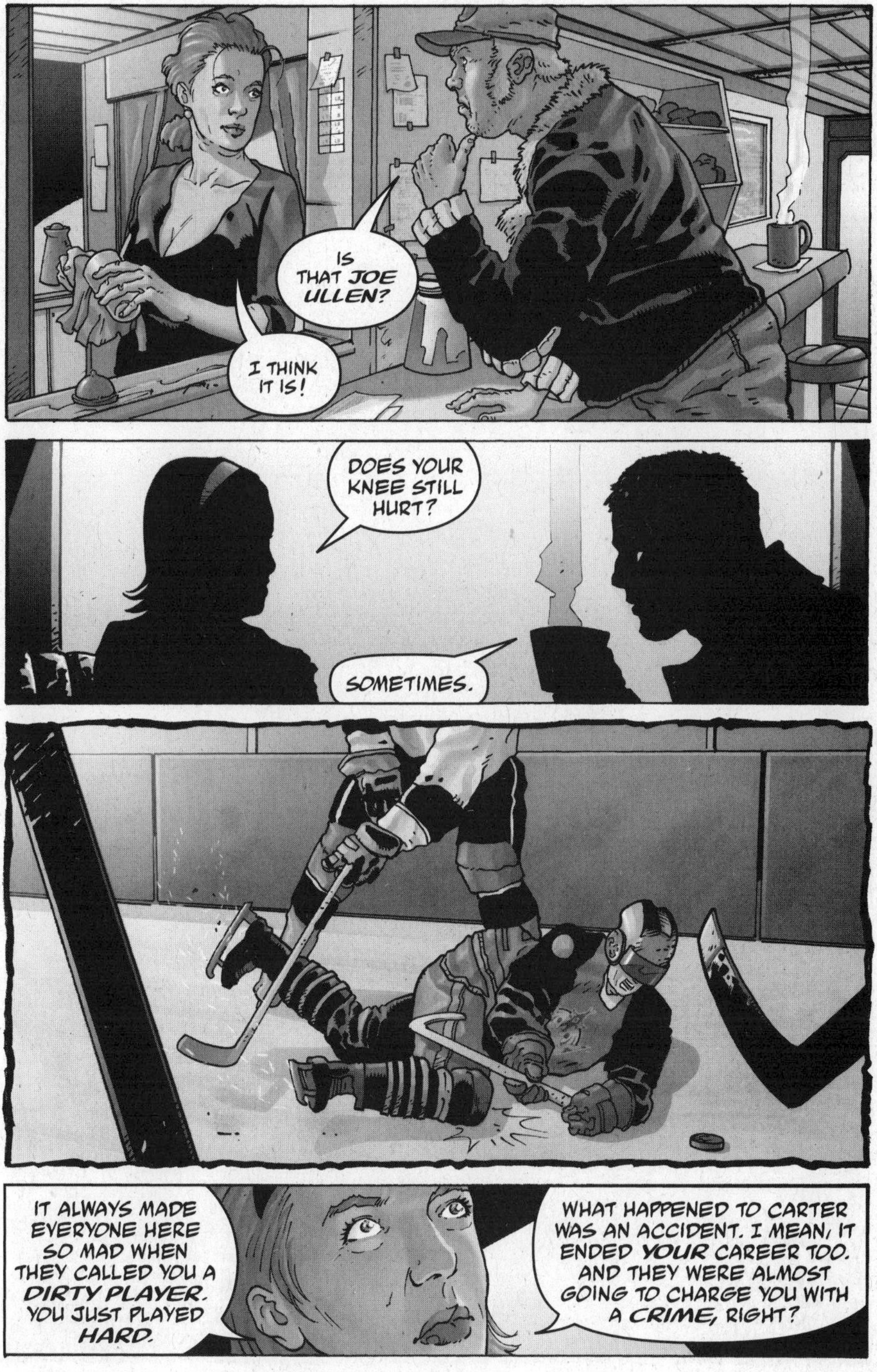
IS THAT JOE ULLEN?
I THINK IT IS!
DOES YOUR KNEE STILL HURT?
SOMETIMES.
IT ALWAYS MADE EVERYONE HERE SO MAD WHEN THEY CALLED YOU A DIRTY PLAYER. YOU JUST PLAYED HARD.
WHAT HAPPENED TO CARTER WAS AN ACCIDENT. I MEAN, IT ENDED YOUR CAREER TOO. AND THEY WERE ALMOST GOING TO CHARGE YOU WITH A CRIME, RIGHT?

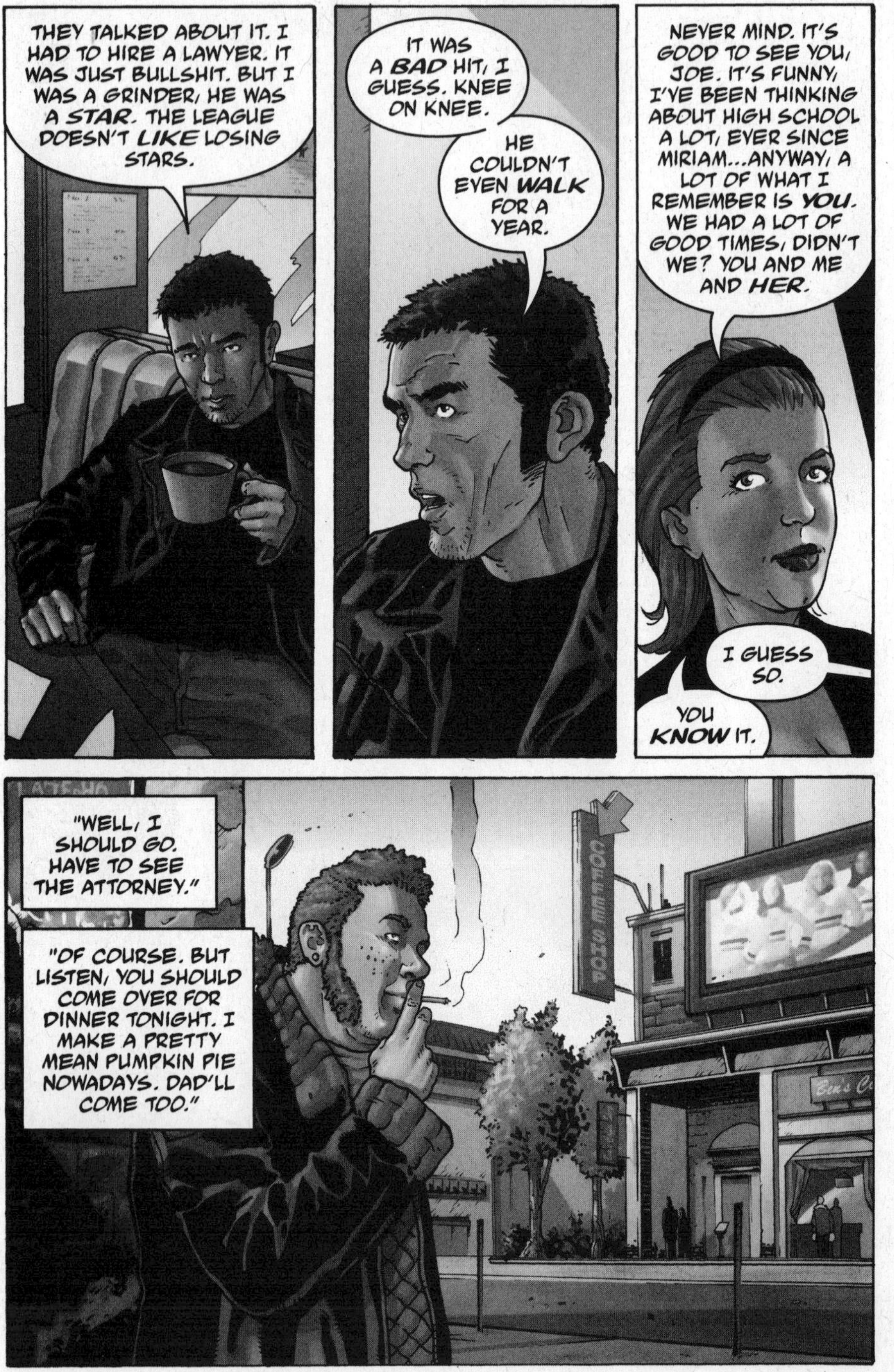
THEY TALKED ABOUT IT. I HAD TO HIRE A LAWYER. IT WAS JUST BULLSHIT. BUT I WAS A GRINDER, HE WAS A **STAR**. THE LEAGUE DOESN'T **LIKE** LOSING STARS.
IT WAS A **BAD** HIT, I GUESS. KNEE ON KNEE.
HE COULDN'T EVEN **WALK** FOR A YEAR.
NEVER MIND. IT'S GOOD TO SEE YOU, JOE. IT'S FUNNY, I'VE BEEN THINKING ABOUT HIGH SCHOOL A LOT, EVER SINCE MIRIAM...ANYWAY, A LOT OF WHAT I REMEMBER IS **YOU**. WE HAD A LOT OF GOOD TIMES, DIDN'T WE? YOU AND ME AND **HER**.
I GUESS SO.
YOU **KNOW** IT.
"WELL, I SHOULD GO. HAVE TO SEE THE ATTORNEY."
"OF COURSE. BUT LISTEN, YOU SHOULD COME OVER FOR DINNER TONIGHT. I MAKE A PRETTY MEAN PUMPKIN PIE NOWADAYS. DAD'LL COME TOO."
COFFEE SHOP

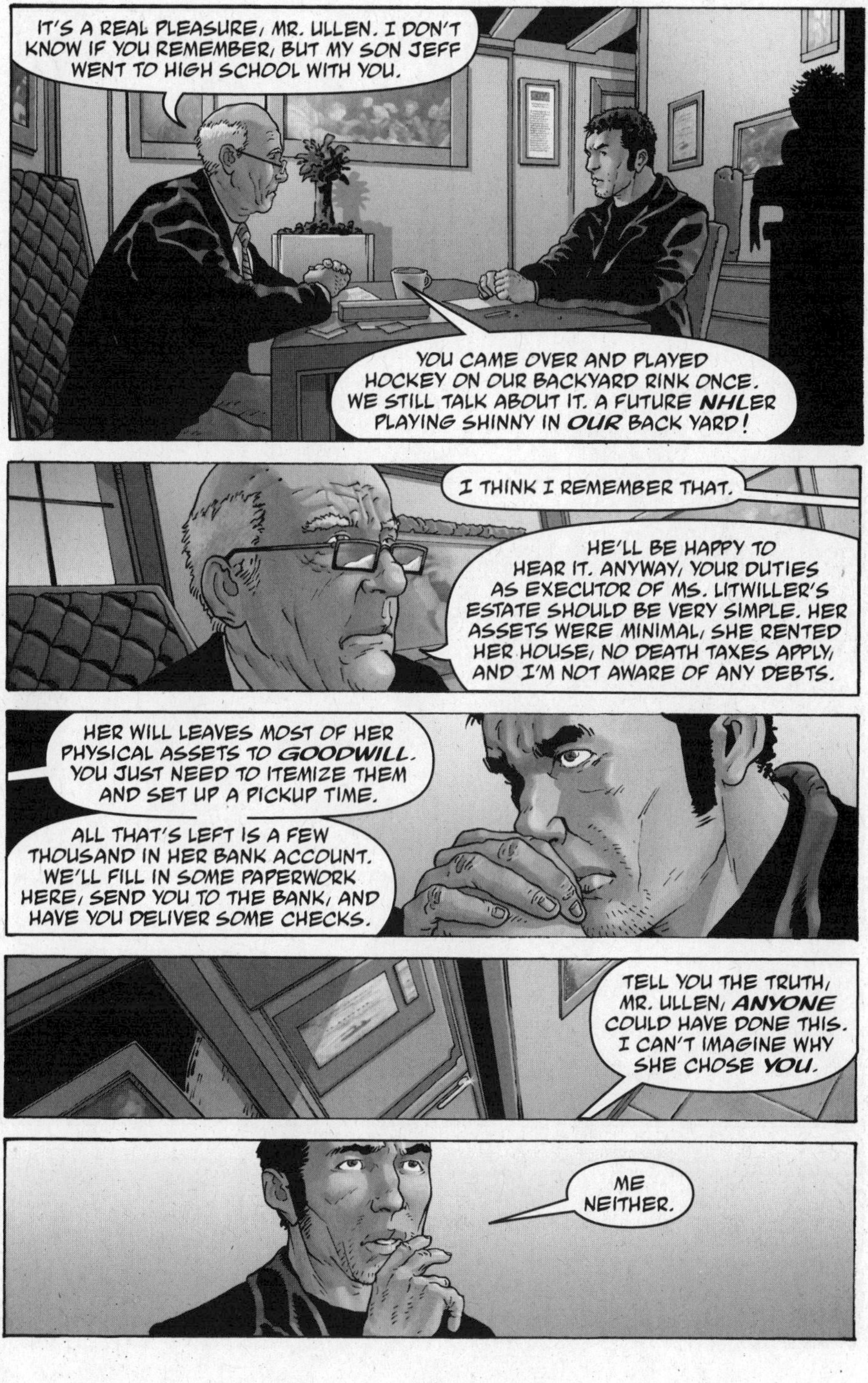
IT'S A REAL PLEASURE, MR. ULLEN. I DON'T KNOW IF YOU REMEMBER, BUT MY SON JEFF WENT TO HIGH SCHOOL WITH YOU.
YOU CAME OVER AND PLAYED HOCKEY ON OUR BACKYARD RINK ONCE. WE STILL TALK ABOUT IT. A FUTURE NHLER PLAYING SHINNY IN OUR BACK YARD!
I THINK I REMEMBER THAT.
HE'LL BE HAPPY TO HEAR IT. ANYWAY, YOUR DUTIES AS EXECUTOR OF MS. LITWILLER'S ESTATE SHOULD BE VERY SIMPLE. HER ASSETS WERE MINIMAL, SHE RENTED HER HOUSE, NO DEATH TAXES APPLY, AND I'M NOT AWARE OF ANY DEBTS.
HER WILL LEAVES MOST OF HER PHYSICAL ASSETS TO GOODWILL. YOU JUST NEED TO ITEMIZE THEM AND SET UP A PICKUP TIME.
ALL THAT'S LEFT IS A FEW THOUSAND IN HER BANK ACCOUNT. WE'LL FILL IN SOME PAPERWORK HERE, SEND YOU TO THE BANK, AND HAVE YOU DELIVER SOME CHECKS.
TELL YOU THE TRUTH, MR. ULLEN, ANYONE COULD HAVE DONE THIS. I CAN'T IMAGINE WHY SHE CHOSE YOU.
ME NEITHER.

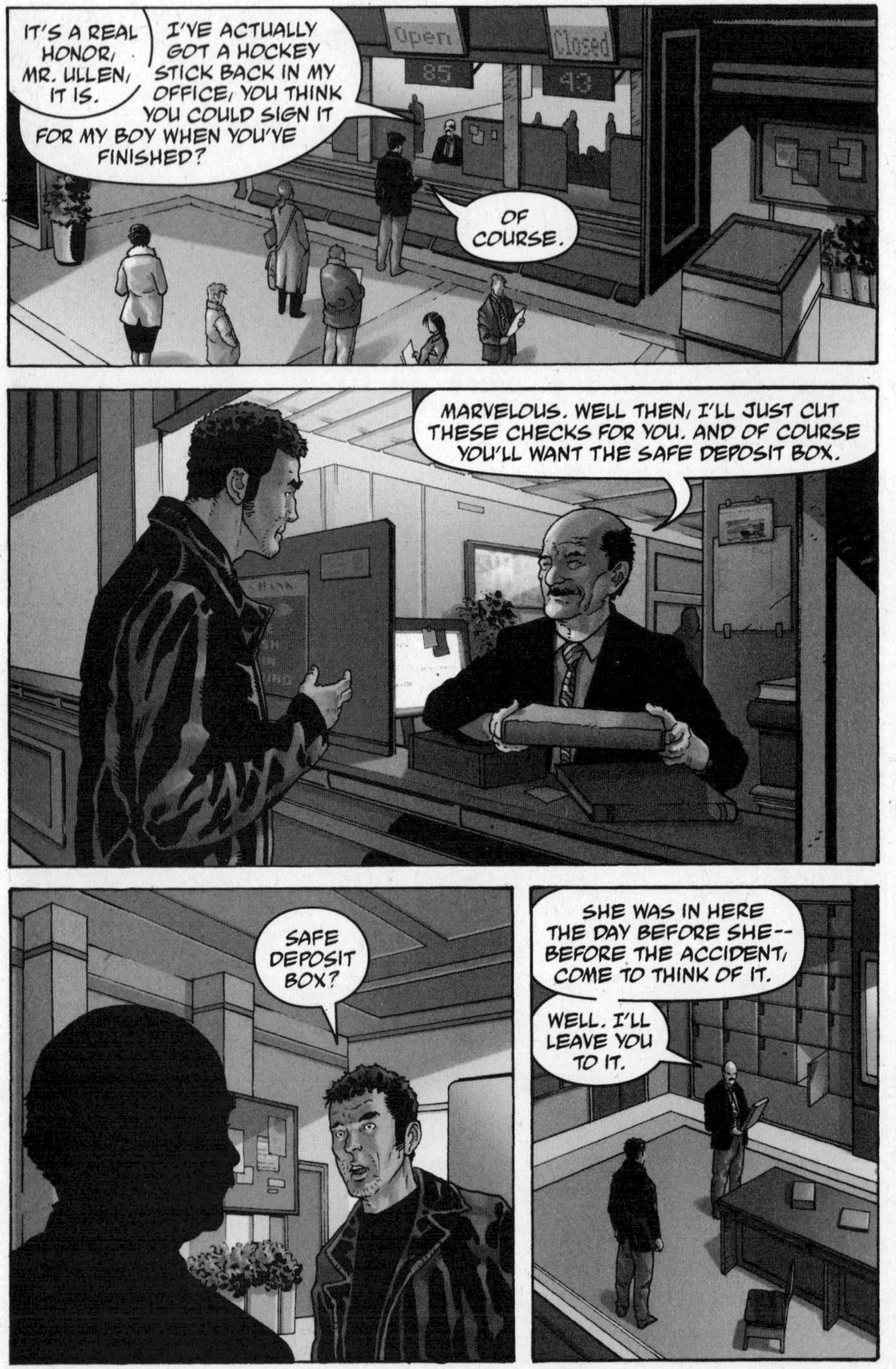
IT'S A REAL HONOR, MR. ULLEN, IT IS.
I'VE ACTUALLY GOT A HOCKEY STICK BACK IN MY OFFICE, YOU THINK YOU COULD SIGN IT FOR MY BOY WHEN YOU'VE FINISHED?
OF COURSE.
Open
Closed
85
43
MARVELOUS. WELL THEN, I'LL JUST CUT THESE CHECKS FOR YOU. AND OF COURSE YOU'LL WANT THE SAFE DEPOSIT BOX.
SAFE DEPOSIT BOX?
SHE WAS IN HERE THE DAY BEFORE SHE-- BEFORE THE ACCIDENT, COME TO THINK OF IT.
WELL. I'LL LEAVE YOU TO IT.

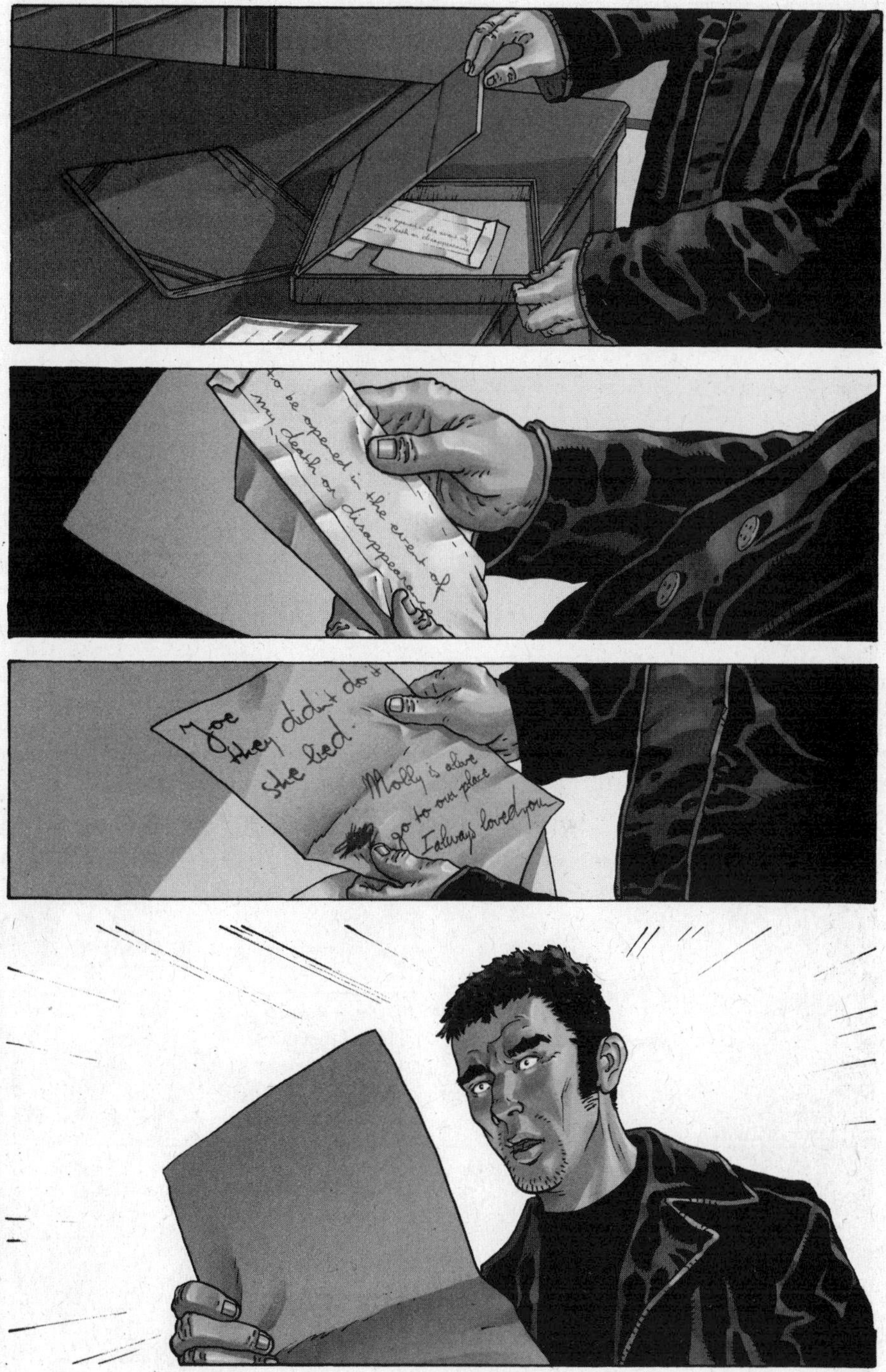
to be opened in the event of
my death or
Joe
They didn't do it
She lied.
Molly is alive
go to our place
I always loved you

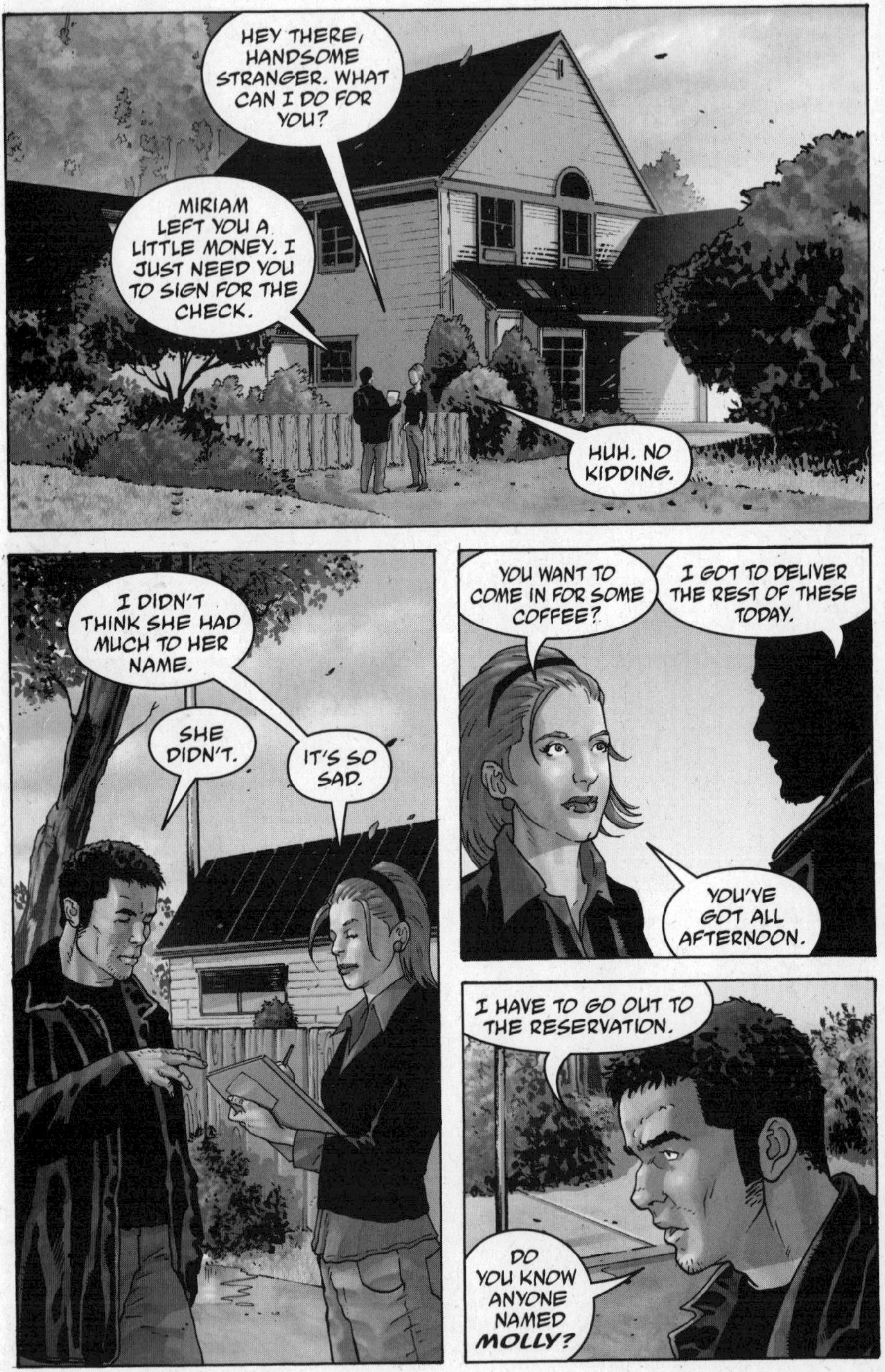
HEY THERE, HANDSOME STRANGER. WHAT CAN I DO FOR YOU?
MIRIAM LEFT YOU A LITTLE MONEY. I JUST NEED YOU TO SIGN FOR THE CHECK.
HUH. NO KIDDING.
I DIDN'T THINK SHE HAD MUCH TO HER NAME.
SHE DIDN'T.
IT'S SO SAD.
YOU WANT TO COME IN FOR SOME COFFEE?
I GOT TO DELIVER THE REST OF THESE TODAY.
YOU'VE GOT ALL AFTERNOON.
I HAVE TO GO OUT TO THE RESERVATION.
DO YOU KNOW ANYONE NAMED MOLLY?

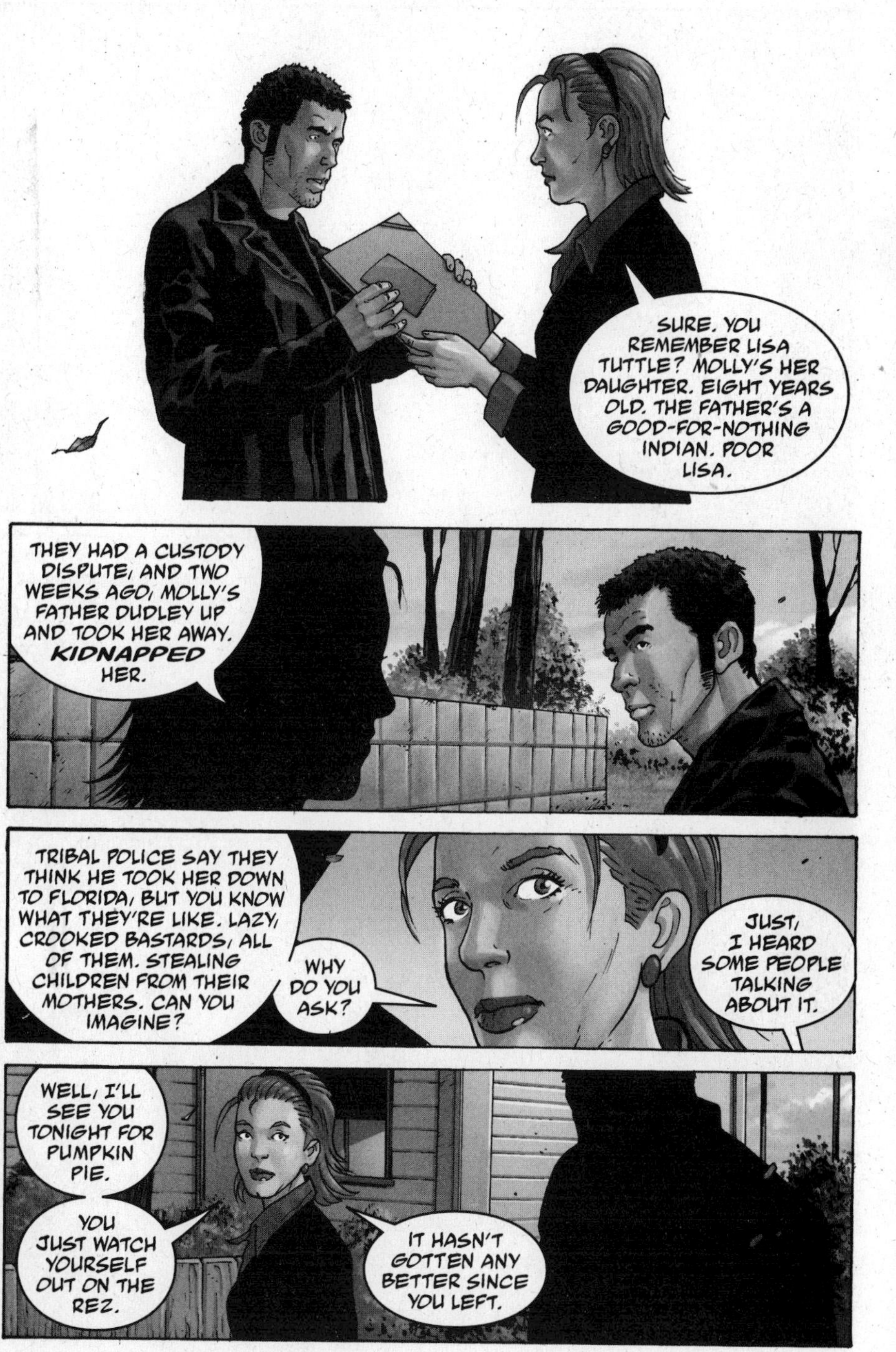
SURE. YOU REMEMBER LISA TUTTLE? MOLLY'S HER DAUGHTER. EIGHT YEARS OLD. THE FATHER'S A GOOD-FOR-NOTHING INDIAN. POOR LISA.
THEY HAD A CUSTODY DISPUTE, AND TWO WEEKS AGO, MOLLY'S FATHER DUDLEY UP AND TOOK HER AWAY. KIDNAPPED HER.
TRIBAL POLICE SAY THEY THINK HE TOOK HER DOWN TO FLORIDA, BUT YOU KNOW WHAT THEY'RE LIKE. LAZY, CROOKED BASTARDS, ALL OF THEM. STEALING CHILDREN FROM THEIR MOTHERS. CAN YOU IMAGINE?
WHY DO YOU ASK?
JUST, I HEARD SOME PEOPLE TALKING ABOUT IT.
WELL, I'LL SEE YOU TONIGHT FOR PUMPKIN PIE.
YOU JUST WATCH YOURSELF OUT ON THE REZ.
IT HASN'T GOTTEN ANY BETTER SINCE YOU LEFT.

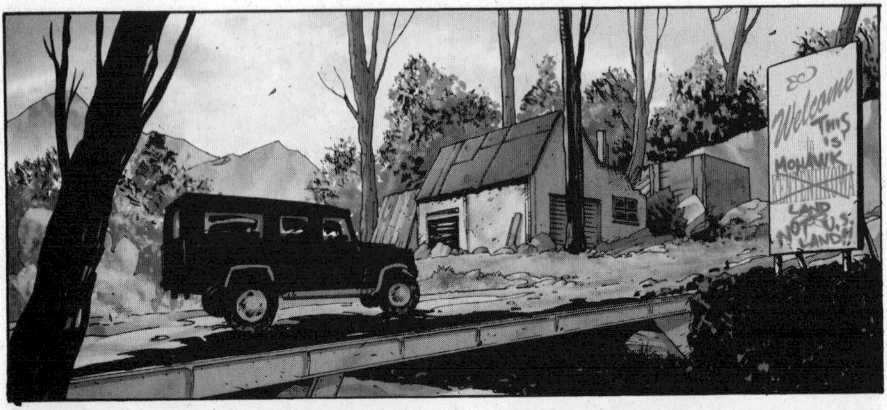
Welcome
THIS IS MOHAWK
LAND NOT U.S. LAND!!

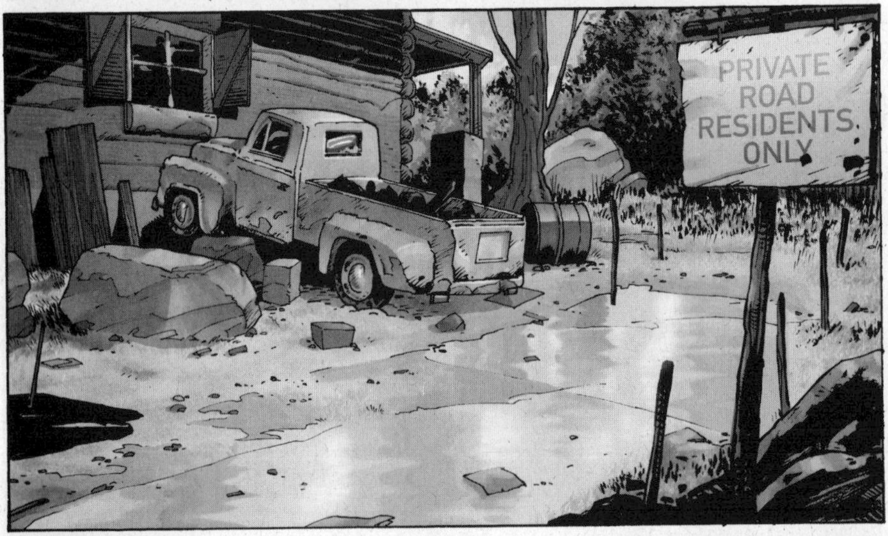
PRIVATE ROAD RESIDENTS ONLY

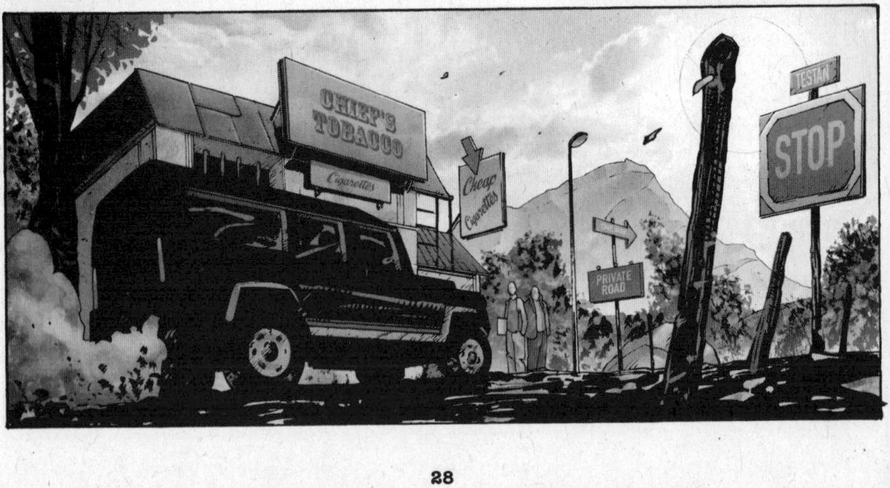
CHIEF'S TOBACCO
Cigarettes
Cheap Cigarettes
PRIVATE ROAD
TESTAN
STOP

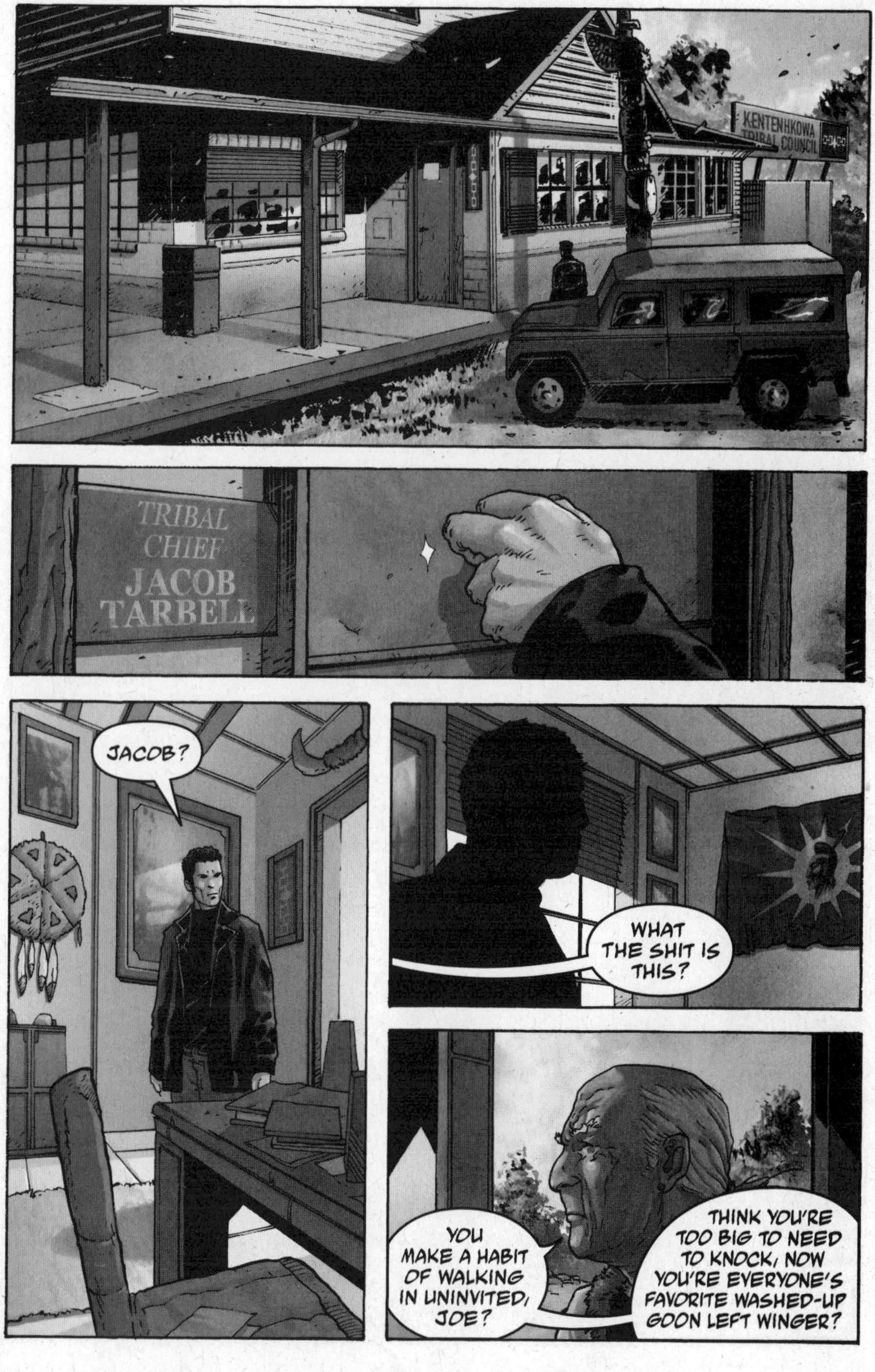
KENTENHKOWA TRIBAL COUNCIL
TRIBAL CHIEF JACOB TARBELL
JACOB?
WHAT THE SHIT IS THIS?
YOU MAKE A HABIT OF WALKING IN UNINVITED, JOE?
THINK YOU'RE TOO BIG TO NEED TO KNOCK, NOW YOU'RE EVERYONE'S FAVORITE WASHED-UP GOON LEFT WINGER?

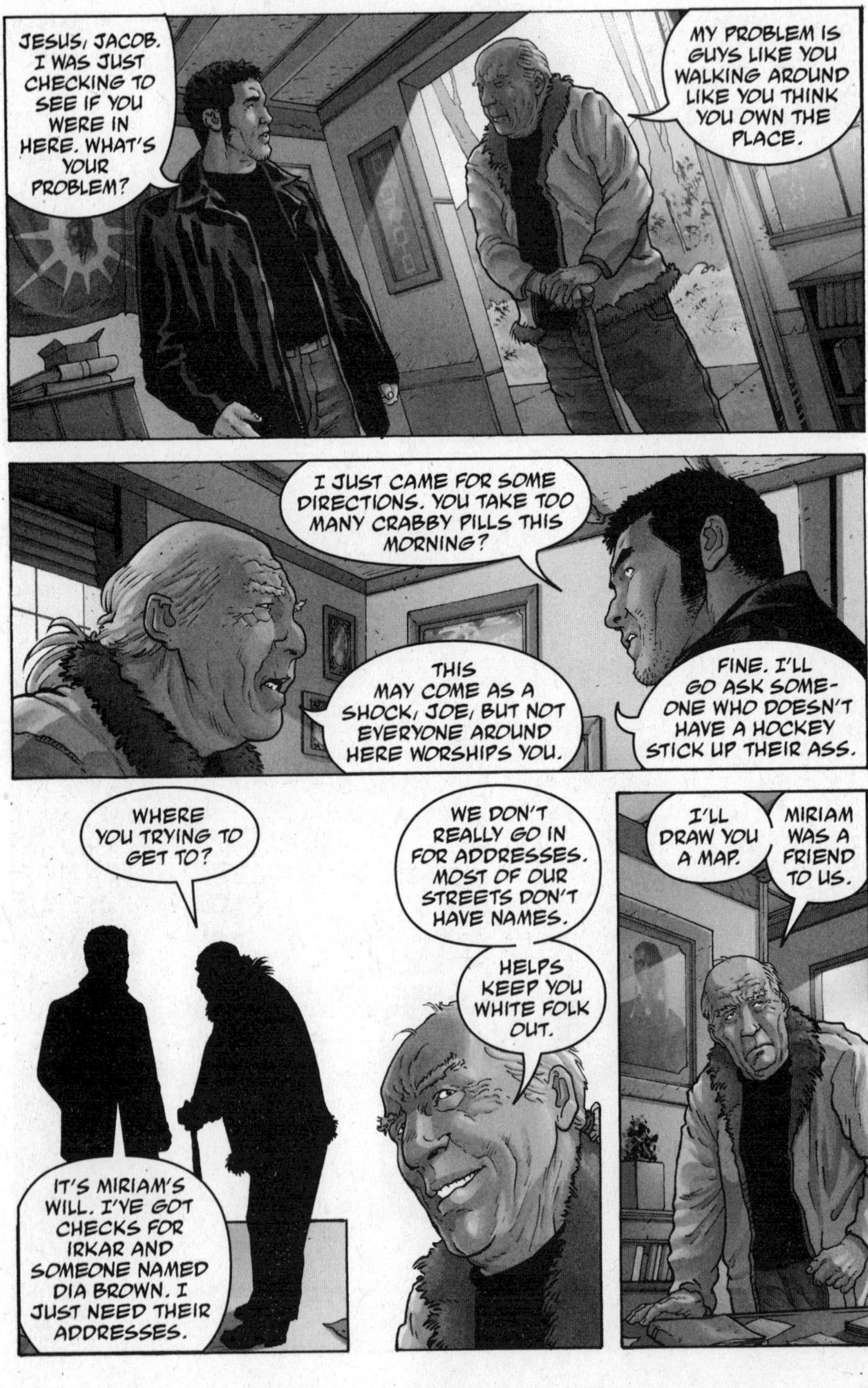
JESUS, JACOB. I WAS JUST CHECKING TO SEE IF YOU WERE IN HERE. WHAT'S YOUR PROBLEM?
MY PROBLEM IS GUYS LIKE YOU WALKING AROUND LIKE YOU THINK YOU OWN THE PLACE.
I JUST CAME FOR SOME DIRECTIONS. YOU TAKE TOO MANY CRABBY PILLS THIS MORNING?
THIS MAY COME AS A SHOCK, JOE, BUT NOT EVERYONE AROUND HERE WORSHIPS YOU.
FINE. I'LL GO ASK SOMEONE WHO DOESN'T HAVE A HOCKEY STICK UP THEIR ASS.
WHERE YOU TRYING TO GET TO?
IT'S MIRIAM'S WILL. I'VE GOT CHECKS FOR IRKAR AND SOMEONE NAMED DIA BROWN. I JUST NEED THEIR ADDRESSES.
WE DON'T REALLY GO IN FOR ADDRESSES. MOST OF OUR STREETS DON'T HAVE NAMES.
HELPS KEEP YOU WHITE FOLK OUT.
MIRIAM WAS A FRIEND TO US.
I'LL DRAW YOU A MAP.

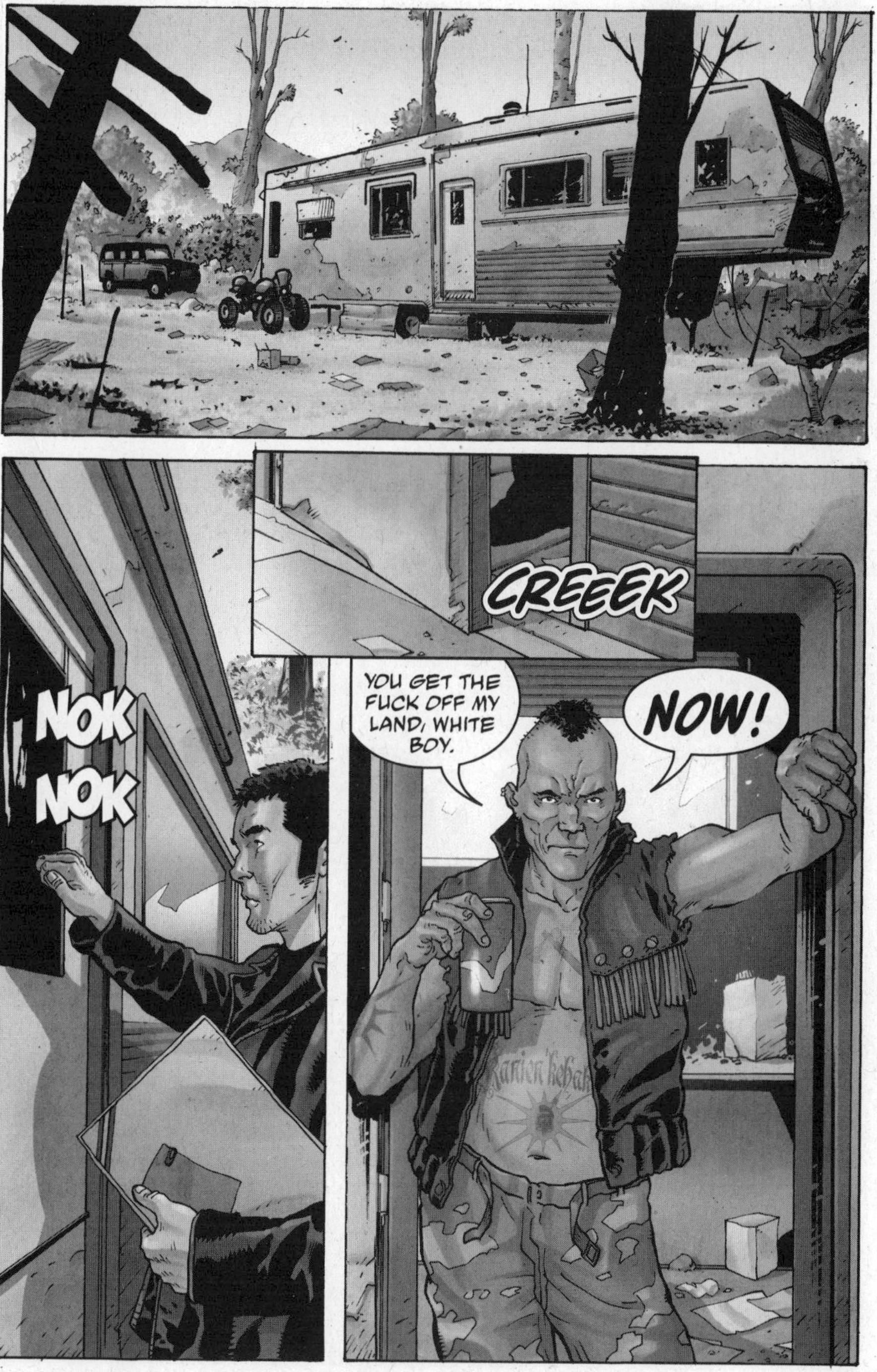
CREEEK
NOK NOK
YOU GET THE FUCK OFF MY LAND, WHITE BOY.
NOW!

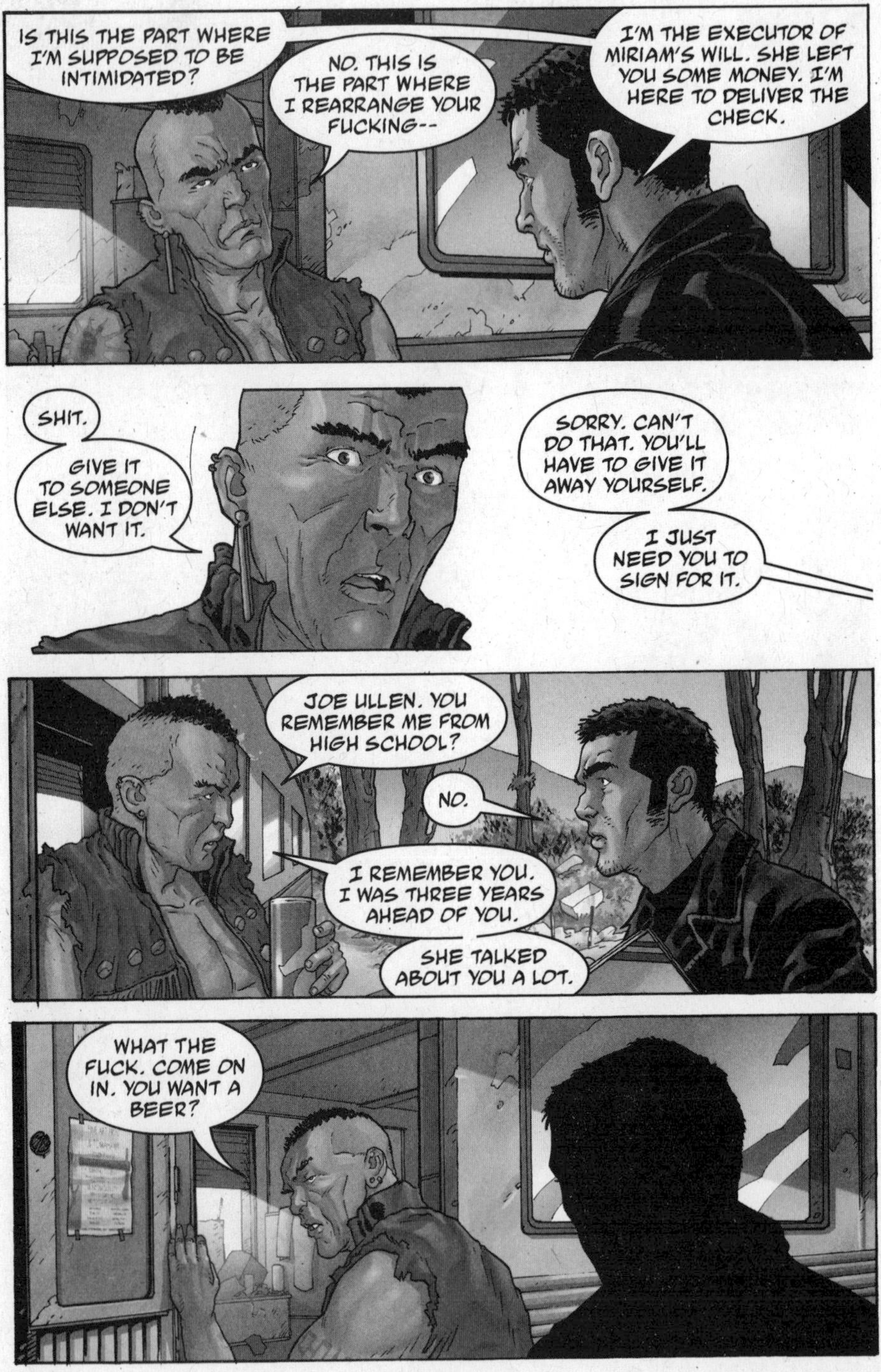
IS THIS THE PART WHERE I'M SUPPOSED TO BE INTIMIDATED?
NO. THIS IS THE PART WHERE I REARRANGE YOUR FUCKING--
I'M THE EXECUTOR OF MIRIAM'S WILL. SHE LEFT YOU SOME MONEY. I'M HERE TO DELIVER THE CHECK.
SHIT.
GIVE IT TO SOMEONE ELSE. I DON'T WANT IT.
SORRY. CAN'T DO THAT. YOU'LL HAVE TO GIVE IT AWAY YOURSELF.
I JUST NEED YOU TO SIGN FOR IT.
JOE ULLEN. YOU REMEMBER ME FROM HIGH SCHOOL?
NO.
I REMEMBER YOU. I WAS THREE YEARS AHEAD OF YOU.
SHE TALKED ABOUT YOU A LOT.
WHAT THE FUCK. COME ON IN. YOU WANT A BEER?

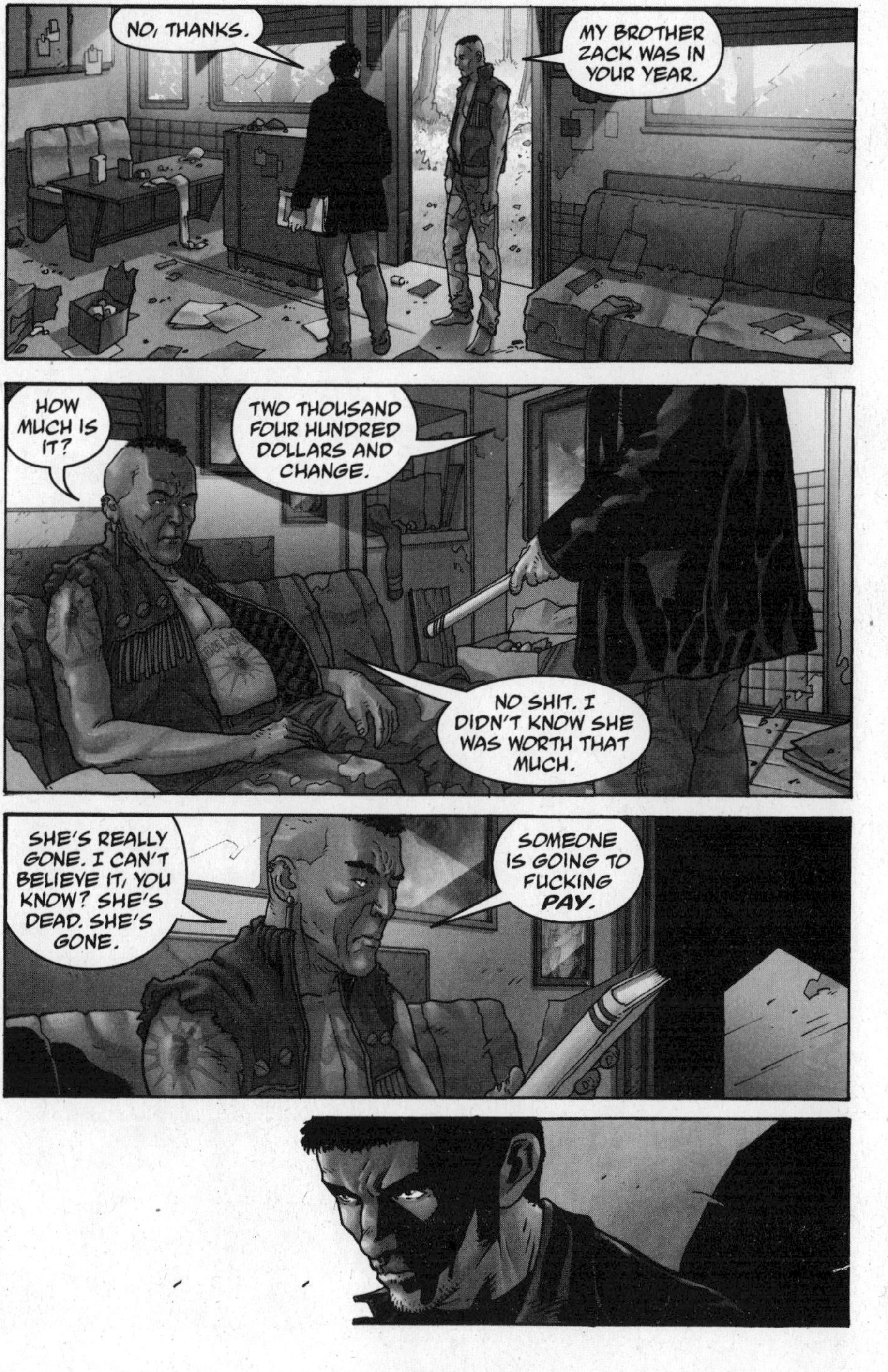
NO, THANKS.
MY BROTHER ZACK WAS IN YOUR YEAR.
HOW MUCH IS IT?
TWO THOUSAND FOUR HUNDRED DOLLARS AND CHANGE.
NO SHIT. I DIDN'T KNOW SHE WAS WORTH THAT MUCH.
SHE'S REALLY GONE. I CAN'T BELIEVE IT, YOU KNOW? SHE'S DEAD. SHE'S GONE.
SOMEONE IS GOING TO FUCKING *PAY.*

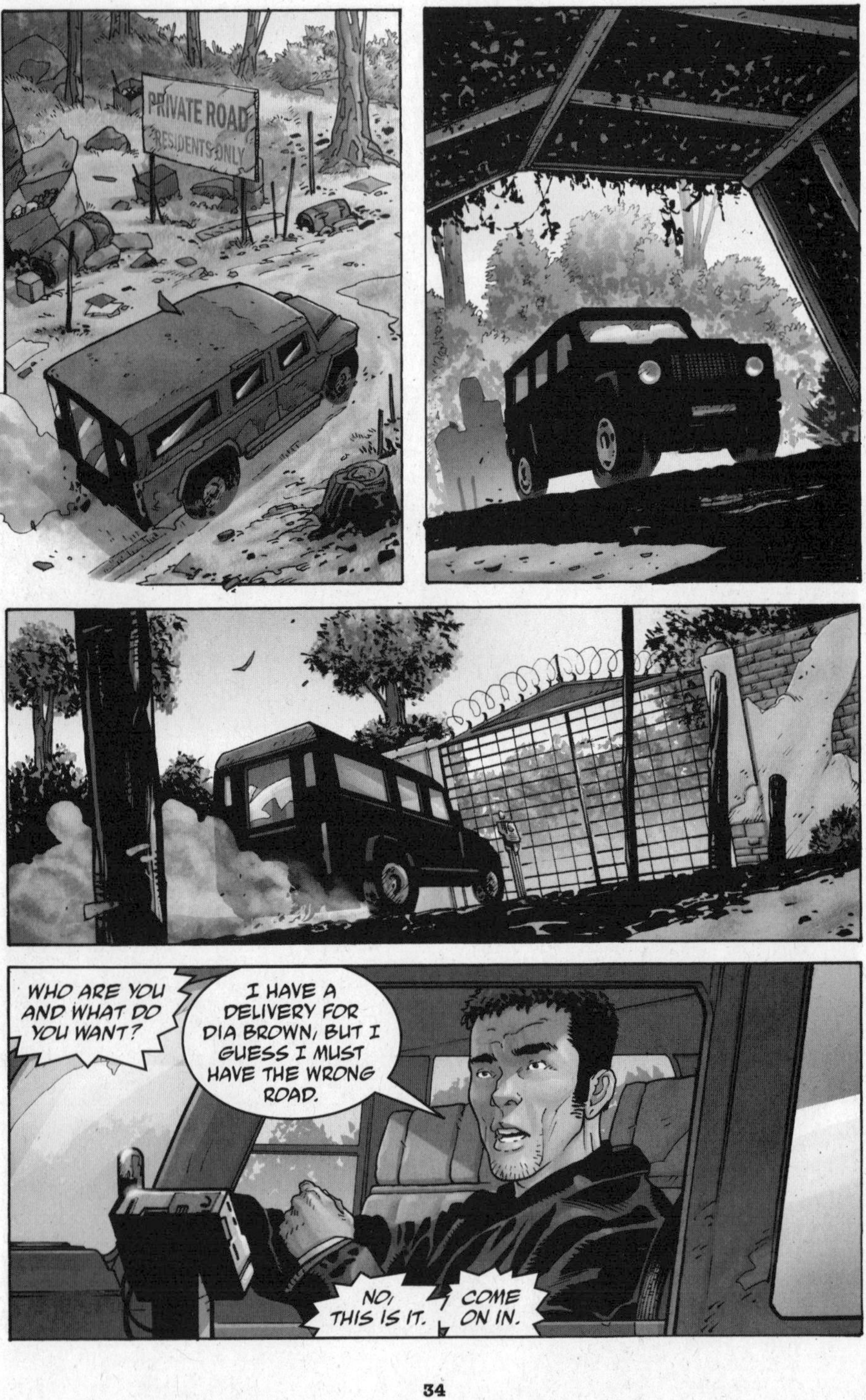
PRIVATE ROAD
RESIDENTS ONLY
WHO ARE YOU AND WHAT DO YOU WANT?
I HAVE A DELIVERY FOR DIA BROWN, BUT I GUESS I MUST HAVE THE WRONG ROAD.
NO, THIS IS IT.
COME ON IN.

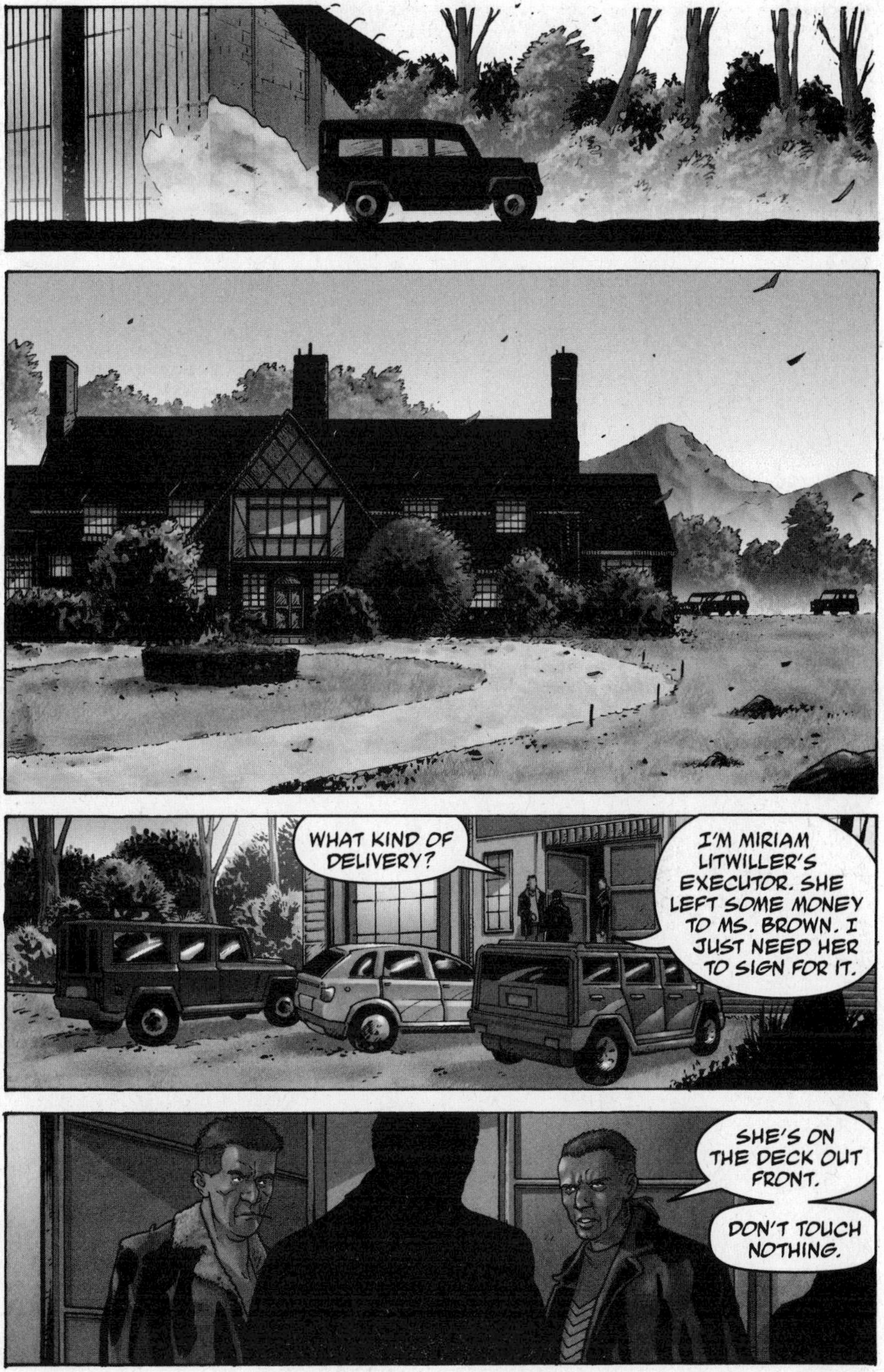
WHAT KIND OF DELIVERY?
I'M MIRIAM LITWILLER'S EXECUTOR. SHE LEFT SOME MONEY TO MS. BROWN. I JUST NEED HER TO SIGN FOR IT.
SHE'S ON THE DECK OUT FRONT.
DON'T TOUCH NOTHING.

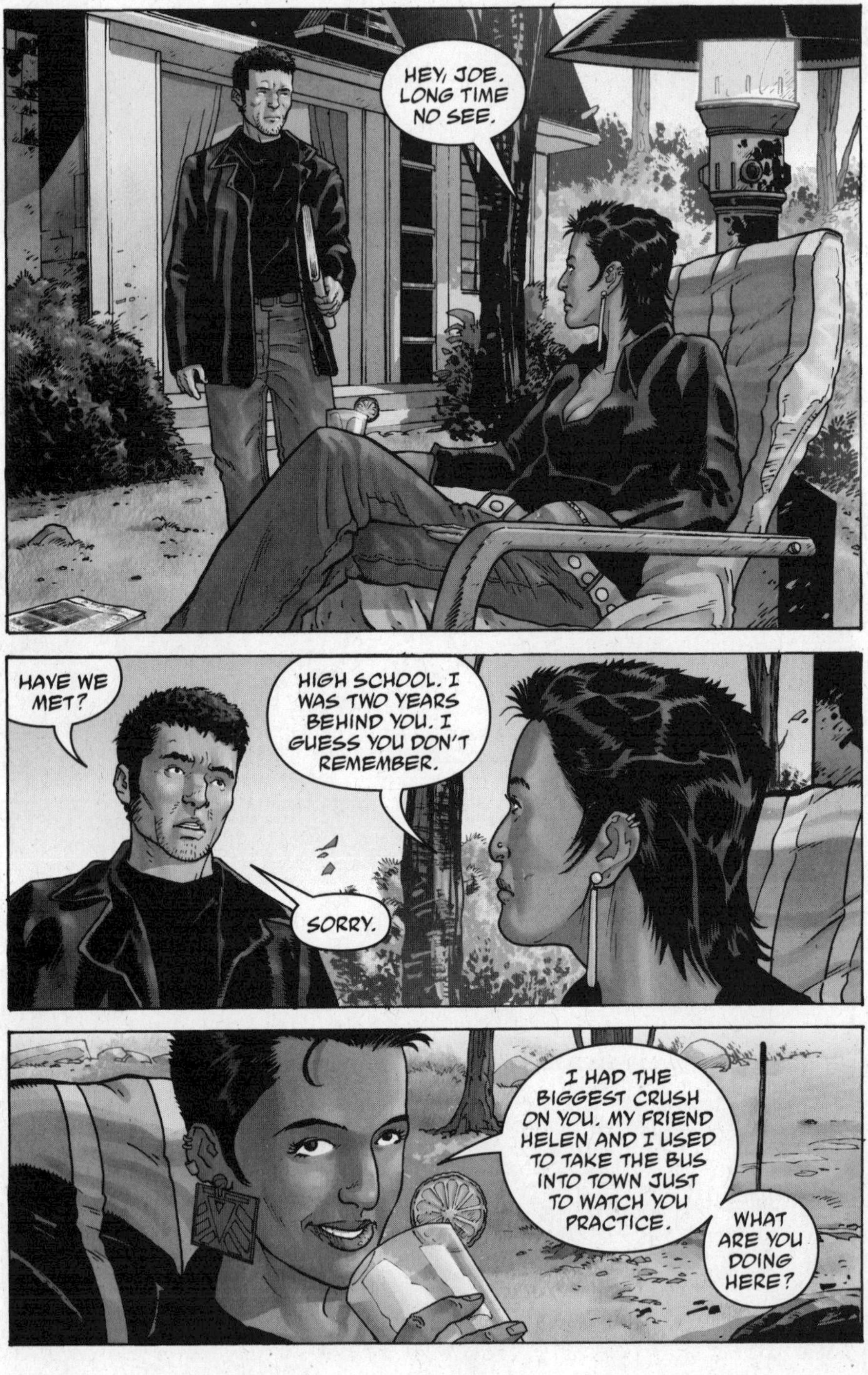
HEY, JOE. LONG TIME NO SEE.
HAVE WE MET?
HIGH SCHOOL. I WAS TWO YEARS BEHIND YOU. I GUESS YOU DON'T REMEMBER.
SORRY.
I HAD THE BIGGEST CRUSH ON YOU. MY FRIEND HELEN AND I USED TO TAKE THE BUS INTO TOWN JUST TO WATCH YOU PRACTICE.
WHAT ARE YOU DOING HERE?

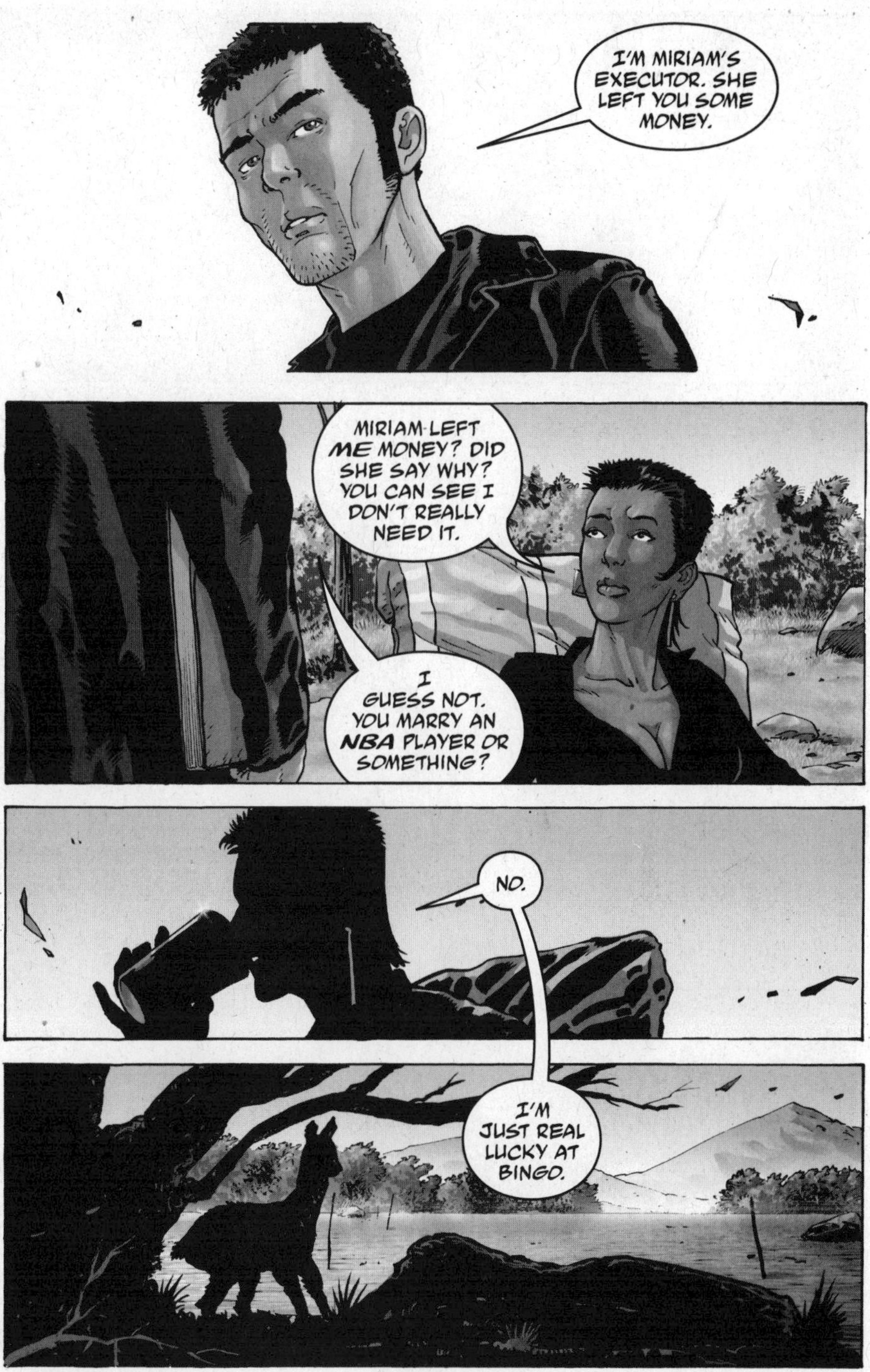
I'M MIRIAM'S EXECUTOR. SHE LEFT YOU SOME MONEY.
MIRIAM LEFT ME MONEY? DID SHE SAY WHY? YOU CAN SEE I DON'T REALLY NEED IT.
I GUESS NOT. YOU MARRY AN NBA PLAYER OR SOMETHING?
NO.
I'M JUST REAL LUCKY AT BINGO.

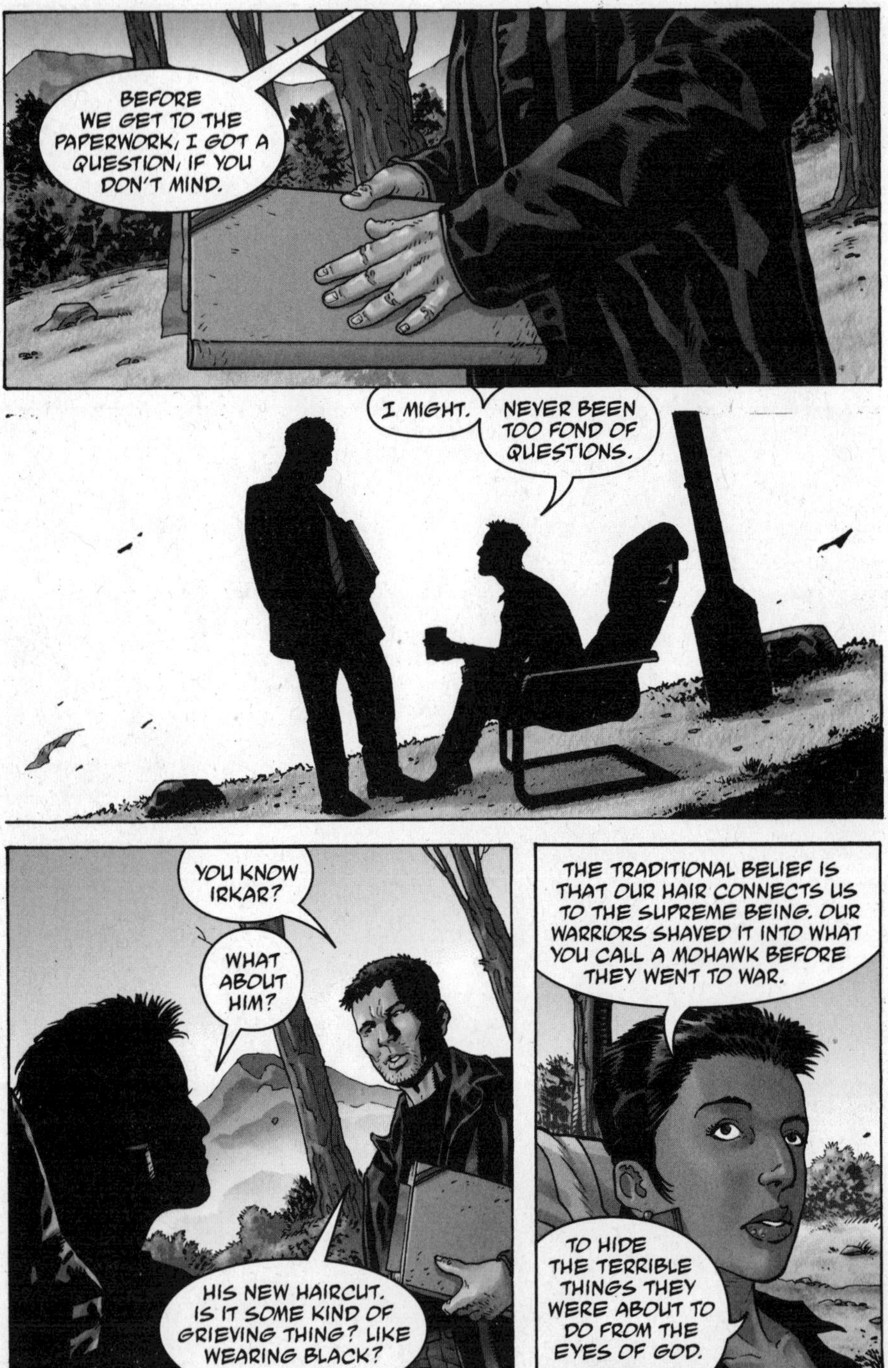
BEFORE WE GET TO THE PAPERWORK, I GOT A QUESTION, IF YOU DON'T MIND.
I MIGHT.
NEVER BEEN TOO FOND OF QUESTIONS.
YOU KNOW IRKAR?
WHAT ABOUT HIM?
HIS NEW HAIRCUT. IS IT SOME KIND OF GRIEVING THING? LIKE WEARING BLACK?
THE TRADITIONAL BELIEF IS THAT OUR HAIR CONNECTS US TO THE SUPREME BEING. OUR WARRIORS SHAVED IT INTO WHAT YOU CALL A MOHAWK BEFORE THEY WENT TO WAR.
TO HIDE THE TERRIBLE THINGS THEY WERE ABOUT TO DO FROM THE EYES OF GOD.

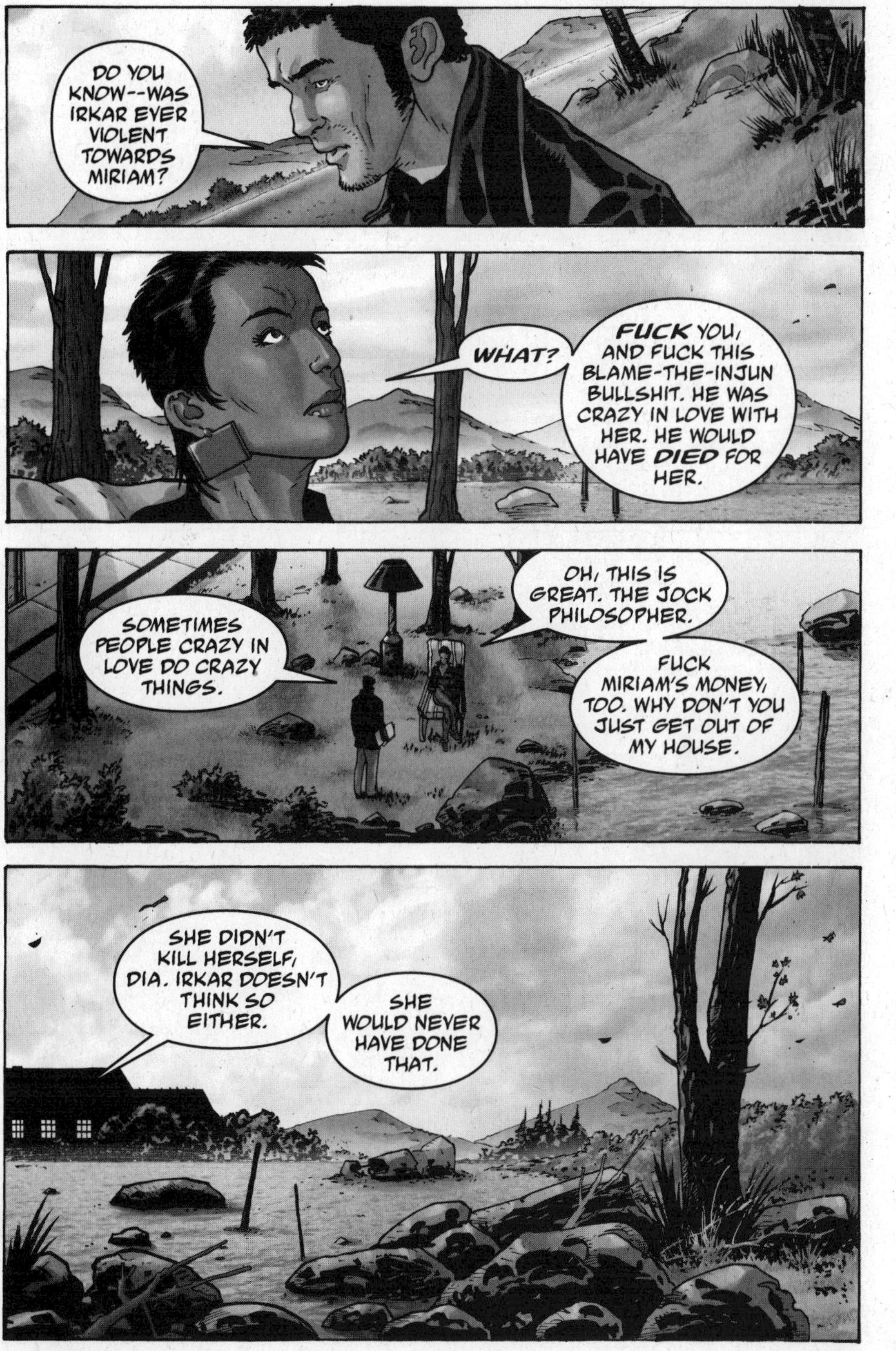
DO YOU KNOW--WAS IRKAR EVER VIOLENT TOWARDS MIRIAM?
WHAT?
FUCK YOU, AND FUCK THIS BLAME-THE-INJUN BULLSHIT. HE WAS CRAZY IN LOVE WITH HER. HE WOULD HAVE DIED FOR HER.
SOMETIMES PEOPLE CRAZY IN LOVE DO CRAZY THINGS.
OH, THIS IS GREAT. THE JOCK PHILOSOPHER.
FUCK MIRIAM'S MONEY, TOO. WHY DON'T YOU JUST GET OUT OF MY HOUSE.
SHE DIDN'T KILL HERSELF, DIA. IRKAR DOESN'T THINK SO EITHER.
SHE WOULD NEVER HAVE DONE THAT.

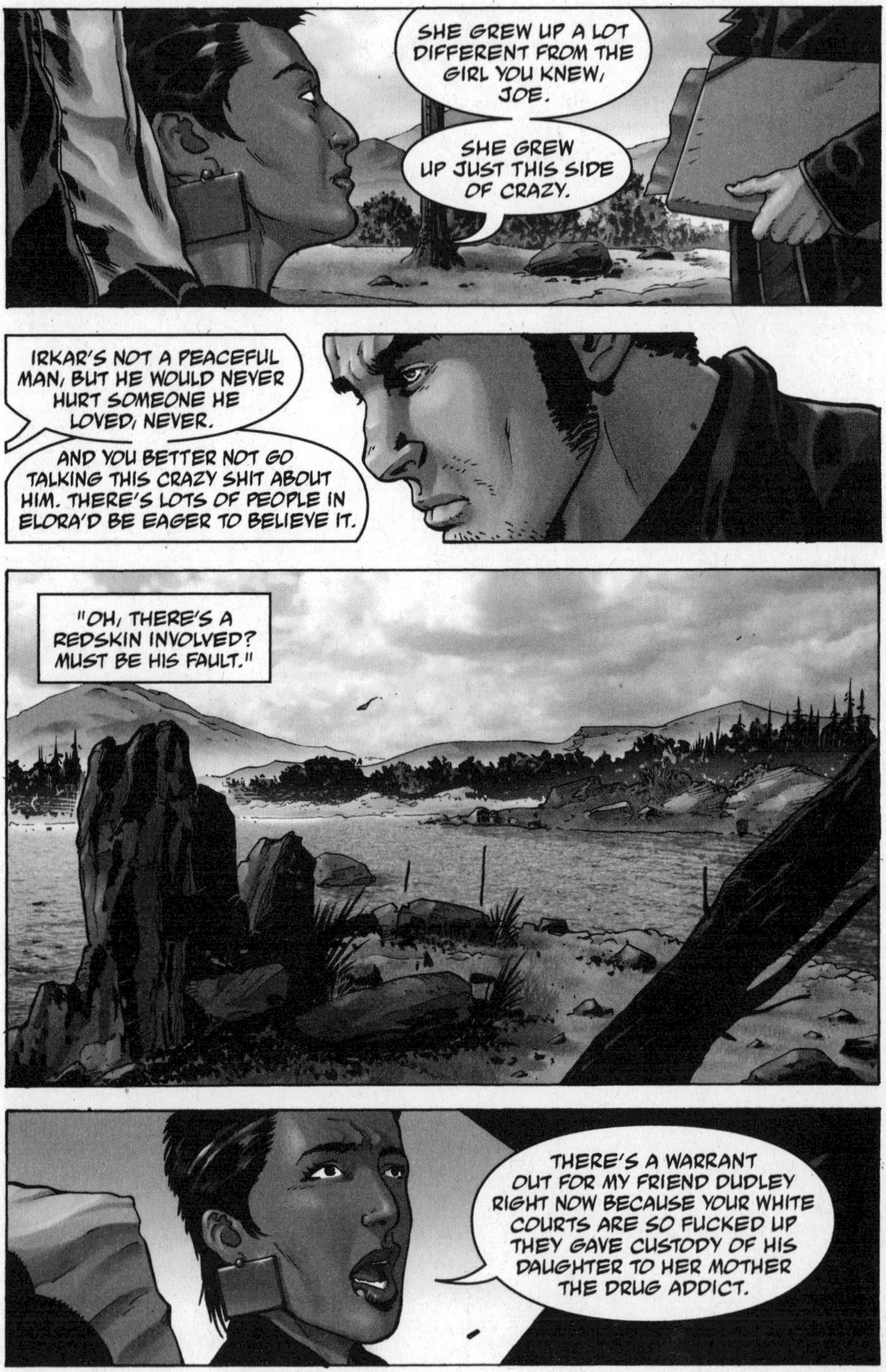
SHE GREW UP A LOT DIFFERENT FROM THE GIRL YOU KNEW, JOE.
SHE GREW UP JUST THIS SIDE OF CRAZY.
IRKAR'S NOT A PEACEFUL MAN, BUT HE WOULD NEVER HURT SOMEONE HE LOVED, NEVER.
AND YOU BETTER NOT GO TALKING THIS CRAZY SHIT ABOUT HIM. THERE'S LOTS OF PEOPLE IN ELORA'D BE EAGER TO BELIEVE IT.
"OH, THERE'S A REDSKIN INVOLVED? MUST BE HIS FAULT."
THERE'S A WARRANT OUT FOR MY FRIEND DUDLEY RIGHT NOW BECAUSE YOUR WHITE COURTS ARE SO FUCKED UP THEY GAVE CUSTODY OF HIS DAUGHTER TO HER MOTHER THE DRUG ADDICT.

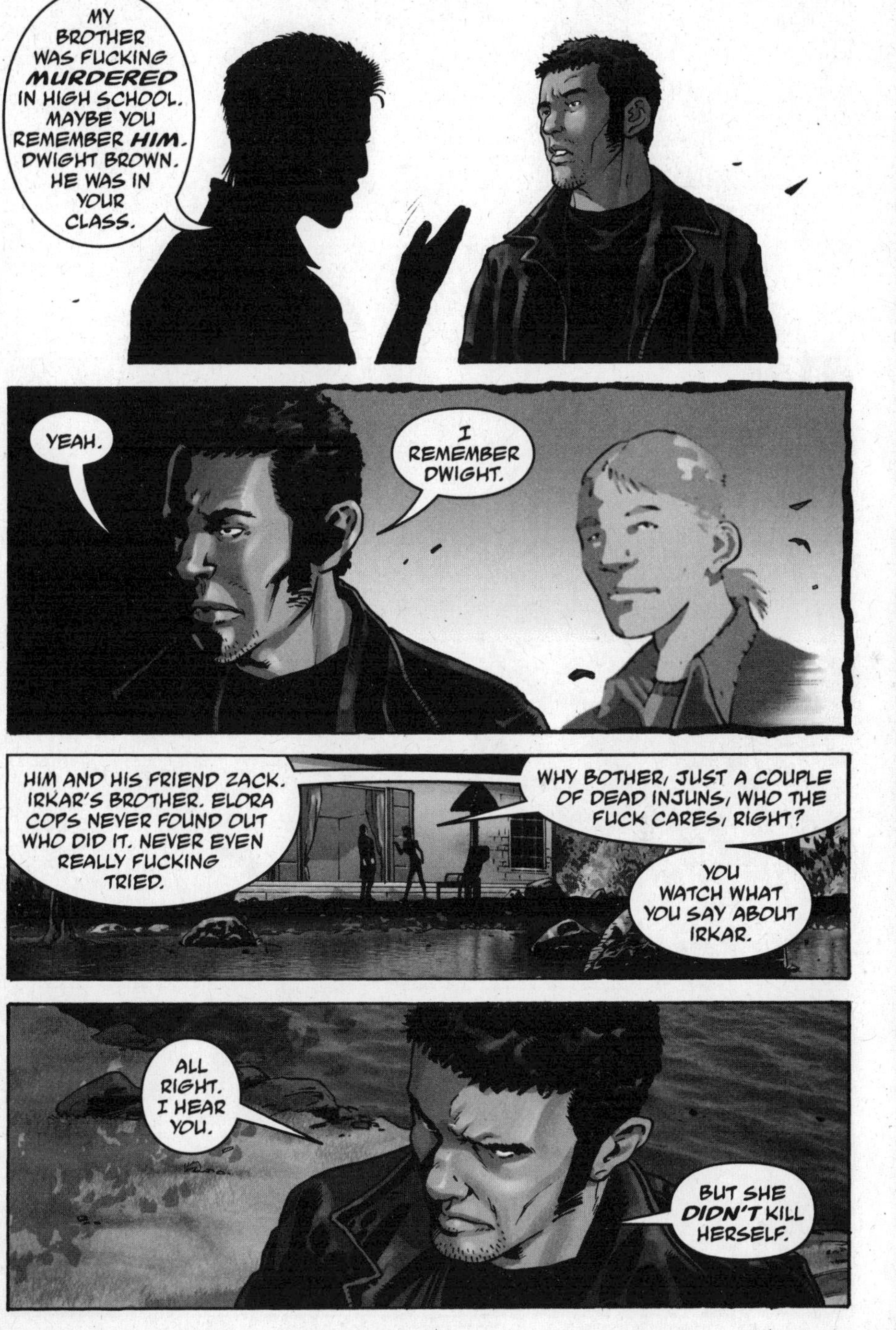
MY BROTHER WAS FUCKING MURDERED IN HIGH SCHOOL. MAYBE YOU REMEMBER HIM. DWIGHT BROWN. HE WAS IN YOUR CLASS.
YEAH.
I REMEMBER DWIGHT.
HIM AND HIS FRIEND ZACK. IRKAR'S BROTHER. ELORA COPS NEVER FOUND OUT WHO DID IT. NEVER EVEN REALLY FUCKING TRIED.
WHY BOTHER, JUST A COUPLE OF DEAD INJUNS, WHO THE FUCK CARES, RIGHT?
YOU WATCH WHAT YOU SAY ABOUT IRKAR.
ALL RIGHT. I HEAR YOU.
BUT SHE DIDN'T KILL HERSELF.

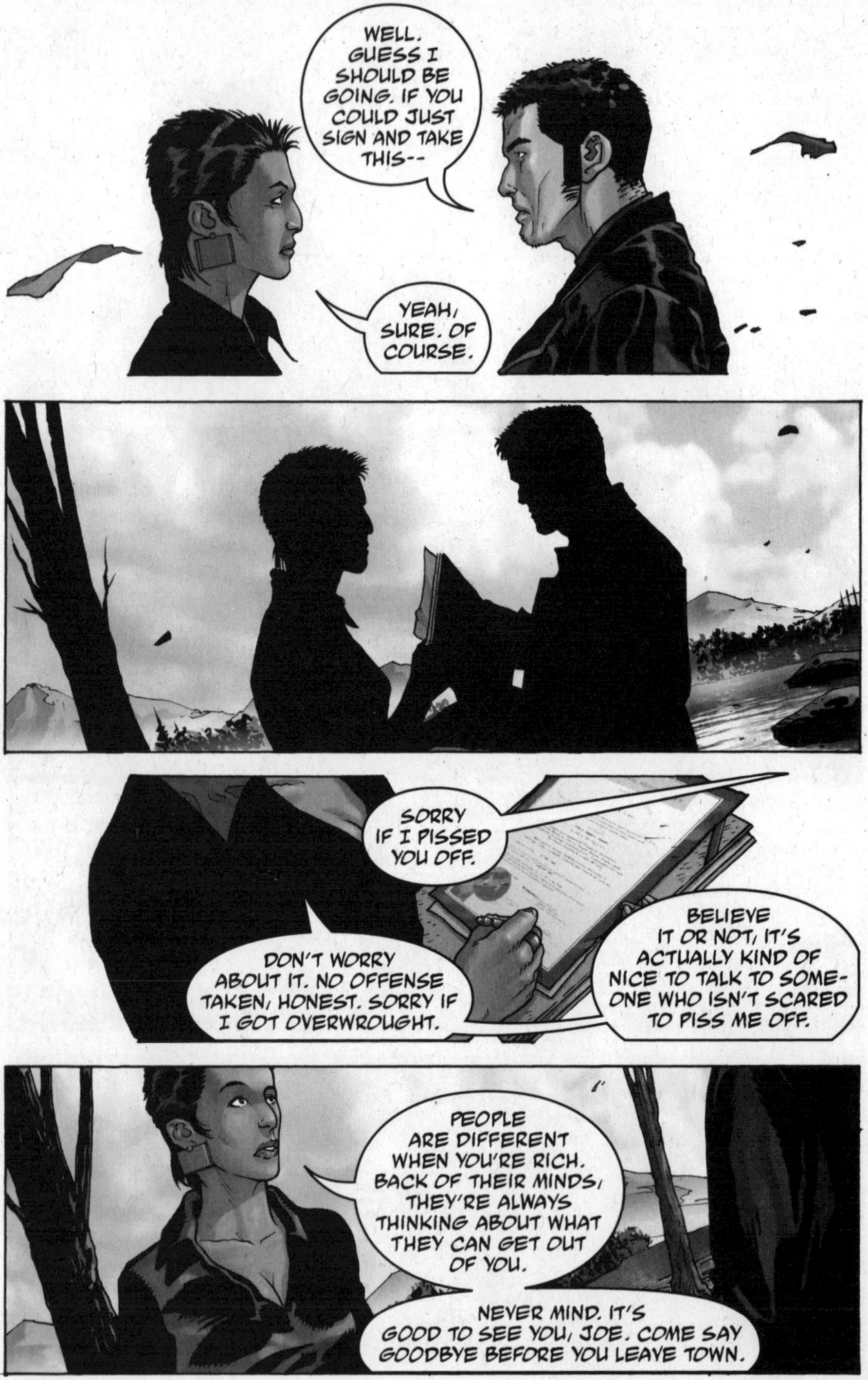
WELL. GUESS I SHOULD BE GOING. IF YOU COULD JUST SIGN AND TAKE THIS--
YEAH, SURE. OF COURSE.
SORRY IF I PISSED YOU OFF.
DON'T WORRY ABOUT IT. NO OFFENSE TAKEN, HONEST. SORRY IF I GOT OVERWROUGHT.
BELIEVE IT OR NOT, IT'S ACTUALLY KIND OF NICE TO TALK TO SOME-ONE WHO ISN'T SCARED TO PISS ME OFF.
PEOPLE ARE DIFFERENT WHEN YOU'RE RICH. BACK OF THEIR MINDS, THEY'RE ALWAYS THINKING ABOUT WHAT THEY CAN GET OUT OF YOU.
NEVER MIND. IT'S GOOD TO SEE YOU, JOE. COME SAY GOODBYE BEFORE YOU LEAVE TOWN.

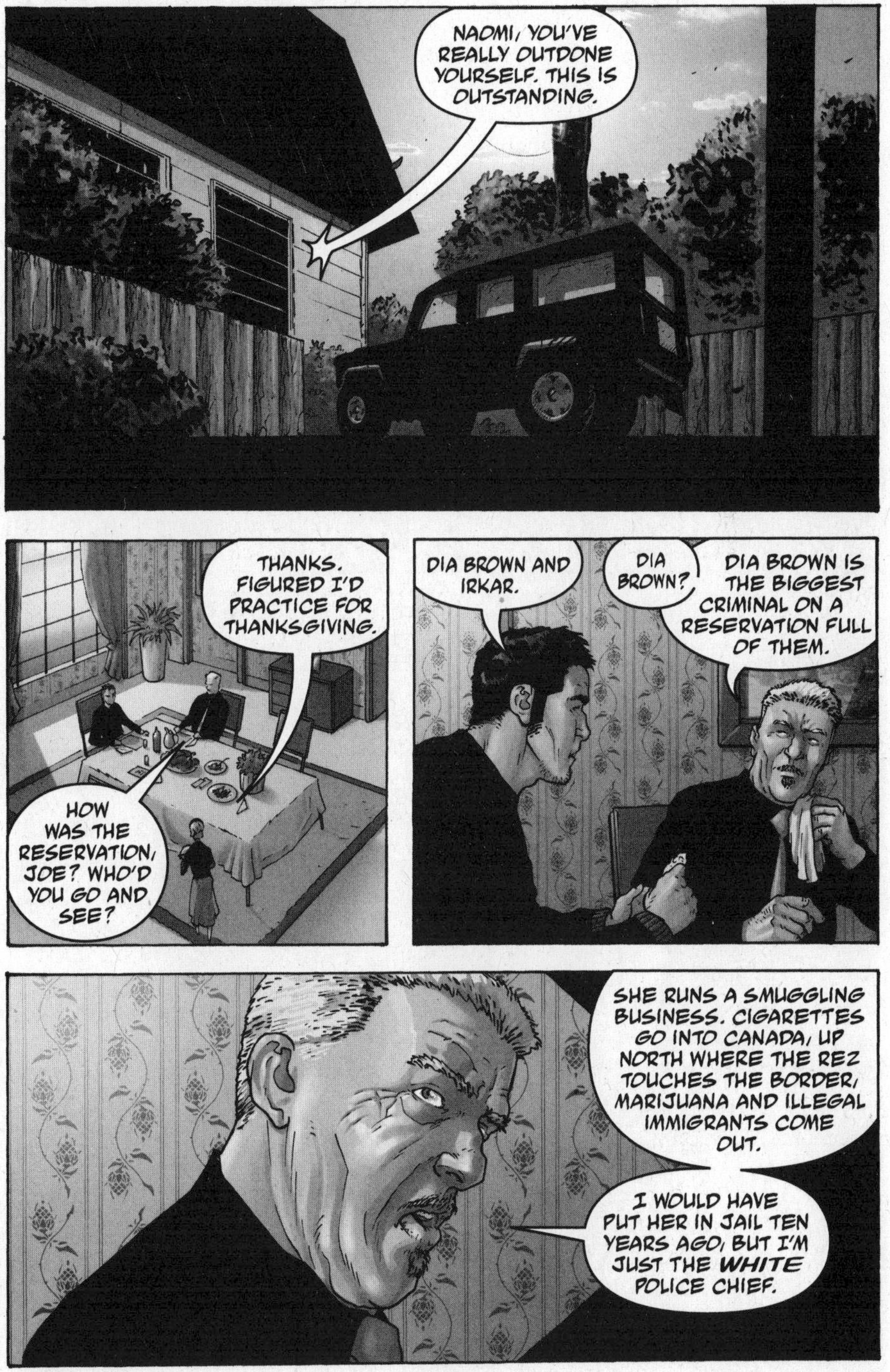
NAOMI, YOU'VE REALLY OUTDONE YOURSELF. THIS IS OUTSTANDING.
THANKS. FIGURED I'D PRACTICE FOR THANKSGIVING.
HOW WAS THE RESERVATION, JOE? WHO'D YOU GO AND SEE?
DIA BROWN AND IRKAR.
DIA BROWN?
DIA BROWN IS THE BIGGEST CRIMINAL ON A RESERVATION FULL OF THEM.
SHE RUNS A SMUGGLING BUSINESS. CIGARETTES GO INTO CANADA, UP NORTH WHERE THE REZ TOUCHES THE BORDER, MARIJUANA AND ILLEGAL IMMIGRANTS COME OUT.
I WOULD HAVE PUT HER IN JAIL TEN YEARS AGO, BUT I'M JUST THE ***WHITE*** POLICE CHIEF.

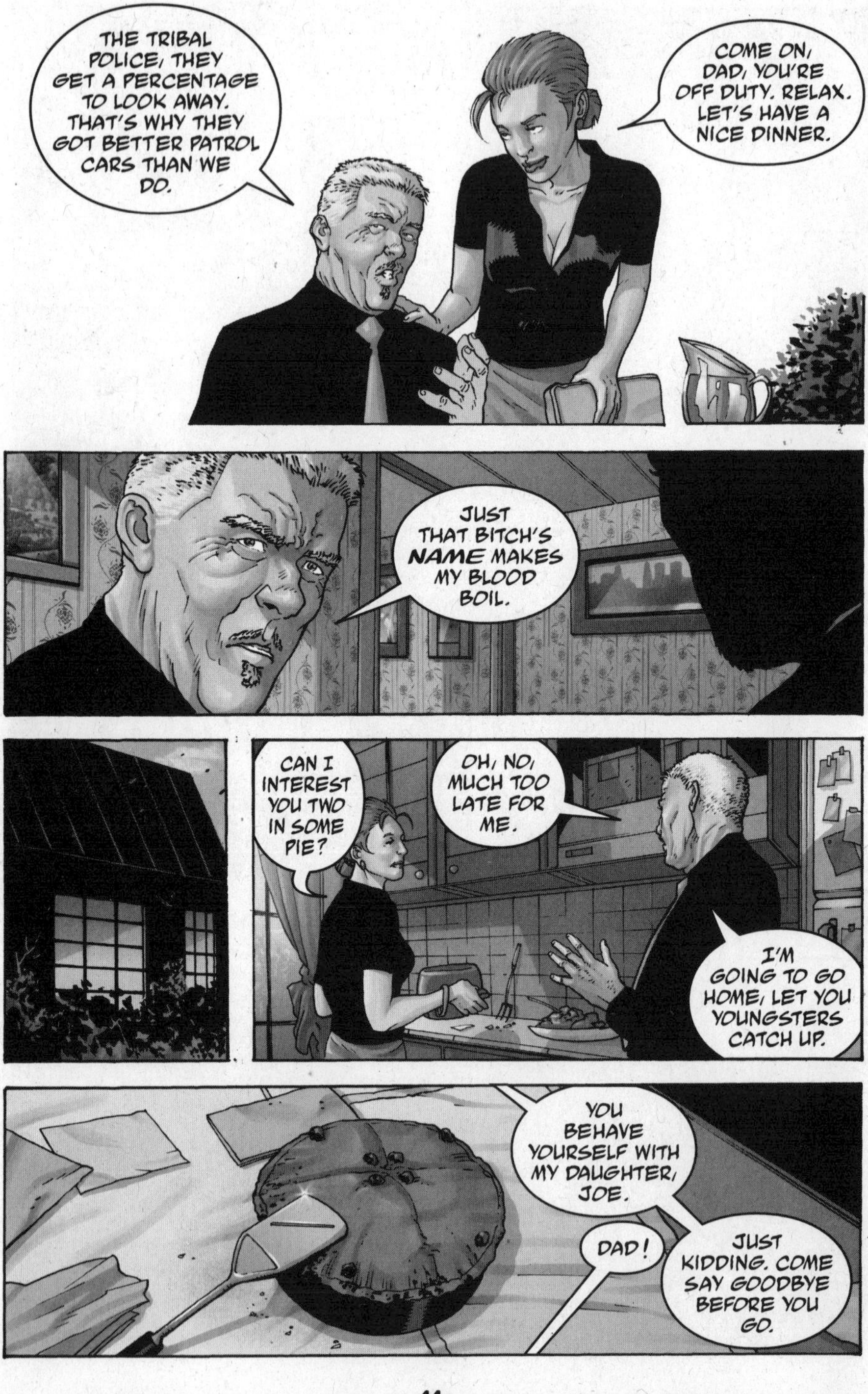
THE TRIBAL POLICE, THEY GET A PERCENTAGE TO LOOK AWAY. THAT'S WHY THEY GOT BETTER PATROL CARS THAN WE DO.
COME ON, DAD, YOU'RE OFF DUTY. RELAX. LET'S HAVE A NICE DINNER.
JUST THAT BITCH'S *NAME* MAKES MY BLOOD BOIL.
CAN I INTEREST YOU TWO IN SOME PIE?
OH, NO, MUCH TOO LATE FOR ME.
I'M GOING TO GO HOME, LET YOU YOUNGSTERS CATCH UP.
YOU BEHAVE YOURSELF WITH MY DAUGHTER, JOE.
DAD!
JUST KIDDING. COME SAY GOODBYE BEFORE YOU GO.

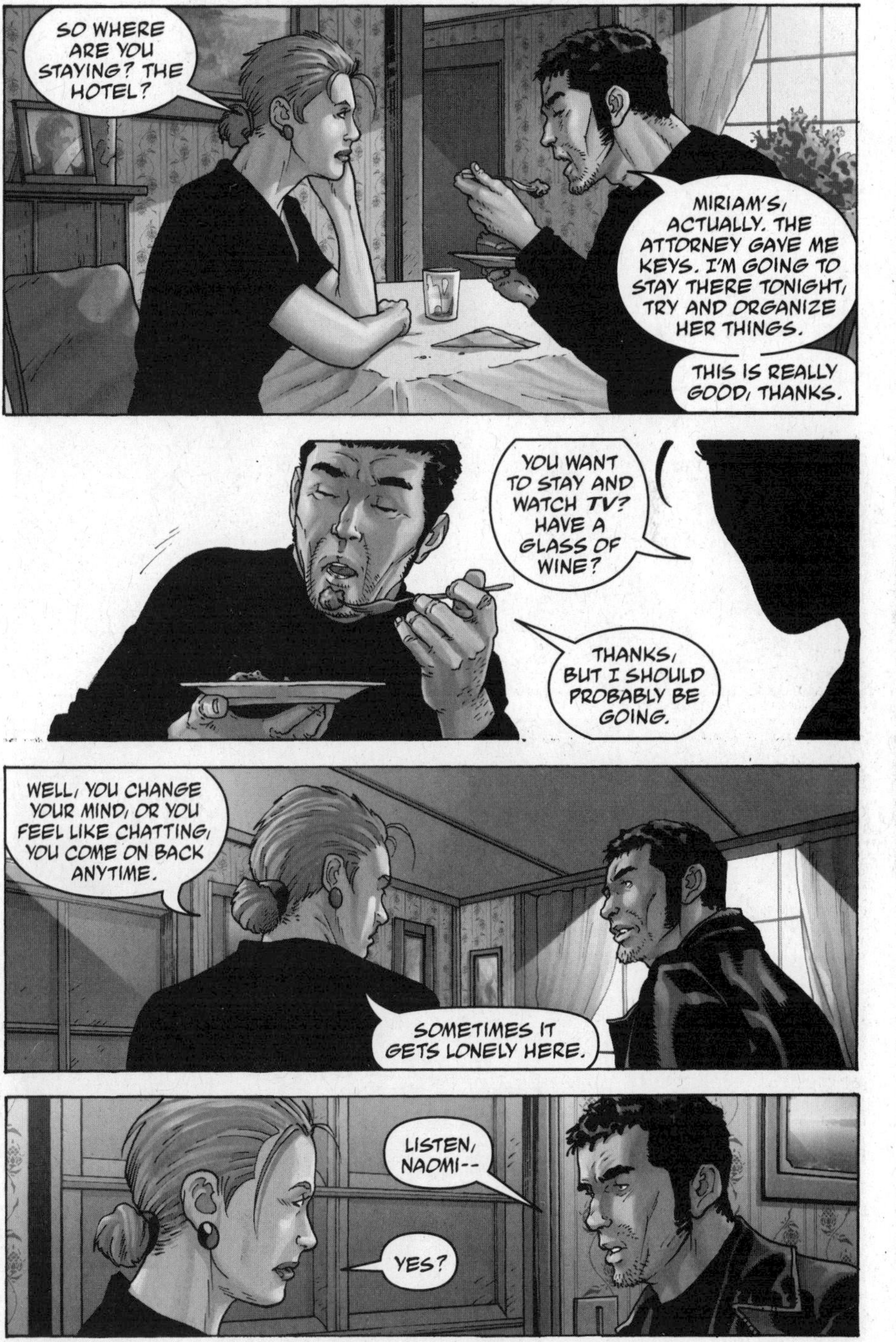
SO WHERE ARE YOU STAYING? THE HOTEL?
MIRIAM'S, ACTUALLY. THE ATTORNEY GAVE ME KEYS. I'M GOING TO STAY THERE TONIGHT, TRY AND ORGANIZE HER THINGS.
THIS IS REALLY GOOD, THANKS.
YOU WANT TO STAY AND WATCH TV? HAVE A GLASS OF WINE?
THANKS, BUT I SHOULD PROBABLY BE GOING.
WELL, YOU CHANGE YOUR MIND, OR YOU FEEL LIKE CHATTING, YOU COME ON BACK ANYTIME.
SOMETIMES IT GETS LONELY HERE.
LISTEN, NAOMI--
YES?

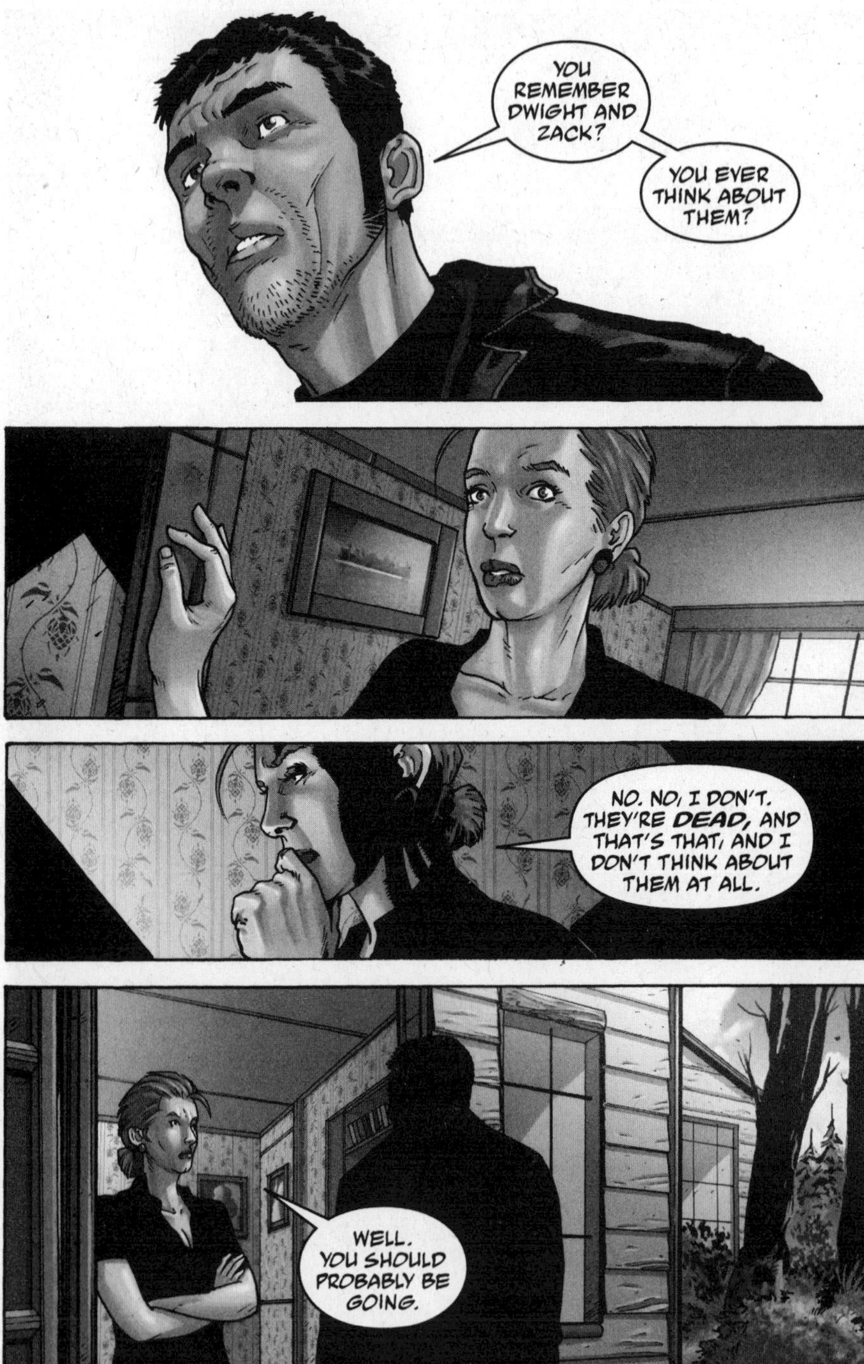
YOU REMEMBER DWIGHT AND ZACK?
YOU EVER THINK ABOUT THEM?
NO. NO, I DON'T. THEY'RE **DEAD,** AND THAT'S THAT, AND I DON'T THINK ABOUT THEM AT ALL.
WELL. YOU SHOULD PROBABLY BE GOING.

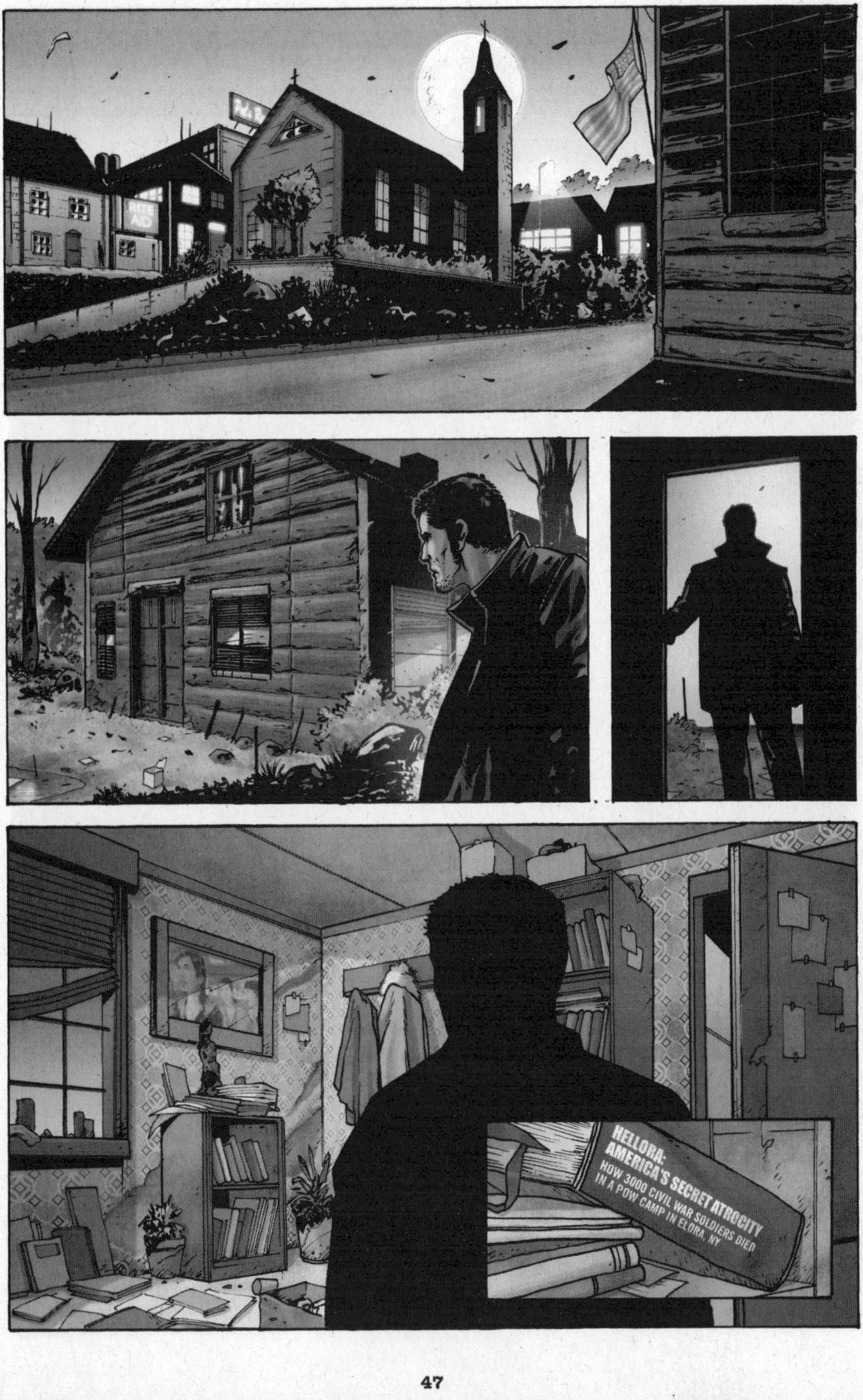
RITE AID
HELLORA: AMERICA'S SECRET ATROCITY
HOW 3000 CIVIL WAR SOLDIERS DIED IN A POW CAMP IN ELORA, NY

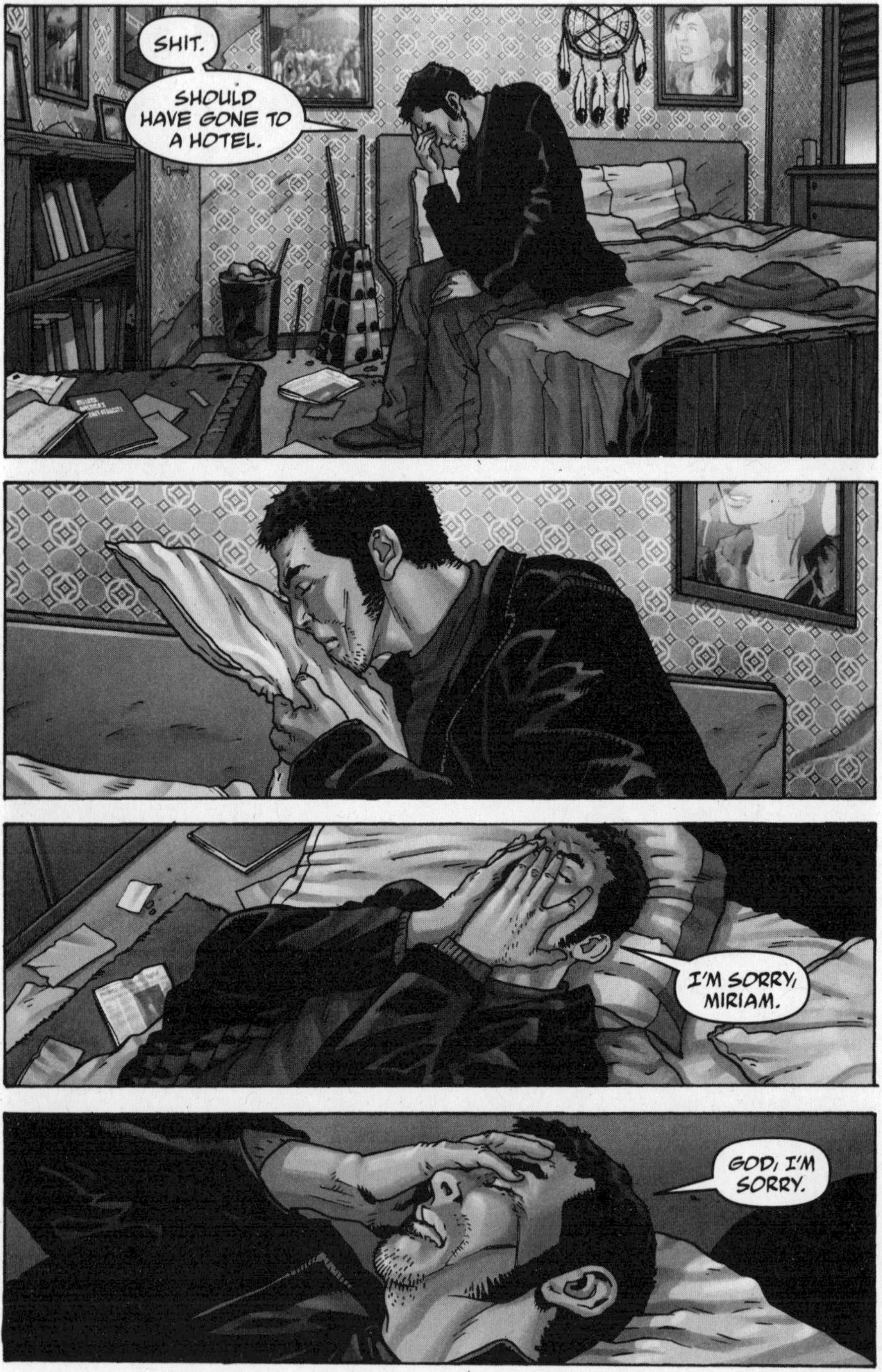
SHIT.
SHOULD HAVE GONE TO A HOTEL.
I'M SORRY, MIRIAM.
GOD, I'M SORRY.

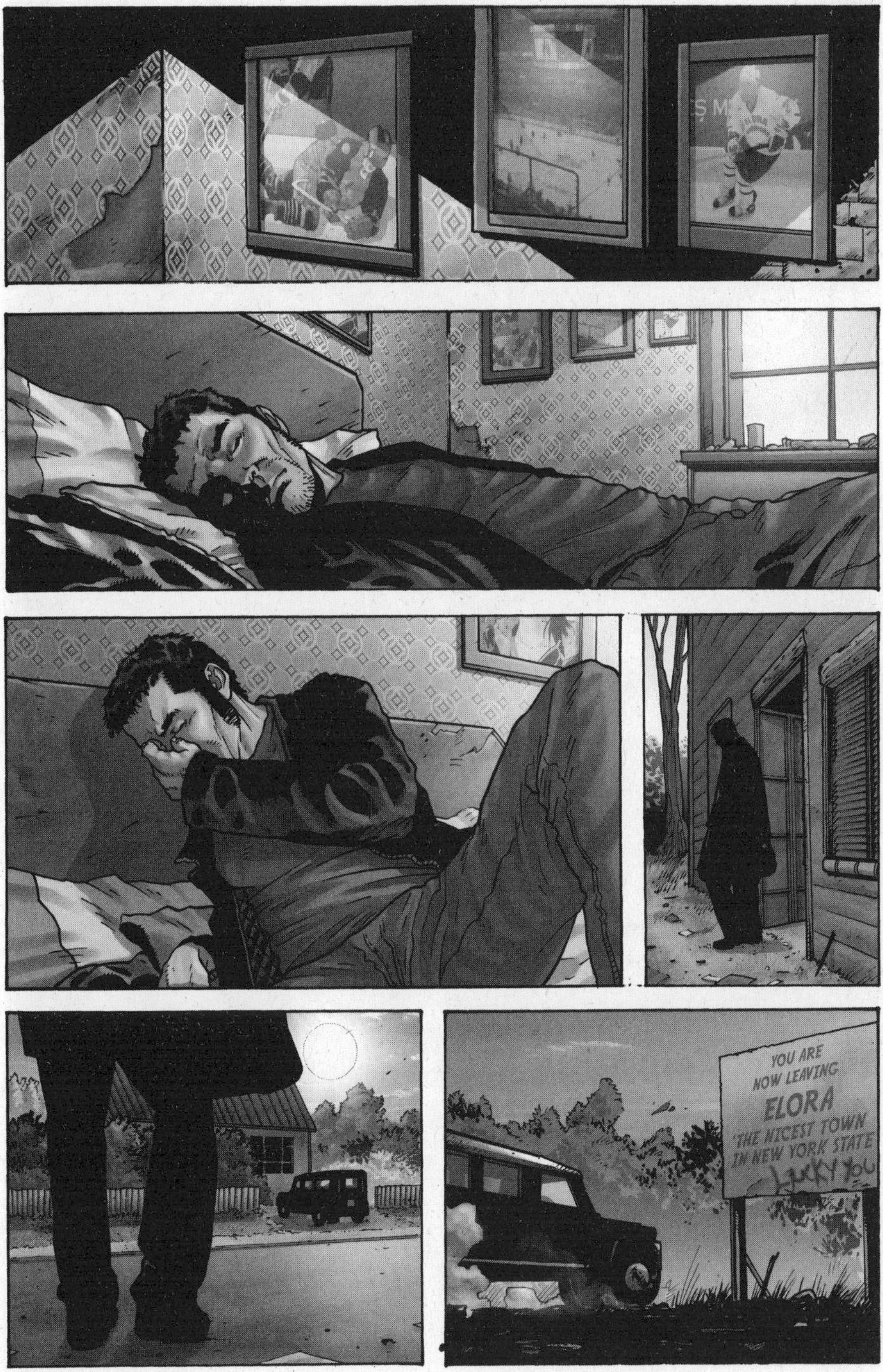
YOU ARE NOW LEAVING
ELORA
'THE NICEST TOWN IN NEW YORK STATE'
LUCKY YOU

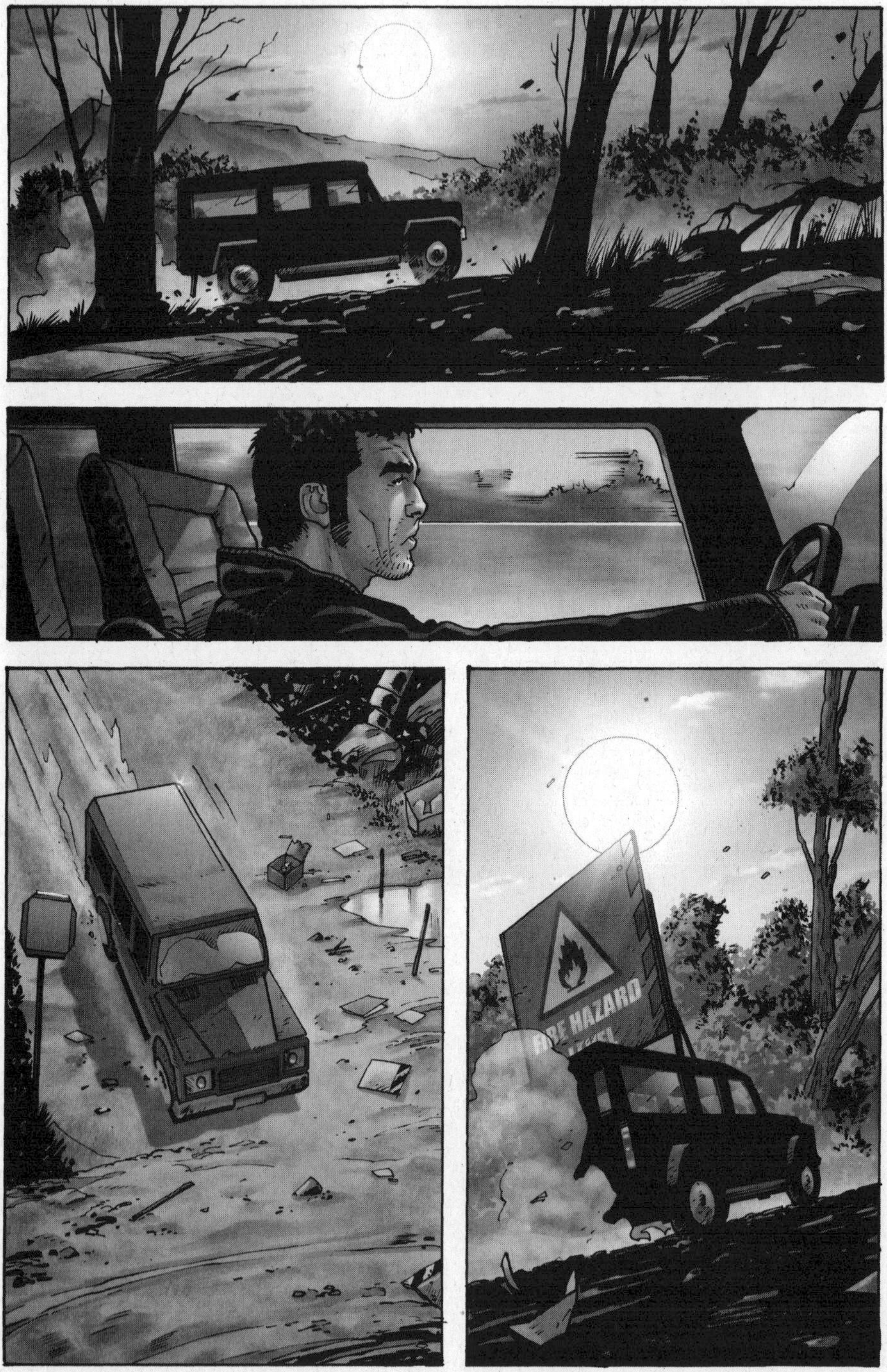
FIRE HAZARD

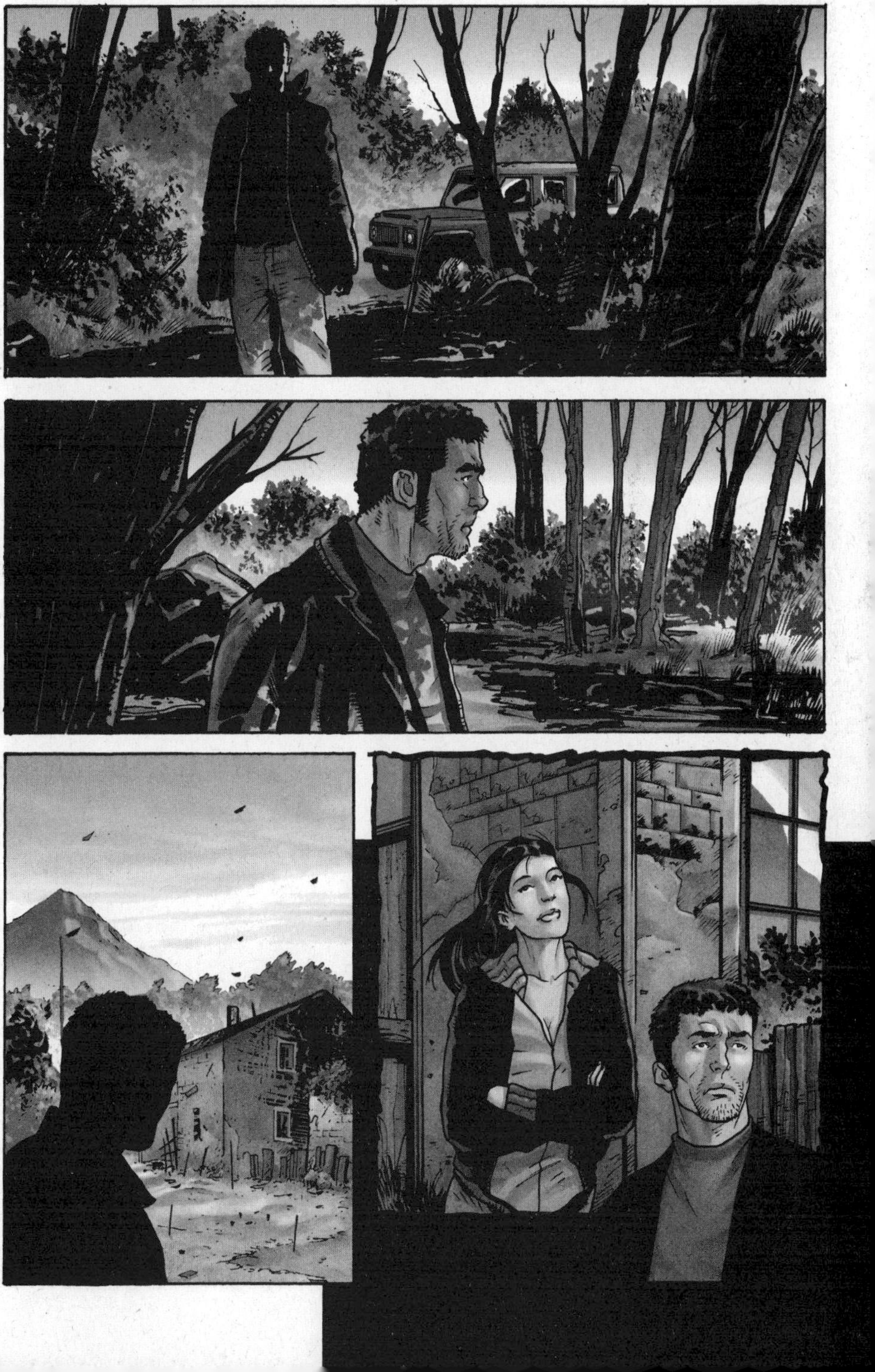

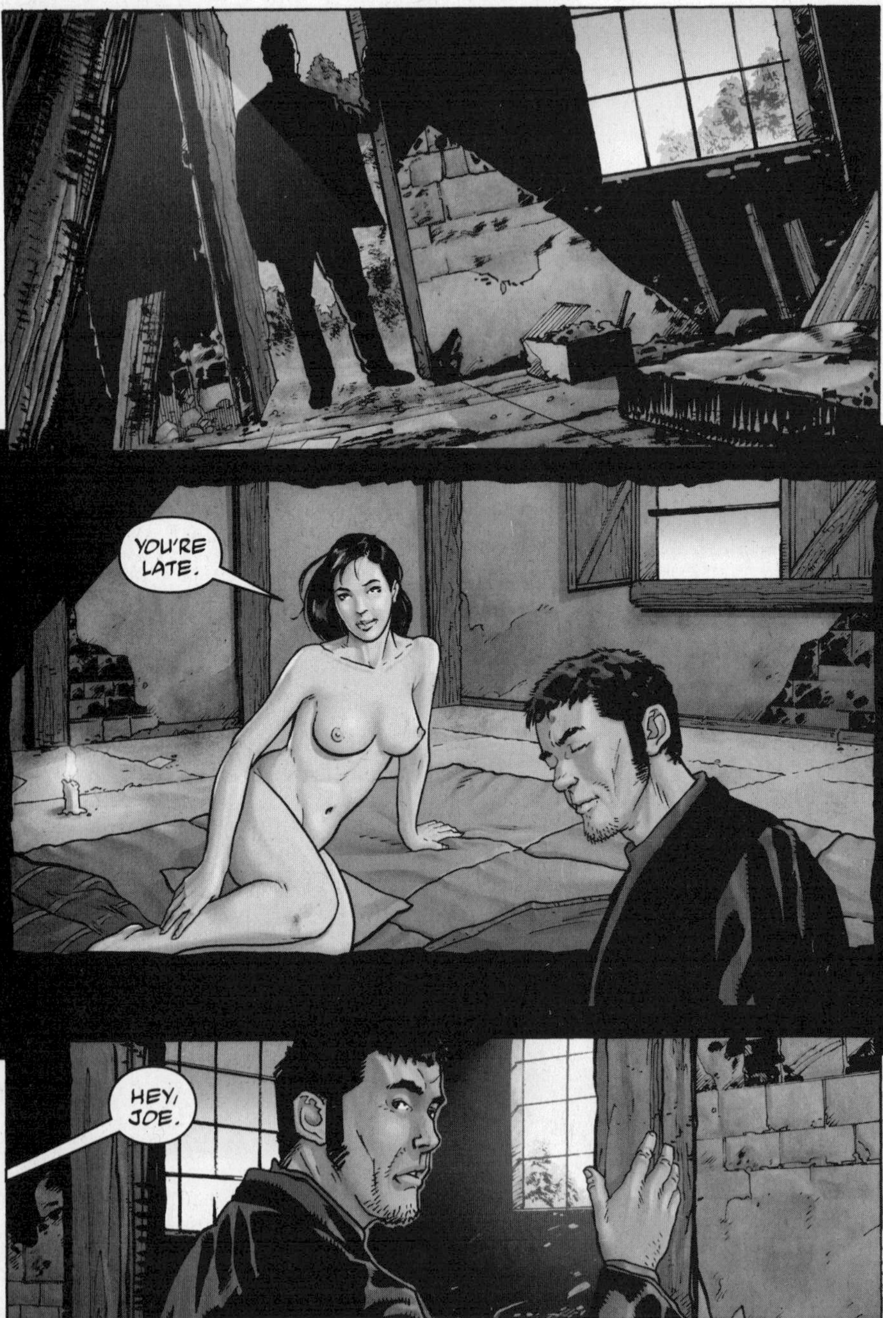
YOU'RE LATE.
HEY, JOE.

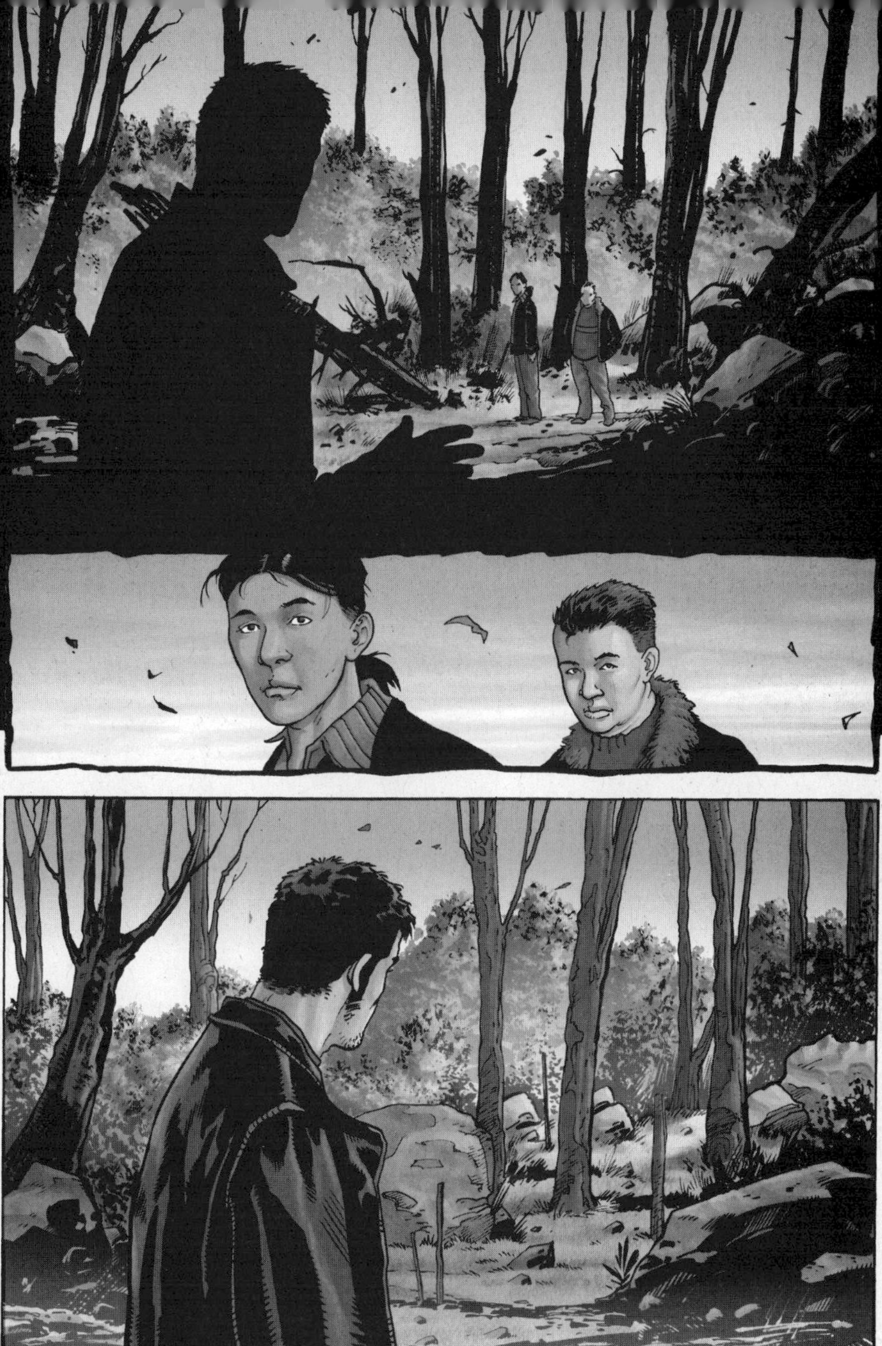

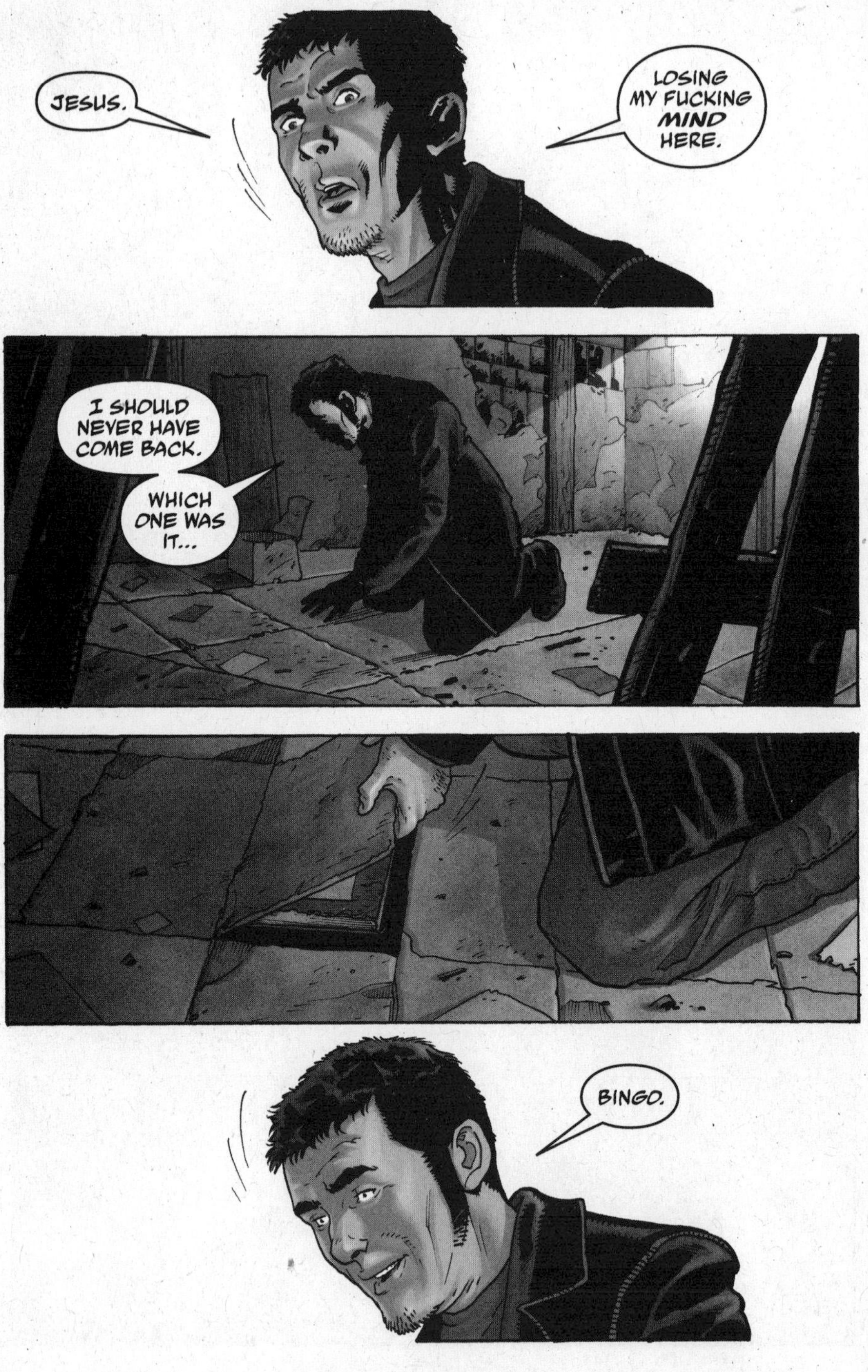
JESUS.
LOSING MY FUCKING MIND HERE.
I SHOULD NEVER HAVE COME BACK.
WHICH ONE WAS IT...
BINGO.

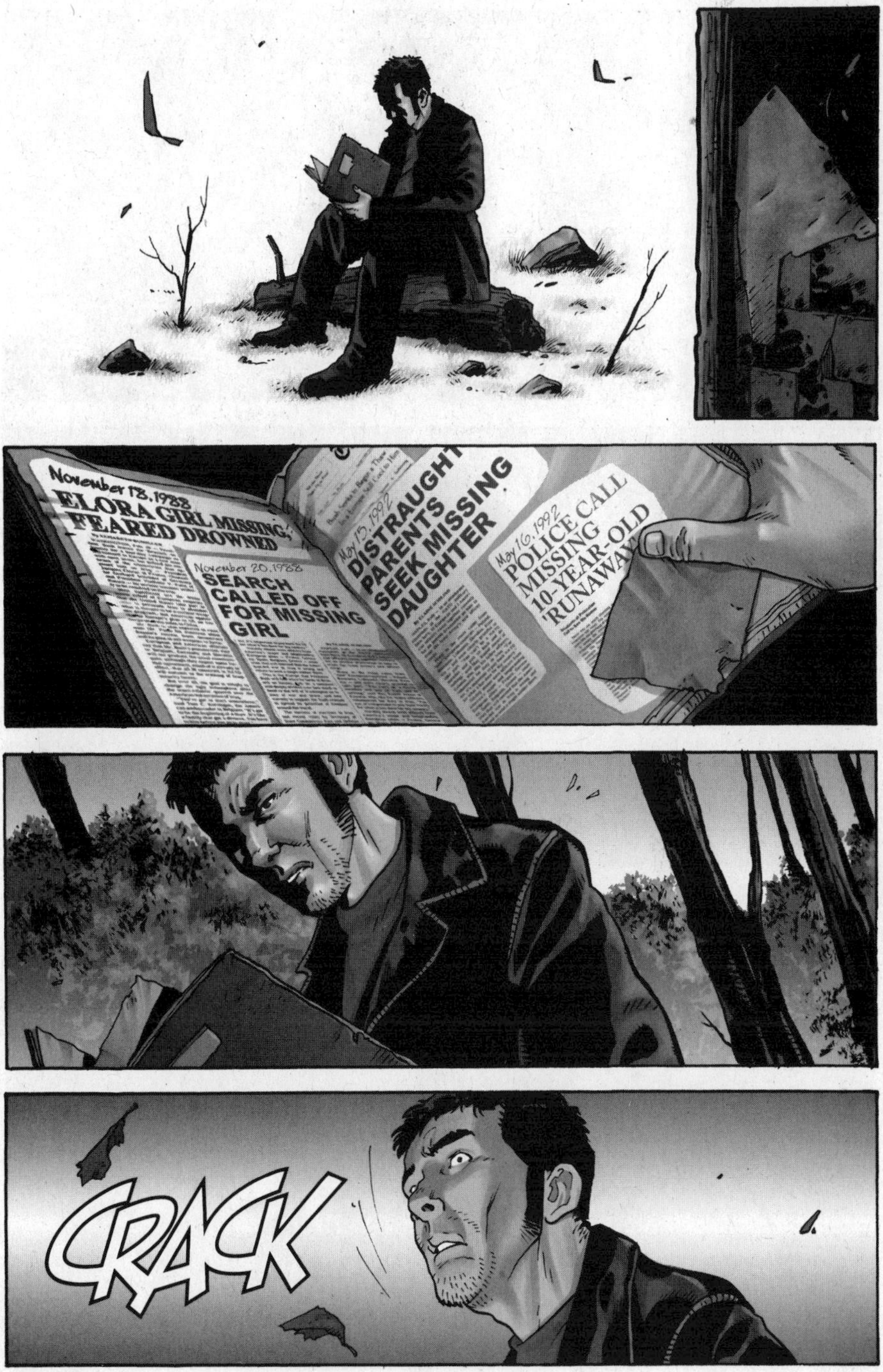
November 18, 1988
ELORA GIRL MISSING; FEARED DROWNED
November 20, 1988
SEARCH CALLED OFF FOR MISSING GIRL
May 15, 1992
DISTRAUGHT PARENTS SEEK MISSING DAUGHTER
May 16, 1992
POLICE CALL MISSING 10-YEAR-OLD 'RUNAWAY'
CRACK

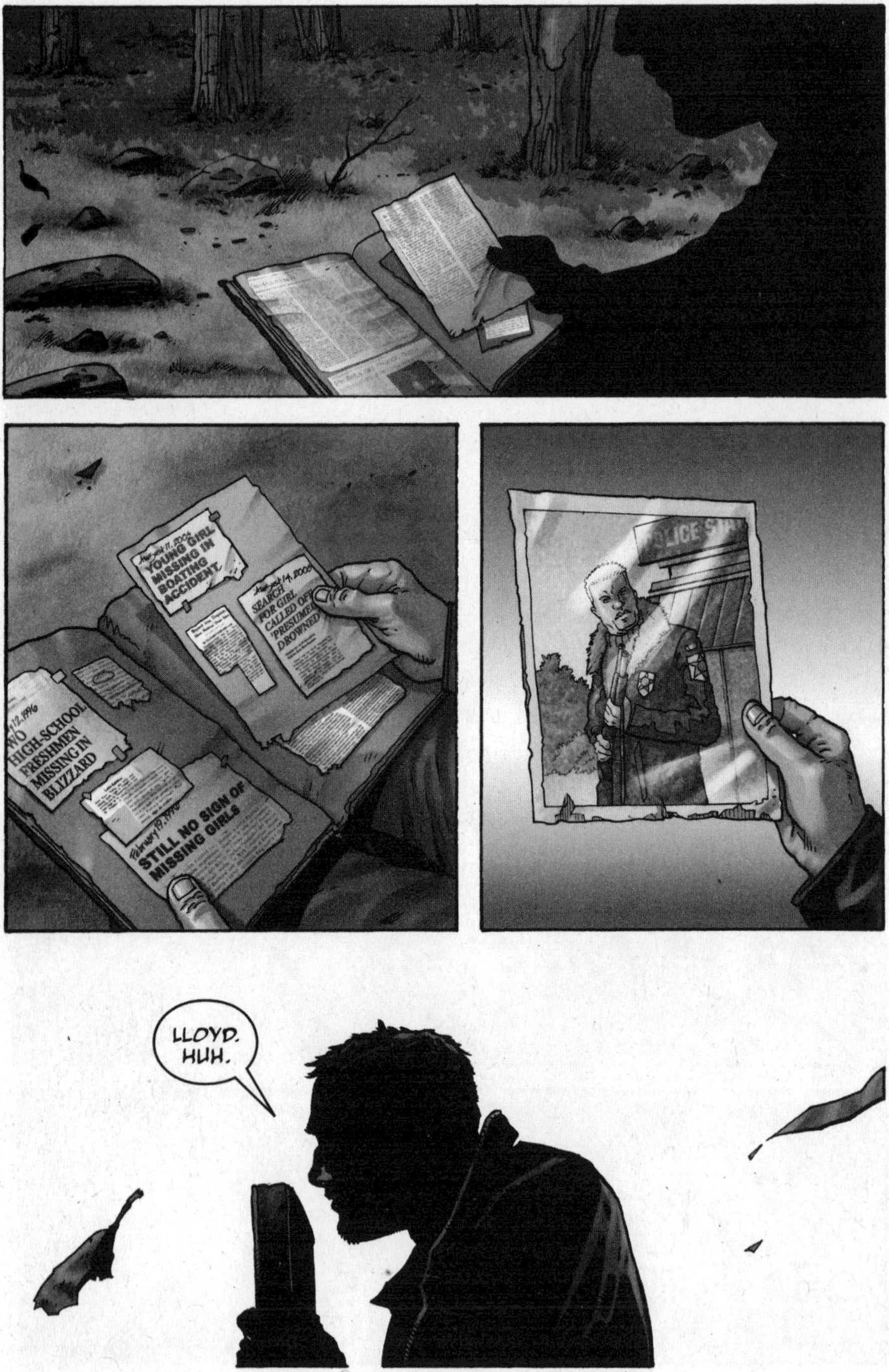
YOUNG GIRL MISSING IN BOATING ACCIDENT
SEARCH FOR GIRL CALLED OFF 'PRESUMED DROWNED'
WO HIGH-SCHOOL FRESHMEN MISSING IN BLIZZARD
STILL NO SIGN OF MISSING GIRLS
LLOYD. HUH.

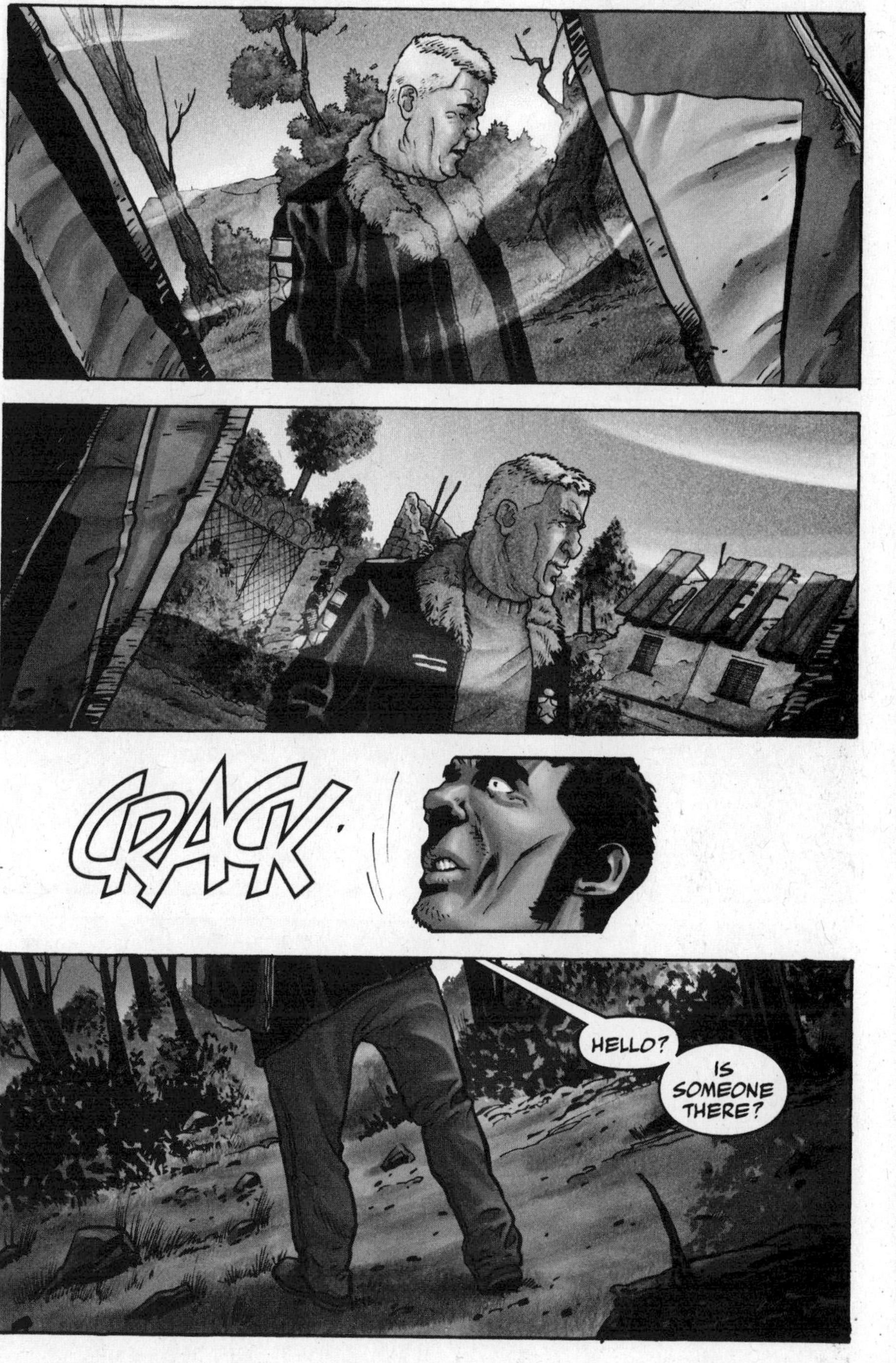
CRACK
HELLO?
IS SOMEONE THERE?

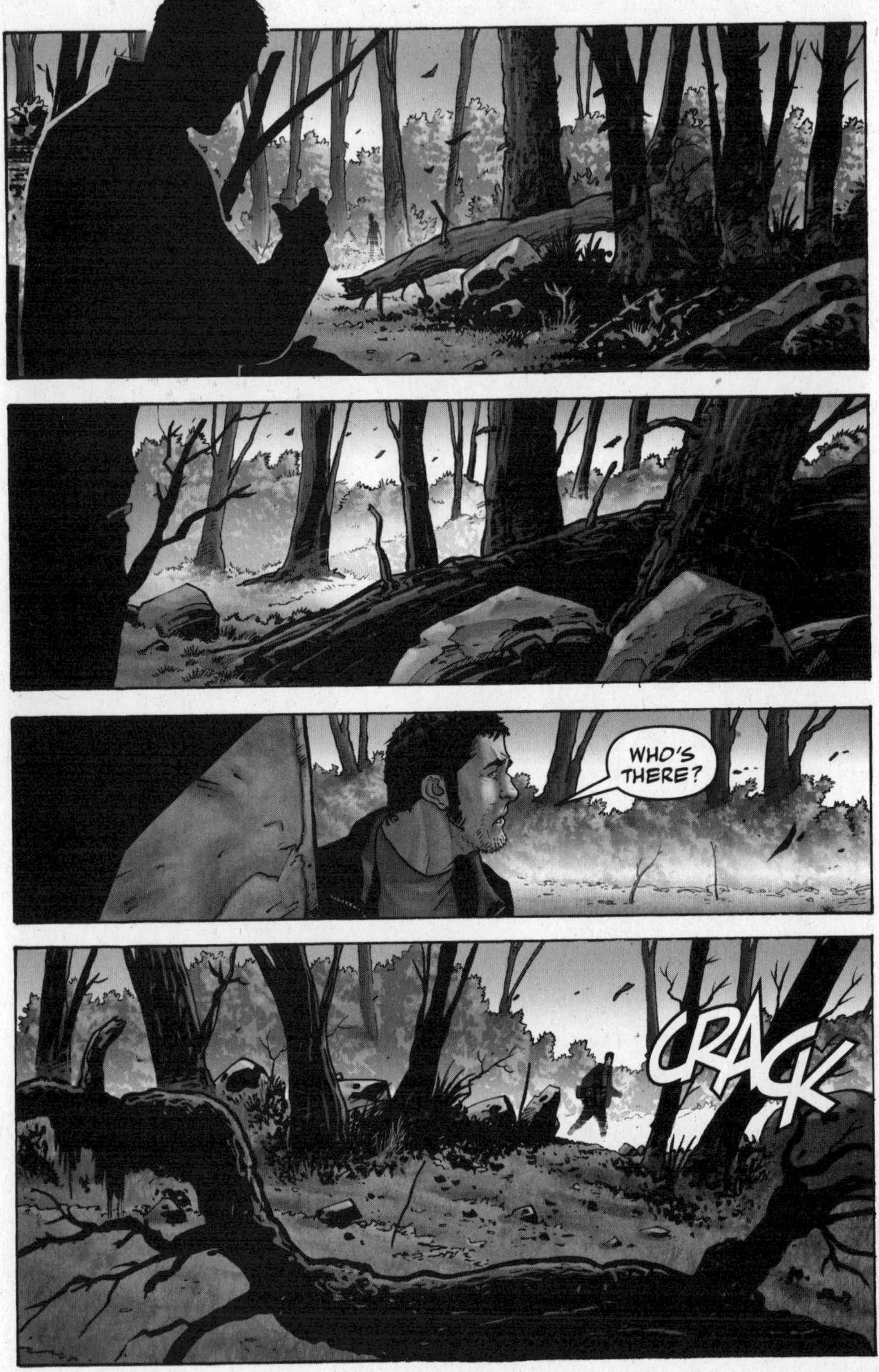
WHO'S THERE?
CRACK

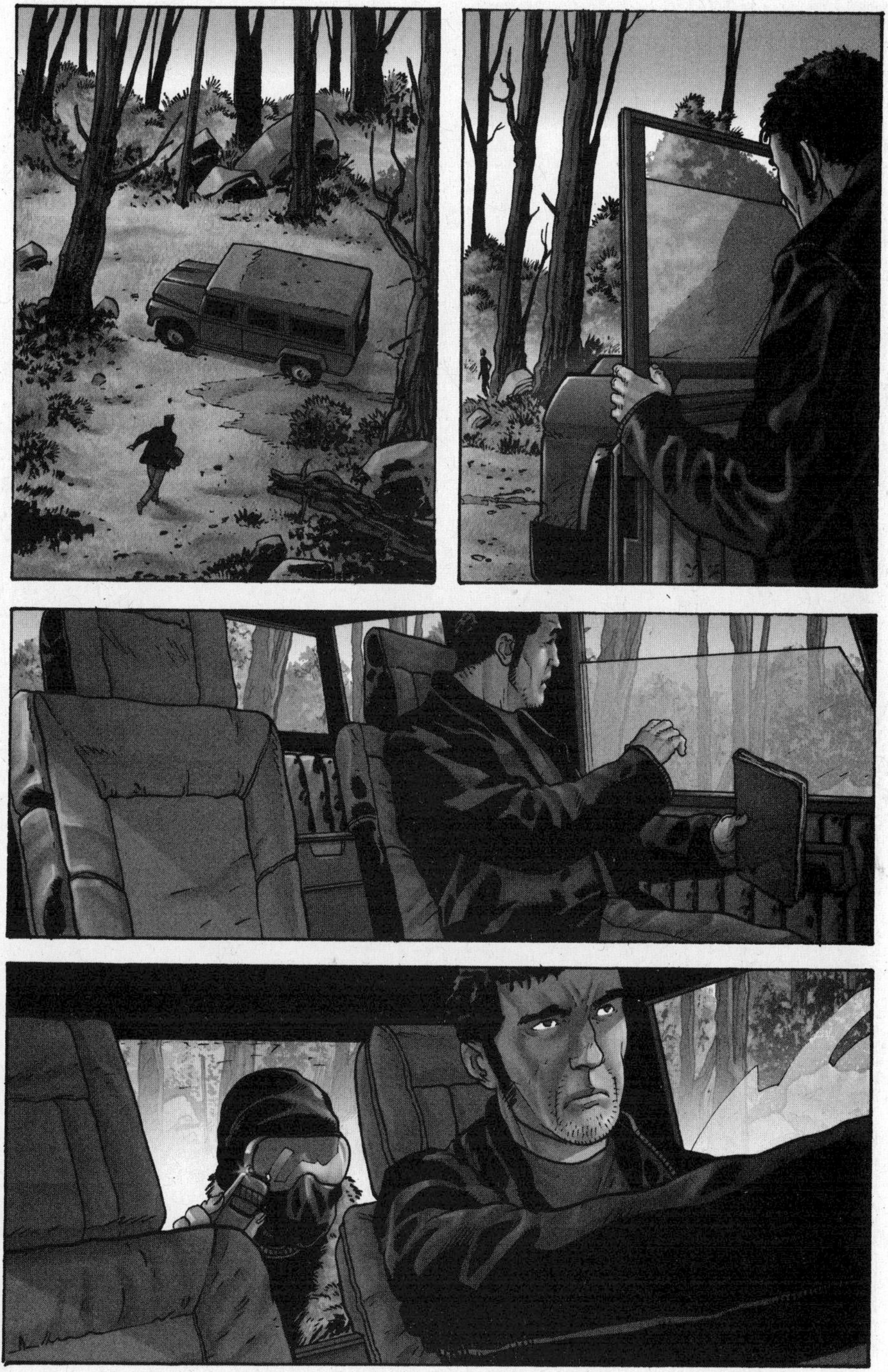

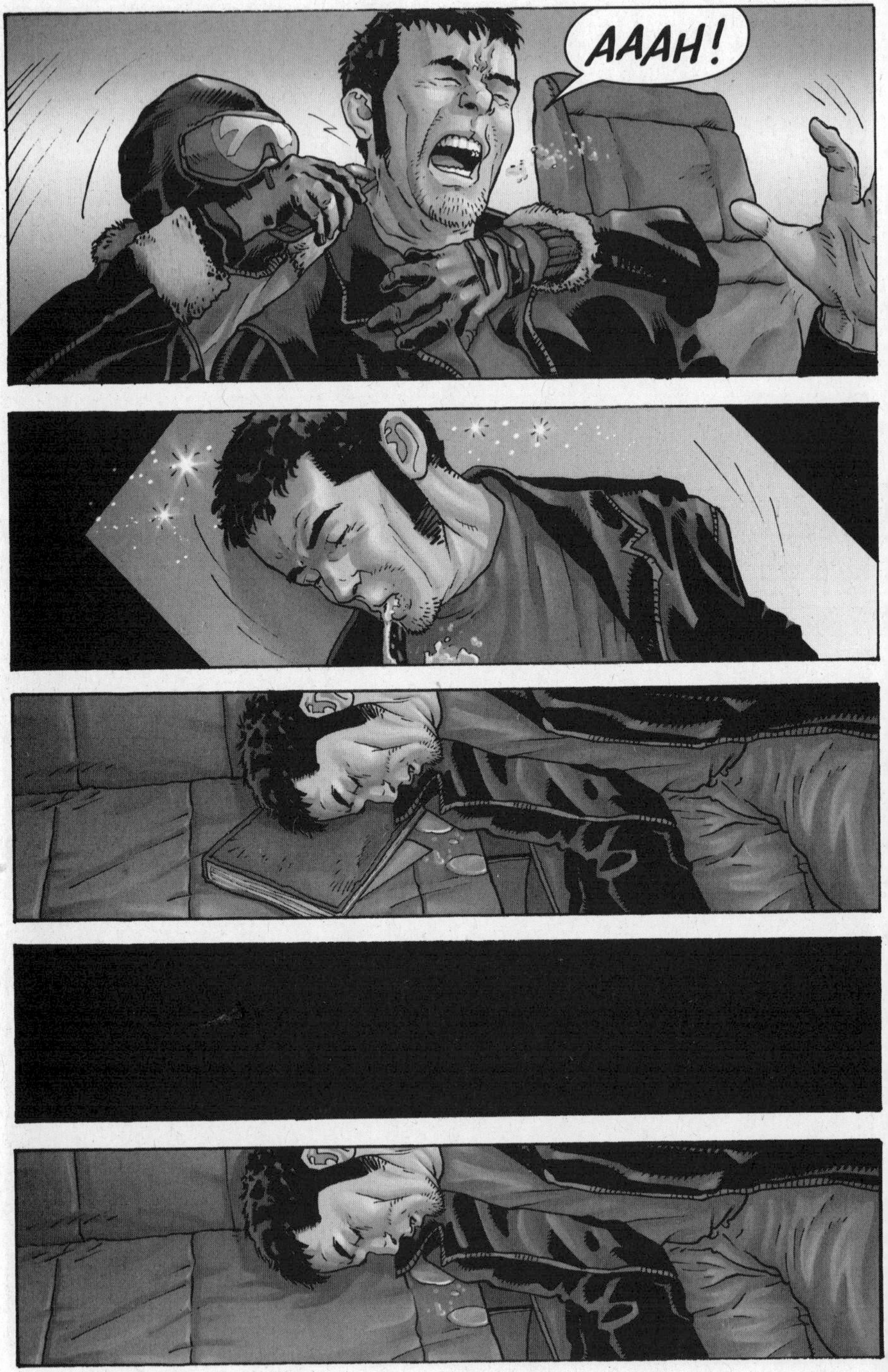
AAAH!

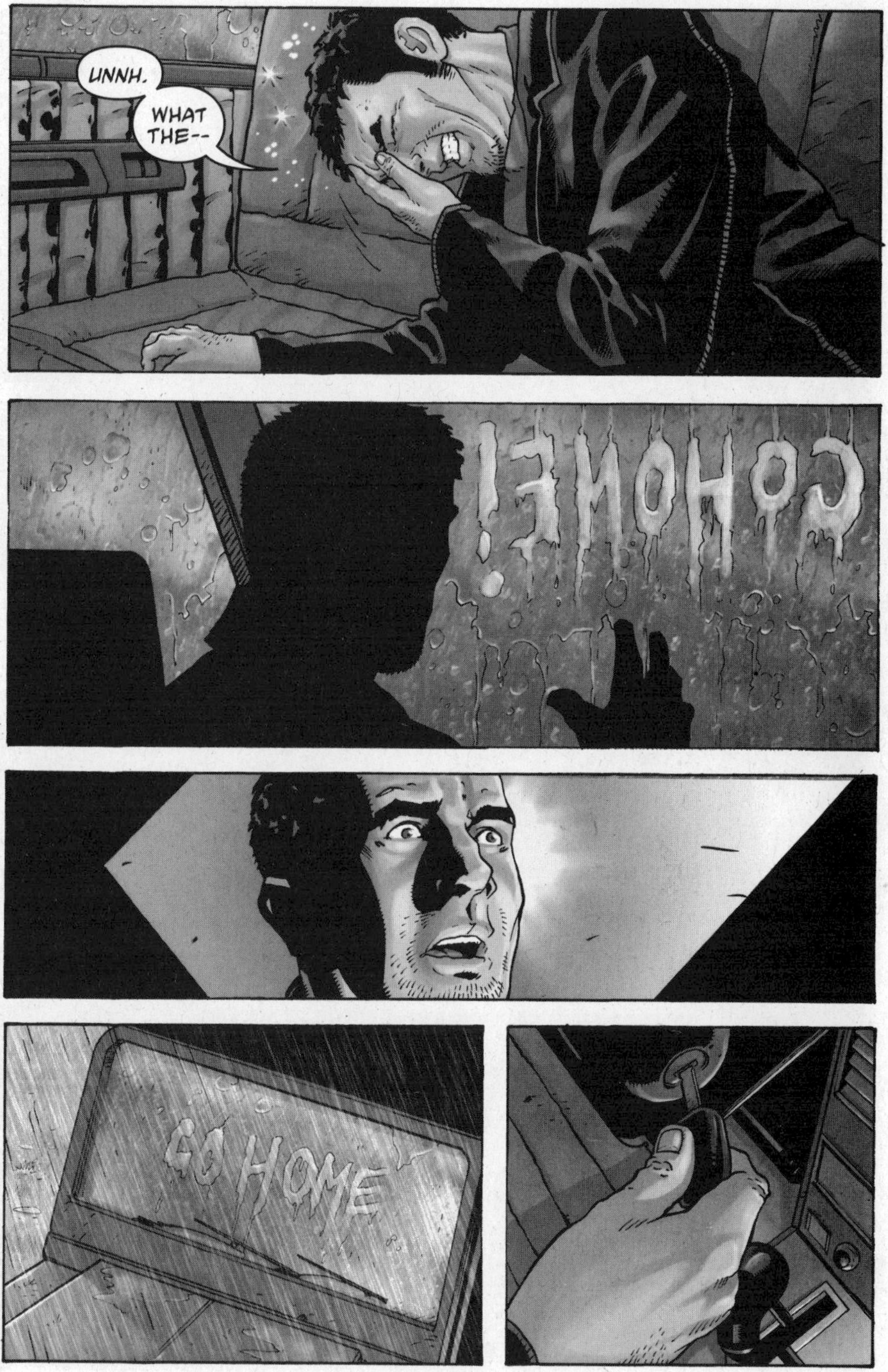
UNNH.
WHAT THE--
GO HOME!
GO HOME

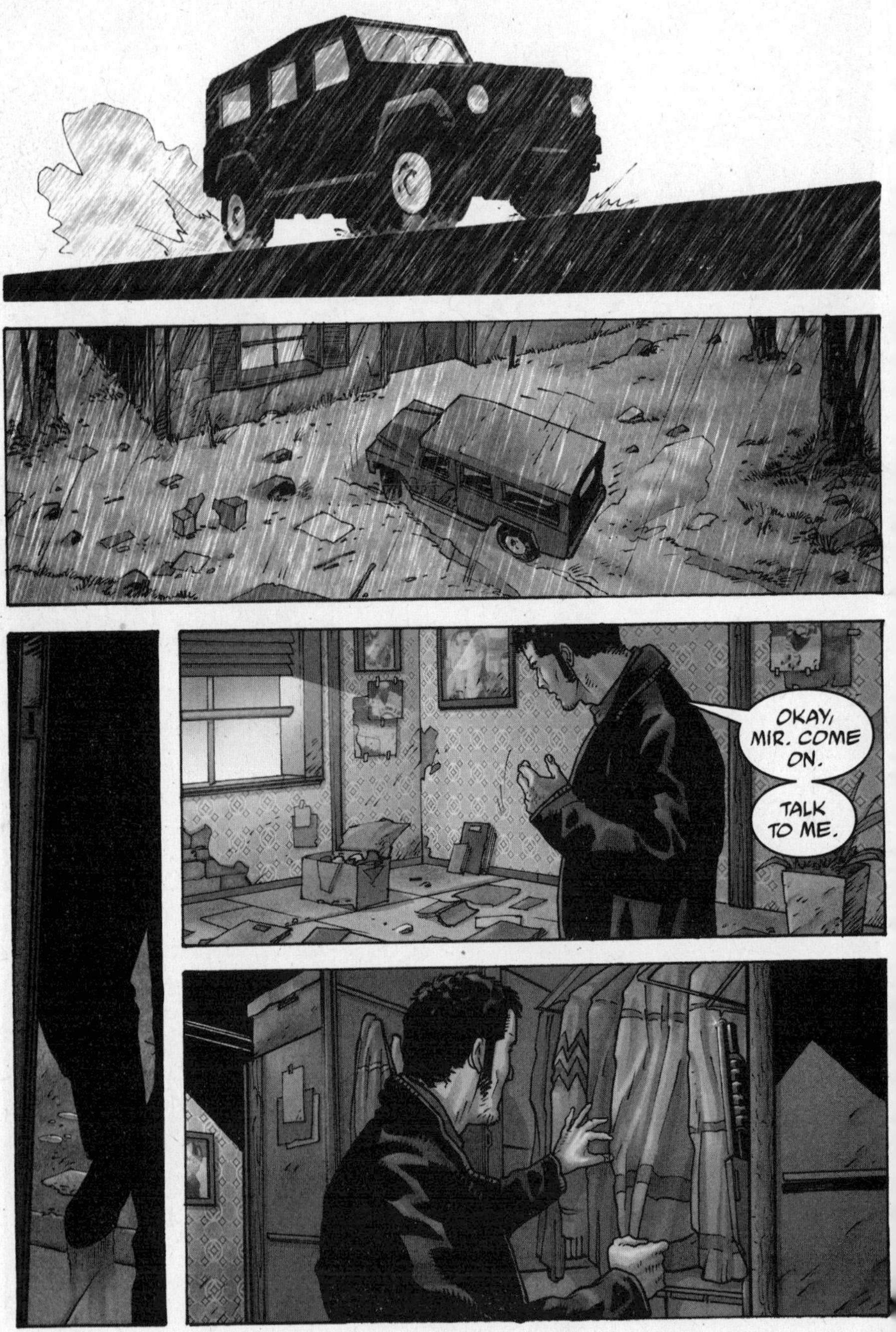
OKAY, MIR. COME ON.
TALK TO ME.

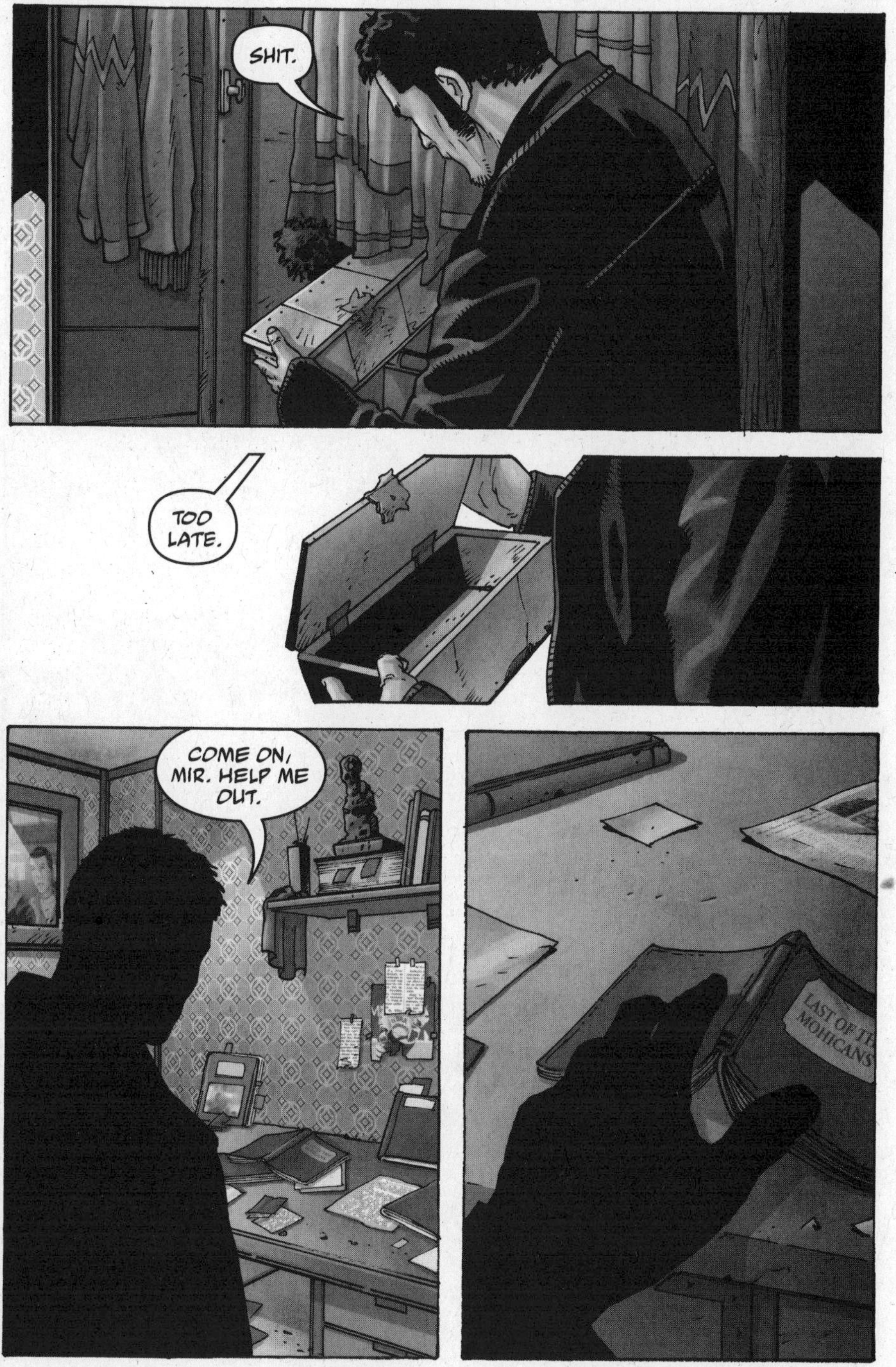
SHIT.
TOO LATE.
COME ON, MIR. HELP ME OUT.
LAST OF THE MOHICANS

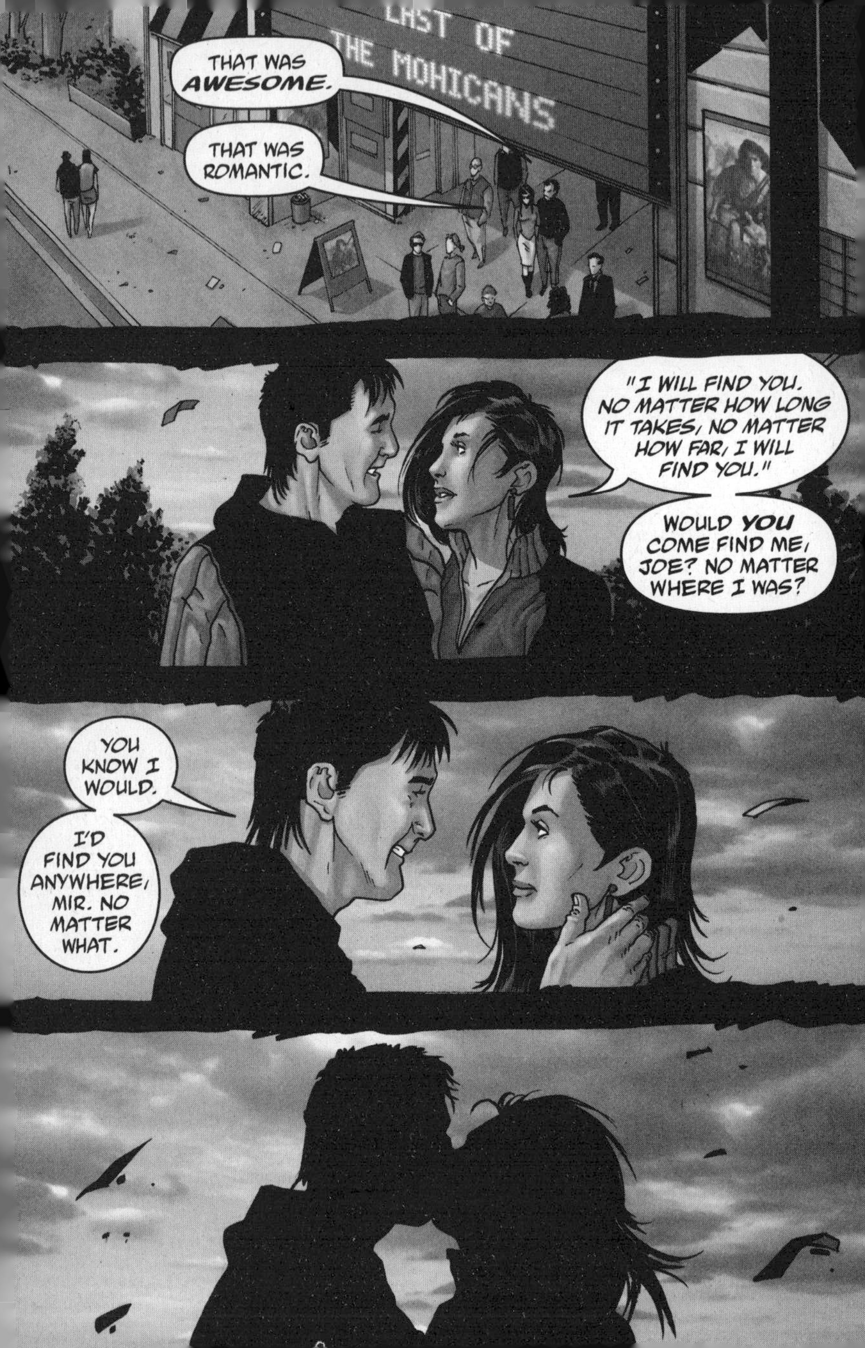
LAST OF THE MOHICANS
THAT WAS AWESOME.
THAT WAS ROMANTIC.
"I WILL FIND YOU. NO MATTER HOW LONG IT TAKES, NO MATTER HOW FAR, I WILL FIND YOU."
WOULD YOU COME FIND ME, JOE? NO MATTER WHERE I WAS?
YOU KNOW I WOULD.
I'D FIND YOU ANYWHERE, MIR. NO MATTER WHAT.

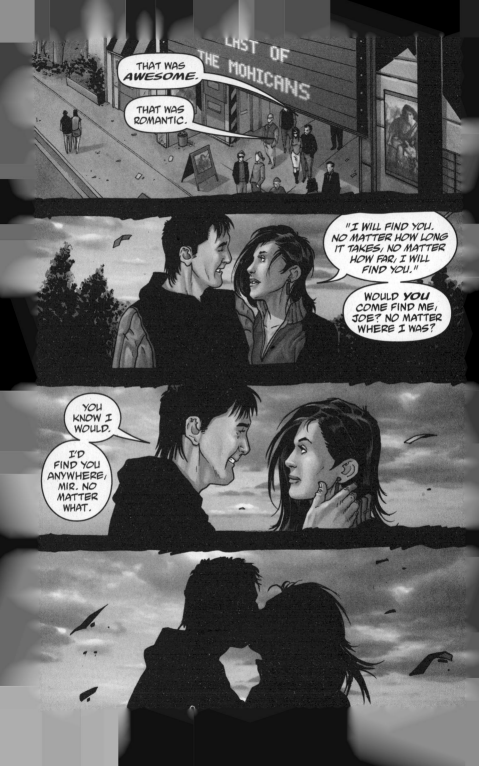

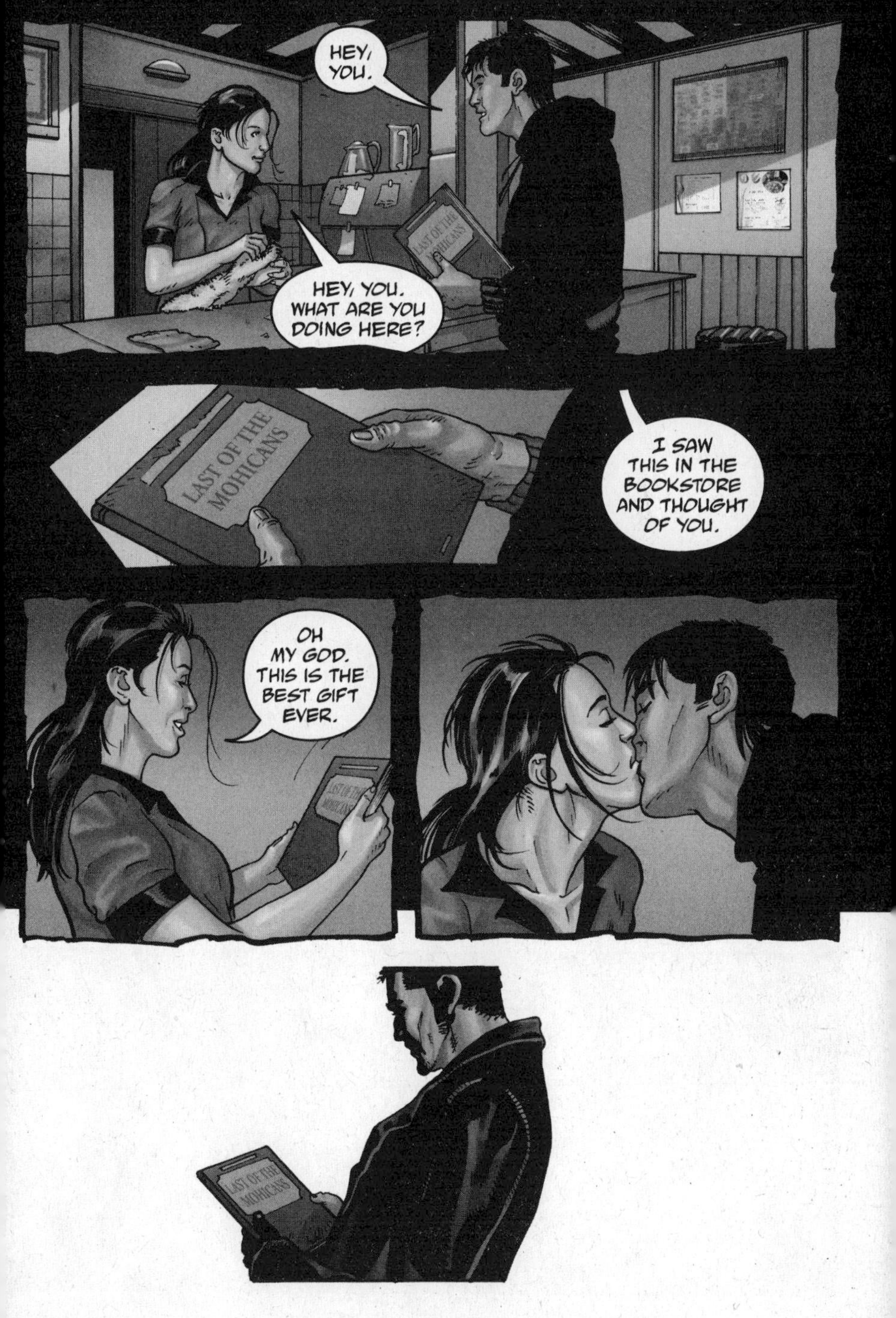
HEY, YOU.
HEY, YOU. WHAT ARE YOU DOING HERE?
I SAW THIS IN THE BOOKSTORE AND THOUGHT OF YOU.
OH MY GOD. THIS IS THE BEST GIFT EVER.

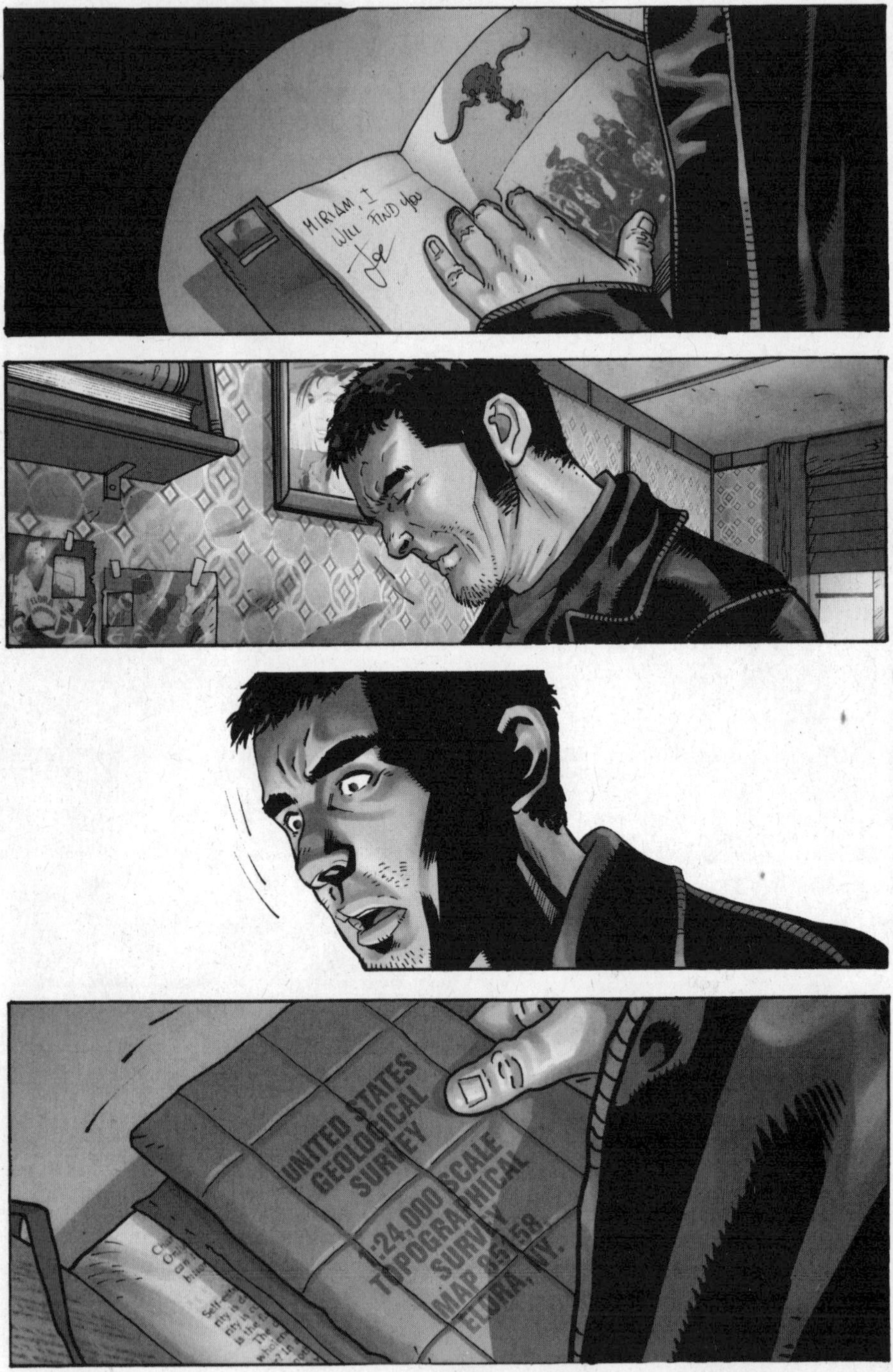
MIRIAM, I WILL FIND YOU
Joe
UNITED STATES GEOLOGICAL SURVEY
1:24,000 SCALE TOPOGRAPHICAL SURVEY
ELORA, NY.

?

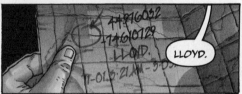

LLOYD.

CLICK

RECEIVING GPS DATA.

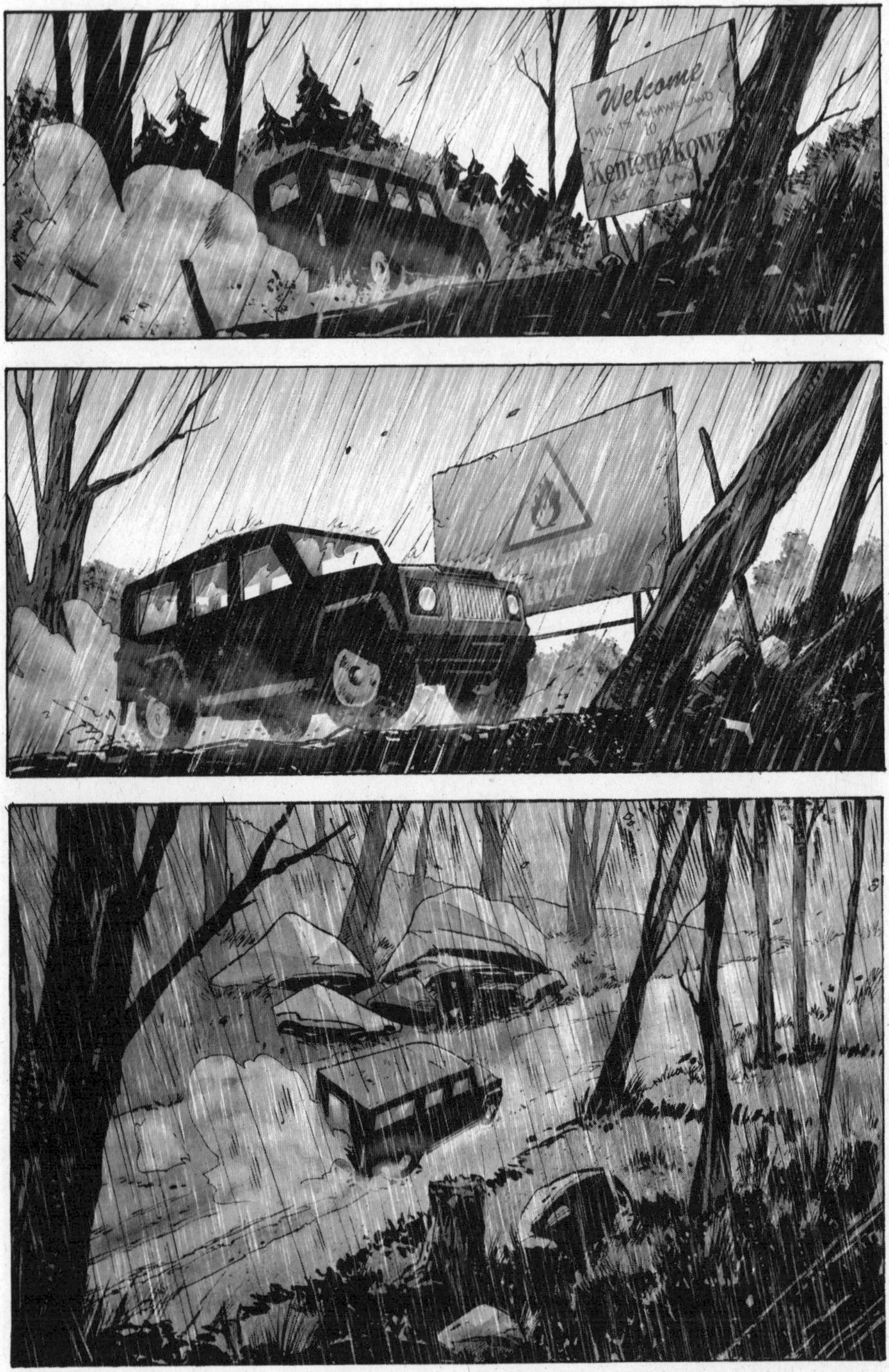
Welcome
to

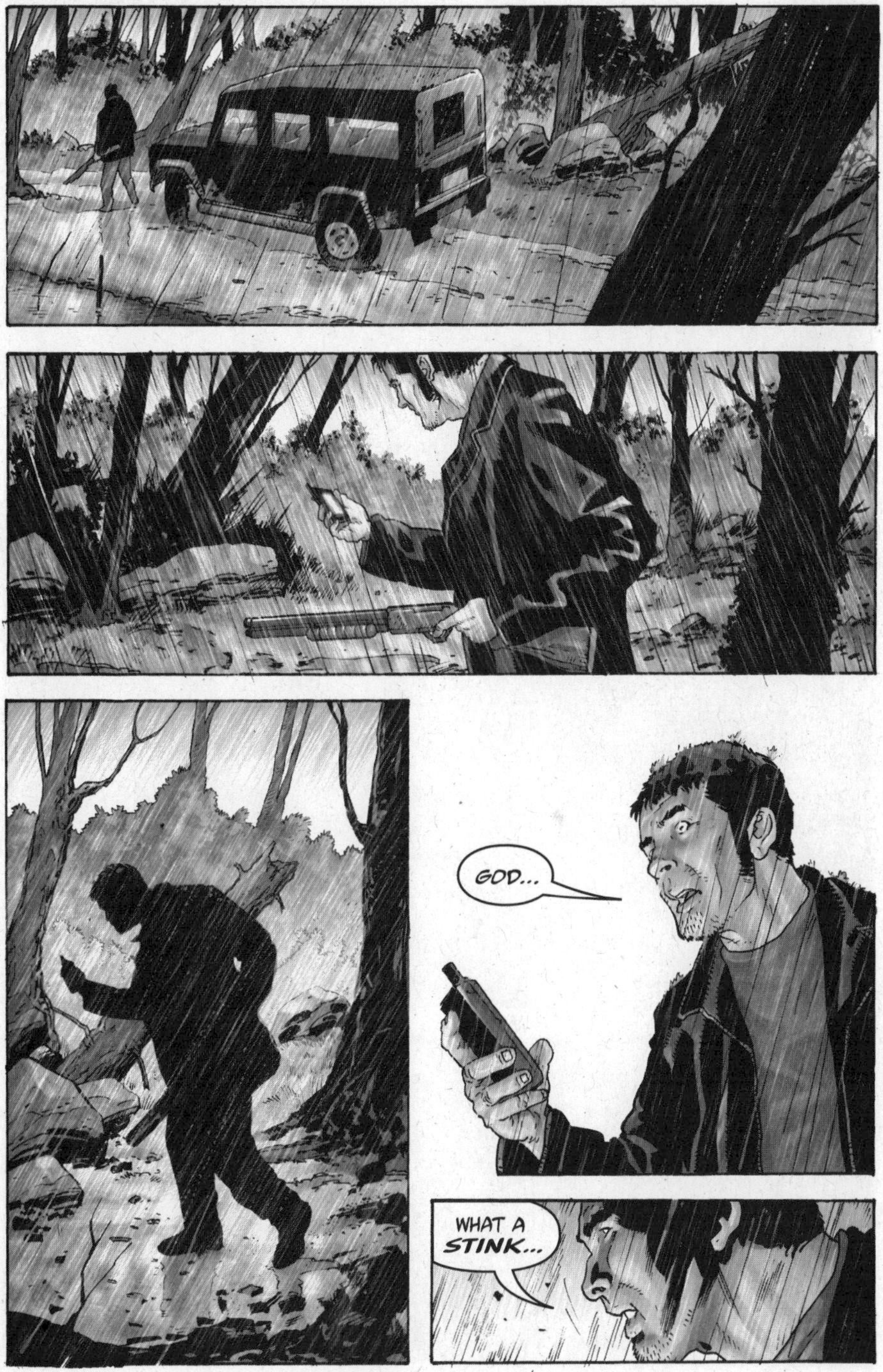
GOD...
WHAT A STINK...

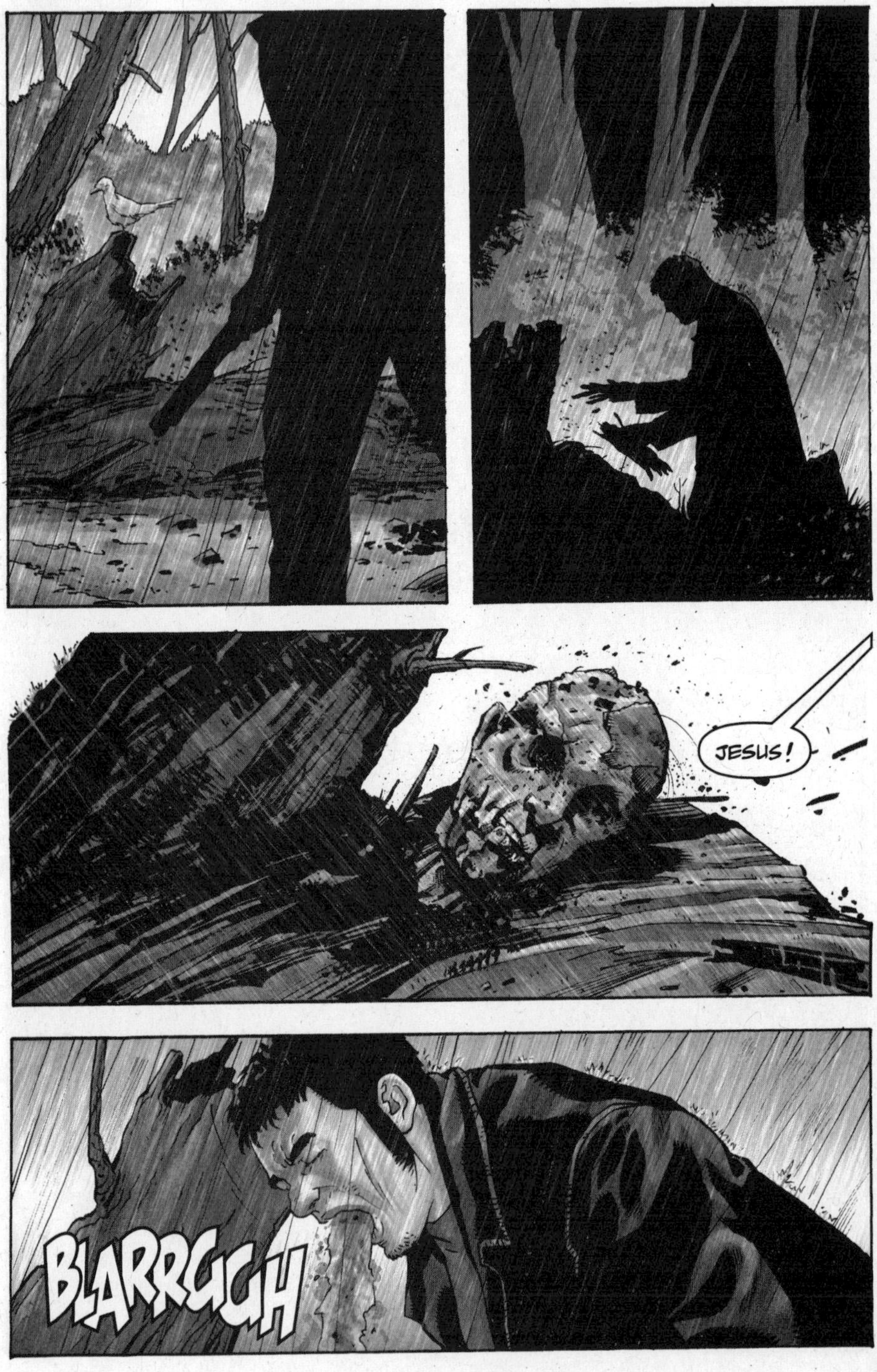
JESUS!
BLARRGGH

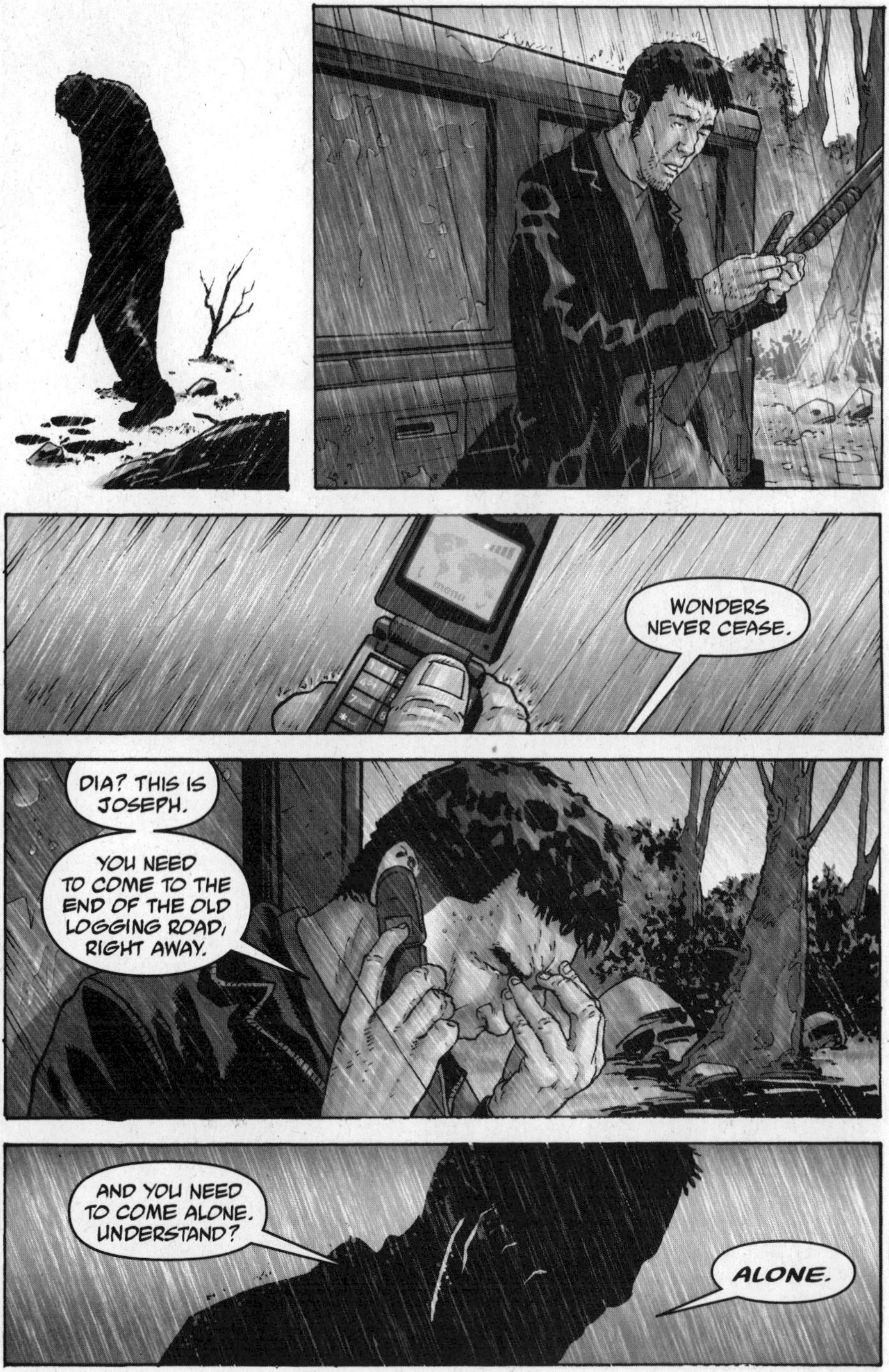
WONDERS NEVER CEASE.
DIA? THIS IS JOSEPH.
YOU NEED TO COME TO THE END OF THE OLD LOGGING ROAD, RIGHT AWAY.
AND YOU NEED TO COME ALONE. UNDERSTAND?
ALONE.

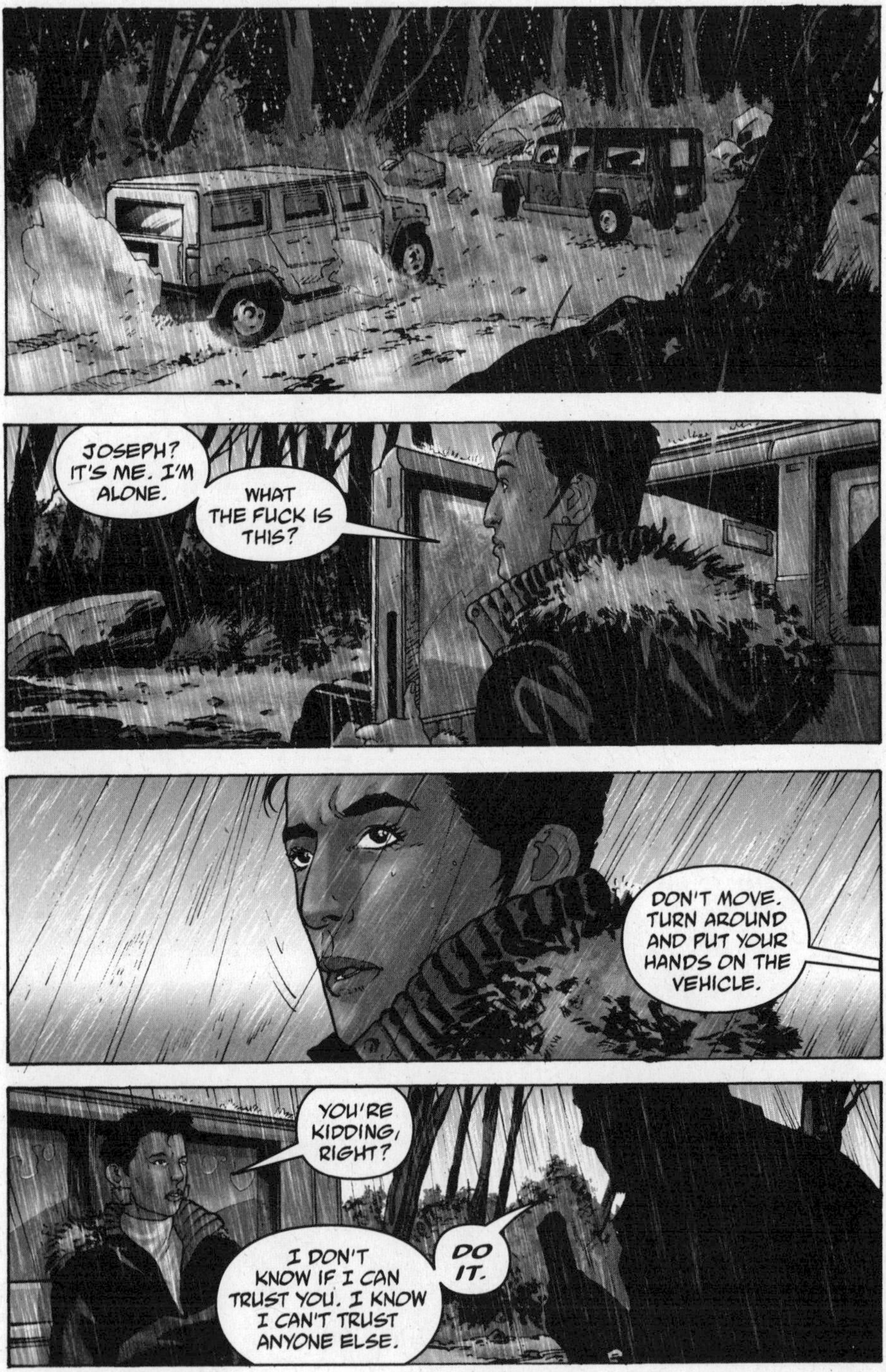
JOSEPH? IT'S ME. I'M ALONE.
WHAT THE FUCK IS THIS?
DON'T MOVE. TURN AROUND AND PUT YOUR HANDS ON THE VEHICLE.
YOU'RE KIDDING, RIGHT?
DO IT.
I DON'T KNOW IF I CAN TRUST YOU. I KNOW I CAN'T TRUST ANYONE ELSE.

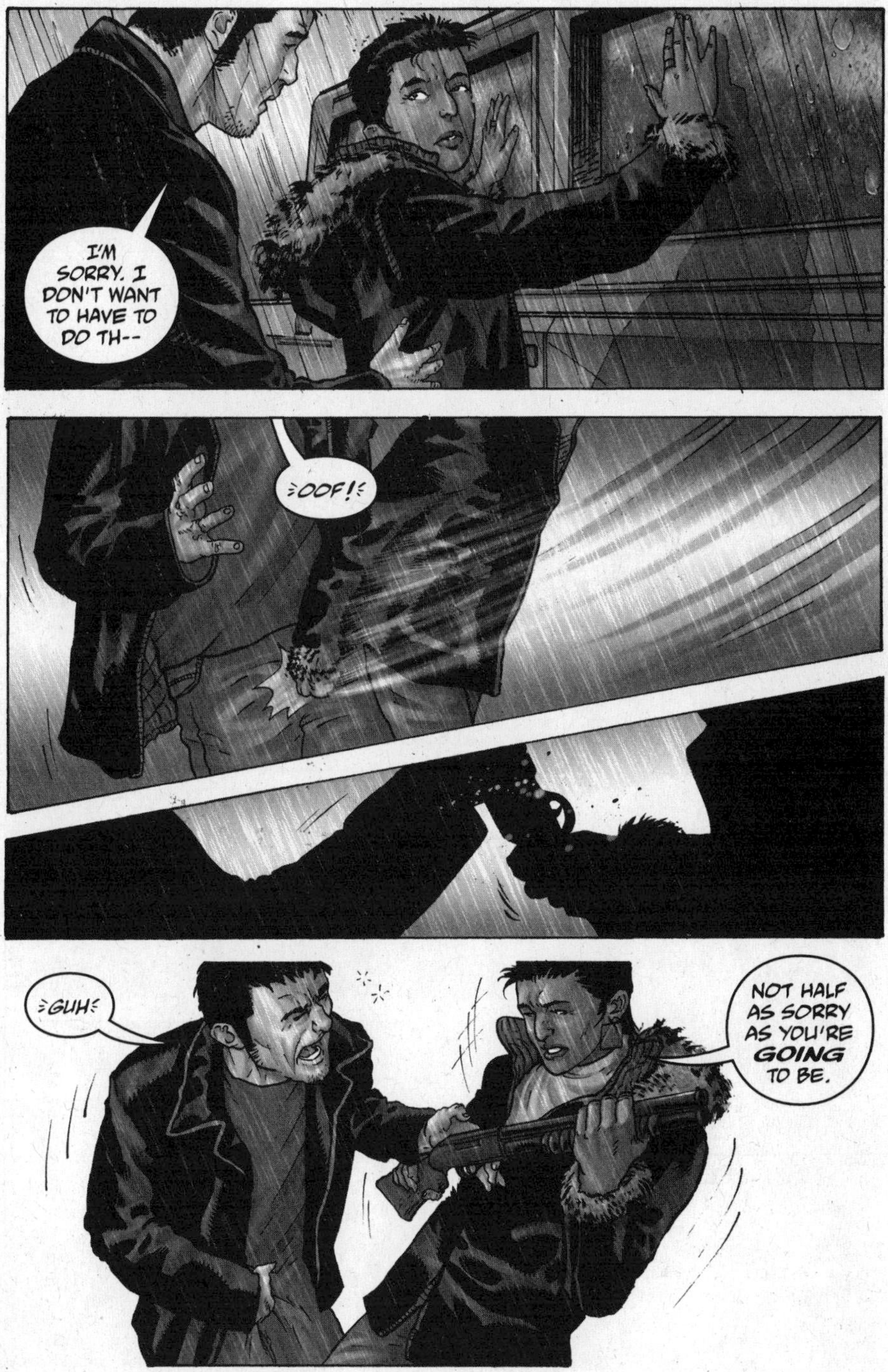
I'M SORRY. I DON'T WANT TO HAVE TO DO TH--
OOF!
GUH
NOT HALF AS SORRY AS YOU'RE GOING TO BE.

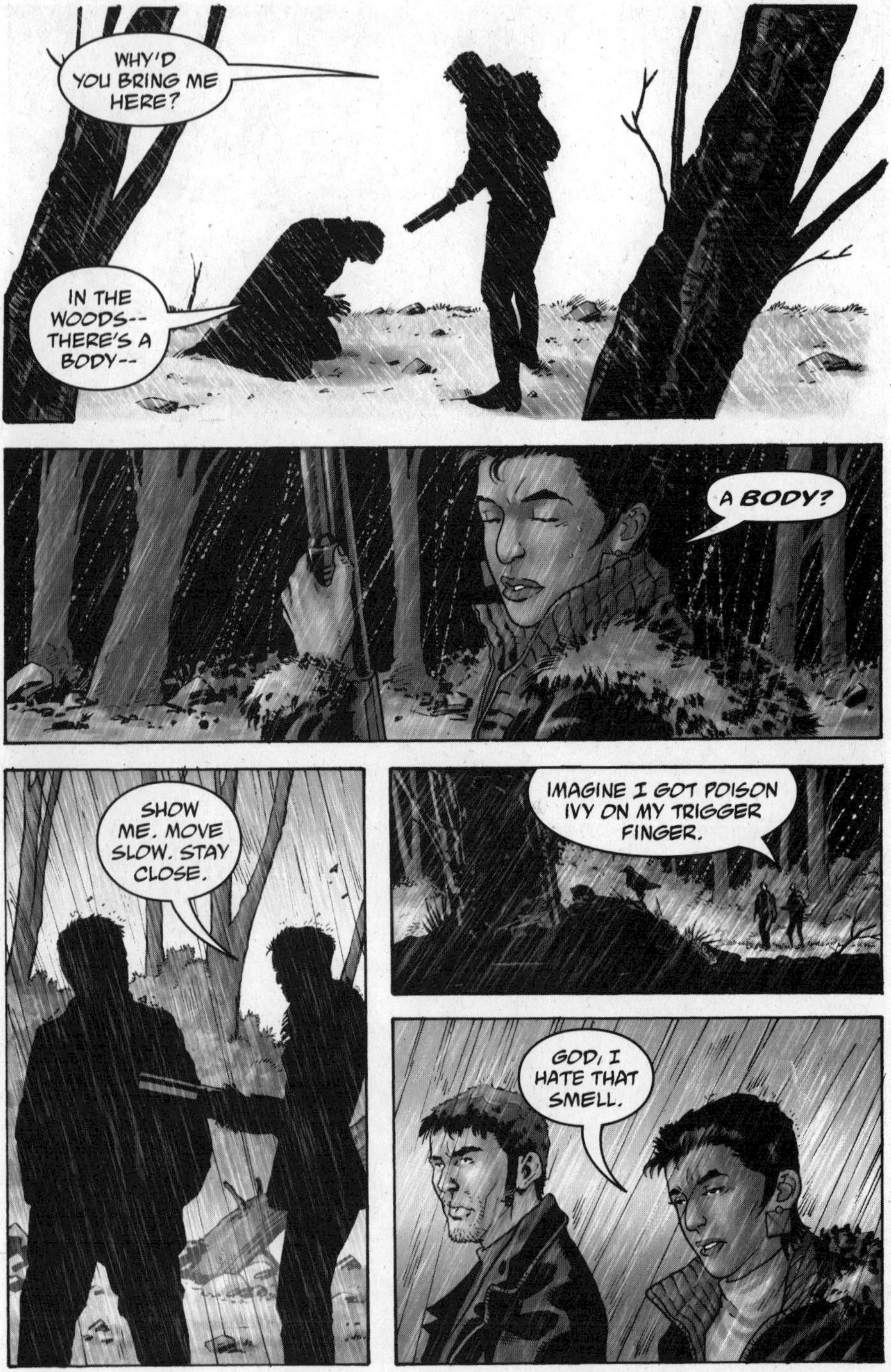
WHY'D YOU BRING ME HERE?
IN THE WOODS-- THERE'S A BODY--
A BODY?
SHOW ME. MOVE SLOW. STAY CLOSE.
IMAGINE I GOT POISON IVY ON MY TRIGGER FINGER.
GOD, I HATE THAT SMELL.

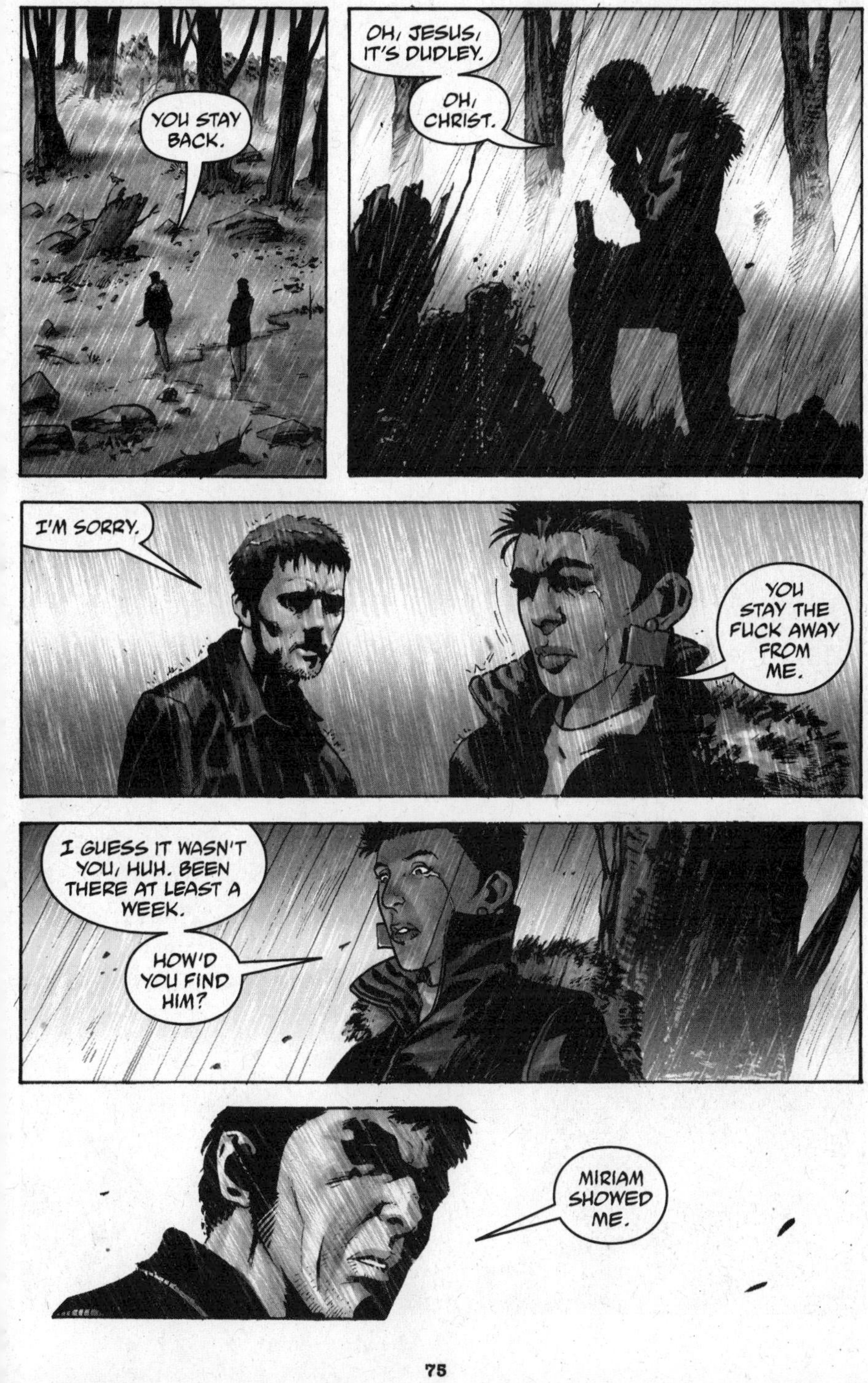
YOU STAY BACK.
OH, JESUS, IT'S DUDLEY.
OH, CHRIST.
I'M SORRY.
YOU STAY THE FUCK AWAY FROM ME.
I GUESS IT WASN'T YOU, HUH. BEEN THERE AT LEAST A WEEK.
HOW'D YOU FIND HIM?
MIRIAM SHOWED ME.

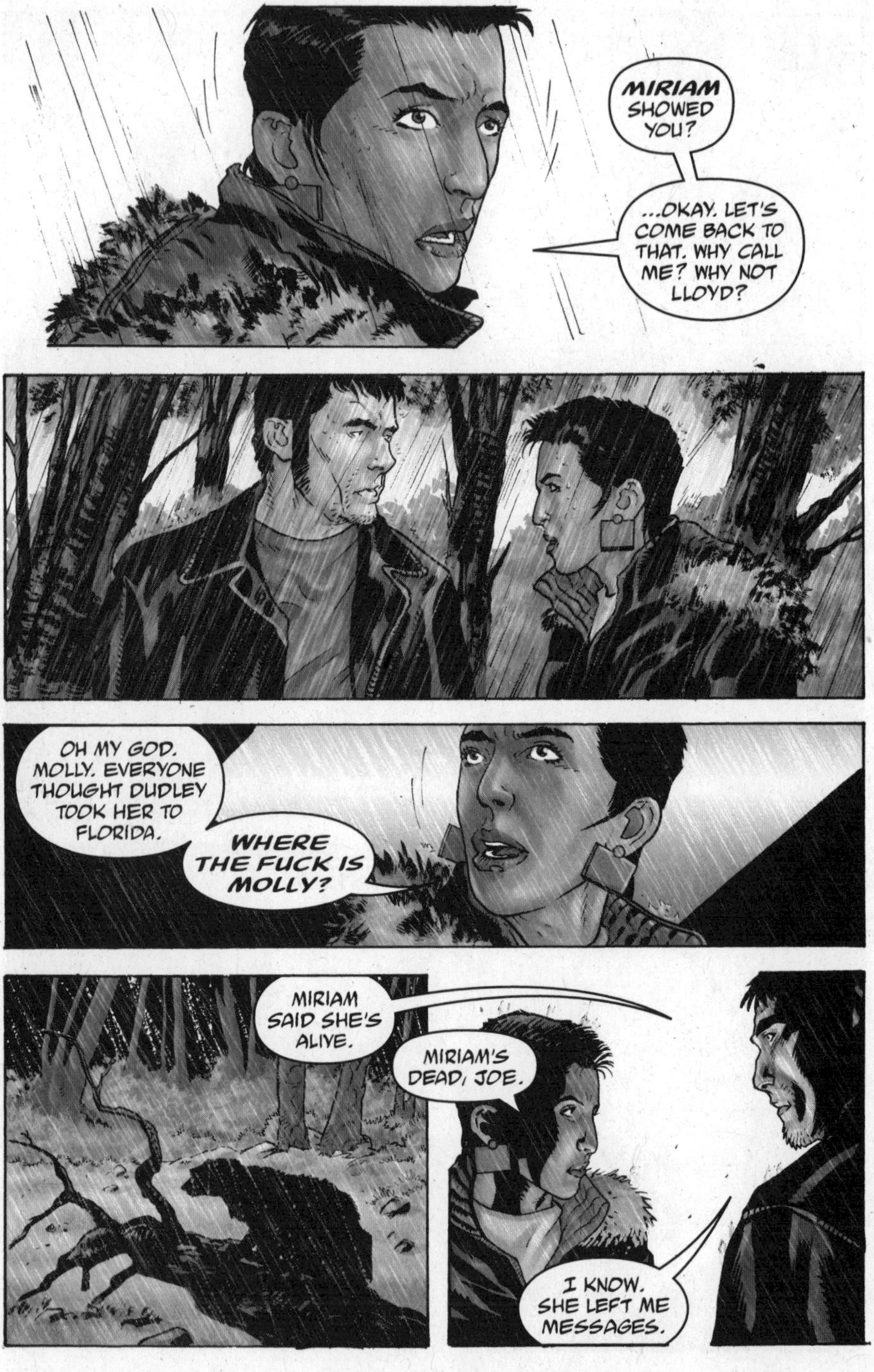
MIRIAM SHOWED YOU?
...OKAY. LET'S COME BACK TO THAT. WHY CALL ME? WHY NOT LLOYD?
OH MY GOD. MOLLY. EVERYONE THOUGHT DUDLEY TOOK HER TO FLORIDA.
WHERE THE FUCK IS MOLLY?
MIRIAM SAID SHE'S ALIVE.
MIRIAM'S DEAD, JOE.
I KNOW. SHE LEFT ME MESSAGES.

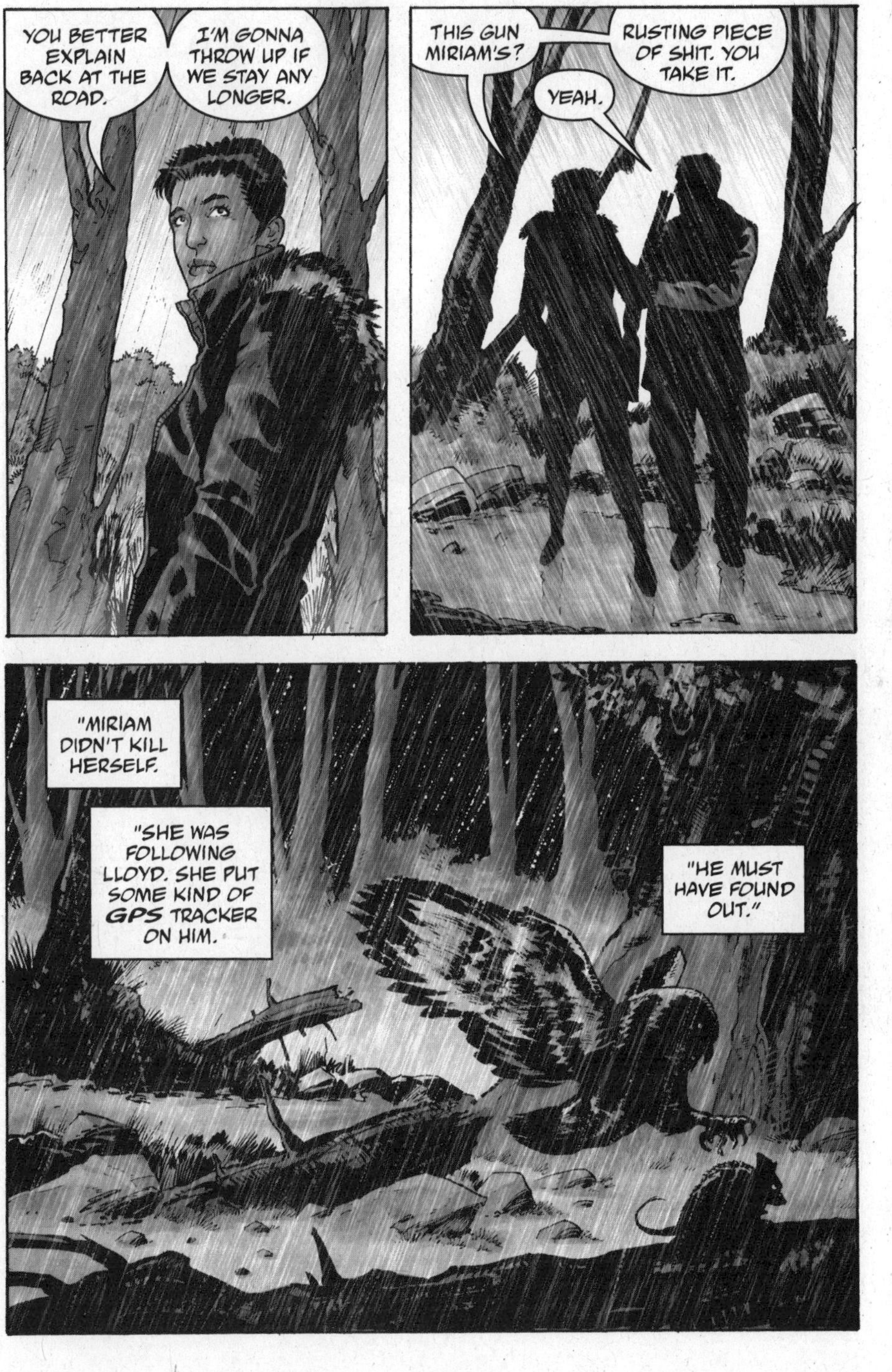
YOU BETTER EXPLAIN BACK AT THE ROAD.
I'M GONNA THROW UP IF WE STAY ANY LONGER.
THIS GUN MIRIAM'S?
YEAH.
RUSTING PIECE OF SHIT. YOU TAKE IT.
"MIRIAM DIDN'T KILL HERSELF.
"SHE WAS FOLLOWING LLOYD. SHE PUT SOME KIND OF GPS TRACKER ON HIM.
"HE MUST HAVE FOUND OUT."

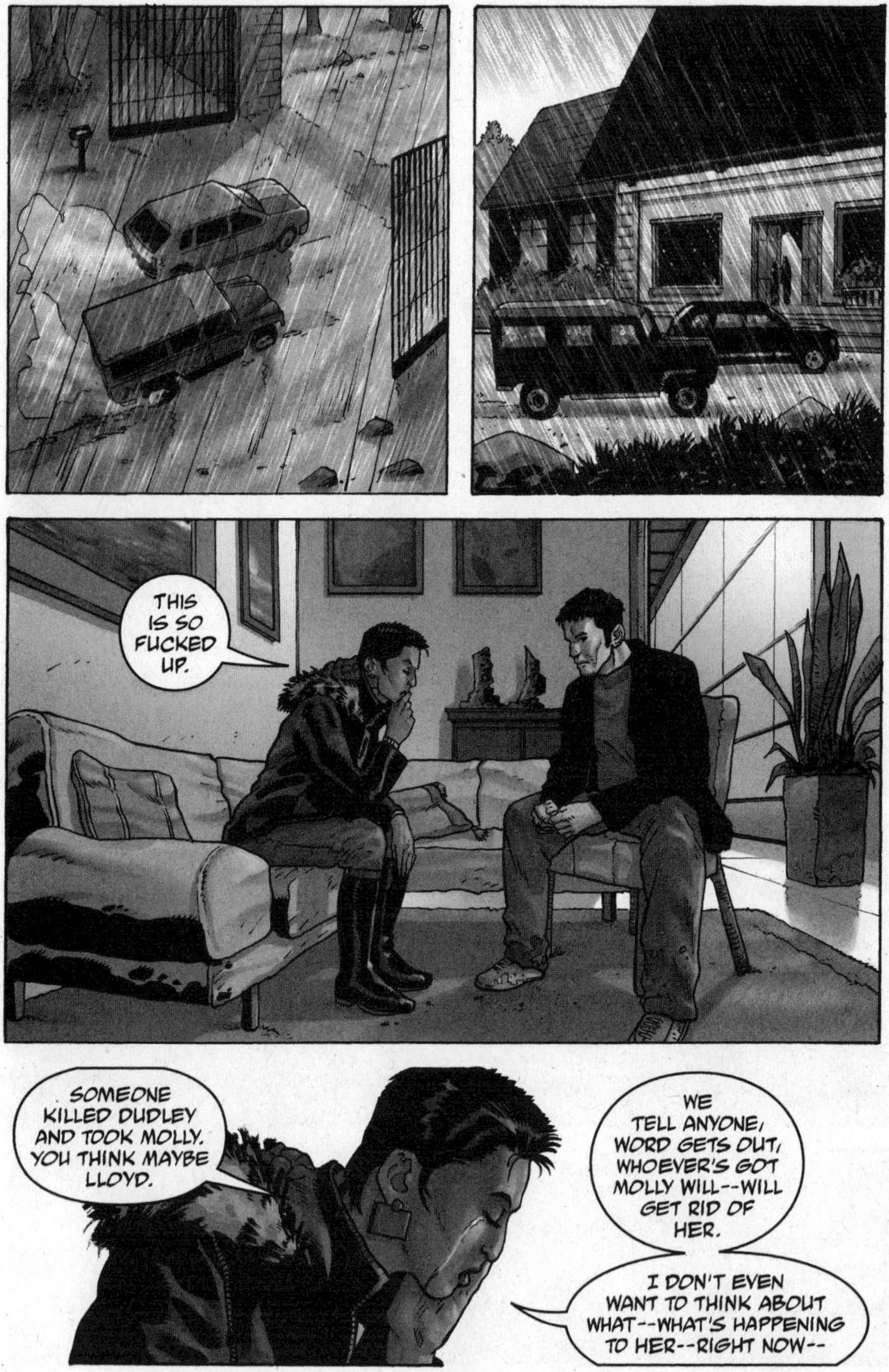
THIS IS SO FUCKED UP.
SOMEONE KILLED DUDLEY AND TOOK MOLLY. YOU THINK MAYBE LLOYD.
WE TELL ANYONE, WORD GETS OUT, WHOEVER'S GOT MOLLY WILL--WILL GET RID OF HER.
I DON'T EVEN WANT TO THINK ABOUT WHAT--WHAT'S HAPPENING TO HER--RIGHT NOW--

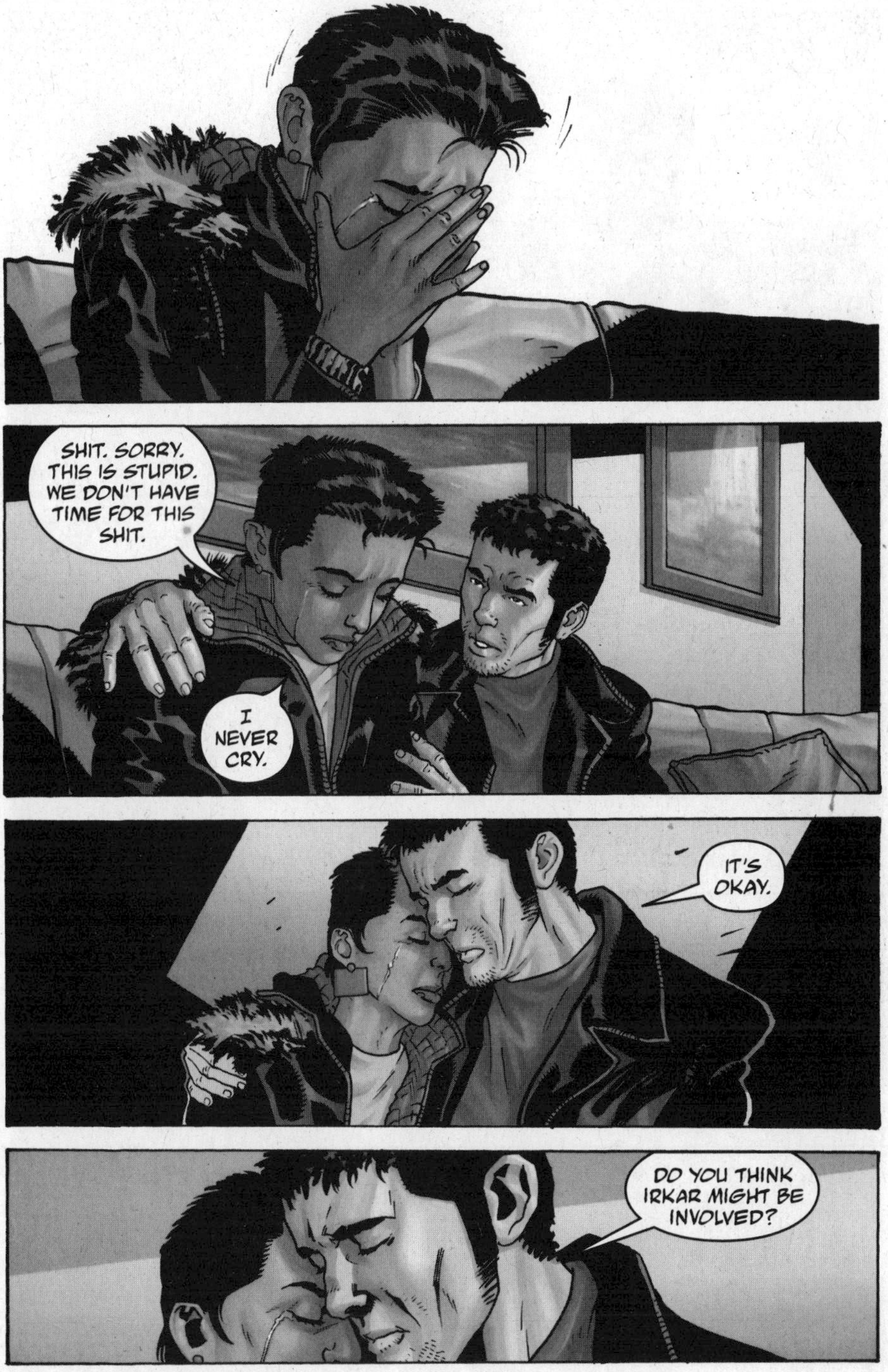
SHIT. SORRY. THIS IS STUPID. WE DON'T HAVE TIME FOR THIS SHIT.
I NEVER CRY.
IT'S OKAY.
DO YOU THINK IRKAR MIGHT BE INVOLVED?

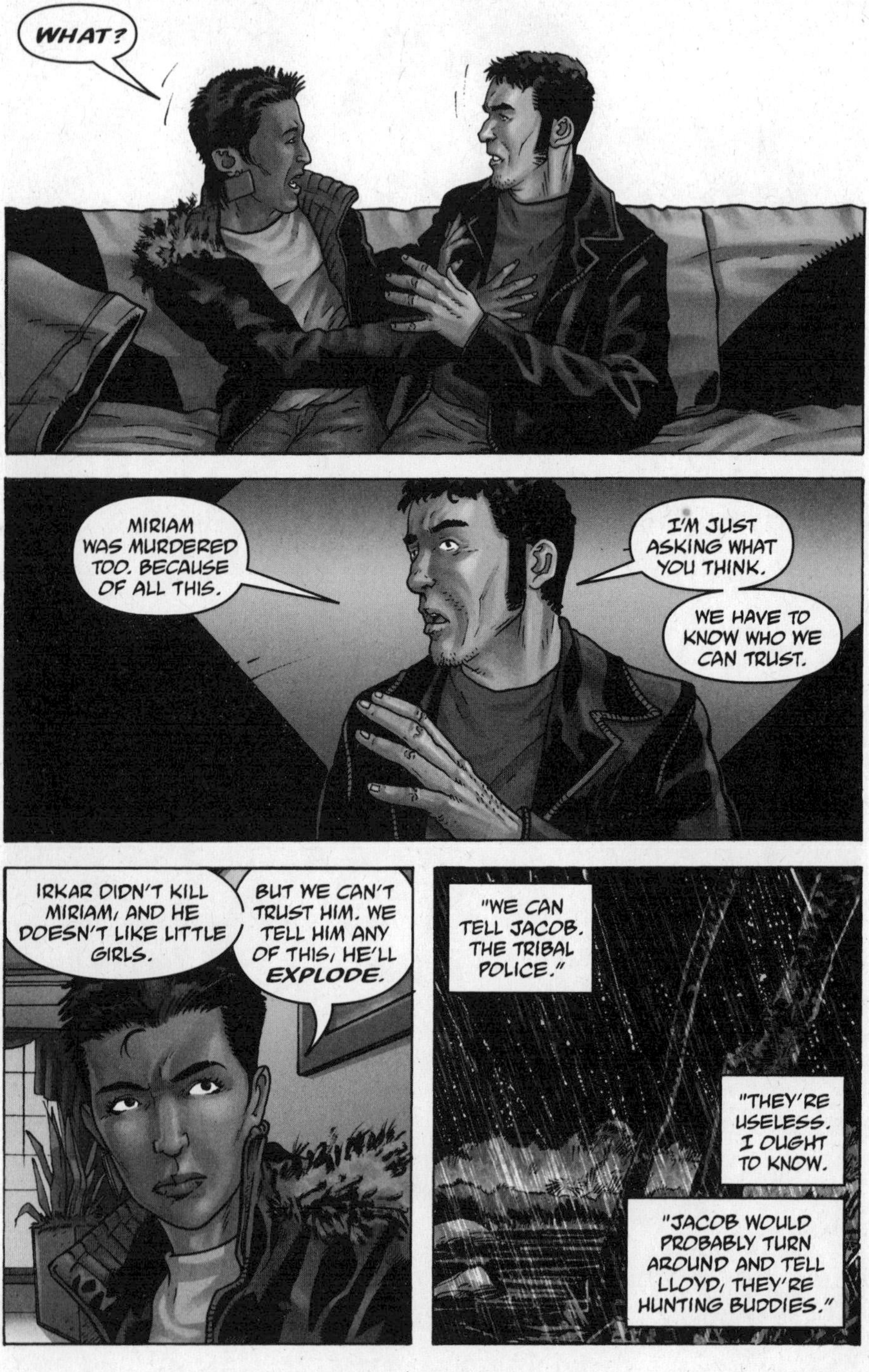
WHAT?
MIRIAM WAS MURDERED TOO. BECAUSE OF ALL THIS.
I'M JUST ASKING WHAT YOU THINK.
WE HAVE TO KNOW WHO WE CAN TRUST.
IRKAR DIDN'T KILL MIRIAM, AND HE DOESN'T LIKE LITTLE GIRLS.
BUT WE CAN'T TRUST HIM. WE TELL HIM ANY OF THIS, HE'LL EXPLODE.
"WE CAN TELL JACOB. THE TRIBAL POLICE."
"THEY'RE USELESS. I OUGHT TO KNOW.
"JACOB WOULD PROBABLY TURN AROUND AND TELL LLOYD, THEY'RE HUNTING BUDDIES."

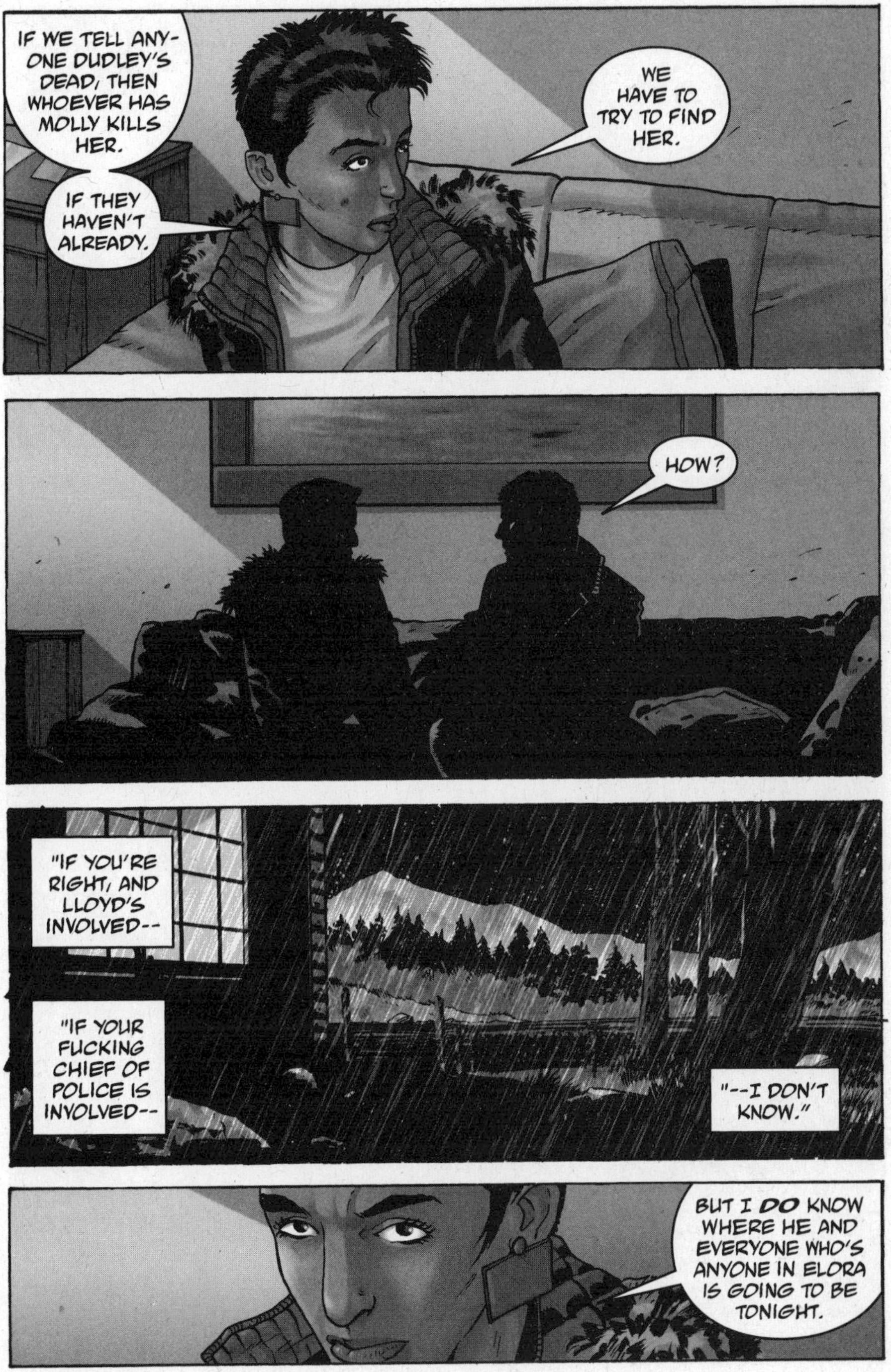
IF WE TELL ANY-ONE DUDLEY'S DEAD, THEN WHOEVER HAS MOLLY KILLS HER.
IF THEY HAVEN'T ALREADY.
WE HAVE TO TRY TO FIND HER.
HOW?
"IF YOU'RE RIGHT, AND LLOYD'S INVOLVED--
"IF YOUR FUCKING CHIEF OF POLICE IS INVOLVED--
"--I DON'T KNOW."
BUT I DO KNOW WHERE HE AND EVERYONE WHO'S ANYONE IN ELORA IS GOING TO BE TONIGHT.

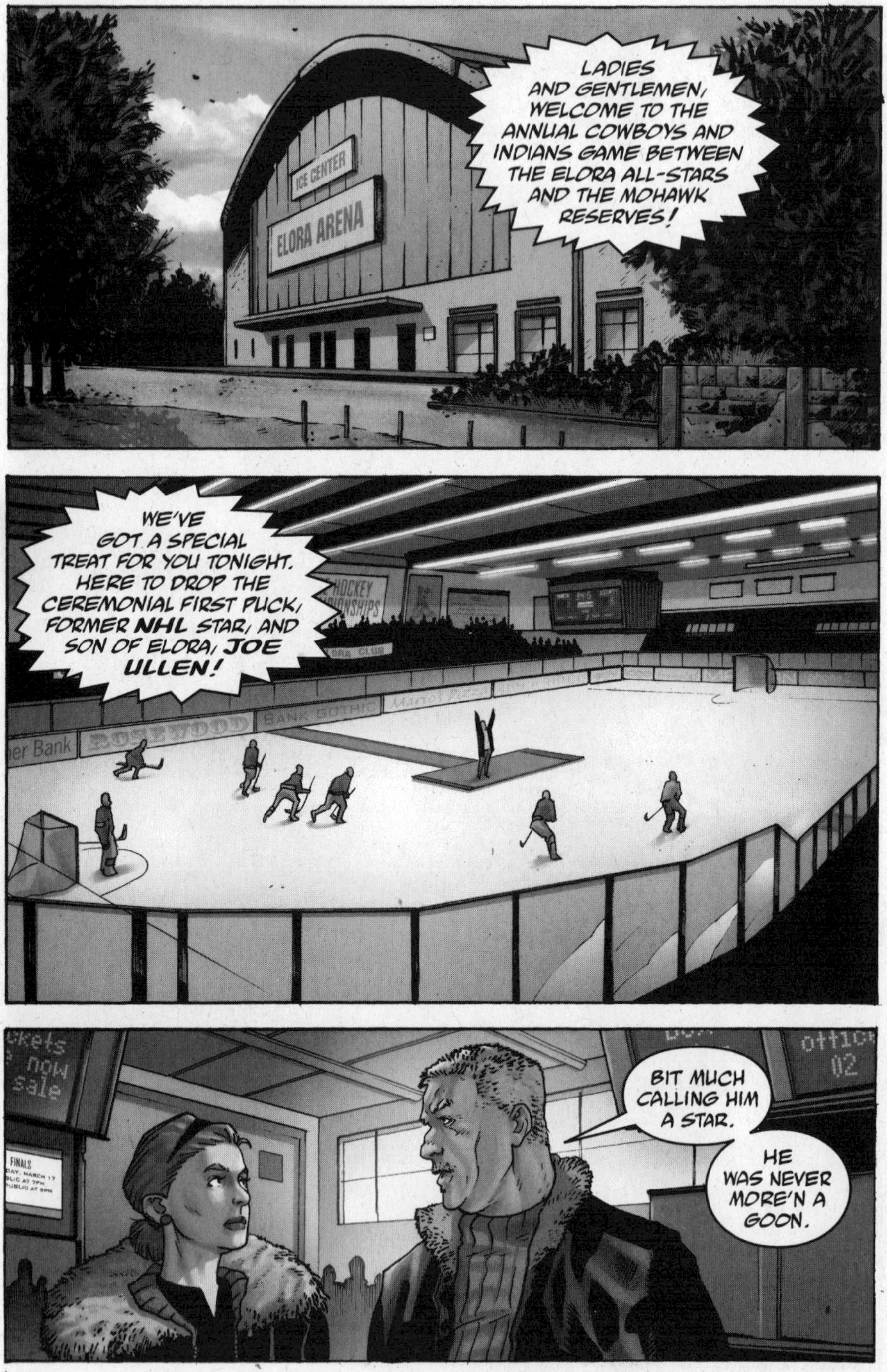
ICE CENTER
ELORA ARENA
LADIES AND GENTLEMEN, WELCOME TO THE ANNUAL COWBOYS AND INDIANS GAME BETWEEN THE ELORA ALL-STARS AND THE MOHAWK RESERVES!
WE'VE GOT A SPECIAL TREAT FOR YOU TONIGHT. HERE TO DROP THE CEREMONIAL FIRST PUCK, FORMER **NHL** STAR, AND SON OF ELORA, **JOE ULLEN!**
BIT MUCH CALLING HIM A STAR.
HE WAS NEVER MORE'N A GOON.

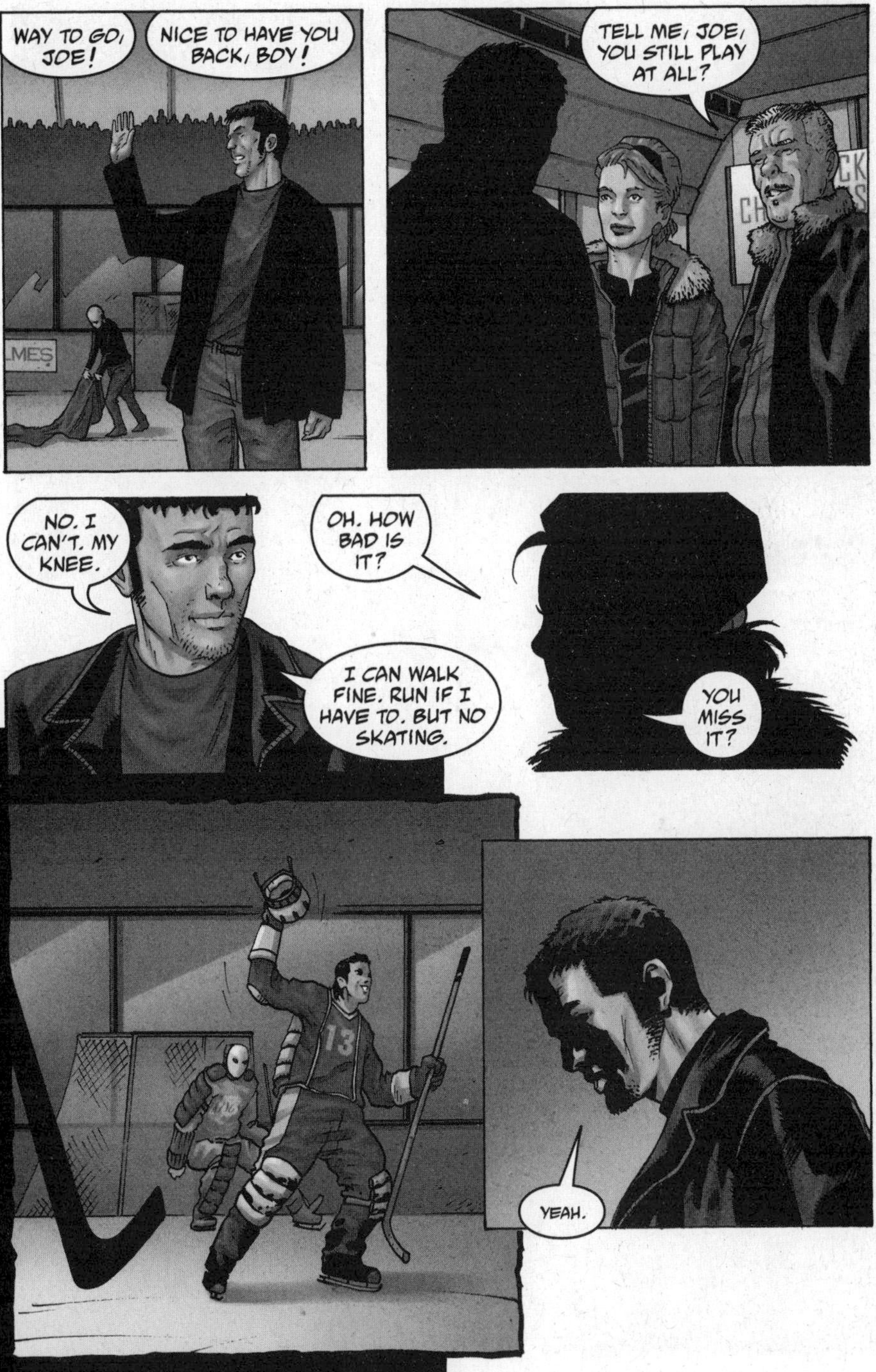
WAY TO GO, JOE!
NICE TO HAVE YOU BACK, BOY!
TELL ME, JOE, YOU STILL PLAY AT ALL?
NO. I CAN'T. MY KNEE.
OH. HOW BAD IS IT?
I CAN WALK FINE. RUN IF I HAVE TO. BUT NO SKATING.
YOU MISS IT?
YEAH.

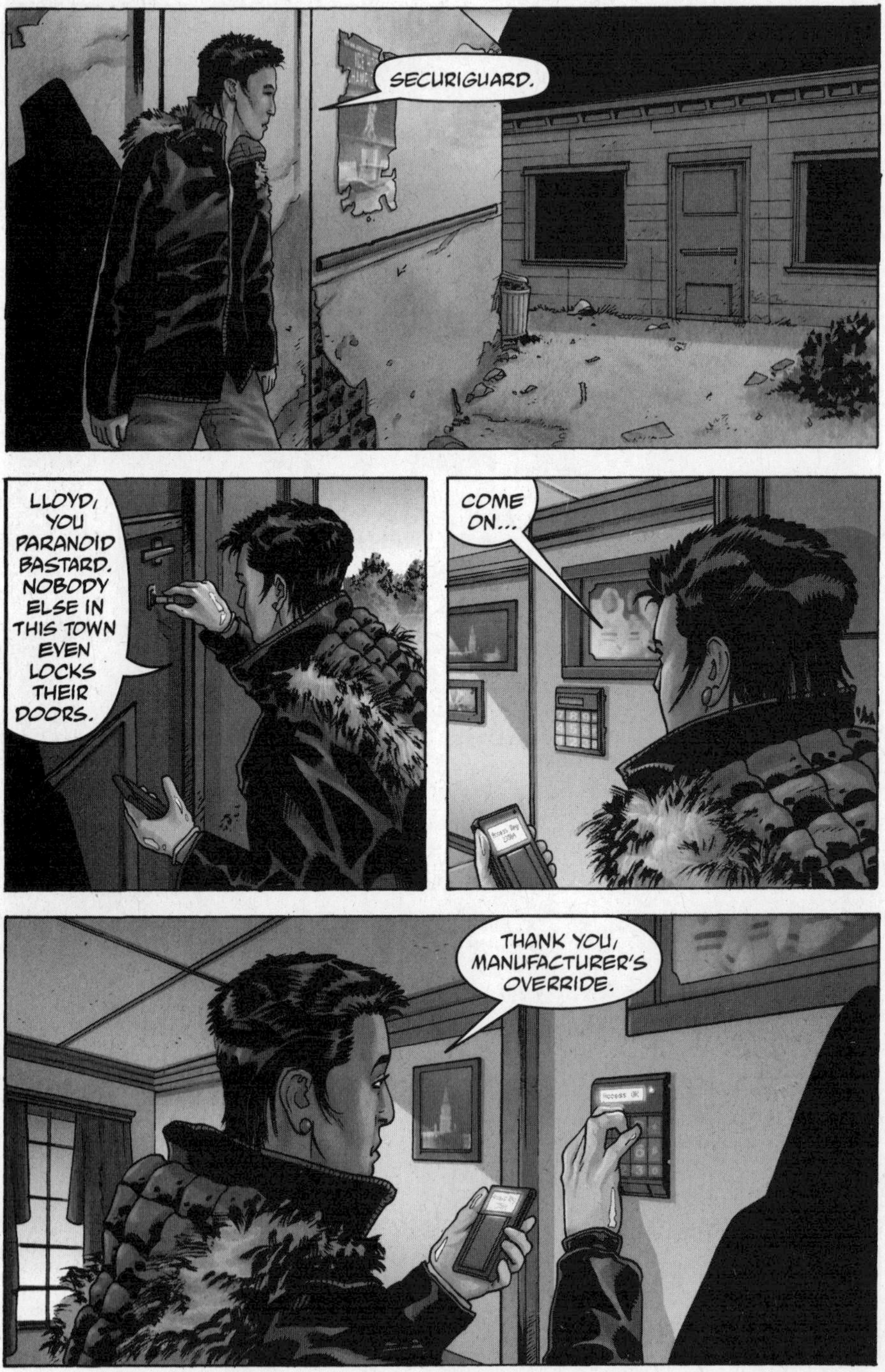
SECURIGUARD.
LLOYD, YOU PARANOID BASTARD. NOBODY ELSE IN THIS TOWN EVEN LOCKS THEIR DOORS.
COME ON...
THANK YOU, MANUFACTURER'S OVERRIDE.

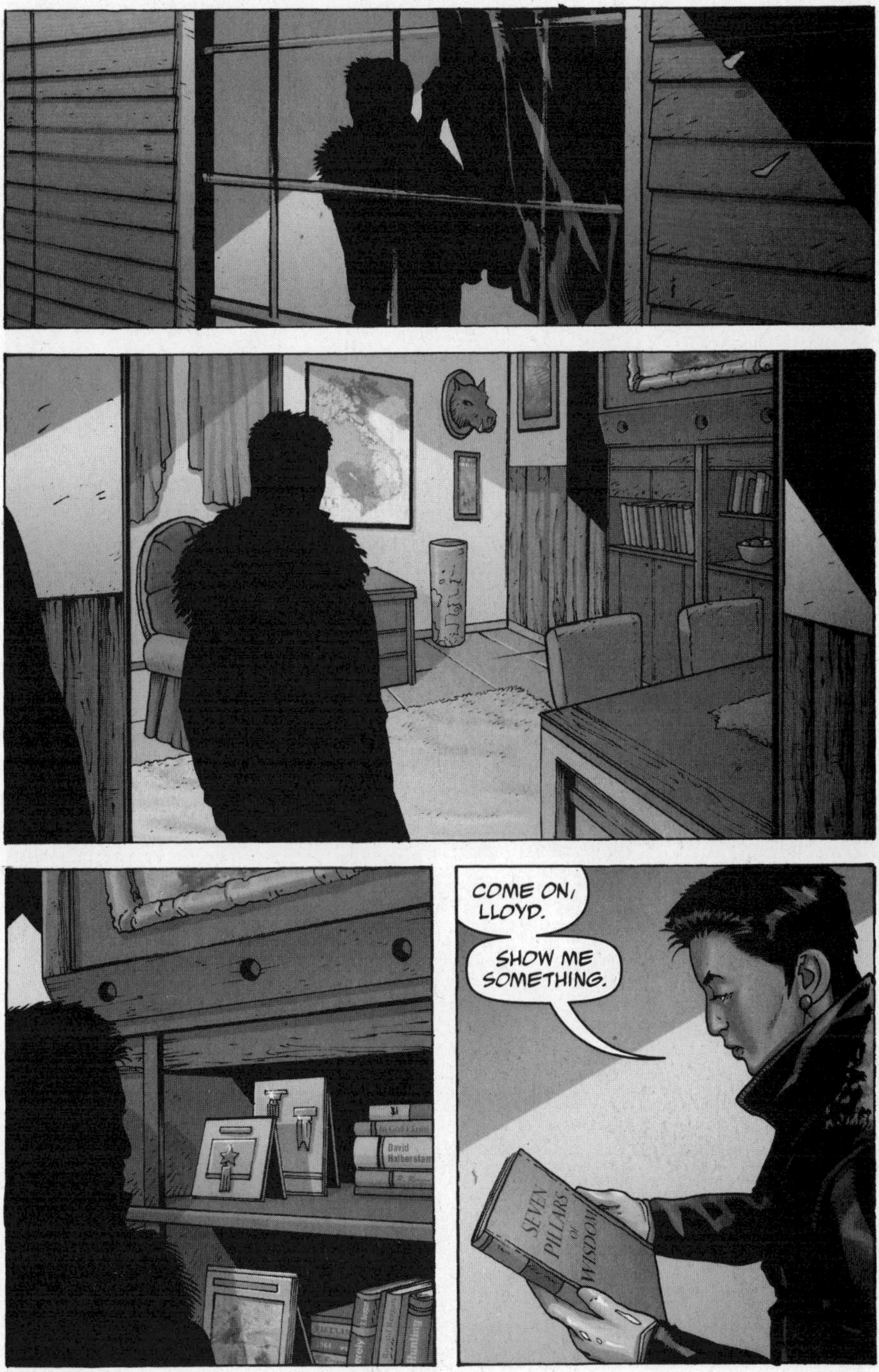
David Halberstam
COME ON, LLOYD.
SHOW ME SOMETHING.
SEVEN PILLARS OF WISDOM

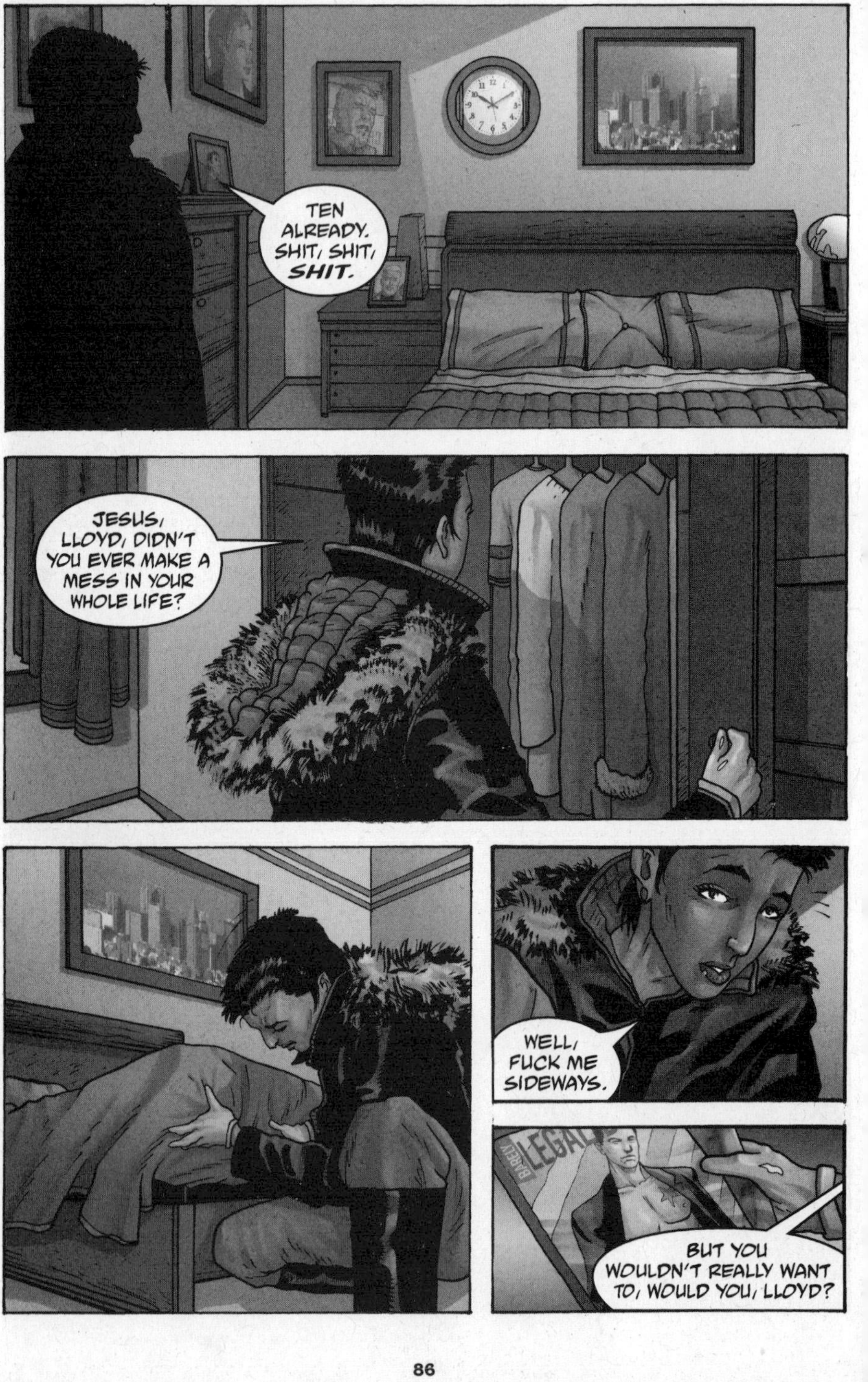
TEN ALREADY. SHIT, SHIT, SHIT.
JESUS, LLOYD, DIDN'T YOU EVER MAKE A MESS IN YOUR WHOLE LIFE?
WELL, FUCK ME SIDEWAYS.
BUT YOU WOULDN'T REALLY WANT TO, WOULD YOU, LLOYD?

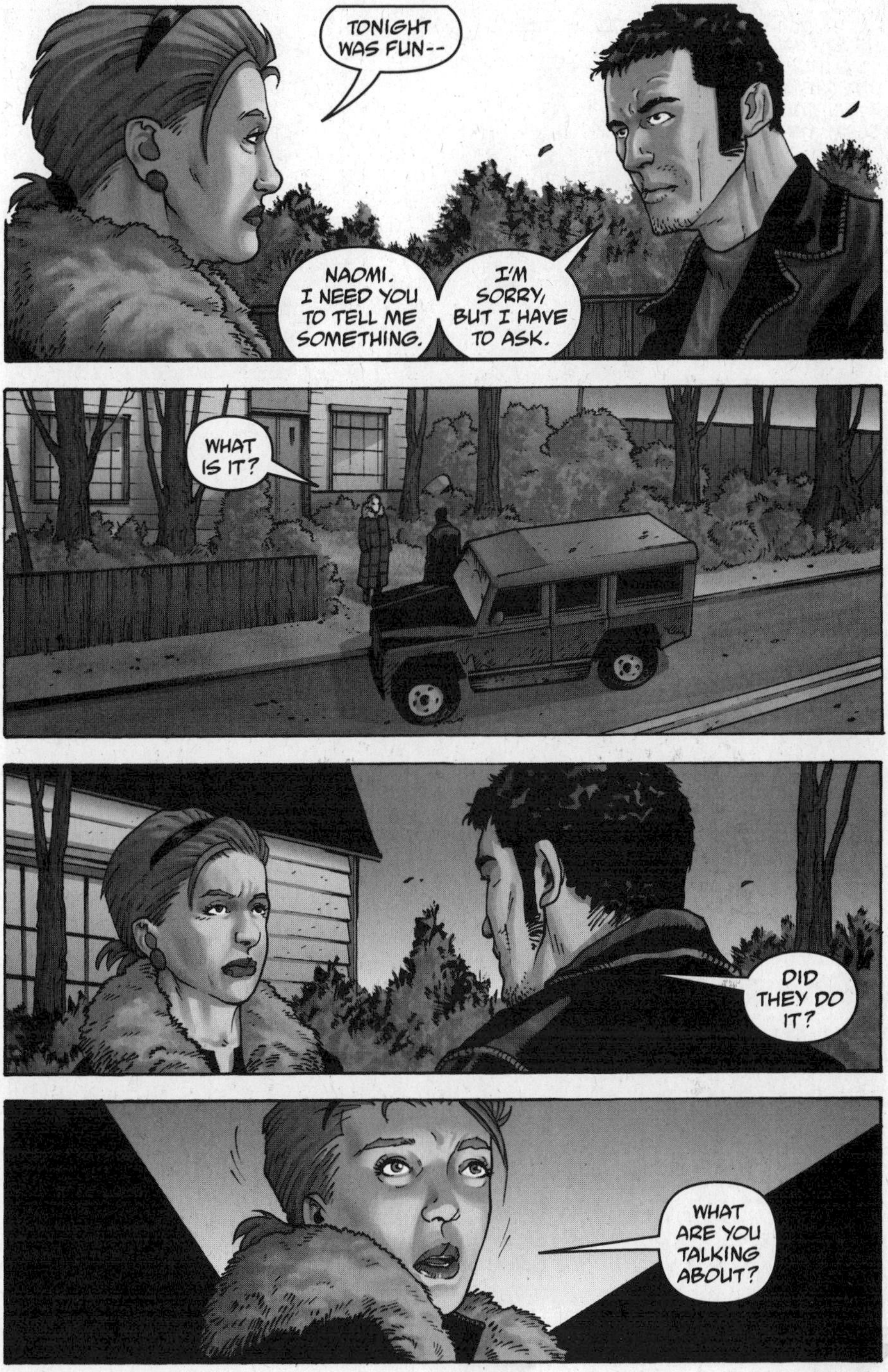
TONIGHT WAS FUN--
I'M SORRY, BUT I HAVE TO ASK.
NAOMI. I NEED YOU TO TELL ME SOMETHING.
WHAT IS IT?
DID THEY DO IT?
WHAT ARE YOU TALKING ABOUT?

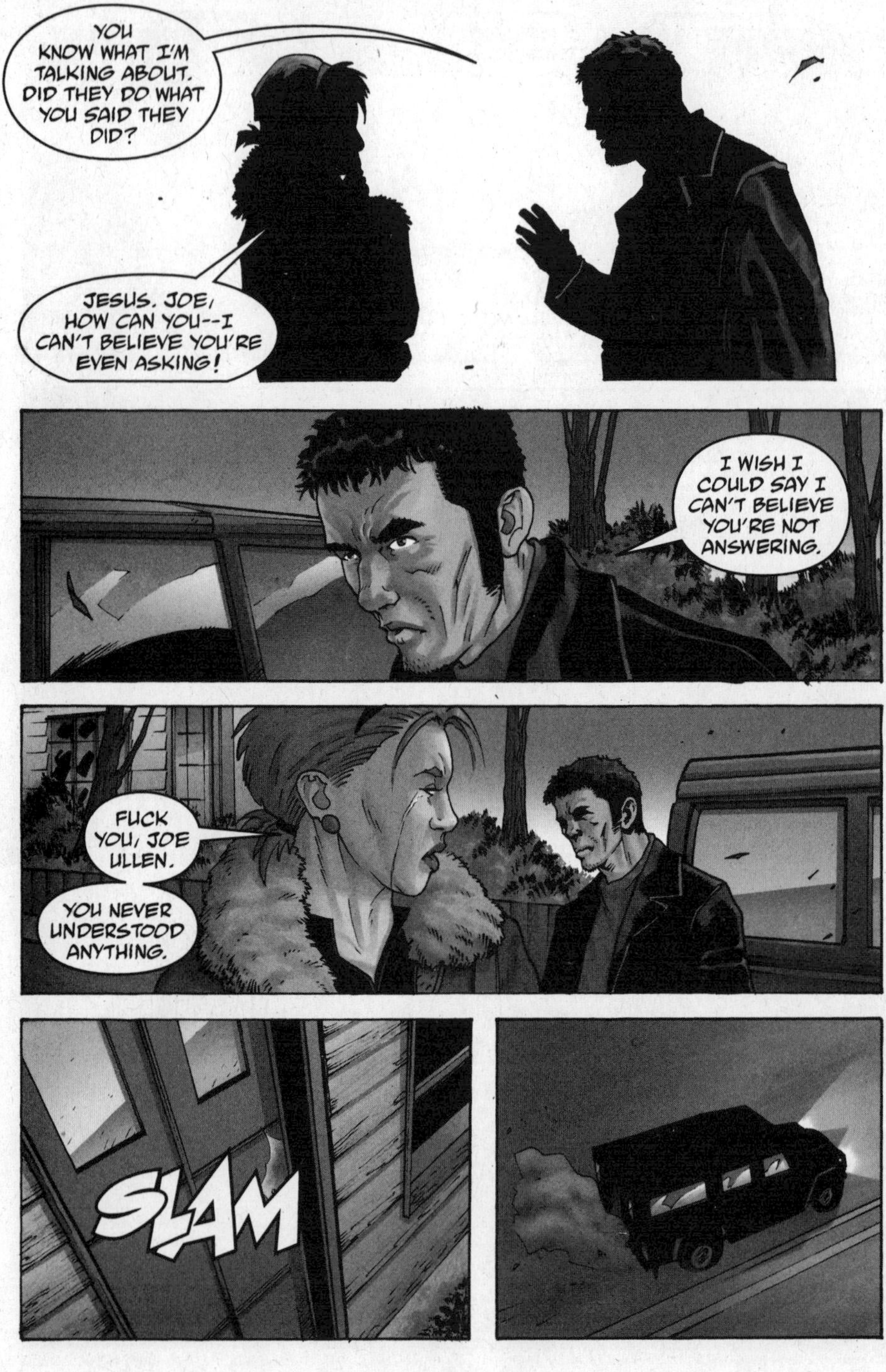
YOU KNOW WHAT I'M TALKING ABOUT. DID THEY DO WHAT YOU SAID THEY DID?
JESUS. JOE, HOW CAN YOU--I CAN'T BELIEVE YOU'RE EVEN ASKING!
I WISH I COULD SAY I CAN'T BELIEVE YOU'RE NOT ANSWERING.
FUCK YOU, JOE ULLEN.
YOU NEVER UNDERSTOOD ANYTHING.
SLAM

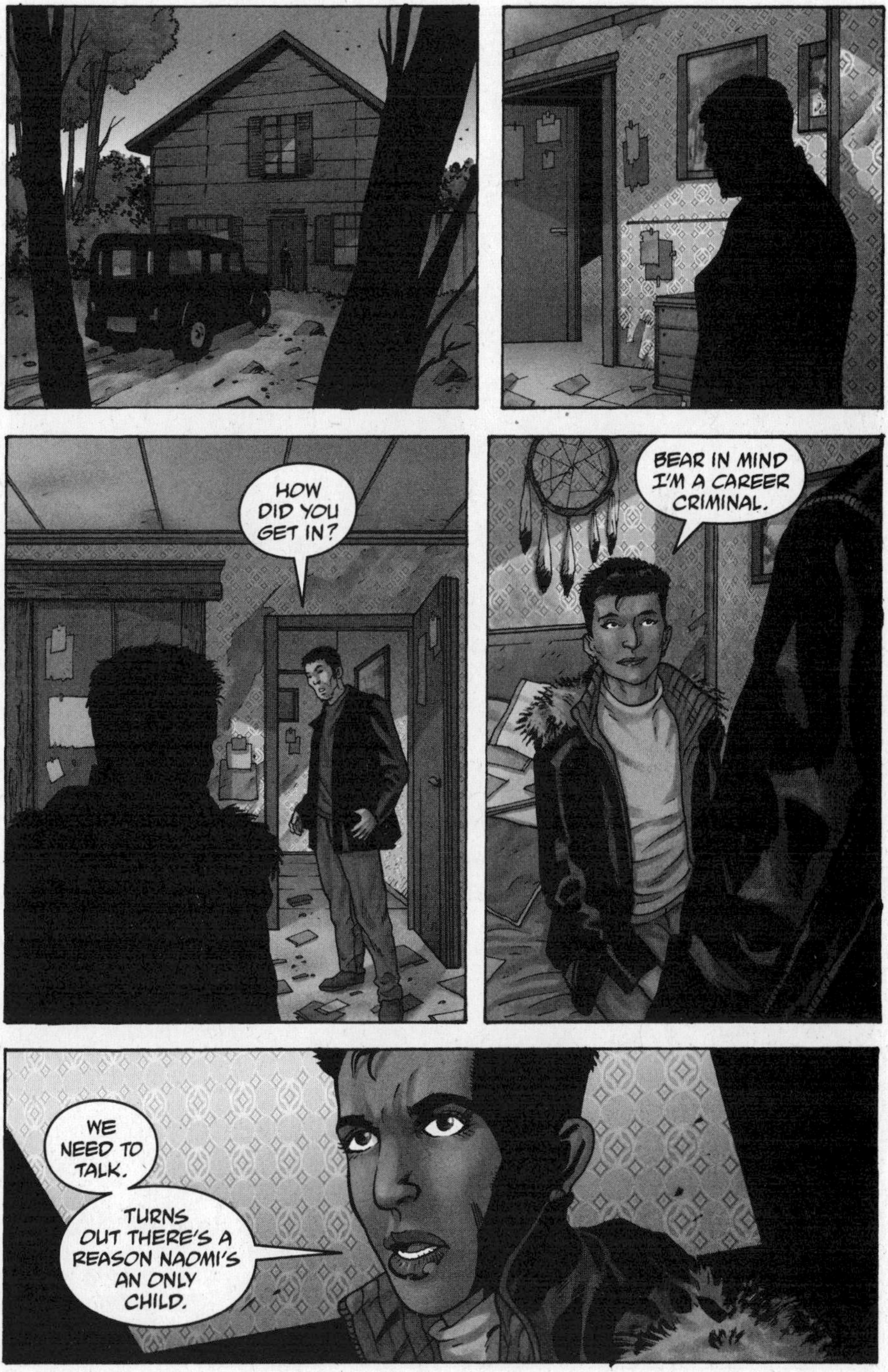
HOW DID YOU GET IN?
BEAR IN MIND I'M A CAREER CRIMINAL.
WE NEED TO TALK.
TURNS OUT THERE'S A REASON NAOMI'S AN ONLY CHILD.

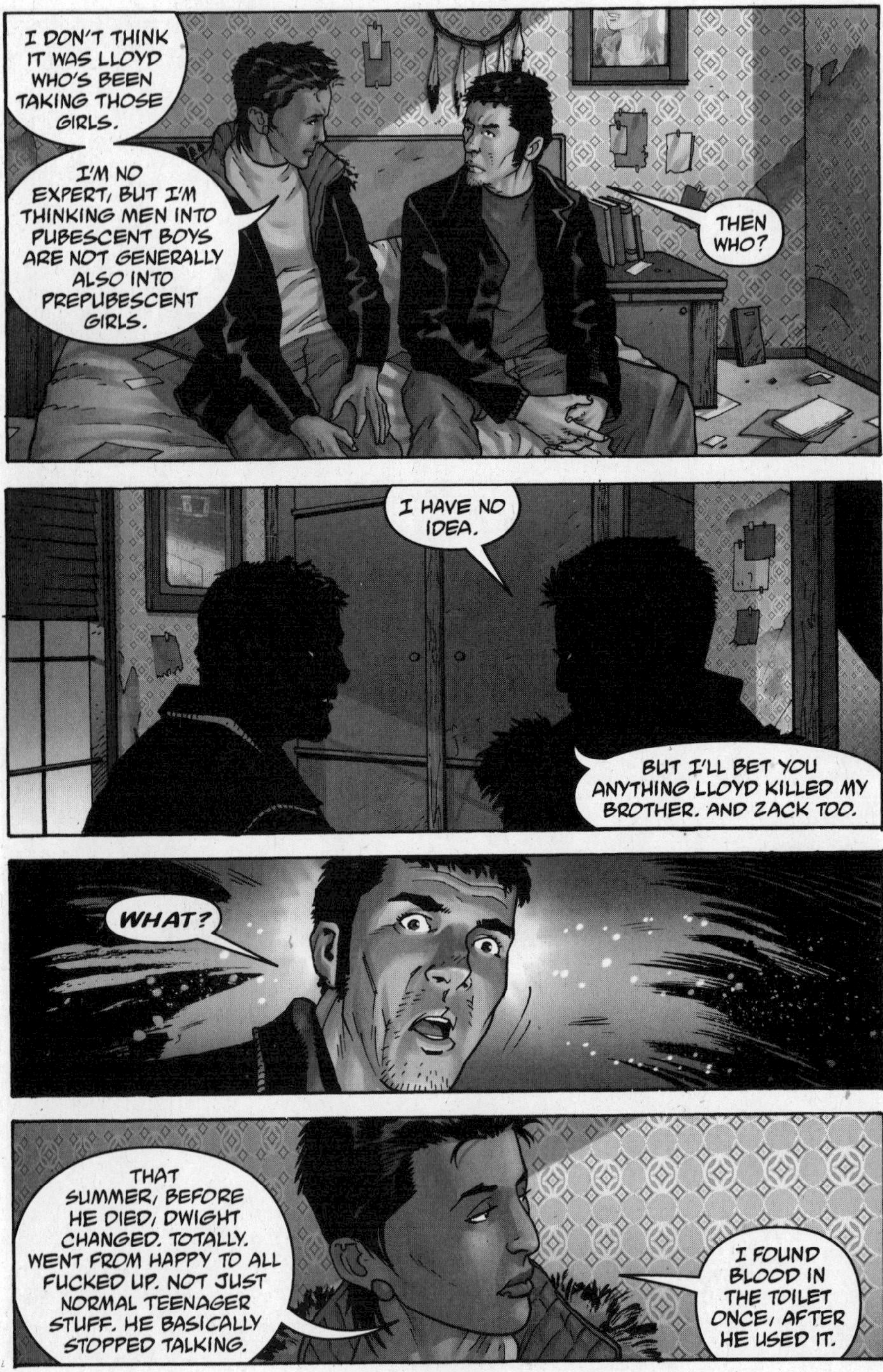

I DON'T THINK IT WAS LLOYD WHO'S BEEN TAKING THOSE GIRLS.
I'M NO EXPERT, BUT I'M THINKING MEN INTO PUBESCENT BOYS ARE NOT GENERALLY ALSO INTO PREPUBESCENT GIRLS.
THEN WHO?
I HAVE NO IDEA.
BUT I'LL BET YOU ANYTHING LLOYD KILLED MY BROTHER. AND ZACK TOO.
WHAT?
THAT SUMMER, BEFORE HE DIED, DWIGHT CHANGED. TOTALLY. WENT FROM HAPPY TO ALL FUCKED UP. NOT JUST NORMAL TEENAGER STUFF. HE BASICALLY STOPPED TALKING.
I FOUND BLOOD IN THE TOILET ONCE, AFTER HE USED IT.

"I DON'T UNDERSTAND."

"YOU THINK CATHOLIC PRIESTS WERE BAD, IMAGINE WHAT IT'S LIKE WHEN IT'S THE CHIEF OF POLICE, SOMEONE WHO CAN THROW YOU INTO JAIL."

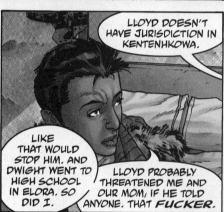

LLOYD DOESN'T HAVE JURISDICTION IN KENTENHKOWA.

LIKE THAT WOULD STOP HIM. AND DWIGHT WENT TO HIGH SCHOOL IN ELORA. SO DID I.

LLOYD PROBABLY THREATENED ME AND OUR MOM, IF HE TOLD ANYONE. THAT *FUCKER.*

YOU'RE INVENTING ALL OF THIS. THERE'S NO EVIDENCE.

TELL ME IT DOESN'T MAKE SENSE.

BUT DWIGHT WAS TOUGHER THAN LLOYD FIGURED. HE WAS GOING TO TALK. GOD, DWIGHT, IF I'M RIGHT, I'M SO FUCKING *PROUD* OF YOU. IT MUST HAVE BEEN SO HARD.

I SHOULD HAVE SEEN SOMETHING. I SHOULD HAVE ASKED.

IT MUST HAVE BEEN SO FUCKING HARD.

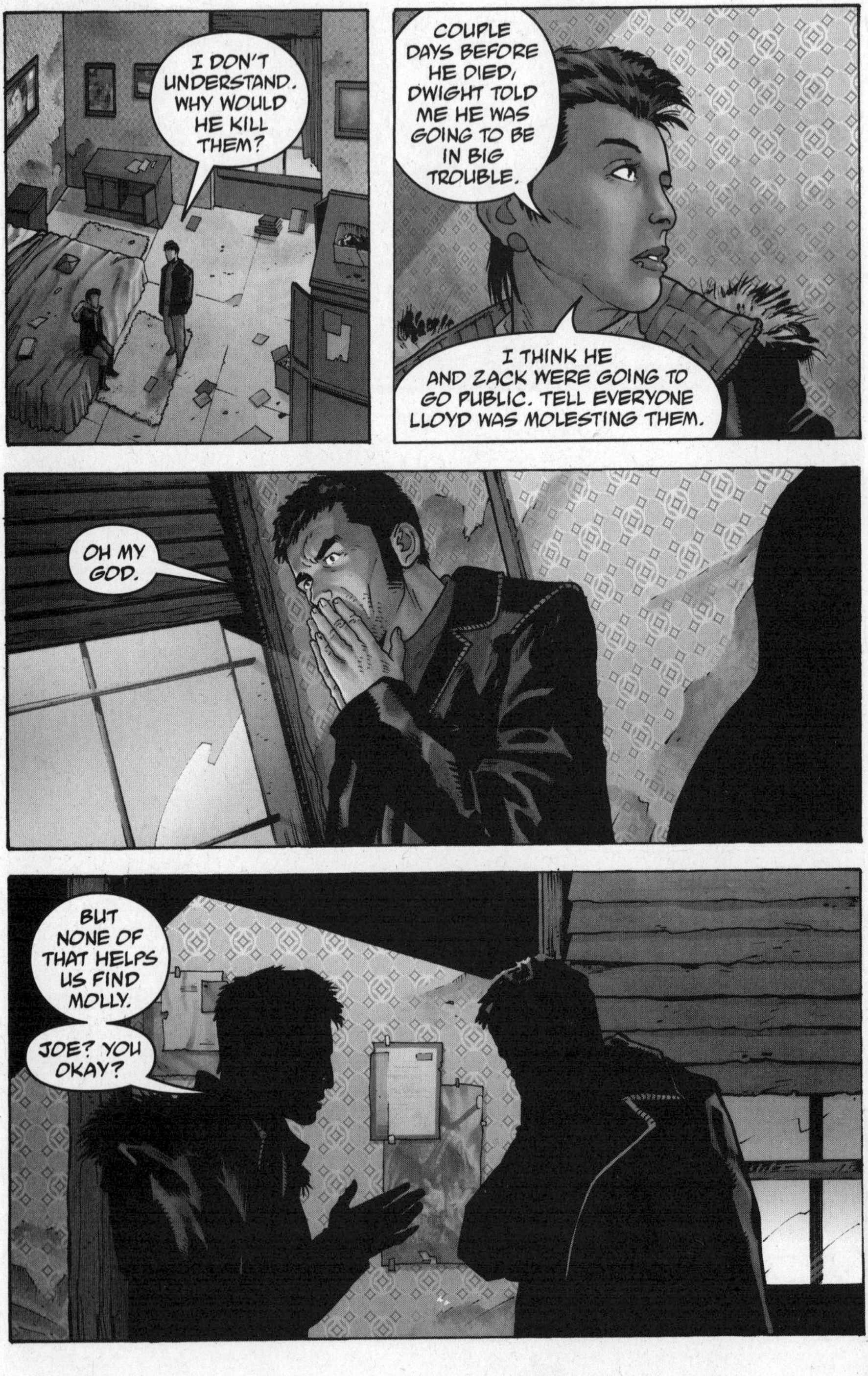
I DON'T UNDERSTAND. WHY WOULD HE KILL THEM?
COUPLE DAYS BEFORE HE DIED, DWIGHT TOLD ME HE WAS GOING TO BE IN BIG TROUBLE.
I THINK HE AND ZACK WERE GOING TO GO PUBLIC. TELL EVERYONE LLOYD WAS MOLESTING THEM.
OH MY GOD.
BUT NONE OF THAT HELPS US FIND MOLLY.
JOE? YOU OKAY?

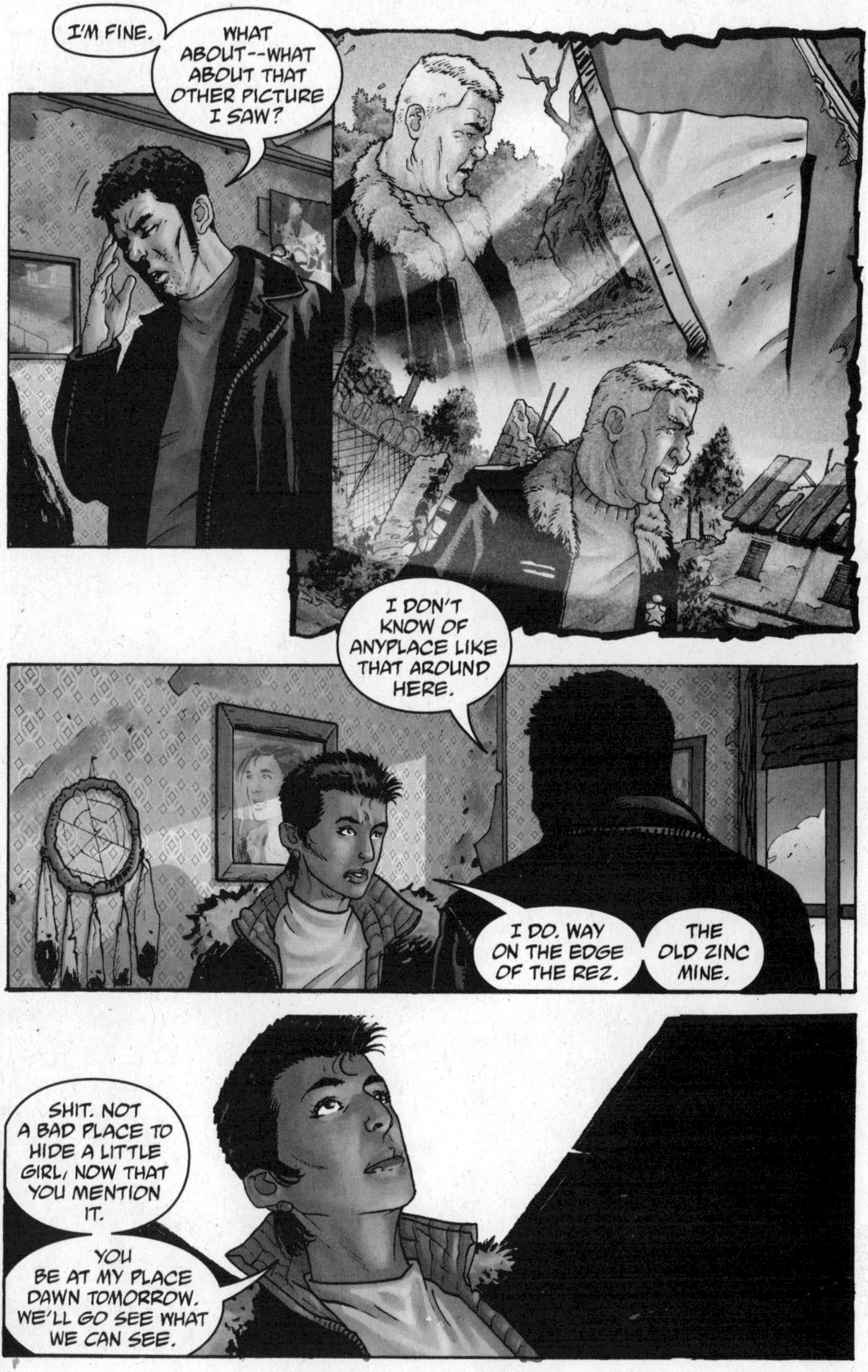
I'M FINE.
WHAT ABOUT--WHAT ABOUT THAT OTHER PICTURE I SAW?
I DON'T KNOW OF ANYPLACE LIKE THAT AROUND HERE.
I DO. WAY ON THE EDGE OF THE REZ.
THE OLD ZINC MINE.
SHIT. NOT A BAD PLACE TO HIDE A LITTLE GIRL, NOW THAT YOU MENTION IT.
YOU BE AT MY PLACE DAWN TOMORROW. WE'LL GO SEE WHAT WE CAN SEE.

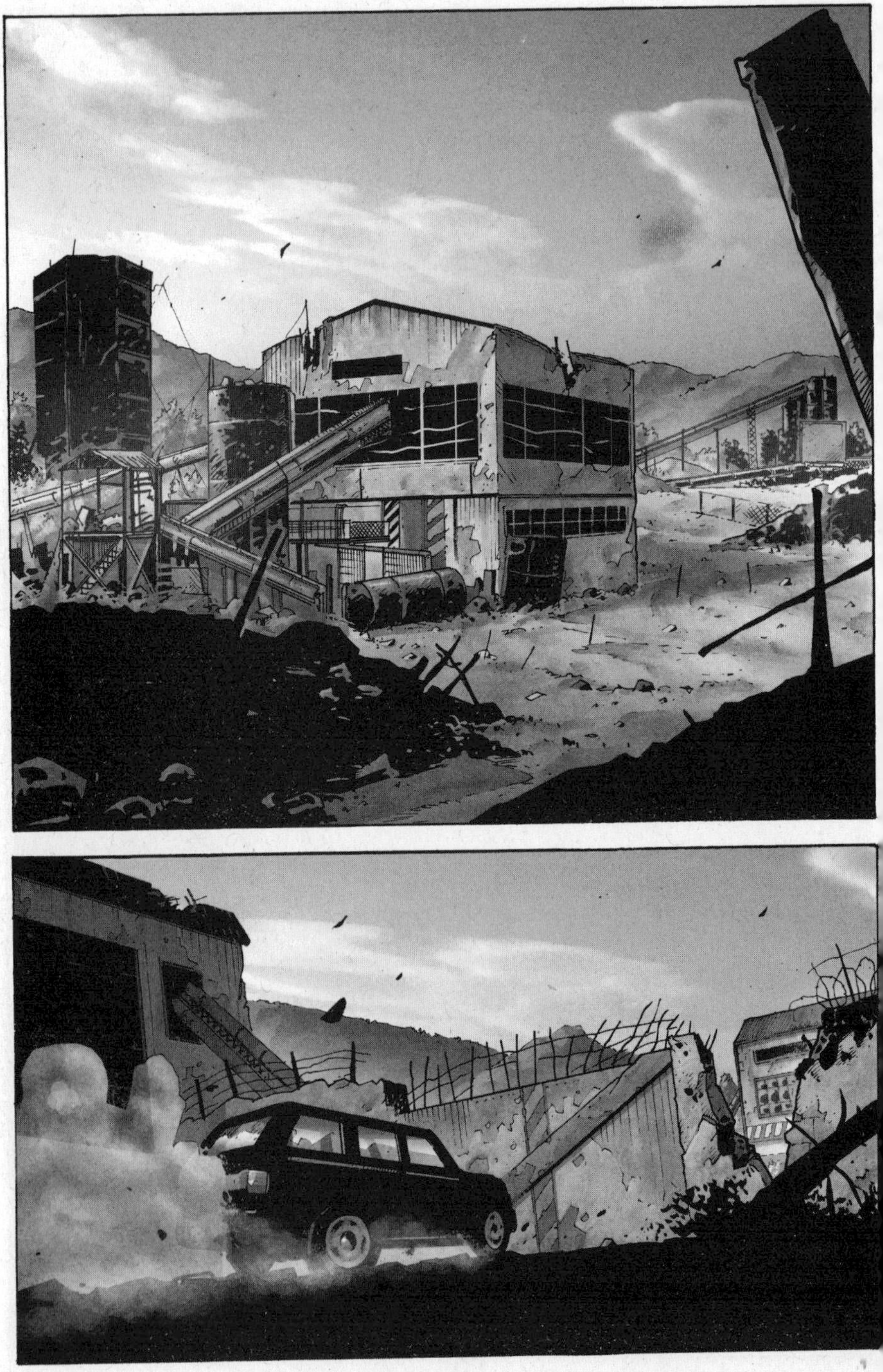

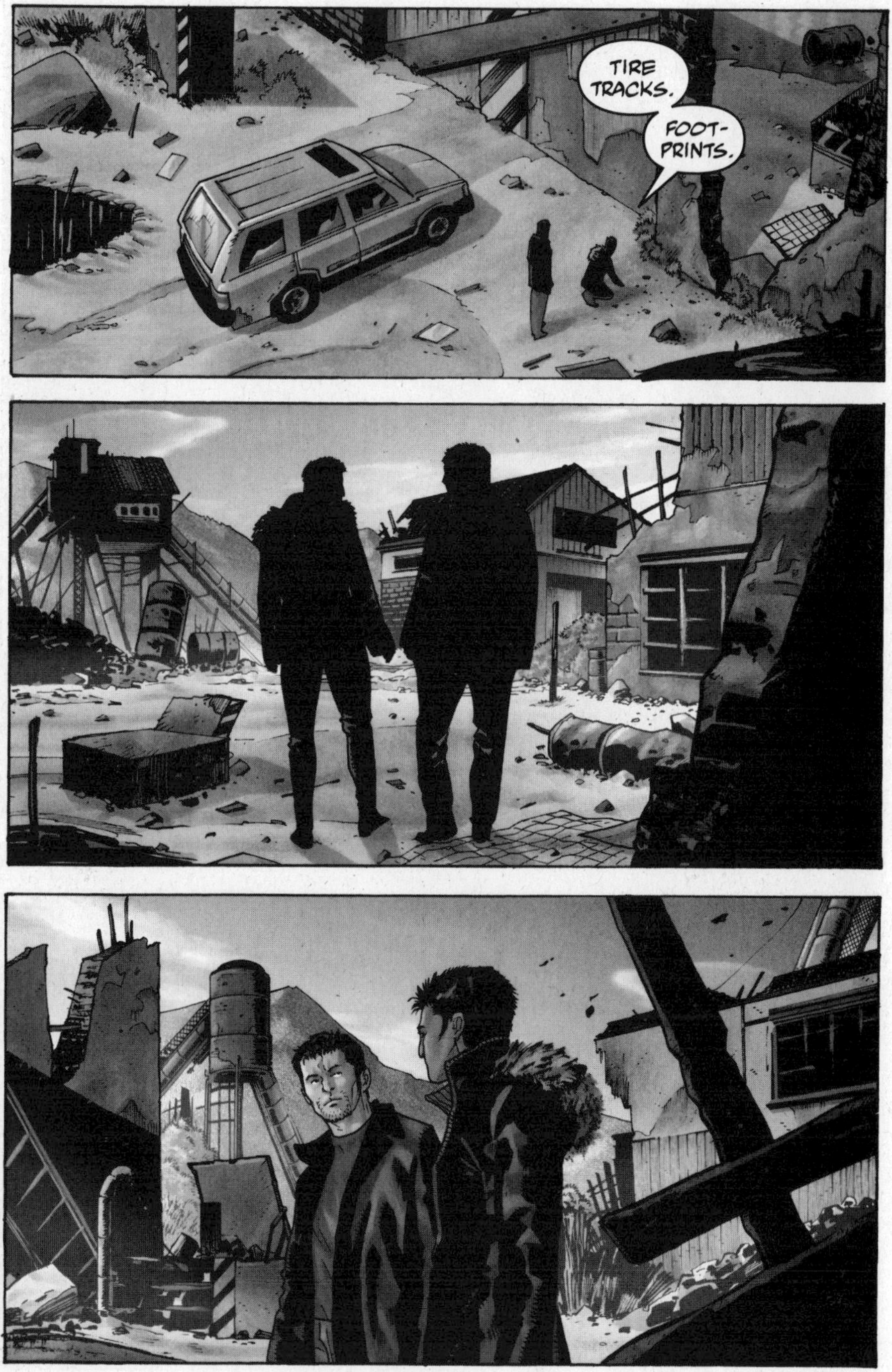
TIRE TRACKS.
FOOT-PRINTS.

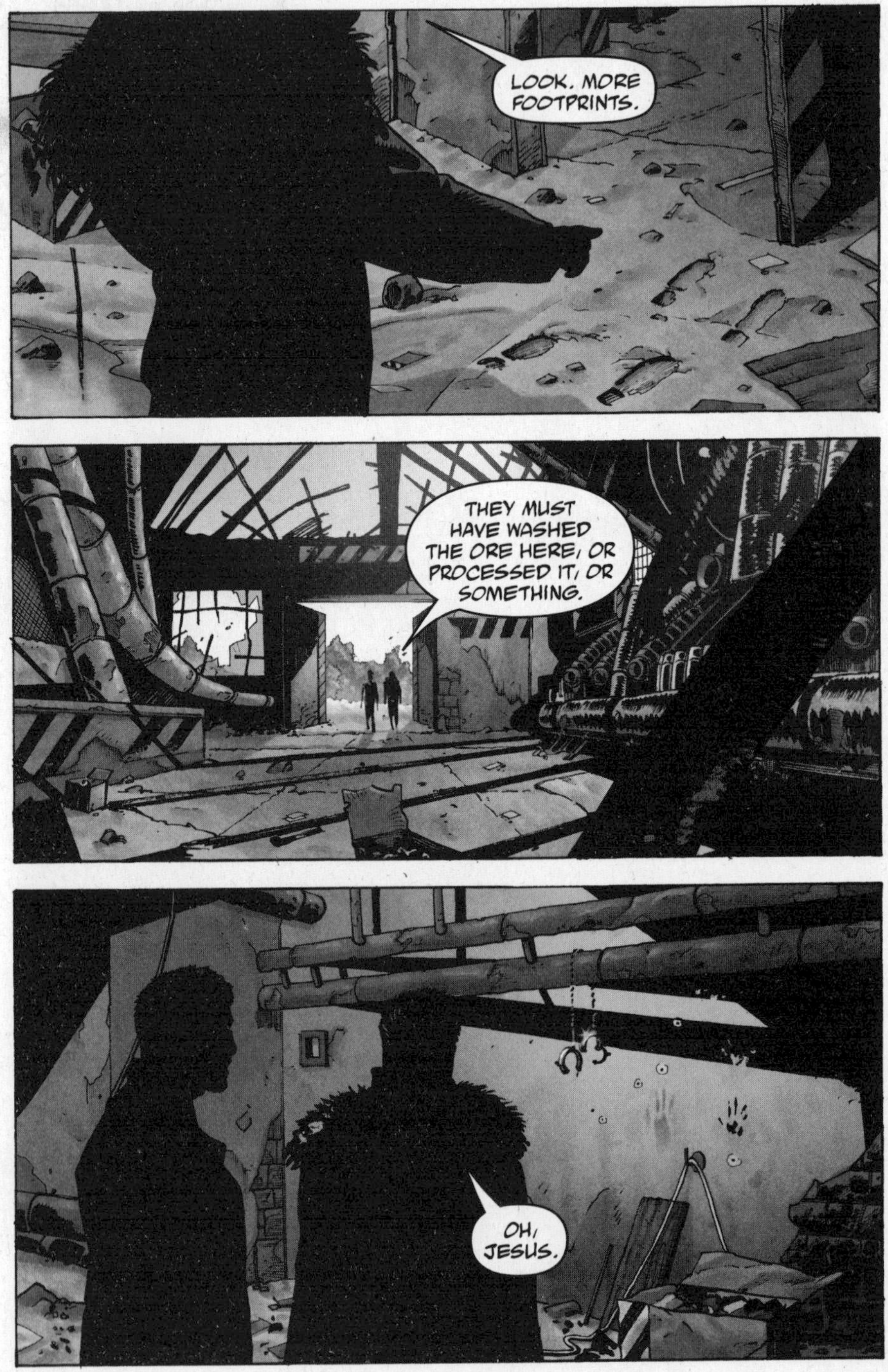
LOOK. MORE FOOTPRINTS.
THEY MUST HAVE WASHED THE ORE HERE, OR PROCESSED IT, OR SOMETHING.
OH, JESUS.

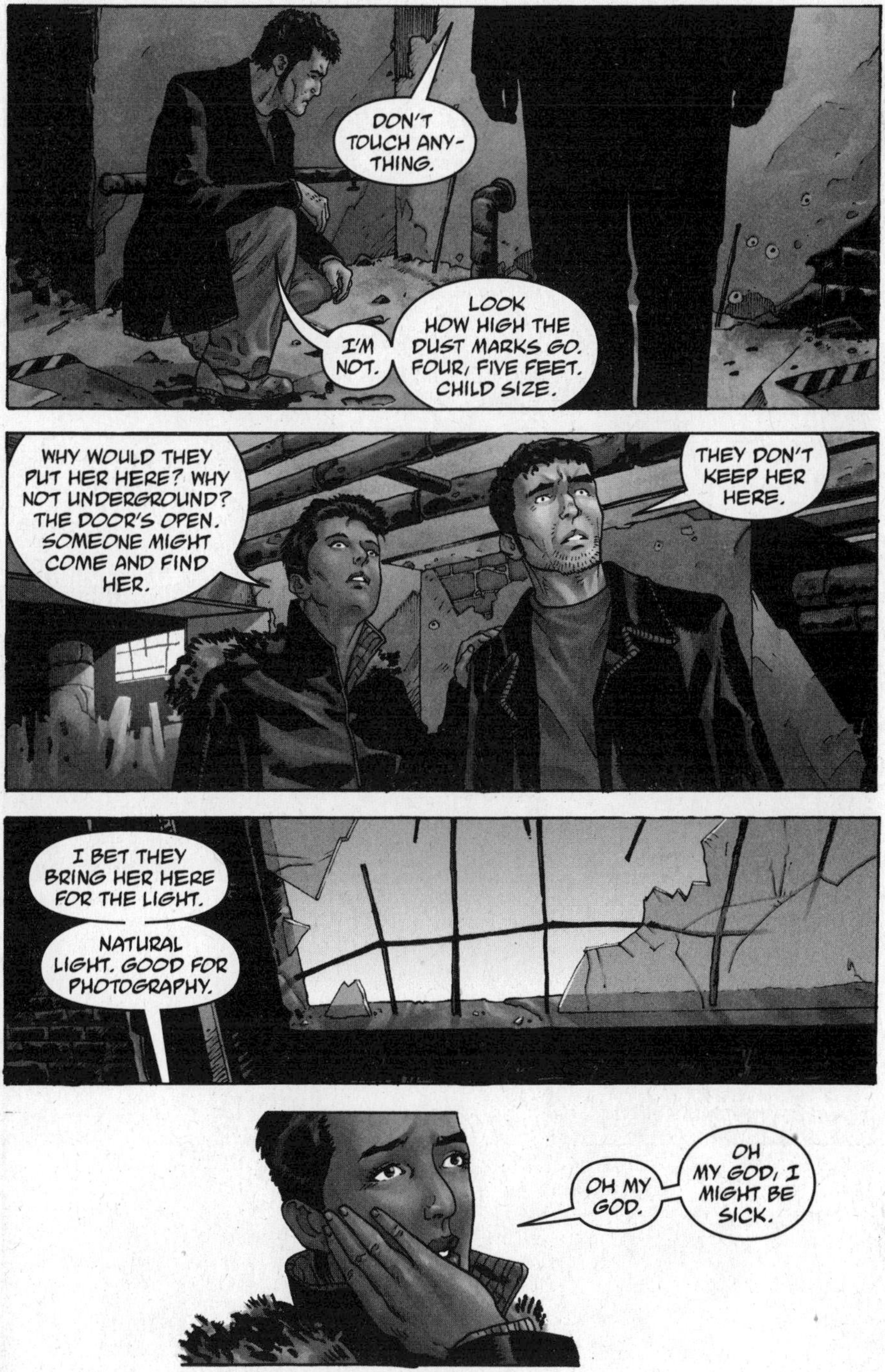
DON'T TOUCH ANY-THING.
I'M NOT.
LOOK HOW HIGH THE DUST MARKS GO. FOUR, FIVE FEET. CHILD SIZE.
WHY WOULD THEY PUT HER HERE? WHY NOT UNDERGROUND? THE DOOR'S OPEN. SOMEONE MIGHT COME AND FIND HER.
THEY DON'T KEEP HER HERE.
I BET THEY BRING HER HERE FOR THE LIGHT.
NATURAL LIGHT. GOOD FOR PHOTOGRAPHY.
OH MY GOD.
OH MY GOD, I MIGHT BE SICK.

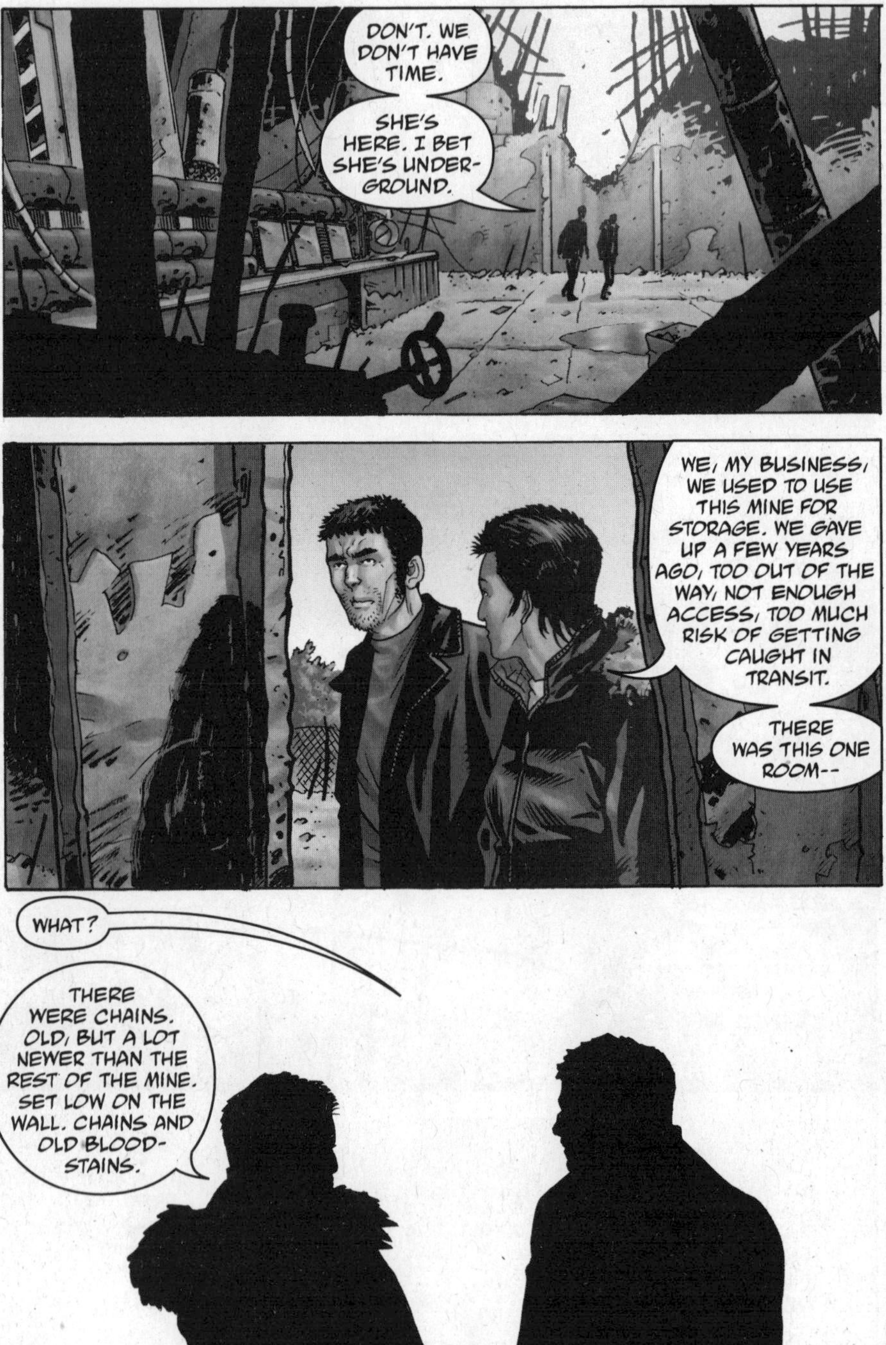
DON'T. WE DON'T HAVE TIME.
SHE'S HERE. I BET SHE'S UNDER-GROUND.
WE, MY BUSINESS, WE USED TO USE THIS MINE FOR STORAGE. WE GAVE UP A FEW YEARS AGO, TOO OUT OF THE WAY, NOT ENOUGH ACCESS, TOO MUCH RISK OF GETTING CAUGHT IN TRANSIT.
THERE WAS THIS ONE ROOM--
WHAT?
THERE WERE CHAINS. OLD, BUT A LOT NEWER THAN THE REST OF THE MINE. SET LOW ON THE WALL. CHAINS AND OLD BLOOD-STAINS.

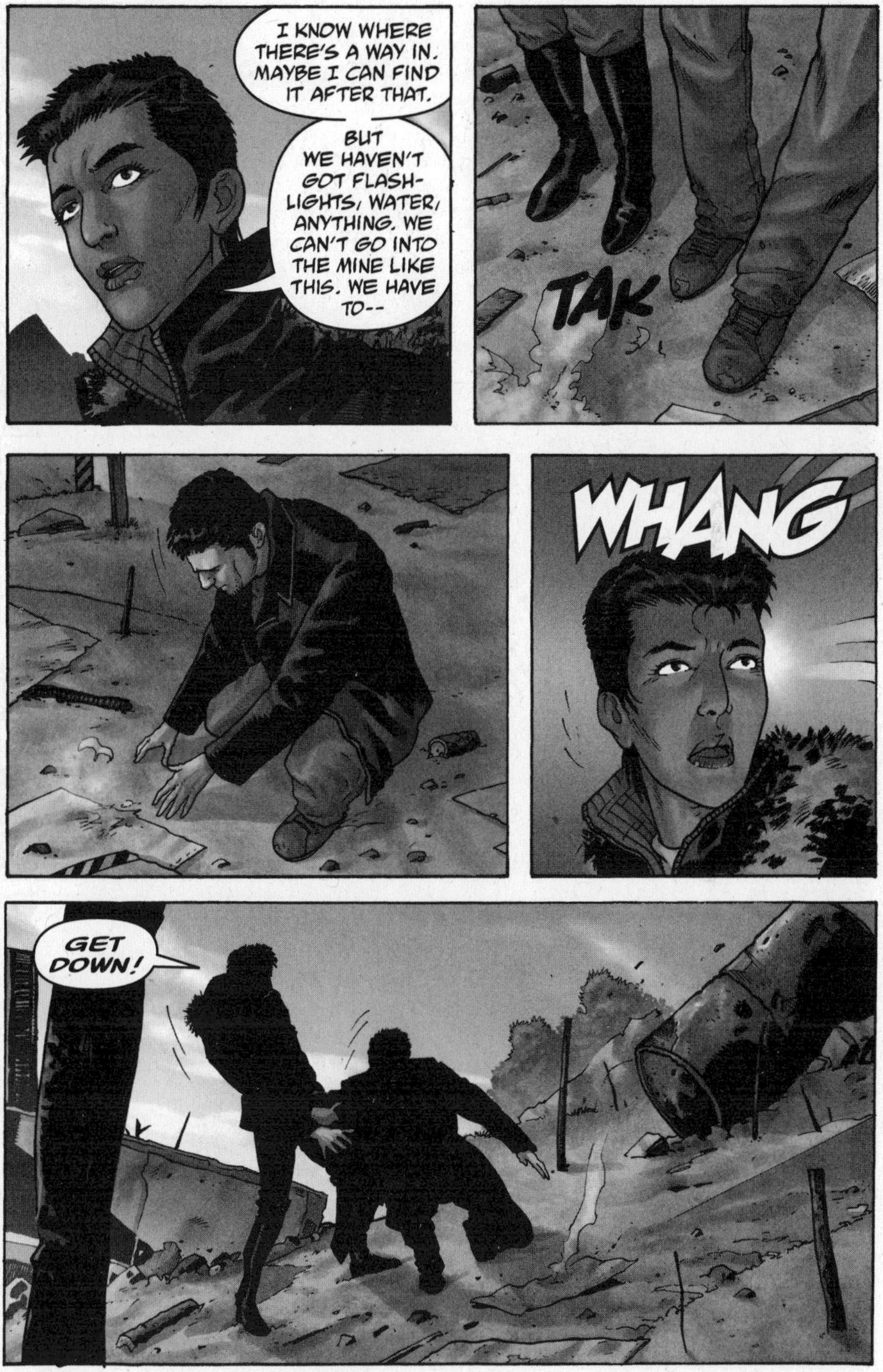
I KNOW WHERE THERE'S A WAY IN. MAYBE I CAN FIND IT AFTER THAT.
BUT WE HAVEN'T GOT FLASH-LIGHTS, WATER, ANYTHING. WE CAN'T GO INTO THE MINE LIKE THIS. WE HAVE TO--
TAK
WHANG
GET DOWN!

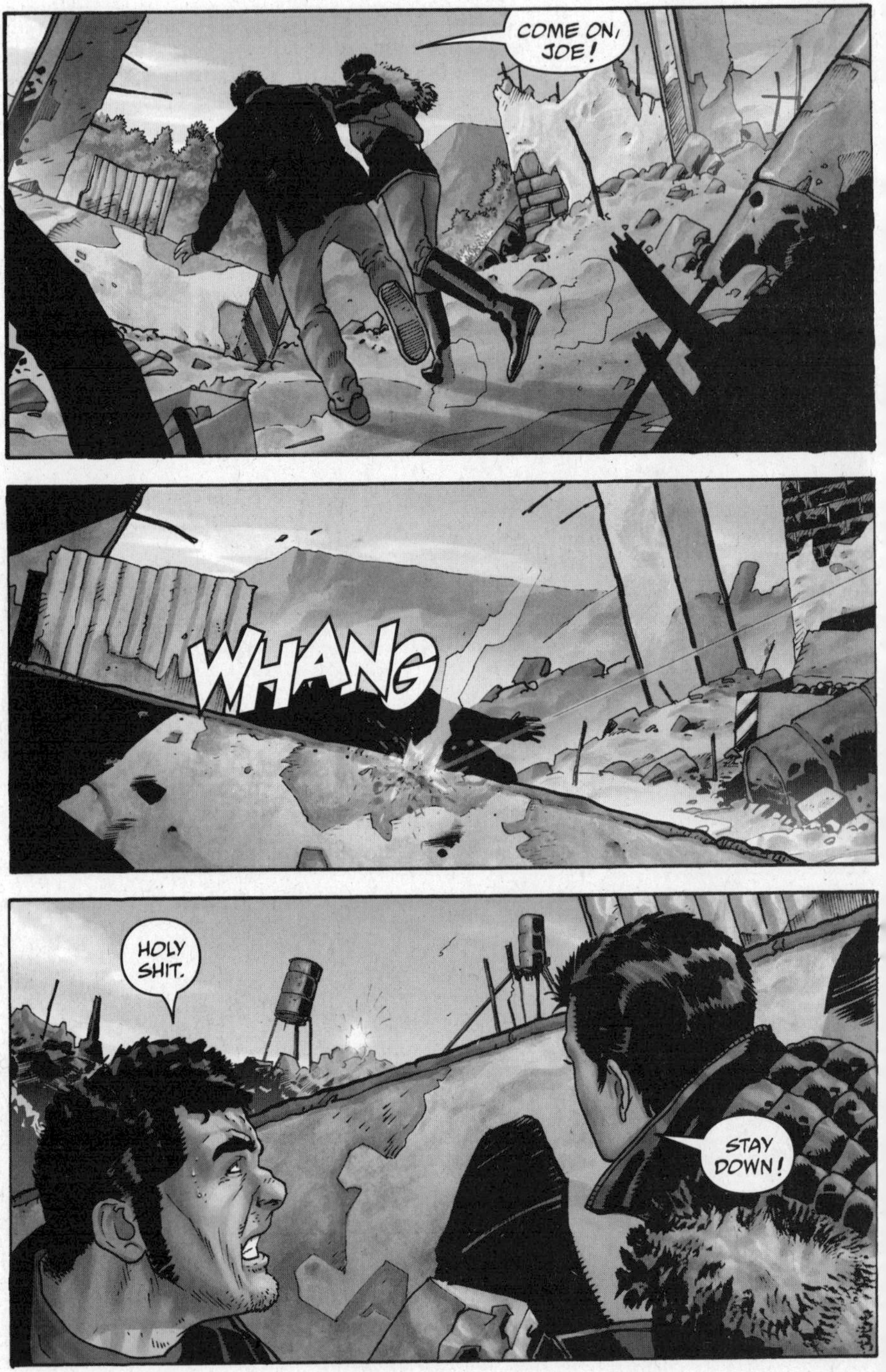
COME ON, JOE!
WHANG
HOLY SHIT.
STAY DOWN!

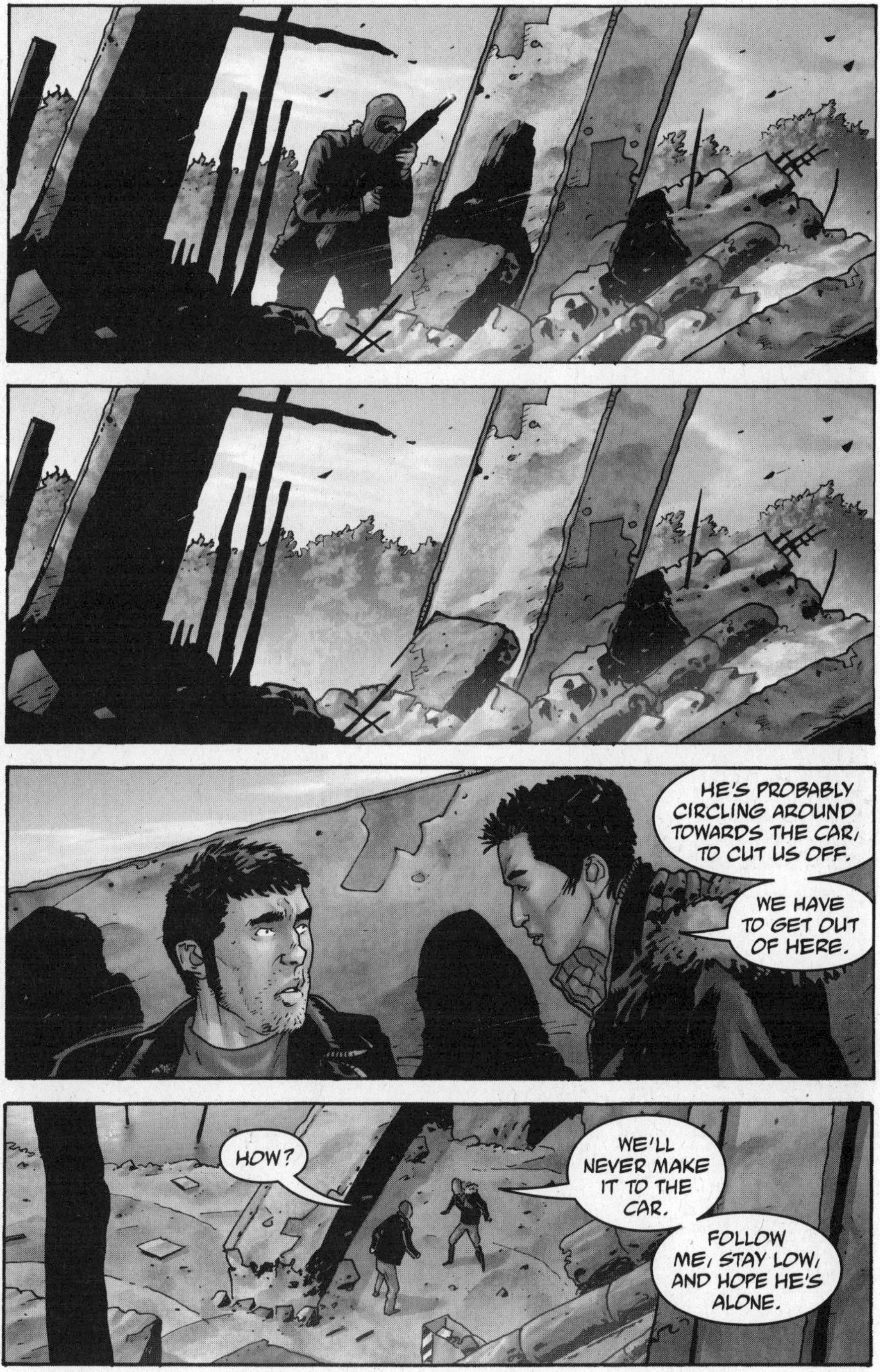
HE'S PROBABLY CIRCLING AROUND TOWARDS THE CAR, TO CUT US OFF.
WE HAVE TO GET OUT OF HERE.
HOW?
WE'LL NEVER MAKE IT TO THE CAR.
FOLLOW ME, STAY LOW, AND HOPE HE'S ALONE.

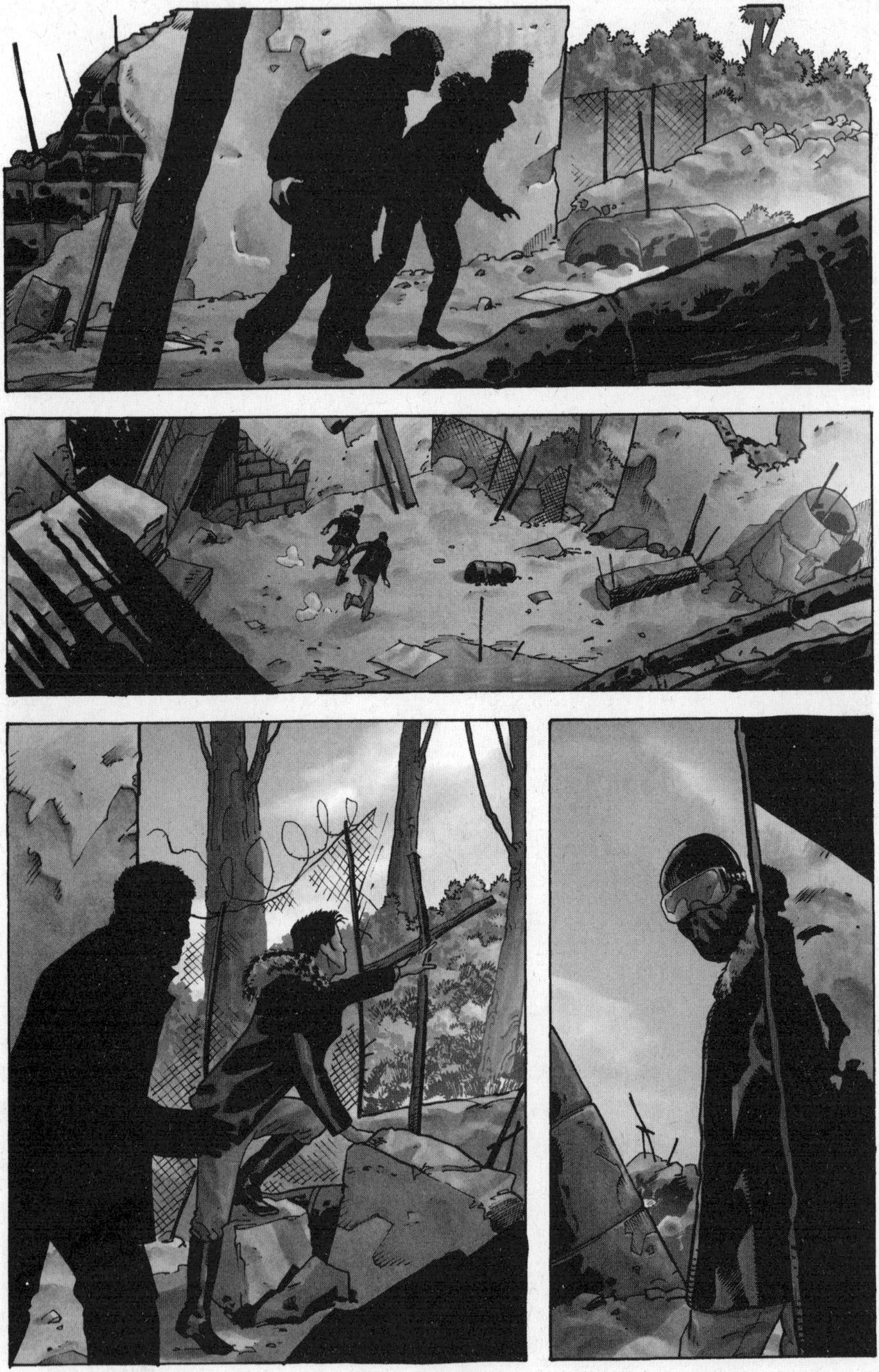

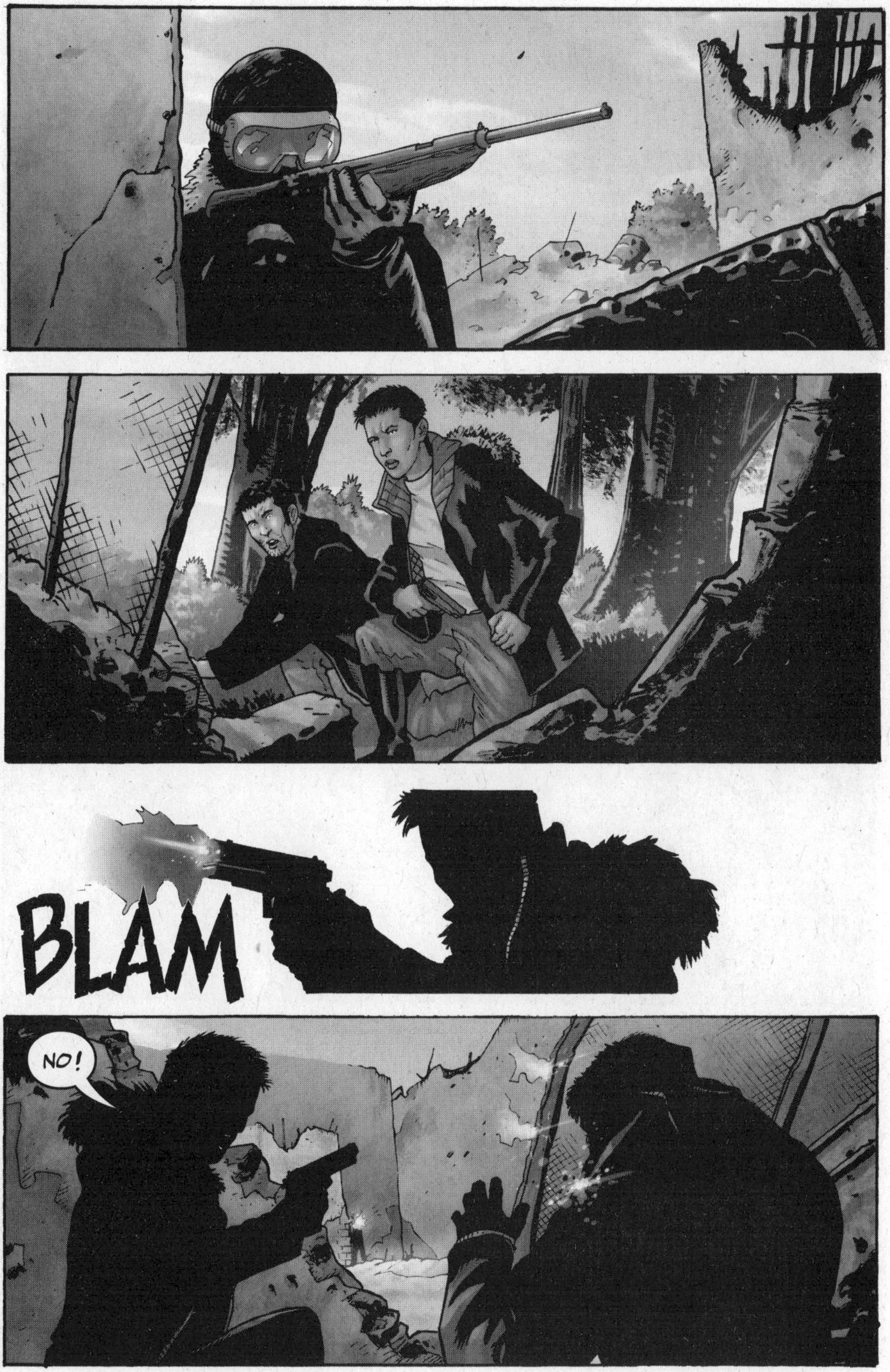
BLAM
NO!

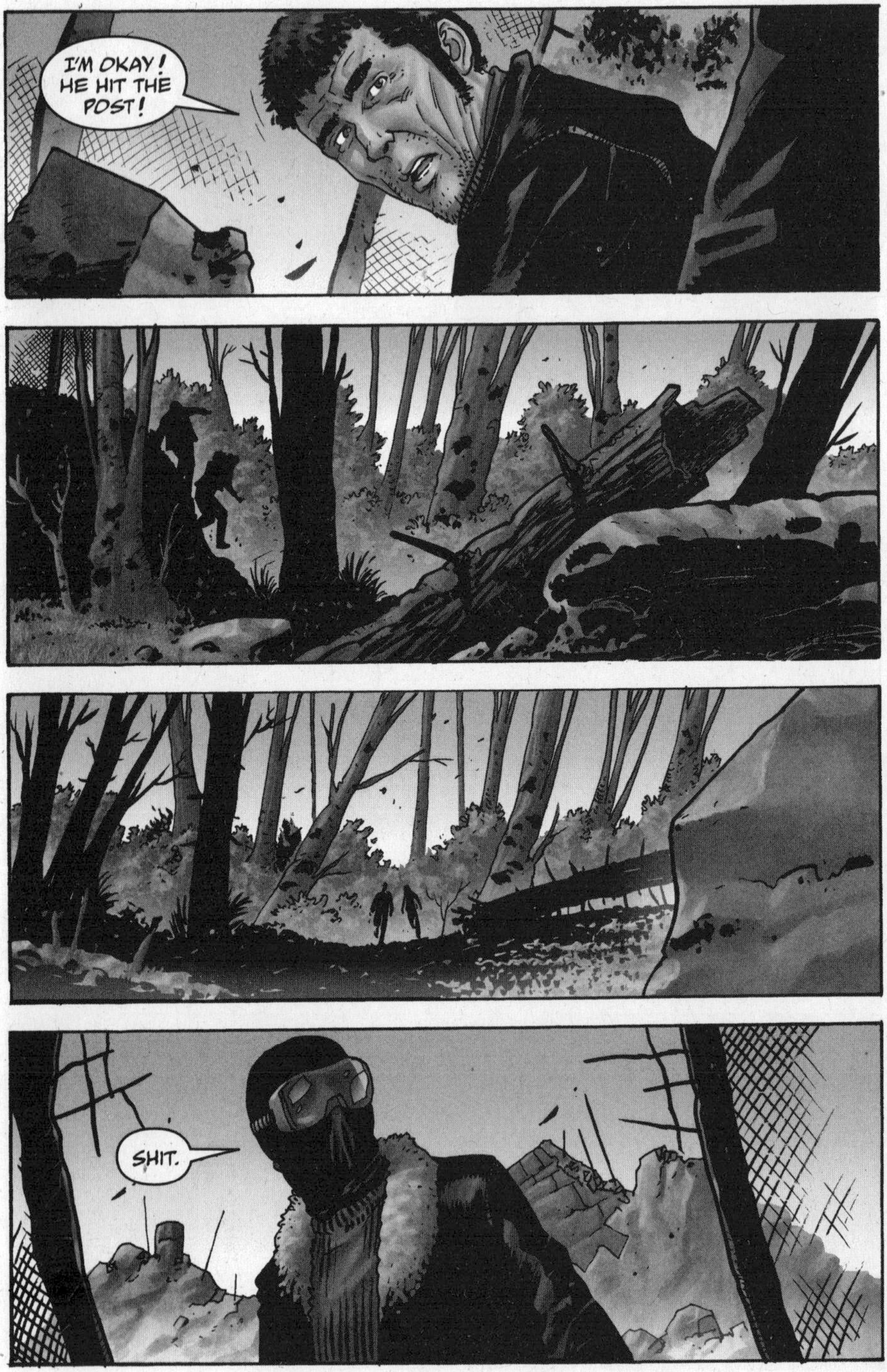
I'M OKAY! HE HIT THE POST!
SHIT.

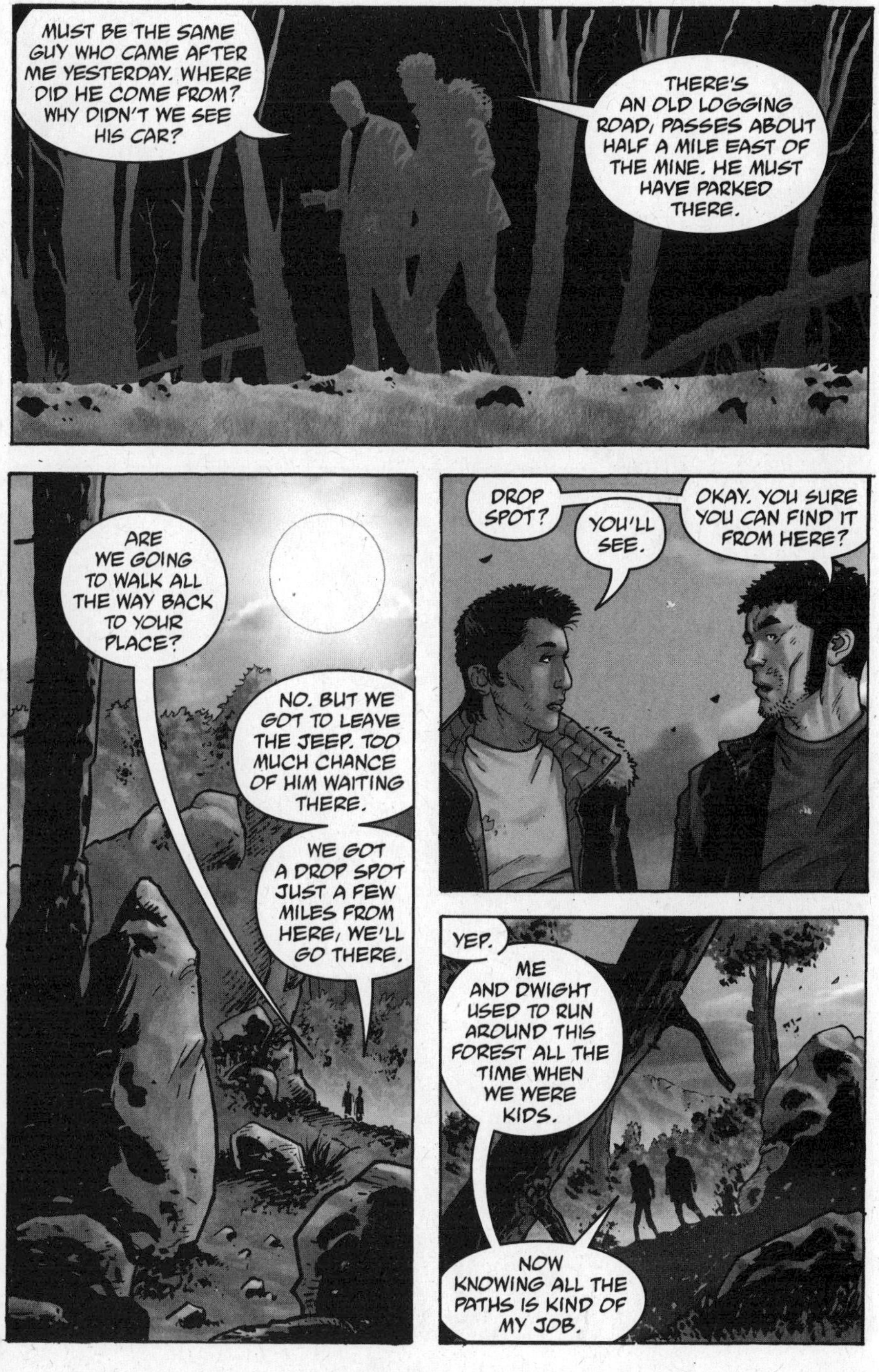

MUST BE THE SAME GUY WHO CAME AFTER ME YESTERDAY. WHERE DID HE COME FROM? WHY DIDN'T WE SEE HIS CAR?
THERE'S AN OLD LOGGING ROAD, PASSES ABOUT HALF A MILE EAST OF THE MINE. HE MUST HAVE PARKED THERE.
ARE WE GOING TO WALK ALL THE WAY BACK TO YOUR PLACE?
NO. BUT WE GOT TO LEAVE THE JEEP. TOO MUCH CHANCE OF HIM WAITING THERE.
WE GOT A DROP SPOT JUST A FEW MILES FROM HERE, WE'LL GO THERE.
DROP SPOT?
YOU'LL SEE.
OKAY. YOU SURE YOU CAN FIND IT FROM HERE?
YEP.
ME AND DWIGHT USED TO RUN AROUND THIS FOREST ALL THE TIME WHEN WE WERE KIDS.
NOW KNOWING ALL THE PATHS IS KIND OF MY JOB.

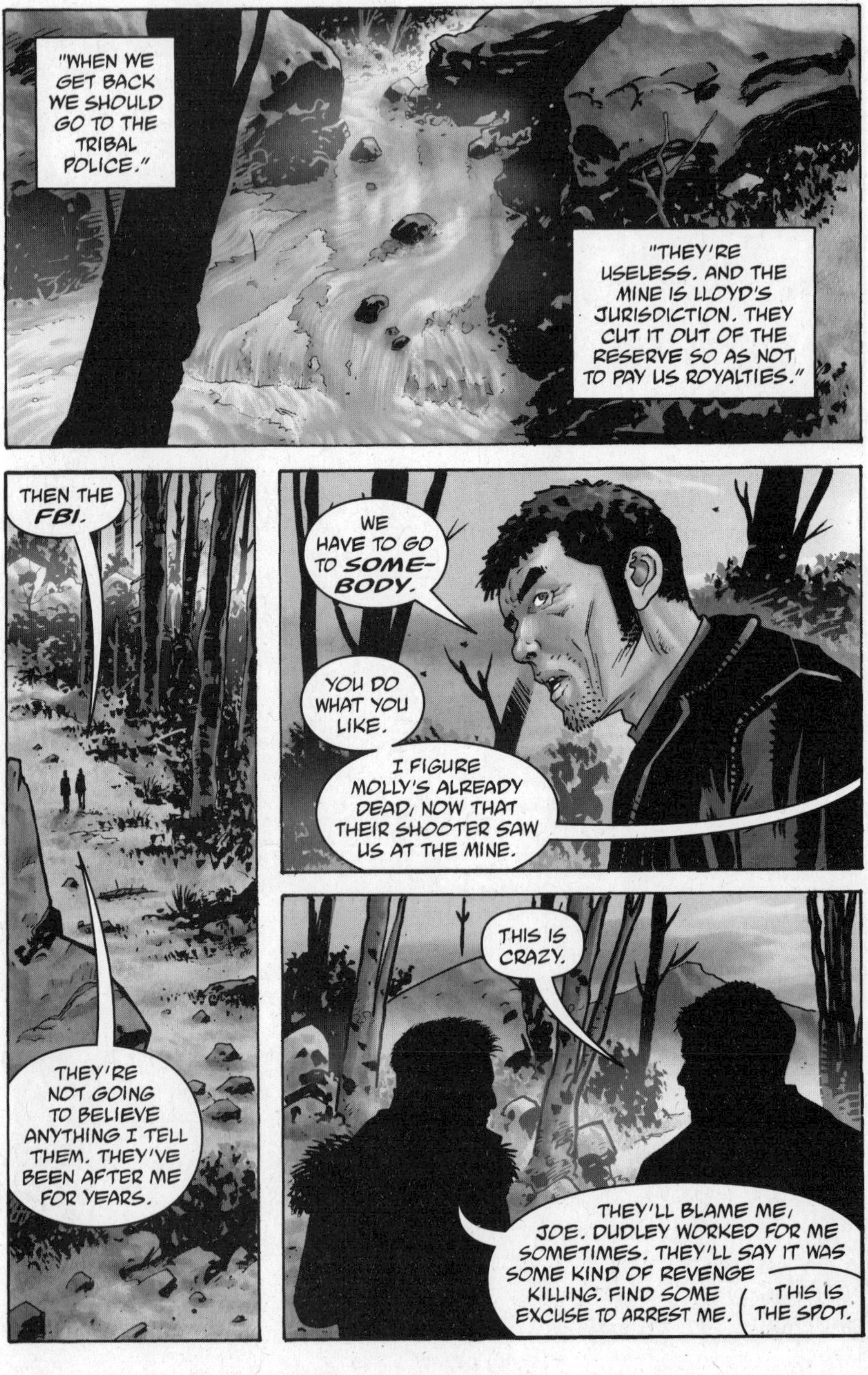
"WHEN WE GET BACK WE SHOULD GO TO THE TRIBAL POLICE."
"THEY'RE USELESS. AND THE MINE IS LLOYD'S JURISDICTION. THEY CUT IT OUT OF THE RESERVE SO AS NOT TO PAY US ROYALTIES."
THEN THE FBI.
THEY'RE NOT GOING TO BELIEVE ANYTHING I TELL THEM. THEY'VE BEEN AFTER ME FOR YEARS.
WE HAVE TO GO TO SOME-BODY.
YOU DO WHAT YOU LIKE.
I FIGURE MOLLY'S ALREADY DEAD, NOW THAT THEIR SHOOTER SAW US AT THE MINE.
THIS IS CRAZY.
THEY'LL BLAME ME, JOE. DUDLEY WORKED FOR ME SOMETIMES. THEY'LL SAY IT WAS SOME KIND OF REVENGE KILLING. FIND SOME EXCUSE TO ARREST ME.
THIS IS THE SPOT.

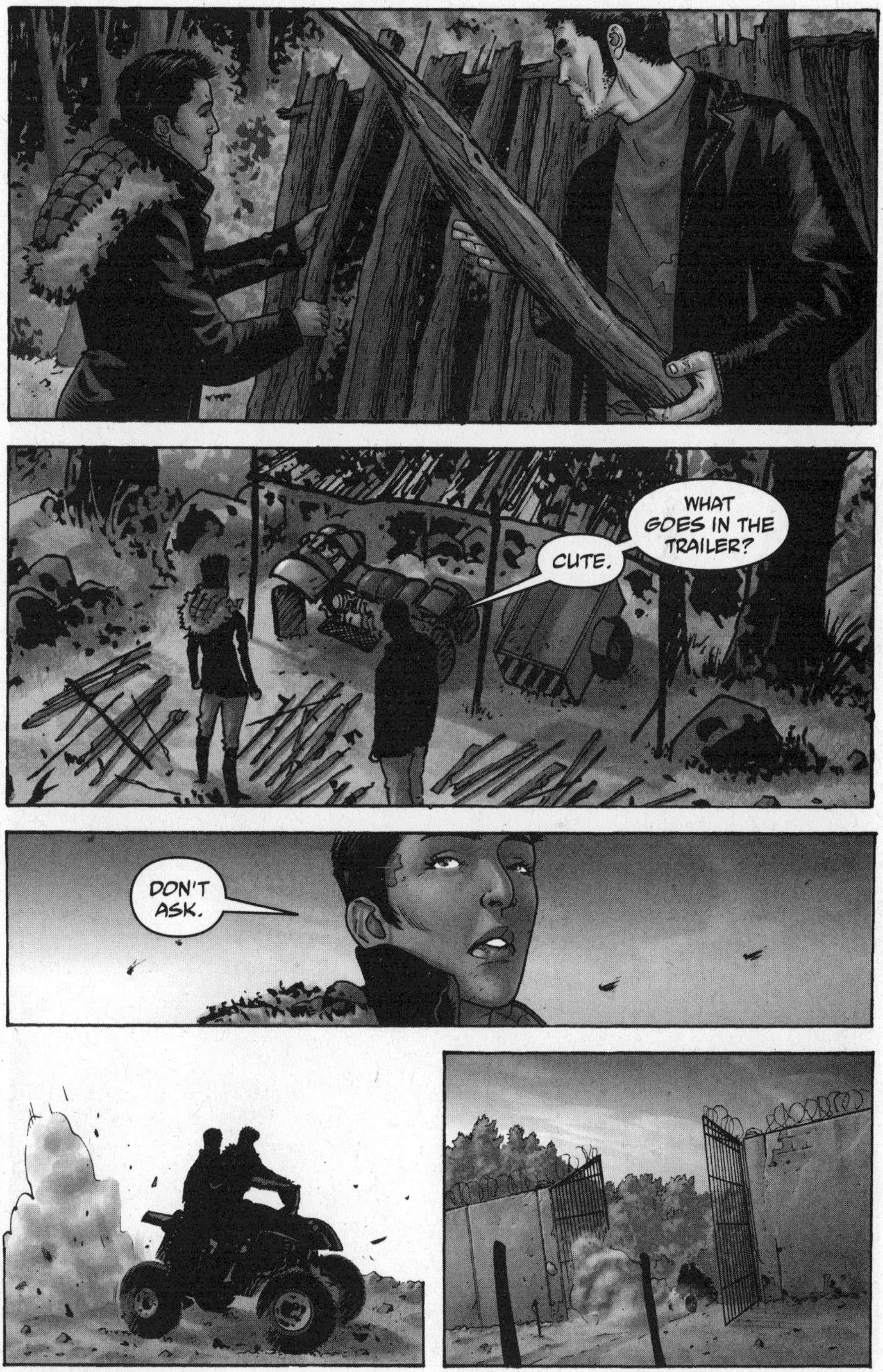
WHAT GOES IN THE TRAILER?
CUTE.
DON'T ASK.

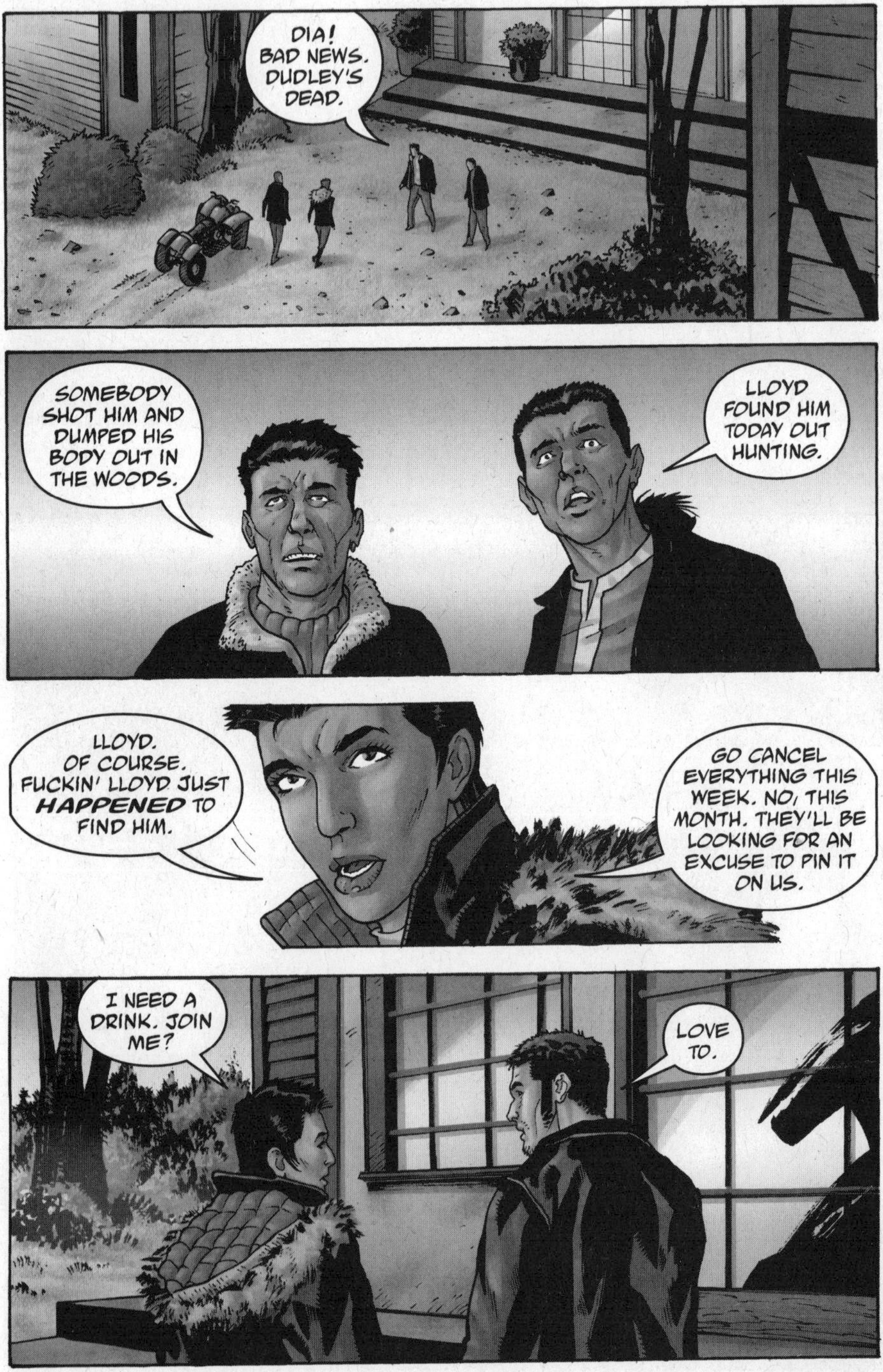
DIA! BAD NEWS. DUDLEY'S DEAD.
SOMEBODY SHOT HIM AND DUMPED HIS BODY OUT IN THE WOODS.
LLOYD FOUND HIM TODAY OUT HUNTING.
LLOYD. OF COURSE. FUCKIN' LLOYD JUST HAPPENED TO FIND HIM.
GO CANCEL EVERYTHING THIS WEEK. NO, THIS MONTH. THEY'LL BE LOOKING FOR AN EXCUSE TO PIN IT ON US.
I NEED A DRINK. JOIN ME?
LOVE TO.

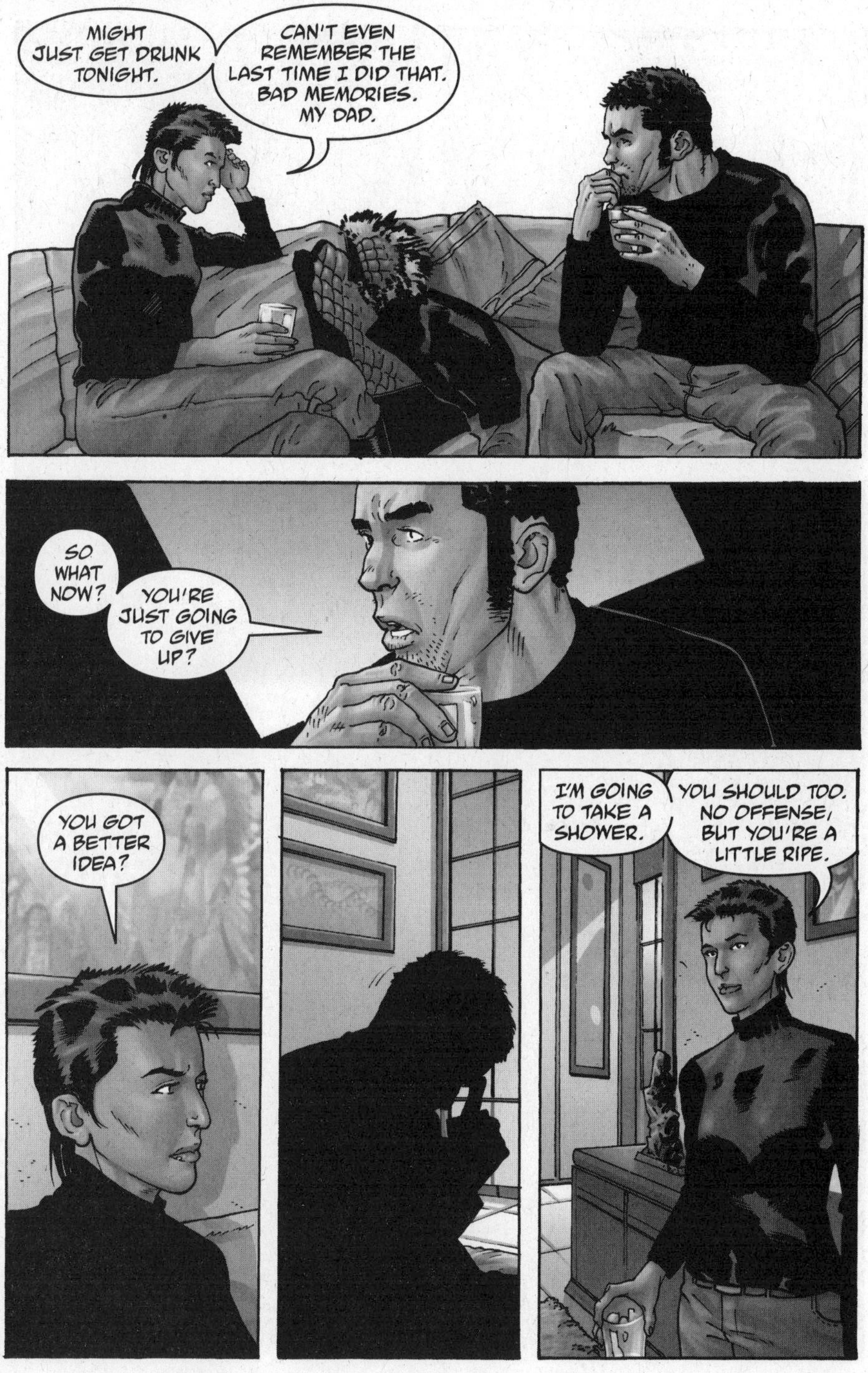
MIGHT JUST GET DRUNK TONIGHT.
CAN'T EVEN REMEMBER THE LAST TIME I DID THAT. BAD MEMORIES. MY DAD.
SO WHAT NOW?
YOU'RE JUST GOING TO GIVE UP?
YOU GOT A BETTER IDEA?
I'M GOING TO TAKE A SHOWER.
YOU SHOULD TOO. NO OFFENSE, BUT YOU'RE A LITTLE RIPE.

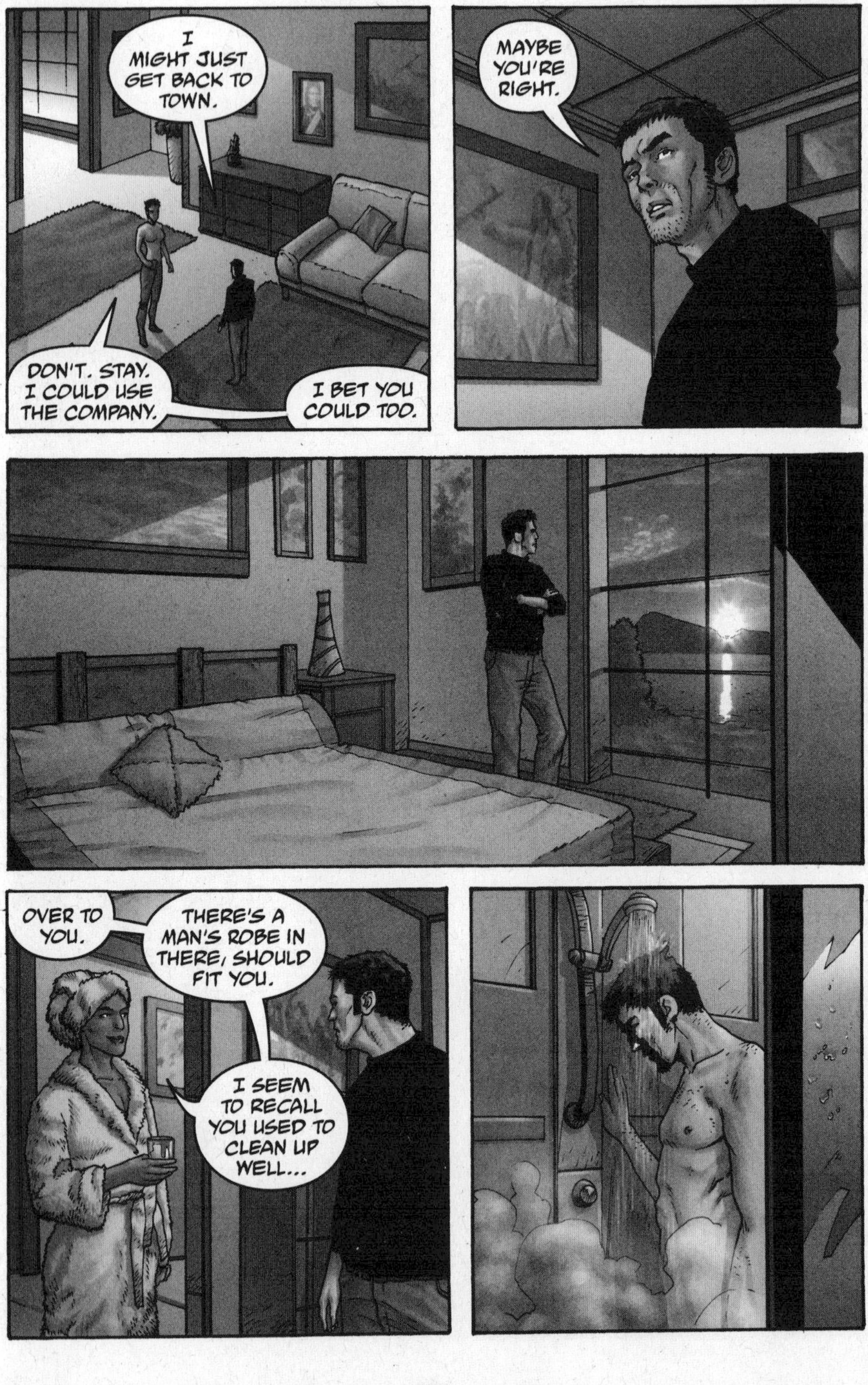
I MIGHT JUST GET BACK TO TOWN.
DON'T. STAY. I COULD USE THE COMPANY.
I BET YOU COULD TOO.
MAYBE YOU'RE RIGHT.
OVER TO YOU.
THERE'S A MAN'S ROBE IN THERE, SHOULD FIT YOU.
I SEEM TO RECALL YOU USED TO CLEAN UP WELL...

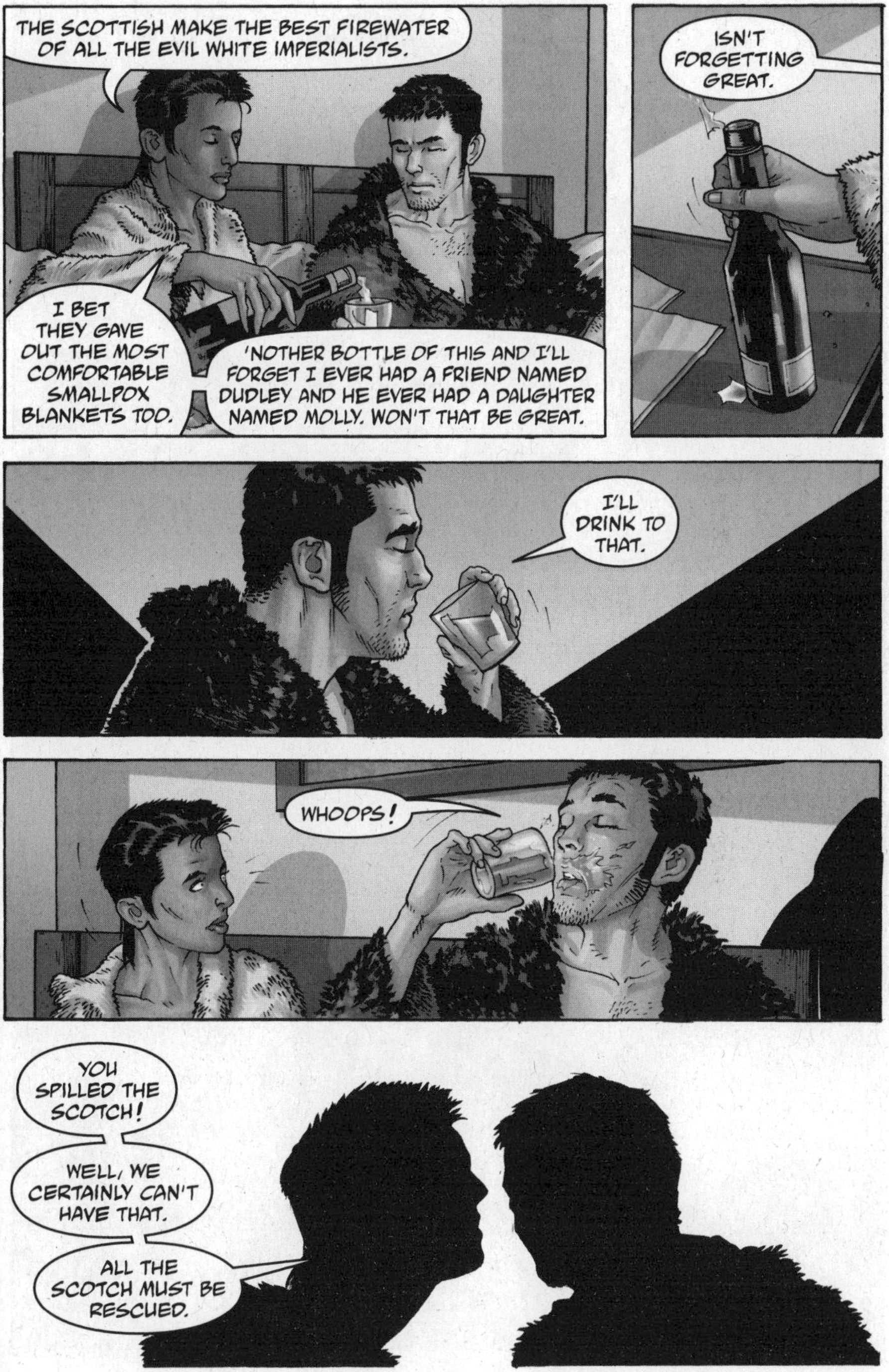
THE SCOTTISH MAKE THE BEST FIREWATER OF ALL THE EVIL WHITE IMPERIALISTS.
I BET THEY GAVE OUT THE MOST COMFORTABLE SMALLPOX BLANKETS TOO.
'NOTHER BOTTLE OF THIS AND I'LL FORGET I EVER HAD A FRIEND NAMED DUDLEY AND HE EVER HAD A DAUGHTER NAMED MOLLY. WON'T THAT BE GREAT.
ISN'T FORGETTING GREAT.
I'LL DRINK TO THAT.
WHOOPS!
YOU SPILLED THE SCOTCH!
WELL, WE CERTAINLY CAN'T HAVE THAT.
ALL THE SCOTCH MUST BE RESCUED.

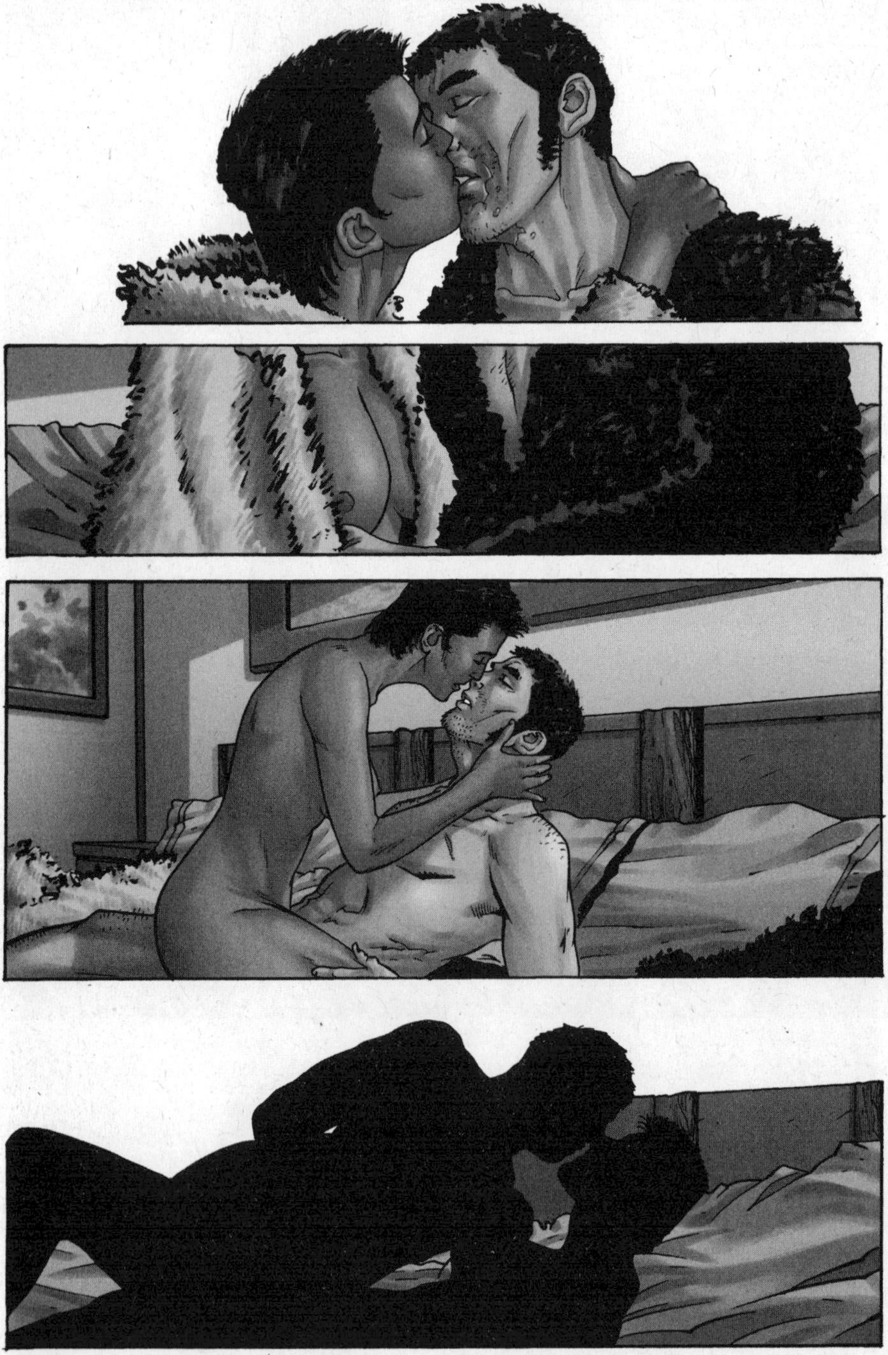

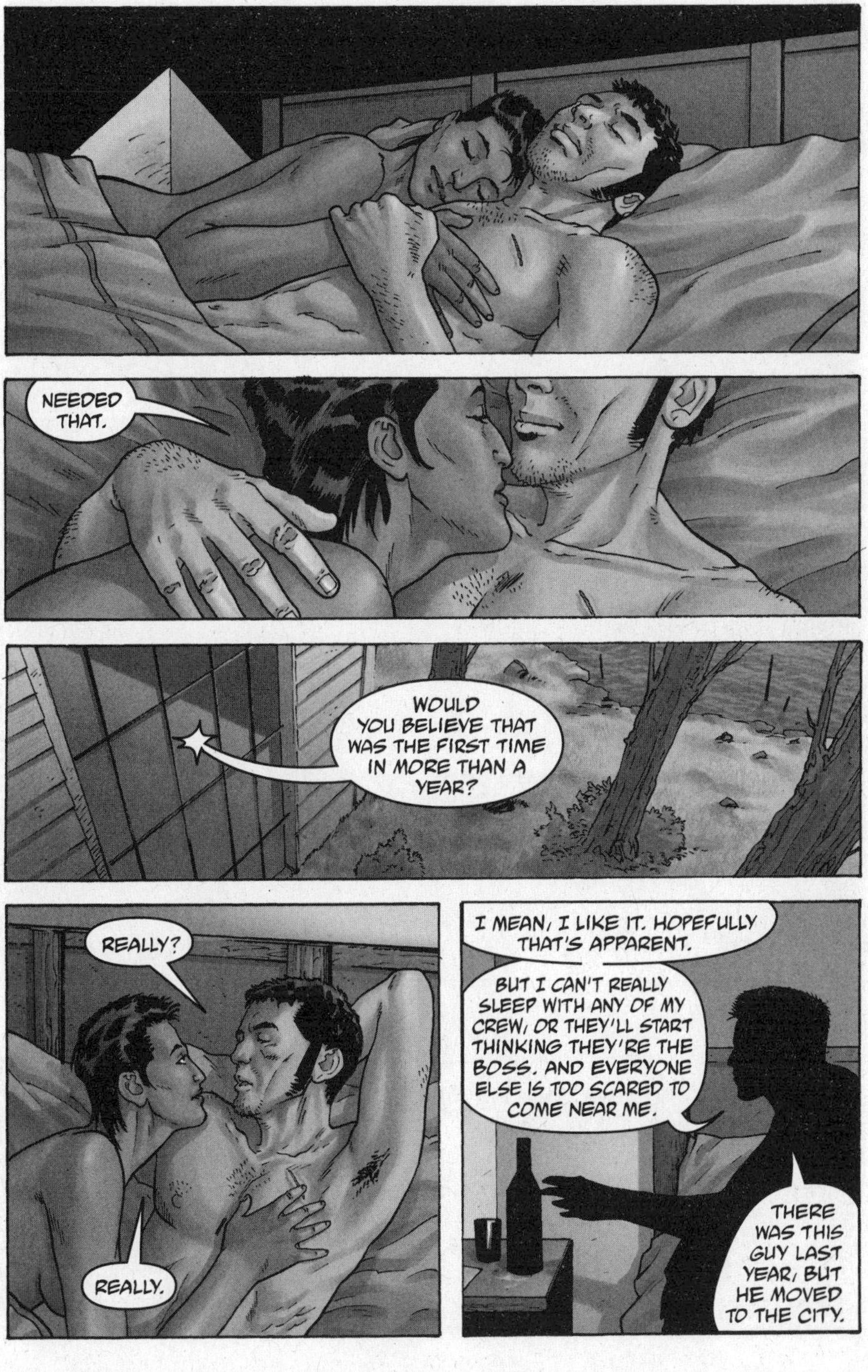
NEEDED THAT.
WOULD YOU BELIEVE THAT WAS THE FIRST TIME IN MORE THAN A YEAR?
REALLY?
REALLY.
I MEAN, I LIKE IT. HOPEFULLY THAT'S APPARENT.
BUT I CAN'T REALLY SLEEP WITH ANY OF MY CREW, OR THEY'LL START THINKING THEY'RE THE BOSS. AND EVERYONE ELSE IS TOO SCARED TO COME NEAR ME.
THERE WAS THIS GUY LAST YEAR, BUT HE MOVED TO THE CITY.

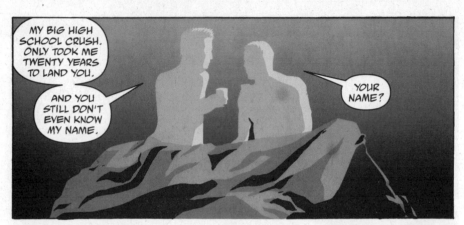

MY BIG HIGH SCHOOL CRUSH. ONLY TOOK ME TWENTY YEARS TO LAND YOU.

AND YOU STILL DON'T EVEN KNOW MY NAME.

YOUR NAME?

MY MOHAWK NAME. KAWISANENTHA.

MEANS "SHE KNOCKS THE ICE OFF THE TREES WITH A STICK," BELIEVE IT OR NOT.

KAWISANENTHA. I LIKE THAT.

SO GLAD IT MEETS WITH YOUR APPROVAL.

WHERE'D YOU GET THIS?

PLAYING HOCKEY?

I'M TIRED. LET'S GET SOME SLEEP.

FUNNY. I ALMOST FORGOT HOW MEN PASS OUT AFTER.

SLEEP TIGHT, JOE.

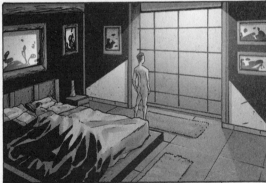

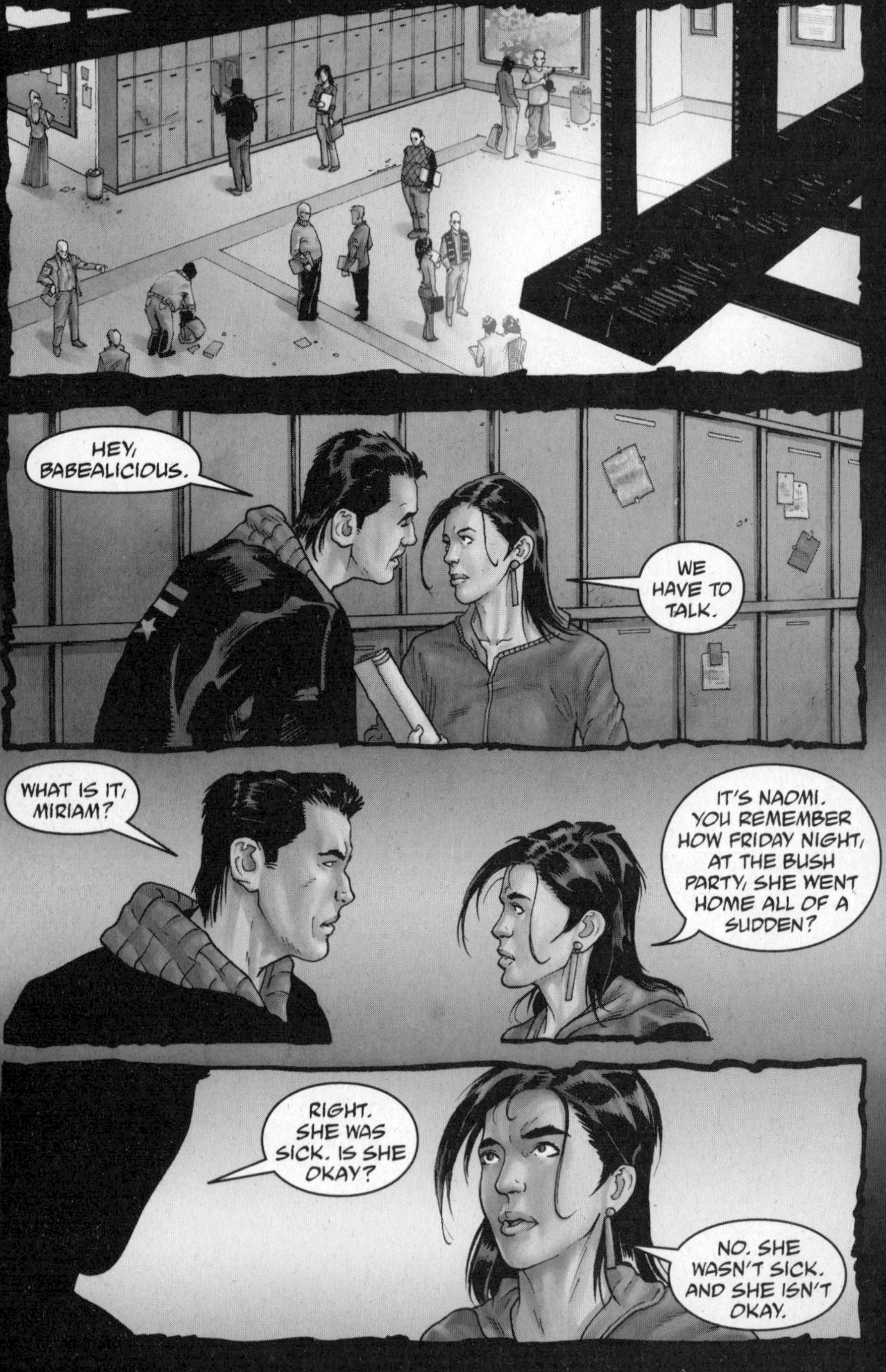
HEY, BABEALICIOUS.
WE HAVE TO TALK.
WHAT IS IT, MIRIAM?
IT'S NAOMI. YOU REMEMBER HOW FRIDAY NIGHT, AT THE BUSH PARTY, SHE WENT HOME ALL OF A SUDDEN?
RIGHT. SHE WAS SICK. IS SHE OKAY?
NO. SHE WASN'T SICK. AND SHE ISN'T OKAY.

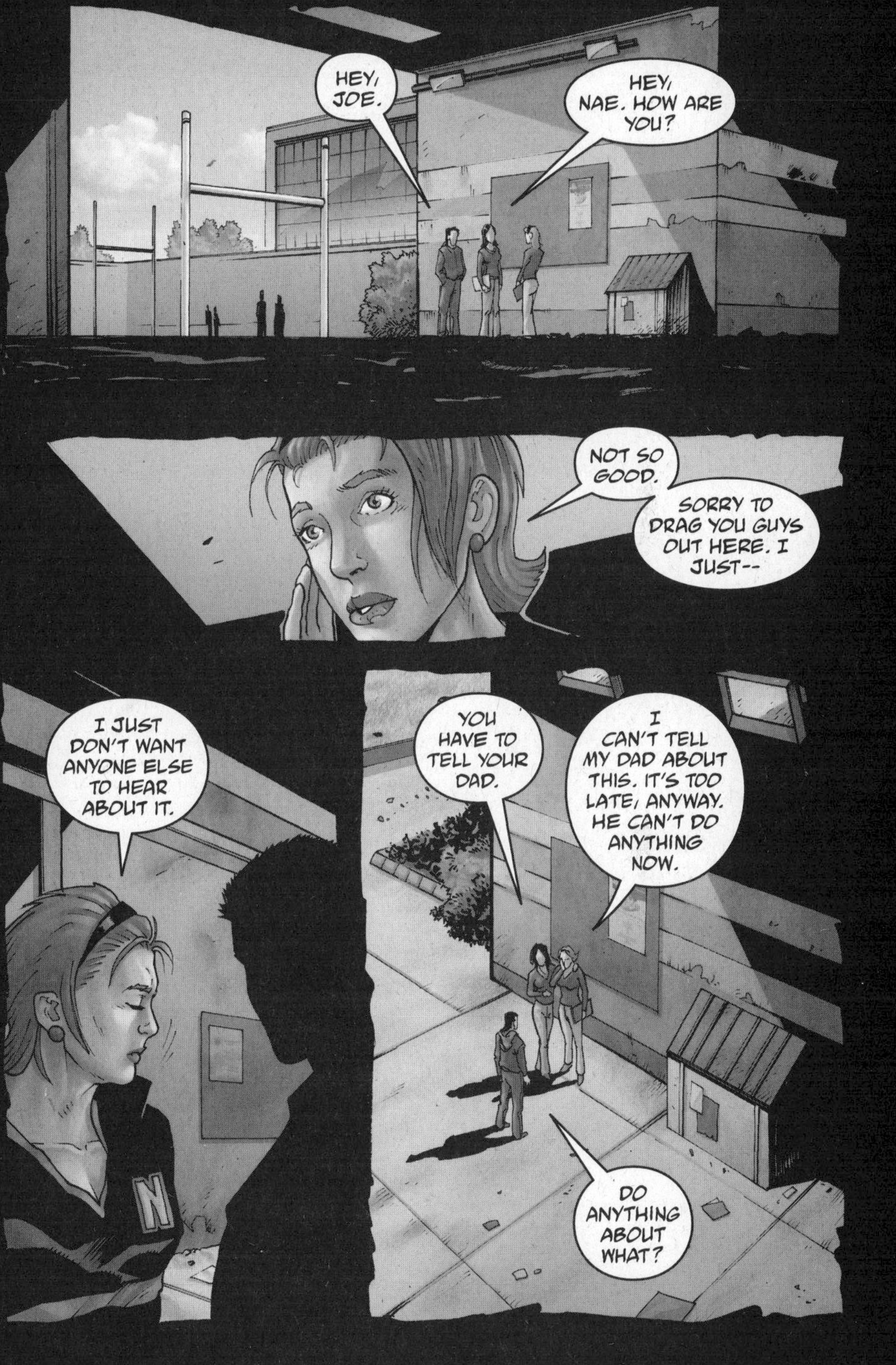

HEY, JOE.
HEY, NAE. HOW ARE YOU?
NOT SO GOOD.
SORRY TO DRAG YOU GUYS OUT HERE. I JUST--
I JUST DON'T WANT ANYONE ELSE TO HEAR ABOUT IT.
YOU HAVE TO TELL YOUR DAD.
I CAN'T TELL MY DAD ABOUT THIS. IT'S TOO LATE, ANYWAY. HE CAN'T DO ANYTHING NOW.
DO ANYTHING ABOUT WHAT?
N

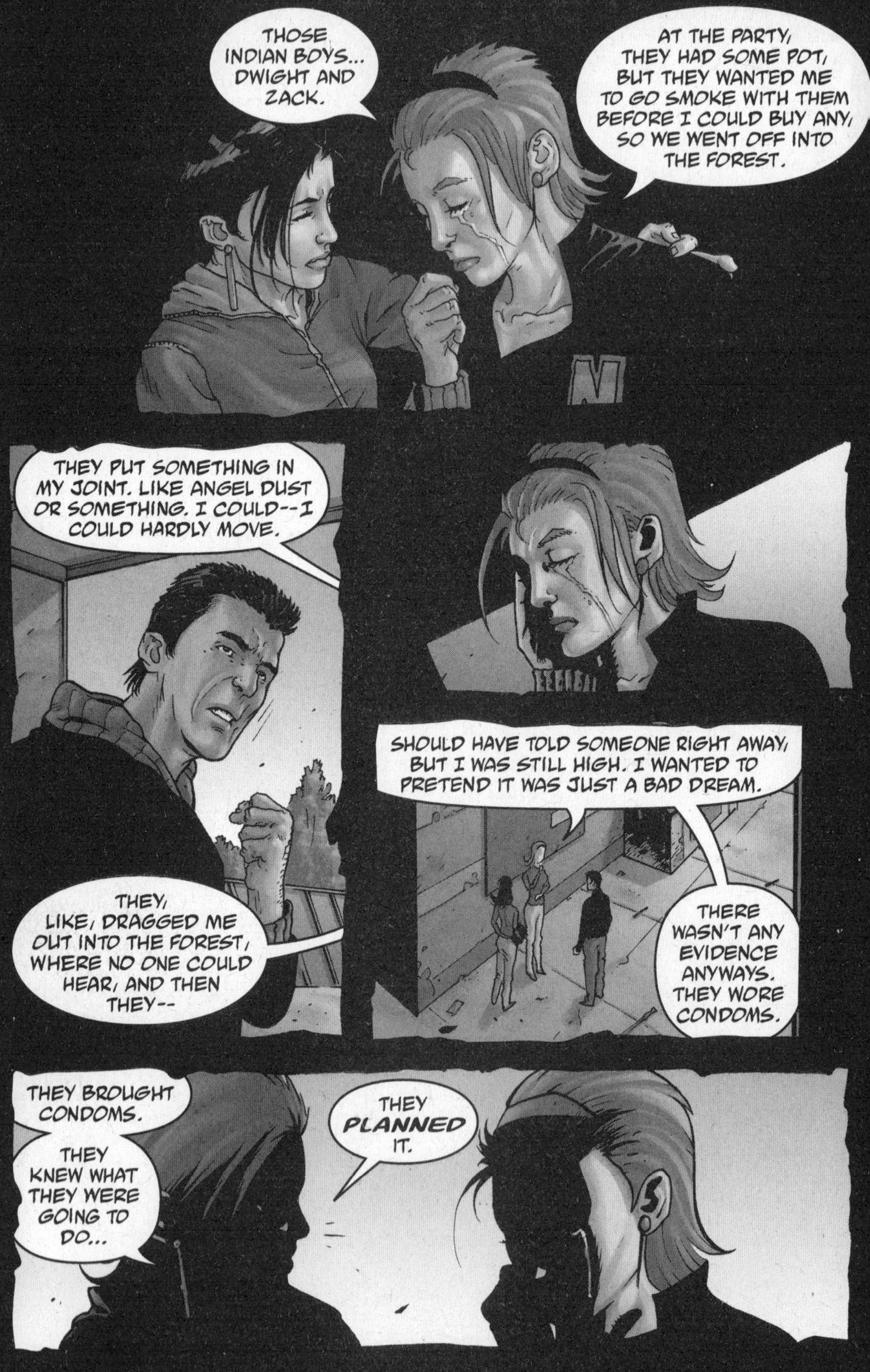
THOSE INDIAN BOYS... DWIGHT AND ZACK.
AT THE PARTY, THEY HAD SOME POT, BUT THEY WANTED ME TO GO SMOKE WITH THEM BEFORE I COULD BUY ANY, SO WE WENT OFF INTO THE FOREST.
THEY PUT SOMETHING IN MY JOINT. LIKE ANGEL DUST OR SOMETHING. I COULD--I COULD HARDLY MOVE.
THEY, LIKE, DRAGGED ME OUT INTO THE FOREST, WHERE NO ONE COULD HEAR, AND THEN THEY--
SHOULD HAVE TOLD SOMEONE RIGHT AWAY, BUT I WAS STILL HIGH. I WANTED TO PRETEND IT WAS JUST A BAD DREAM.
THERE WASN'T ANY EVIDENCE ANYWAYS. THEY WORE CONDOMS.
THEY BROUGHT CONDOMS.
THEY KNEW WHAT THEY WERE GOING TO DO...
THEY PLANNED IT.

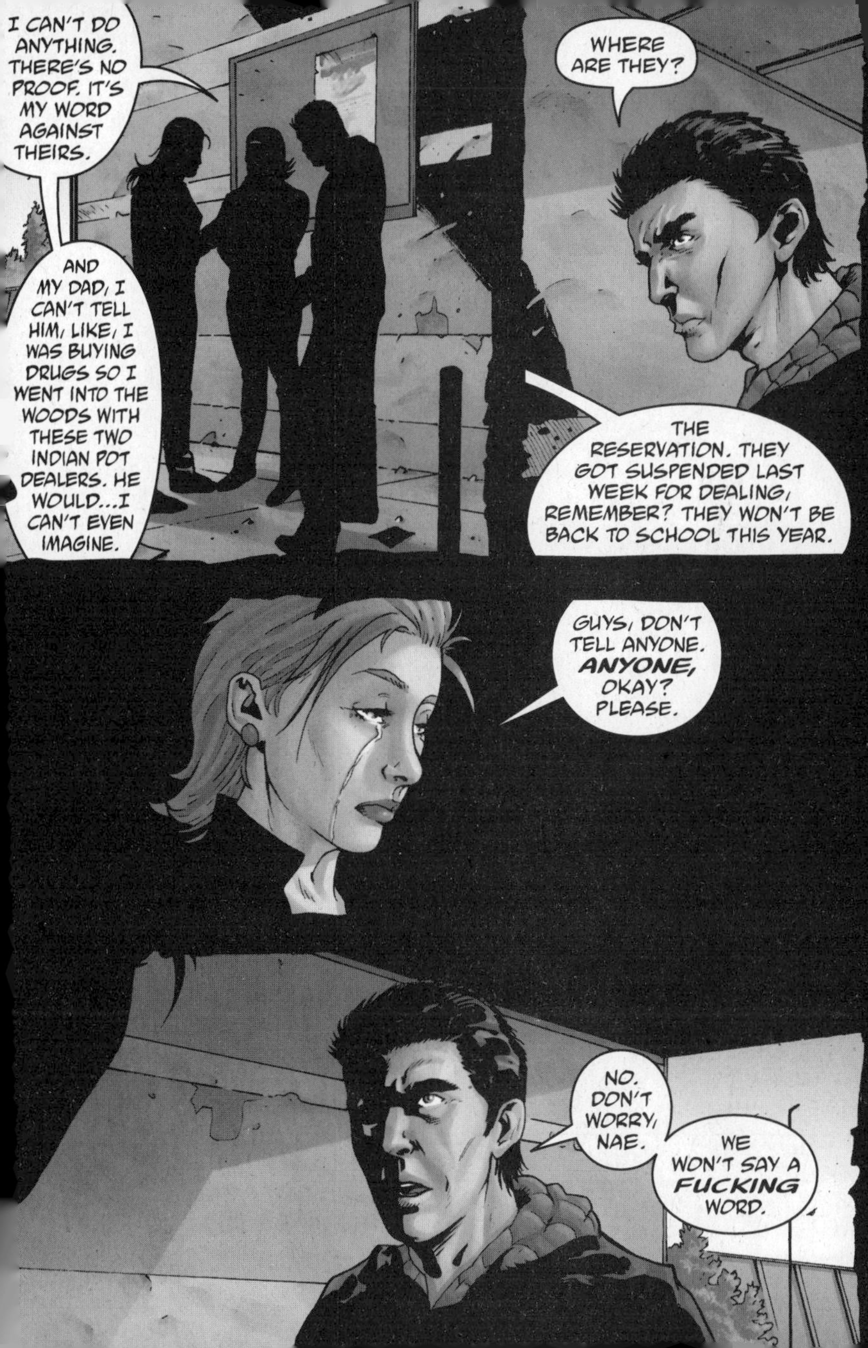
I CAN'T DO ANYTHING. THERE'S NO PROOF. IT'S MY WORD AGAINST THEIRS.
AND MY DAD, I CAN'T TELL HIM, LIKE, I WAS BUYING DRUGS SO I WENT INTO THE WOODS WITH THESE TWO INDIAN POT DEALERS. HE WOULD...I CAN'T EVEN IMAGINE.
WHERE ARE THEY?
THE RESERVATION. THEY GOT SUSPENDED LAST WEEK FOR DEALING, REMEMBER? THEY WON'T BE BACK TO SCHOOL THIS YEAR.
GUYS, DON'T TELL ANYONE. ***ANYONE,*** OKAY? PLEASE.
NO. DON'T WORRY, NAE.
WE WON'T SAY A ***FUCKING*** WORD.

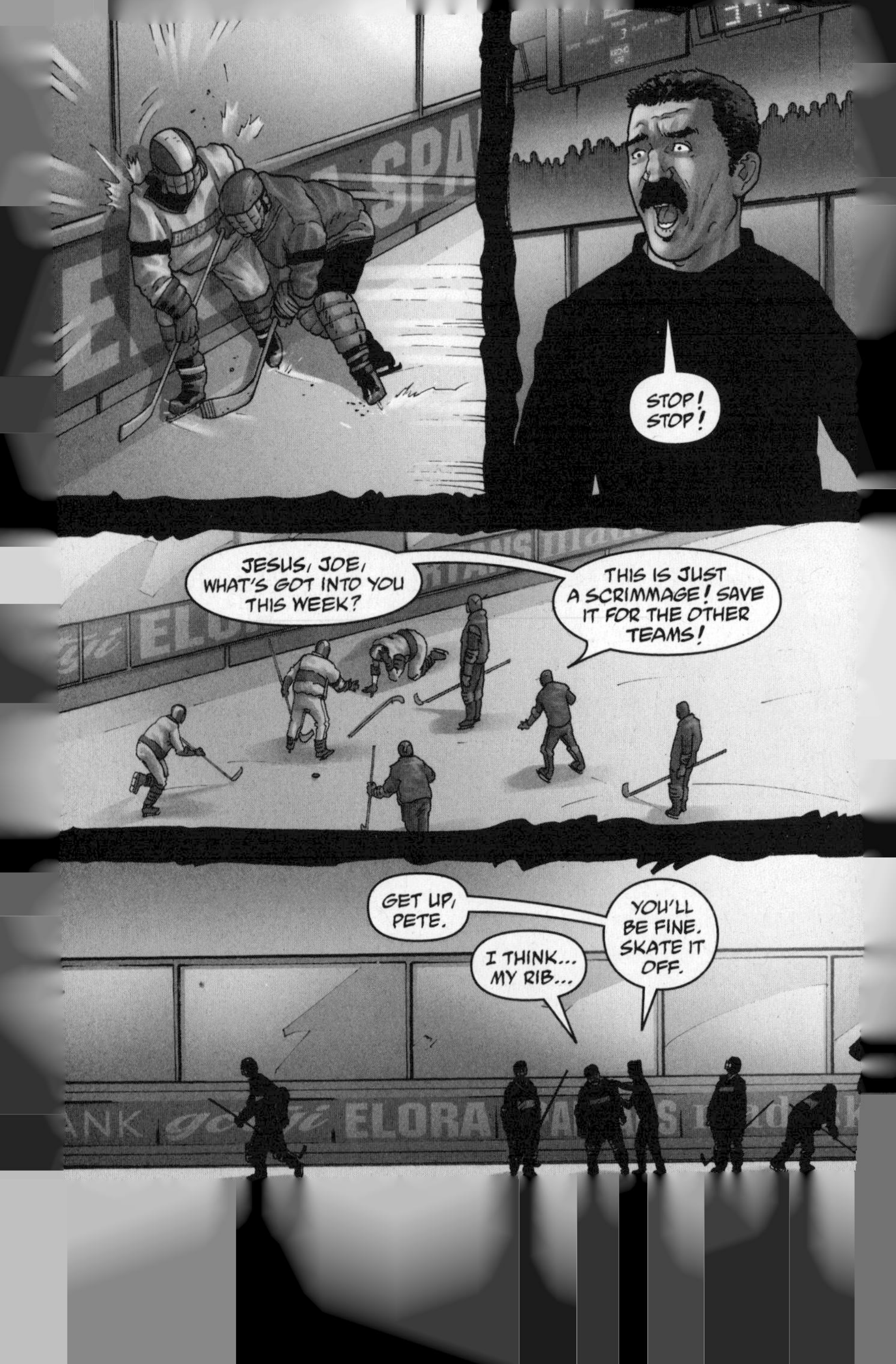
STOP! STOP!
JESUS, JOE, WHAT'S GOT INTO YOU THIS WEEK?
THIS IS JUST A SCRIMMAGE! SAVE IT FOR THE OTHER TEAMS!
GET UP, PETE.
YOU'LL BE FINE. SKATE IT OFF.
I THINK... MY RIB...

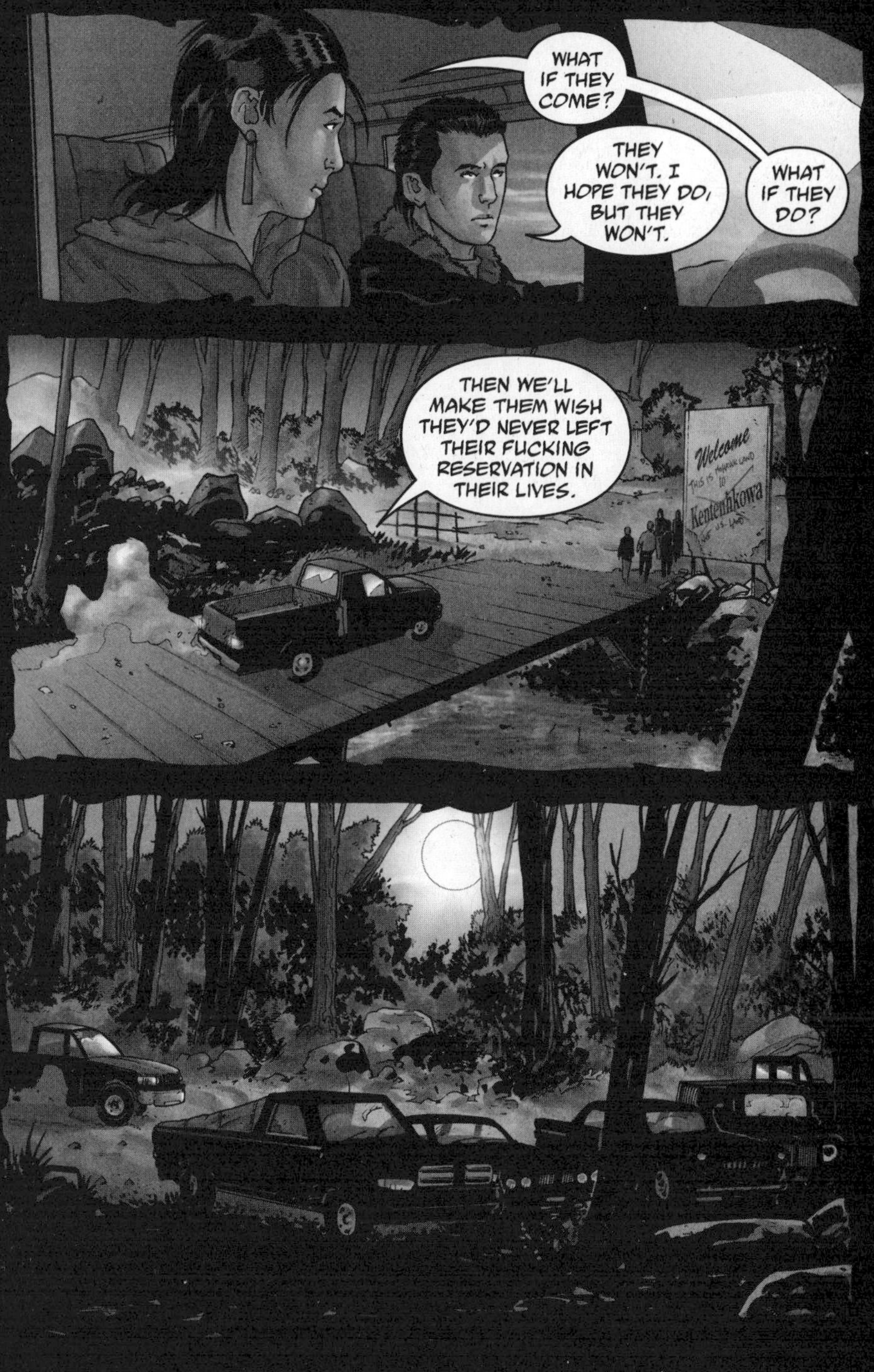
WHAT IF THEY COME?
THEY WON'T. I HOPE THEY DO, BUT THEY WON'T.
WHAT IF THEY DO?
THEN WE'LL MAKE THEM WISH THEY'D NEVER LEFT THEIR FUCKING RESERVATION IN THEIR LIVES.
Welcome
to
Kentenhkowa

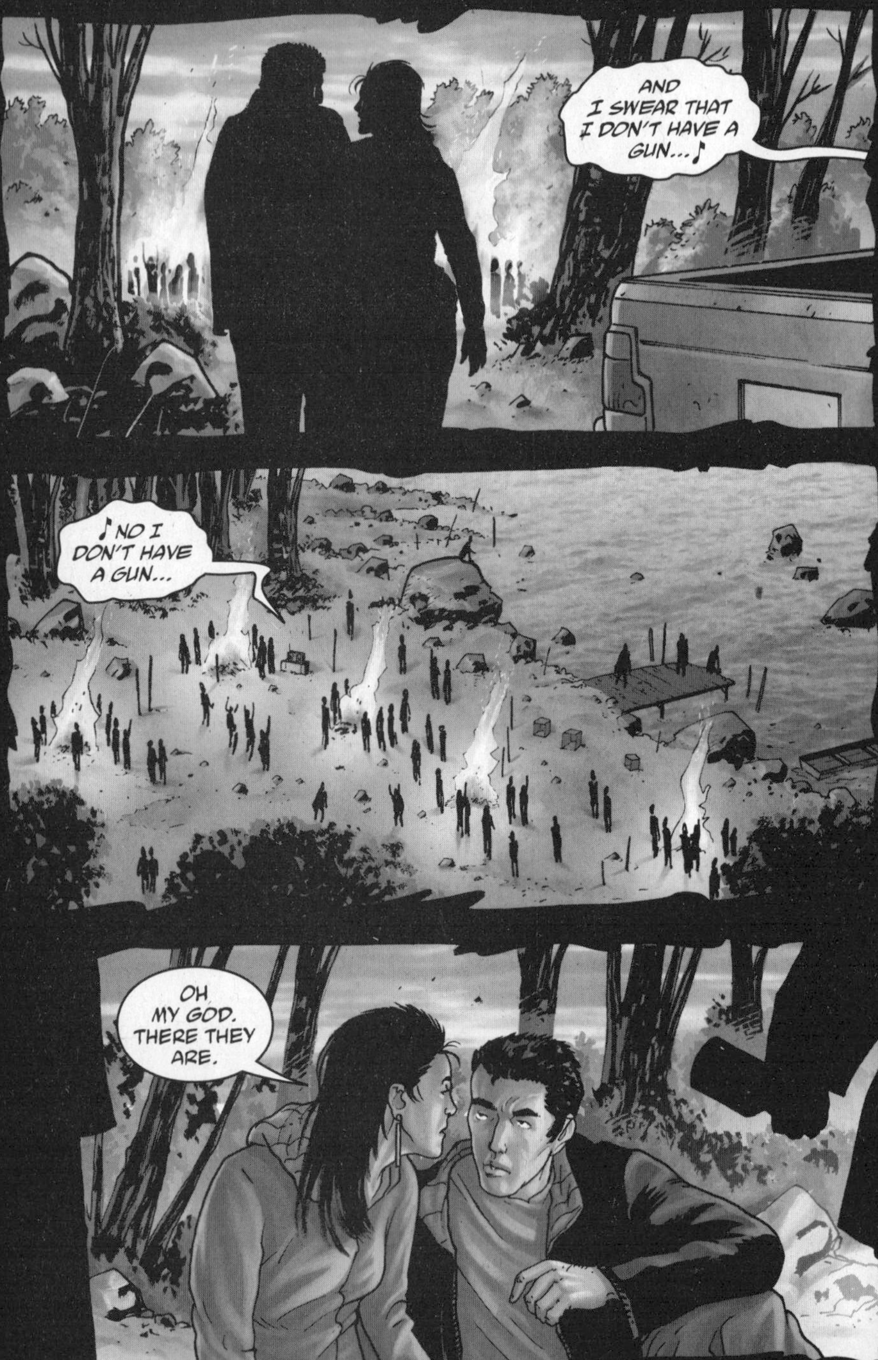
AND I SWEAR THAT I DON'T HAVE A GUN...♪
♪NO I DON'T HAVE A GUN...
OH MY GOD. THERE THEY ARE.

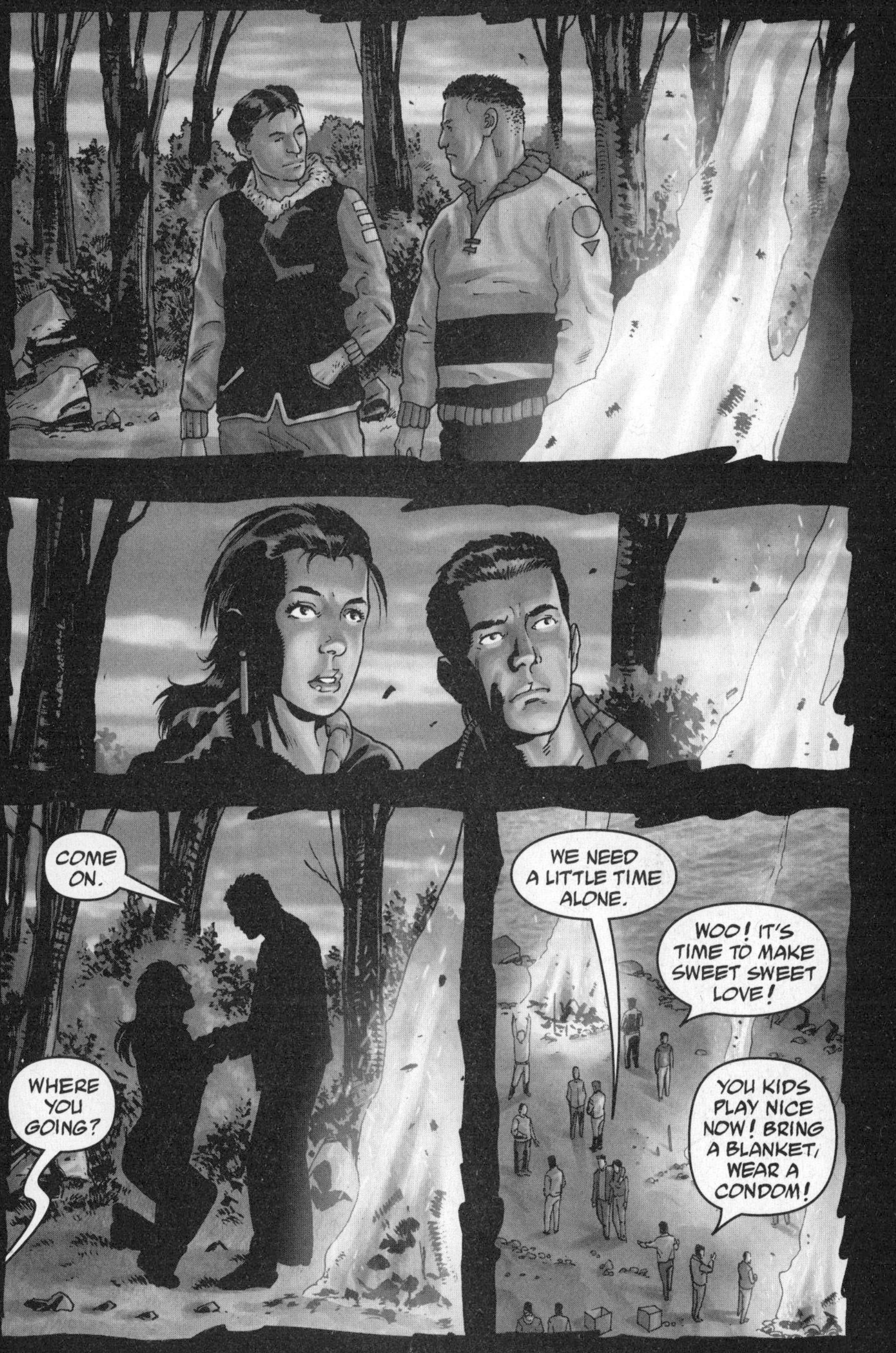
COME ON.
WHERE YOU GOING?
WE NEED A LITTLE TIME ALONE.
WOO! IT'S TIME TO MAKE SWEET SWEET LOVE!
YOU KIDS PLAY NICE NOW! BRING A BLANKET, WEAR A CONDOM!

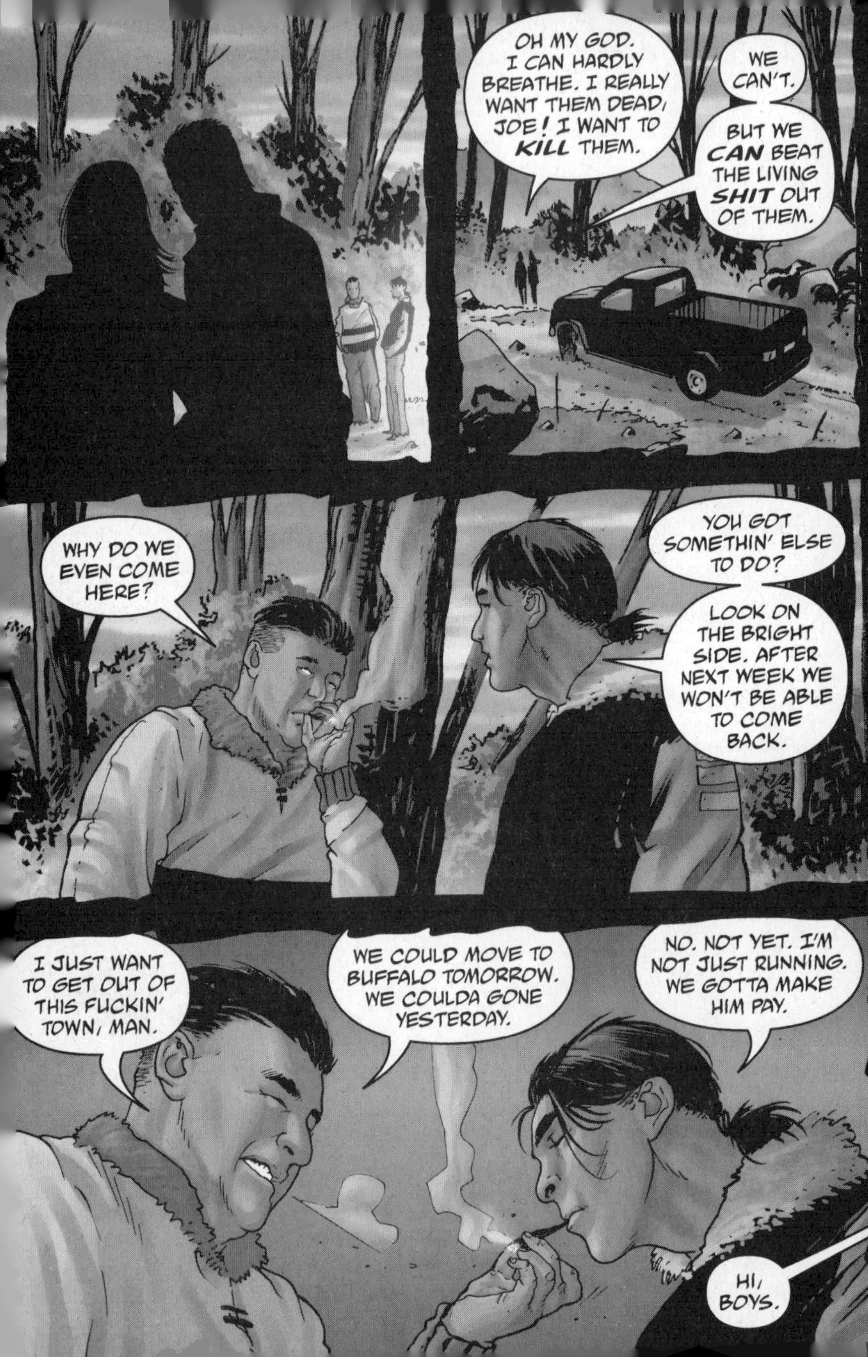
OH MY GOD. I CAN HARDLY BREATHE. I REALLY WANT THEM DEAD, JOE! I WANT TO KILL THEM.
WE CAN'T.
BUT WE CAN BEAT THE LIVING SHIT OUT OF THEM.
WHY DO WE EVEN COME HERE?
YOU GOT SOMETHIN' ELSE TO DO?
LOOK ON THE BRIGHT SIDE. AFTER NEXT WEEK WE WON'T BE ABLE TO COME BACK.
I JUST WANT TO GET OUT OF THIS FUCKIN' TOWN, MAN.
WE COULD MOVE TO BUFFALO TOMORROW. WE COULDA GONE YESTERDAY.
NO. NOT YET. I'M NOT JUST RUNNING. WE GOTTA MAKE HIM PAY.
HI, BOYS.

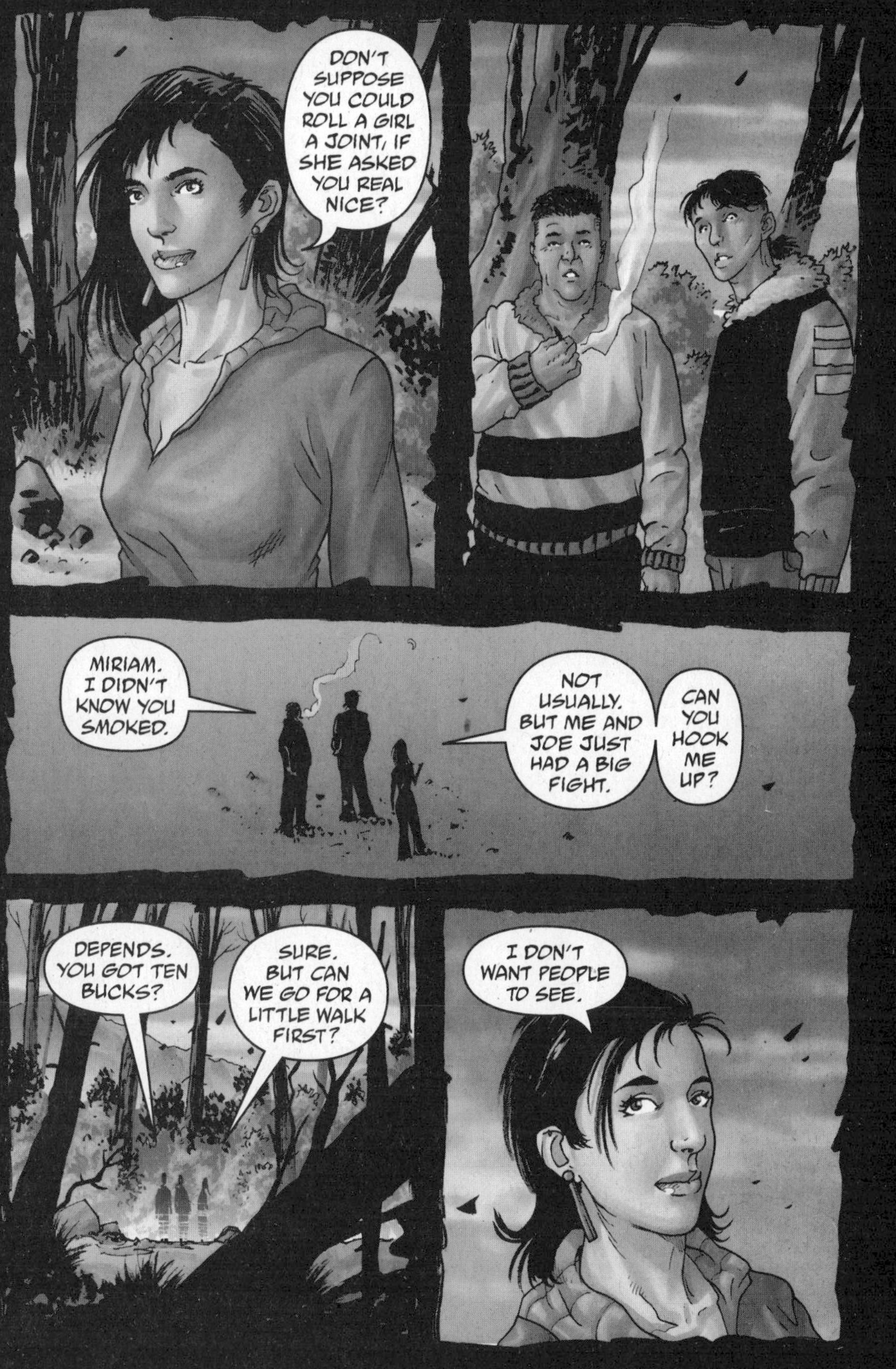
DON'T SUPPOSE YOU COULD ROLL A GIRL A JOINT, IF SHE ASKED YOU REAL NICE?
MIRIAM. I DIDN'T KNOW YOU SMOKED.
NOT USUALLY. BUT ME AND JOE JUST HAD A BIG FIGHT.
CAN YOU HOOK ME UP?
DEPENDS. YOU GOT TEN BUCKS?
SURE. BUT CAN WE GO FOR A LITTLE WALK FIRST?
I DON'T WANT PEOPLE TO SEE.

THIS PRIVATE ENOUGH FOR YOU?
I GUESS.
WAIT. YOU WANT TO SEE SOMETHING?
COME ON, MAN, LET'S JUST ROLL HER A JOINT AND--
MAYBE. SEE WHAT?
WHO'S THAT?
THOUGHT I SAW SOMEONE. NEVER MIND.

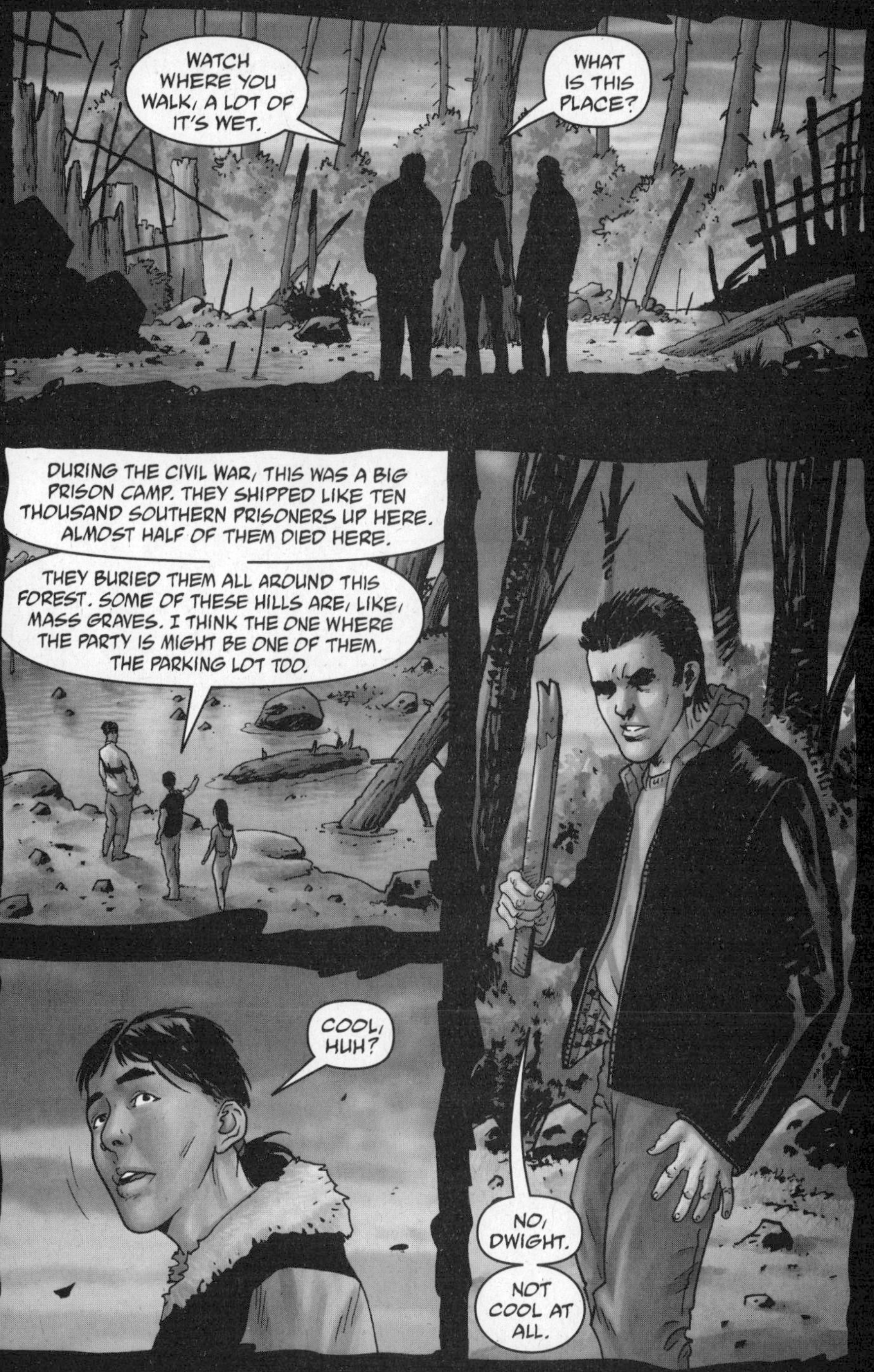
WATCH WHERE YOU WALK, A LOT OF IT'S WET.
WHAT IS THIS PLACE?
DURING THE CIVIL WAR, THIS WAS A BIG PRISON CAMP. THEY SHIPPED LIKE TEN THOUSAND SOUTHERN PRISONERS UP HERE. ALMOST HALF OF THEM DIED HERE.
THEY BURIED THEM ALL AROUND THIS FOREST. SOME OF THESE HILLS ARE, LIKE, MASS GRAVES. I THINK THE ONE WHERE THE PARTY IS MIGHT BE ONE OF THEM. THE PARKING LOT TOO.
COOL, HUH?
NO, DWIGHT.
NOT COOL AT ALL.

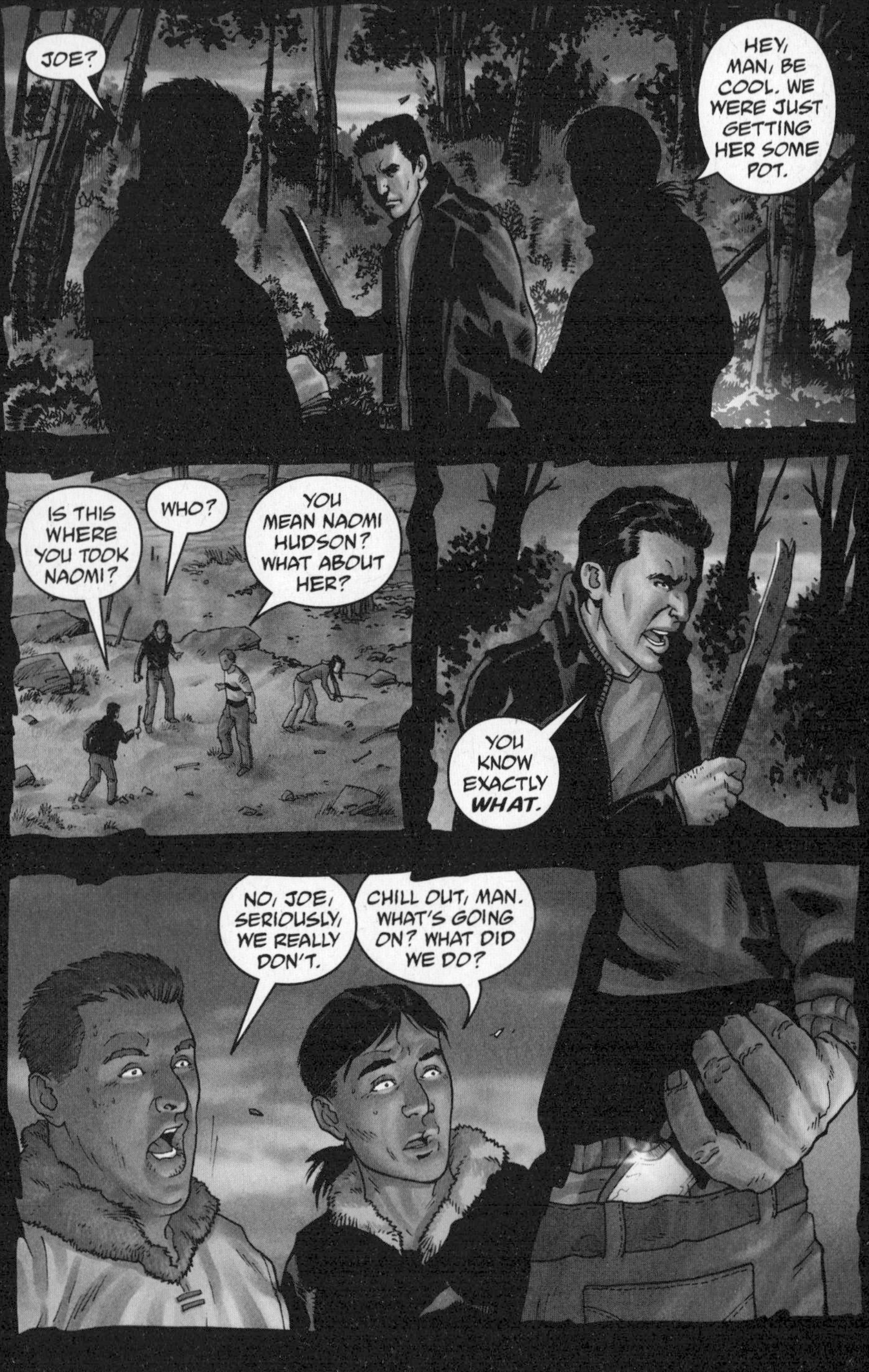
JOE?
HEY, MAN, BE COOL. WE WERE JUST GETTING HER SOME POT.
IS THIS WHERE YOU TOOK NAOMI?
WHO?
YOU MEAN NAOMI HUDSON? WHAT ABOUT HER?
YOU KNOW EXACTLY WHAT.
NO, JOE, SERIOUSLY, WE REALLY DON'T.
CHILL OUT, MAN. WHAT'S GOING ON? WHAT DID WE DO?

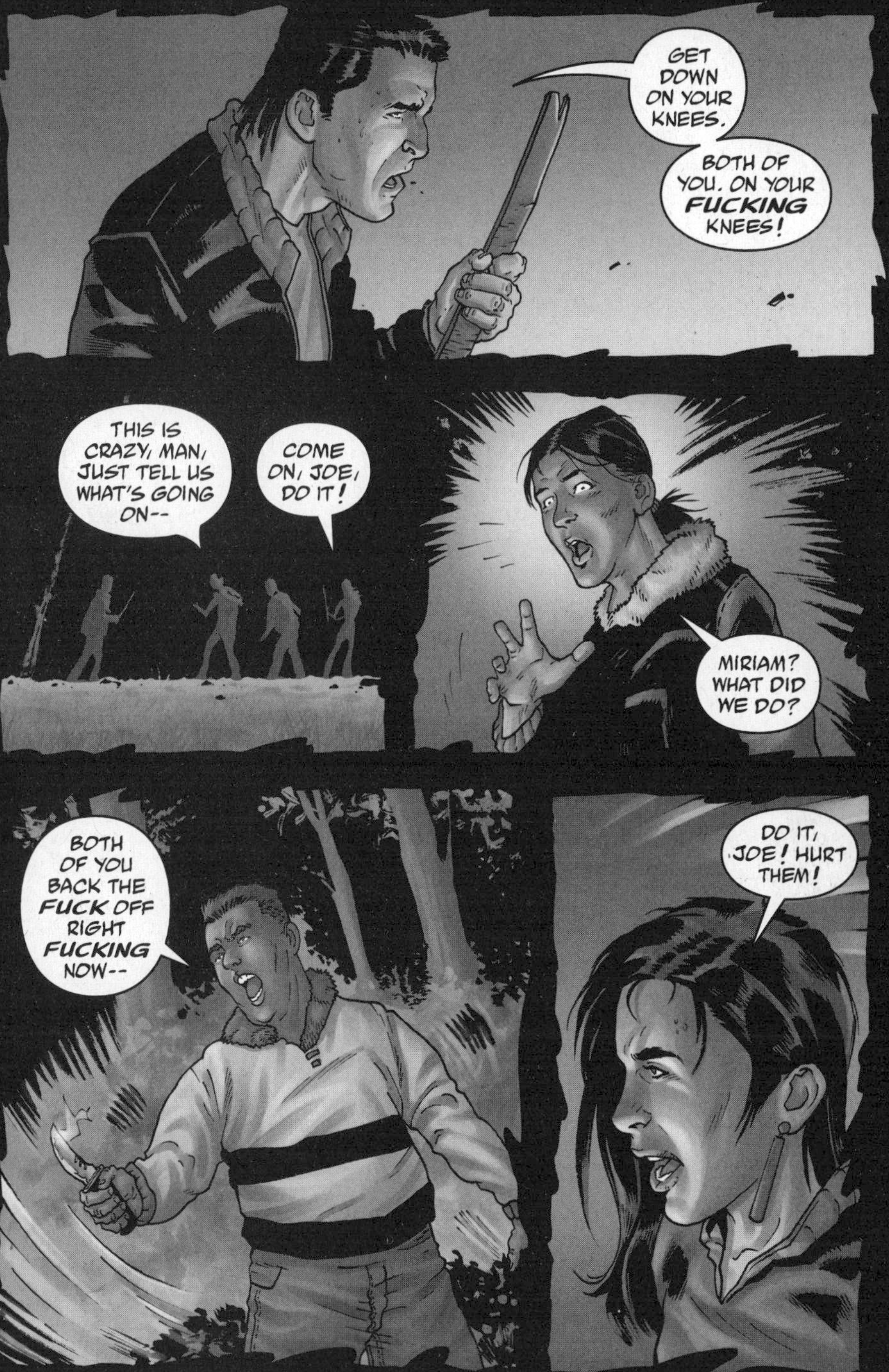
GET DOWN ON YOUR KNEES.
BOTH OF YOU. ON YOUR FUCKING KNEES!
THIS IS CRAZY, MAN, JUST TELL US WHAT'S GOING ON--
COME ON, JOE, DO IT!
MIRIAM? WHAT DID WE DO?
BOTH OF YOU BACK THE FUCK OFF RIGHT FUCKING NOW--
DO IT, JOE! HURT THEM!

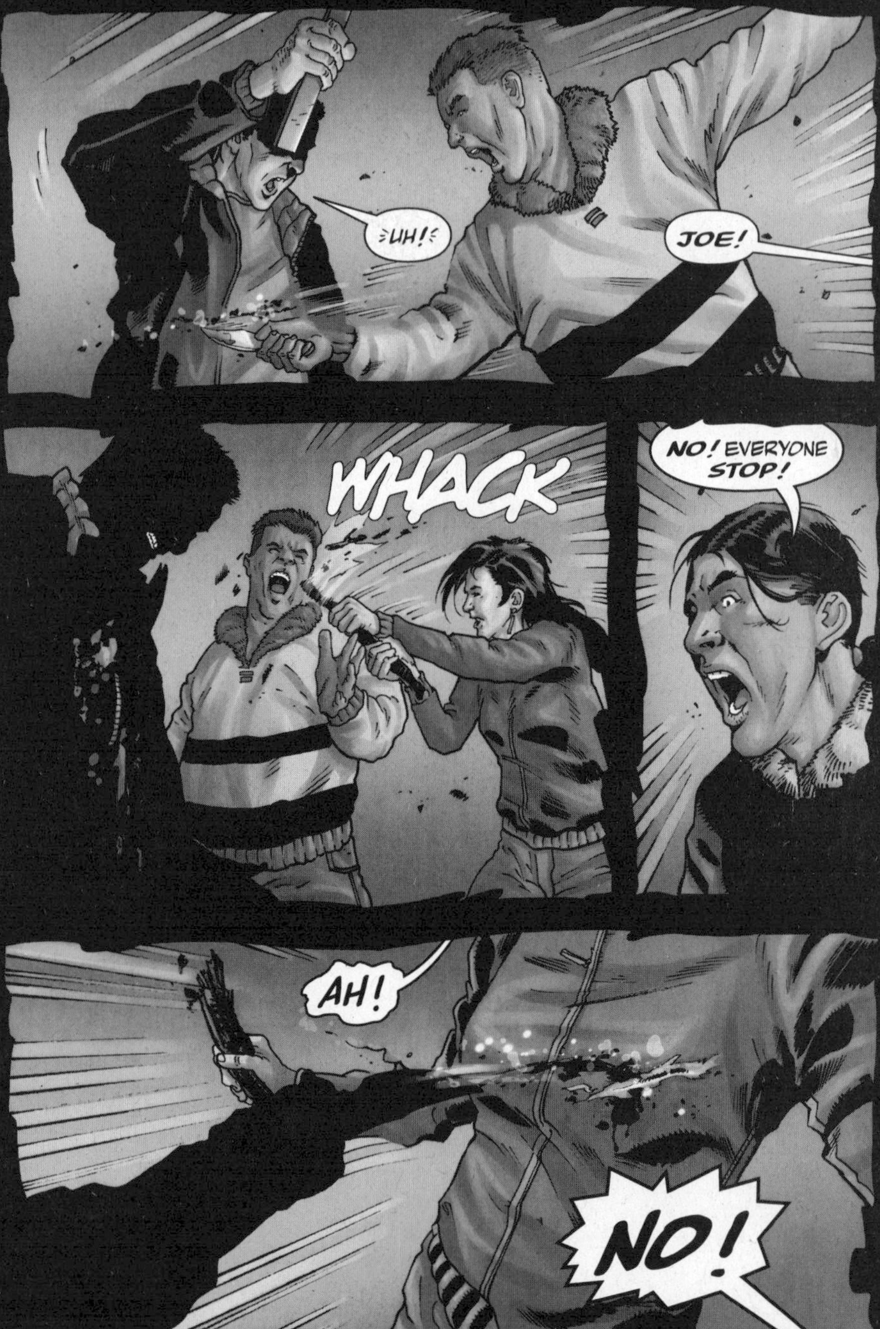
UH!
JOE!
WHACK
NO! EVERYONE STOP!
AH!
NO!

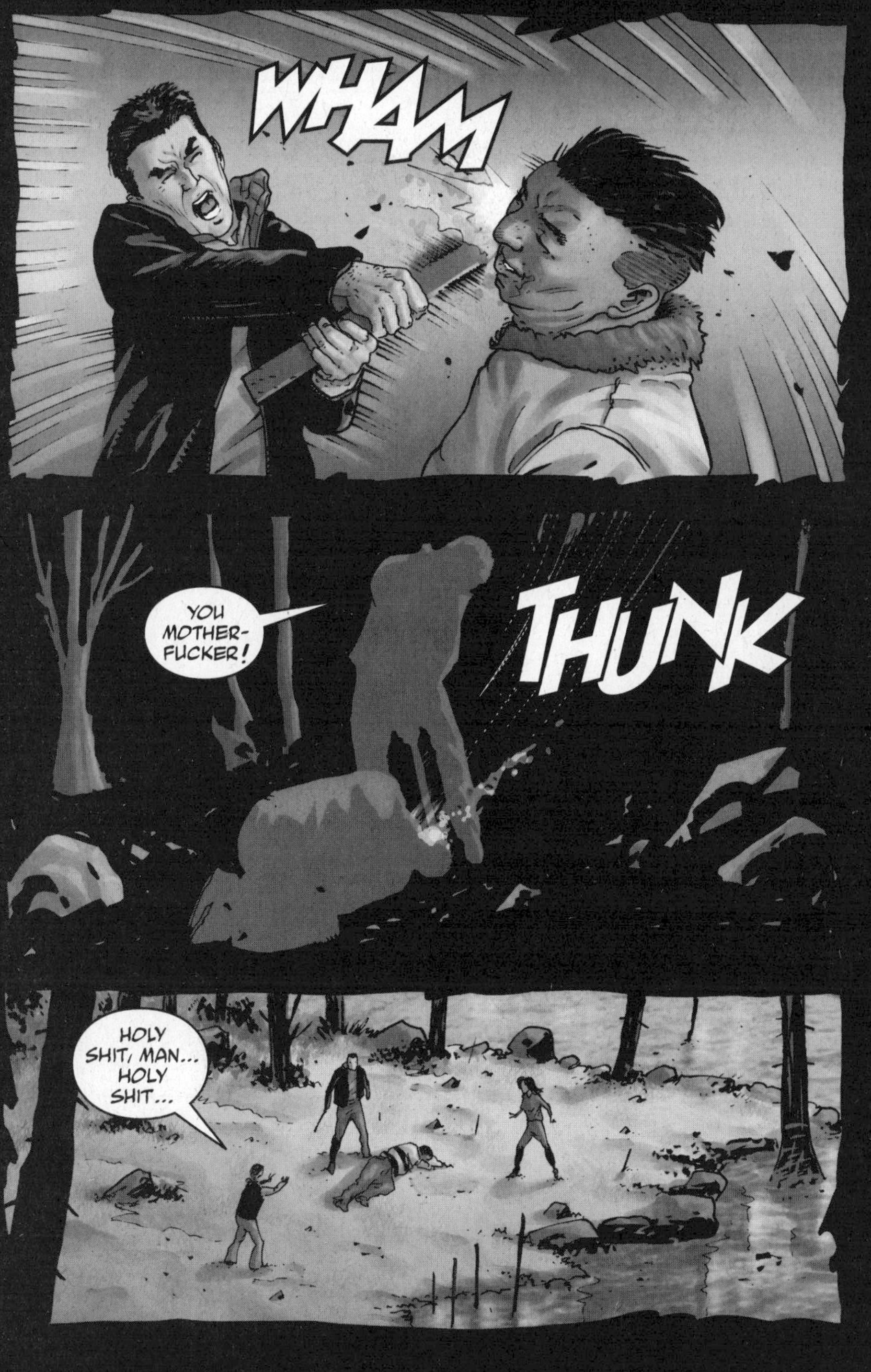
WHAM
YOU MOTHER-FUCKER!
THUNK
HOLY SHIT, MAN... HOLY SHIT...

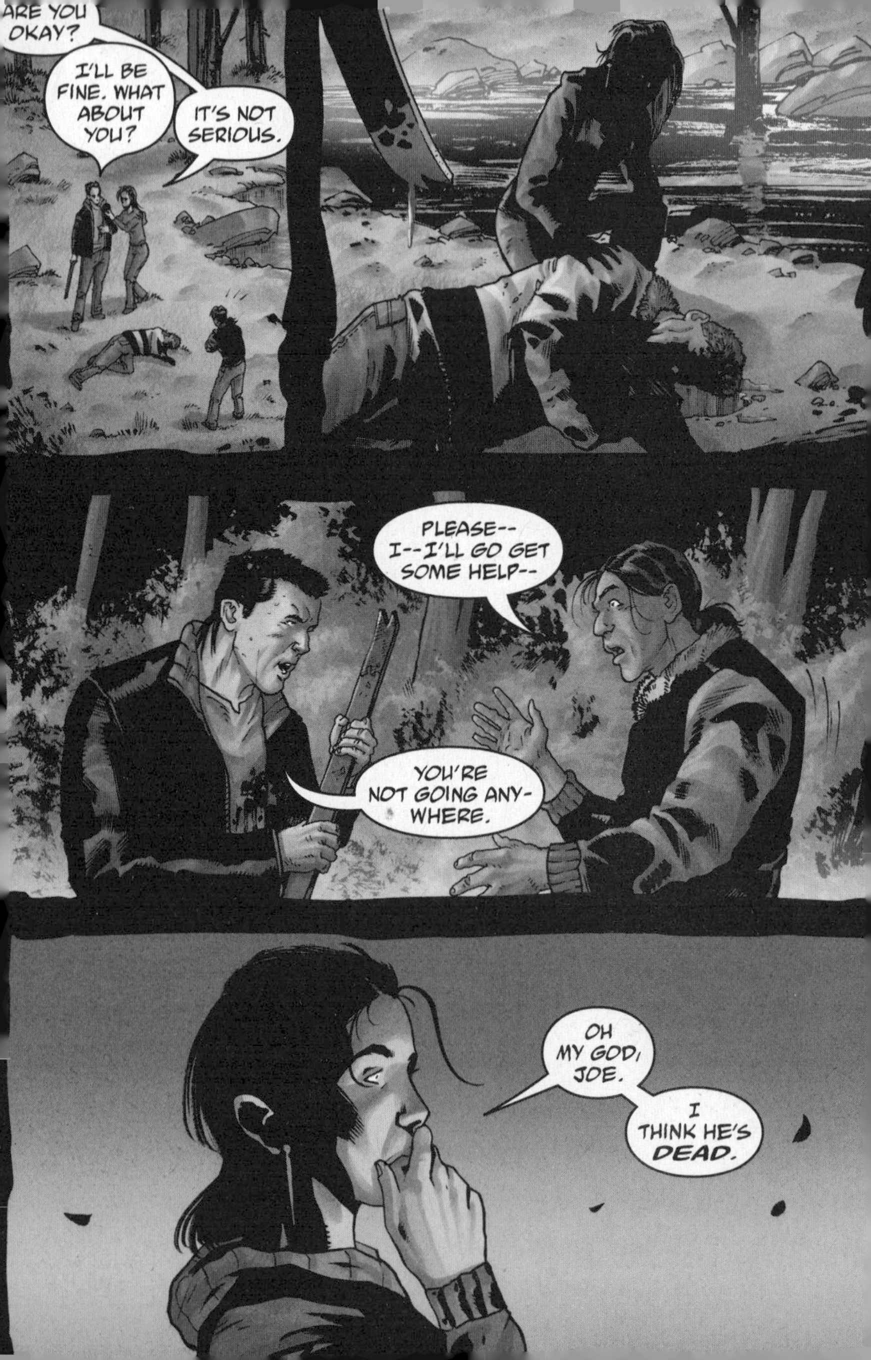
ARE YOU OKAY?
I'LL BE FINE. WHAT ABOUT YOU?
IT'S NOT SERIOUS.
PLEASE-- I--I'LL GO GET SOME HELP--
YOU'RE NOT GOING ANY-WHERE.
OH MY GOD, JOE.
I THINK HE'S DEAD.

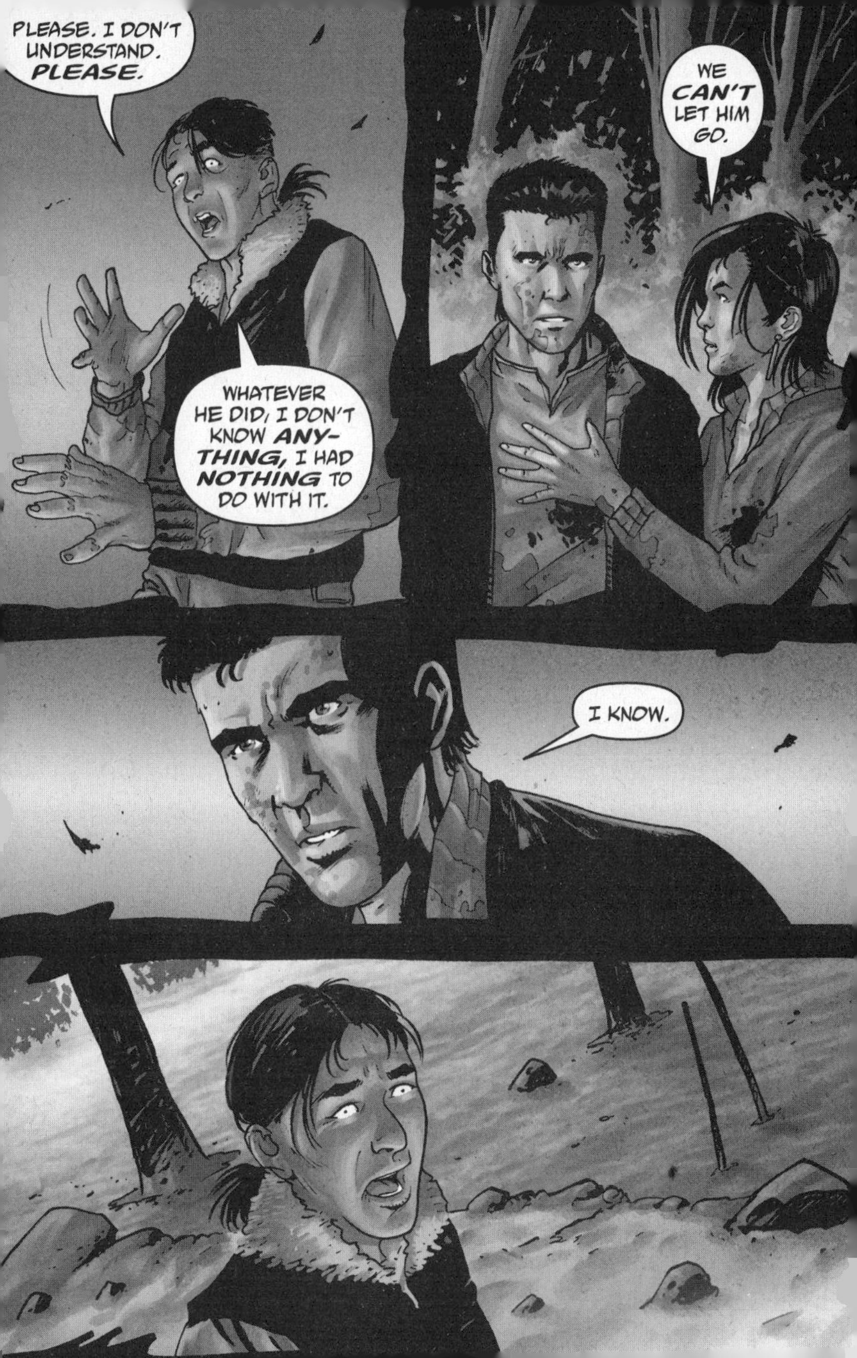
PLEASE. I DON'T UNDERSTAND. PLEASE.
WHATEVER HE DID, I DON'T KNOW ANY-THING, I HAD NOTHING TO DO WITH IT.
WE CAN'T LET HIM GO.
I KNOW.

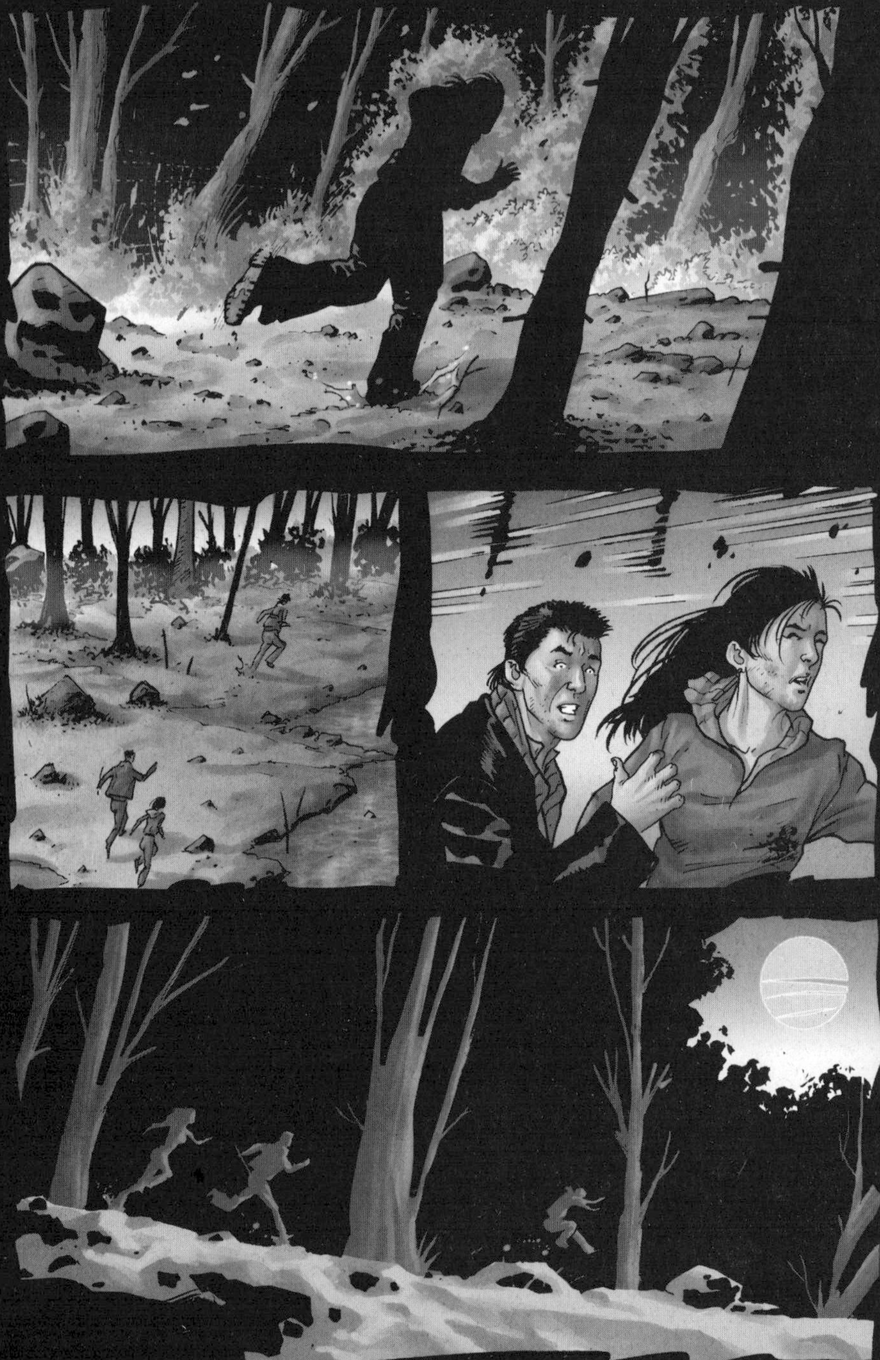

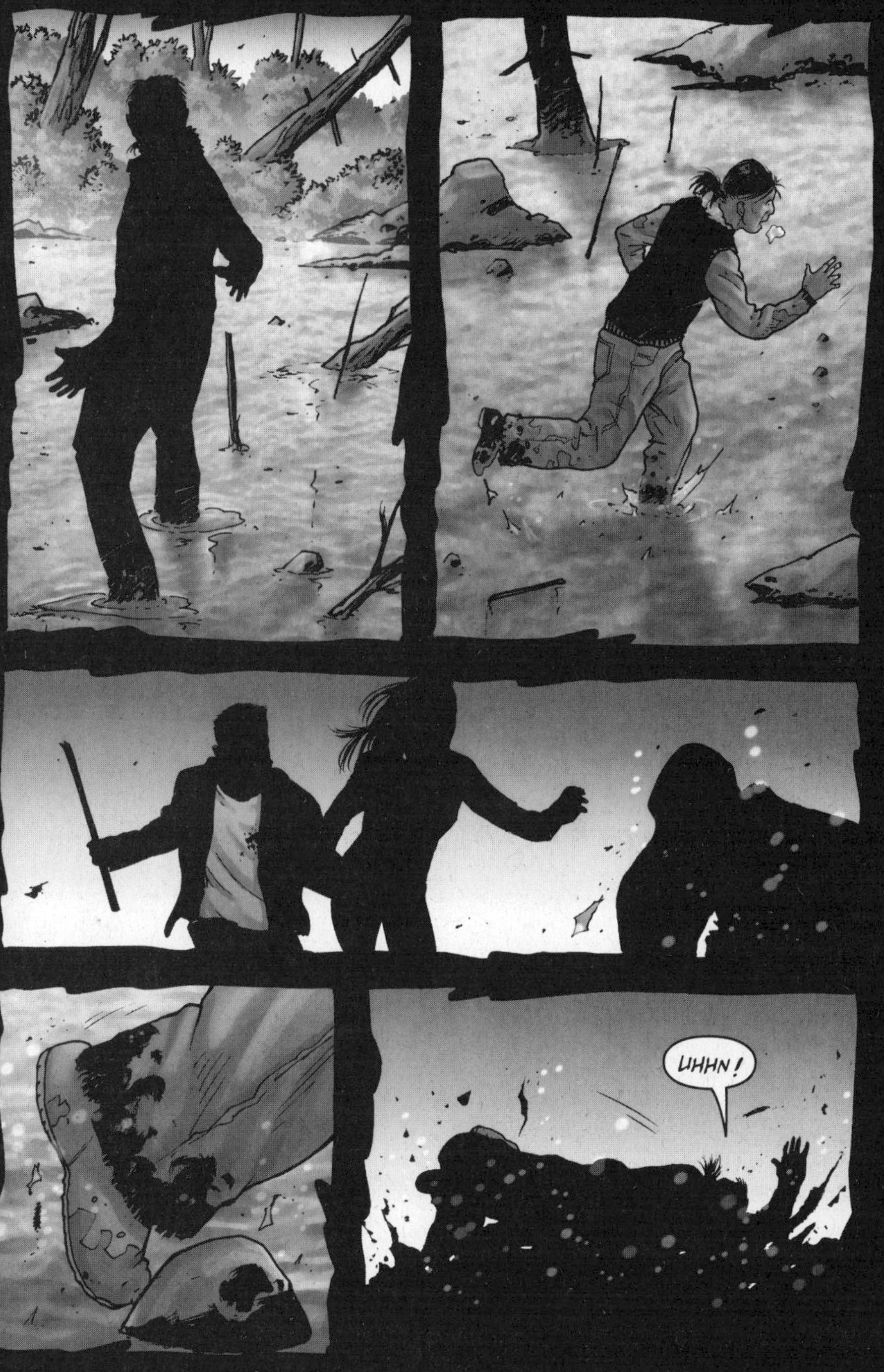
UHHN!

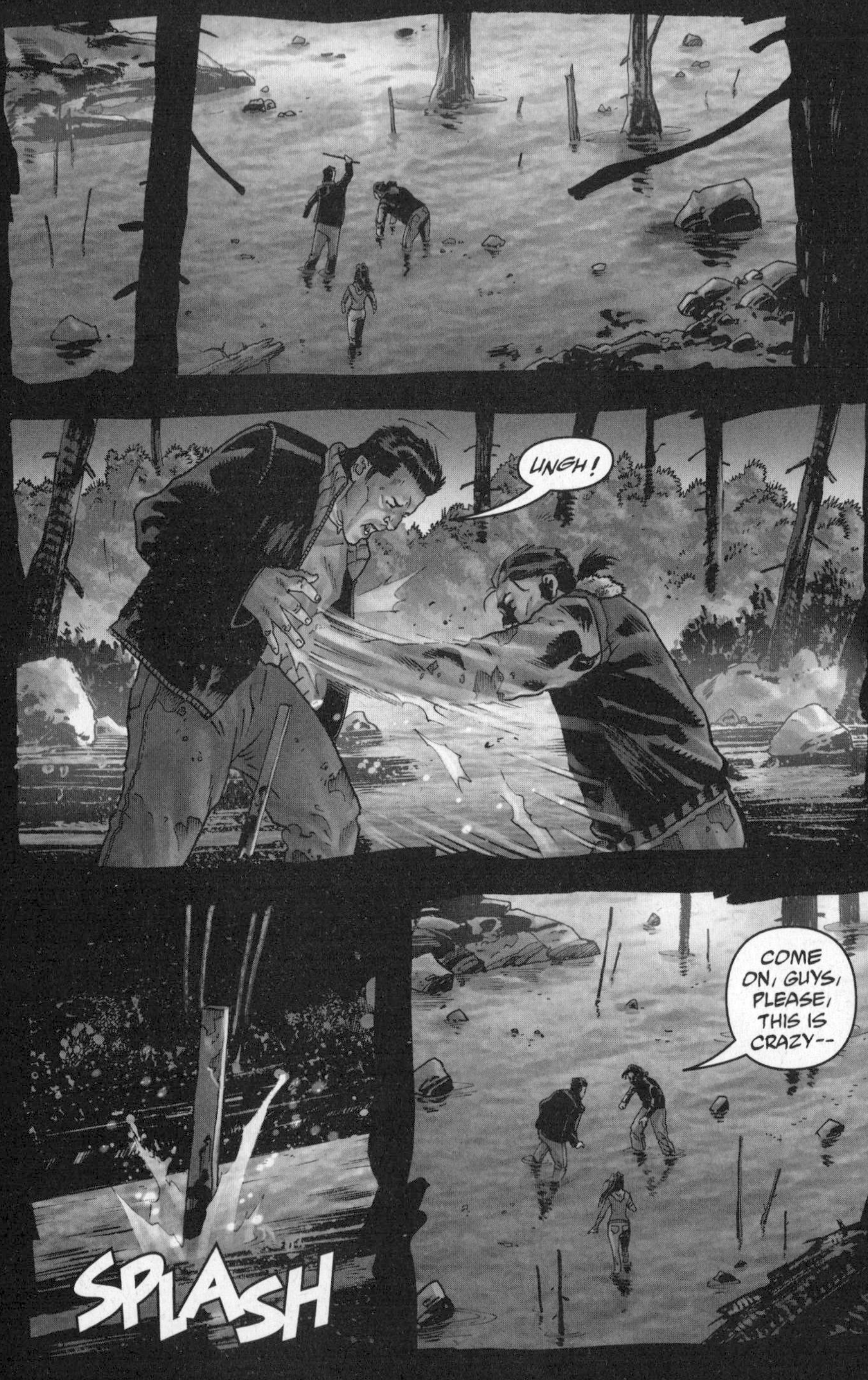
UNGH!
SPLASH
COME ON, GUYS, PLEASE, THIS IS CRAZY--

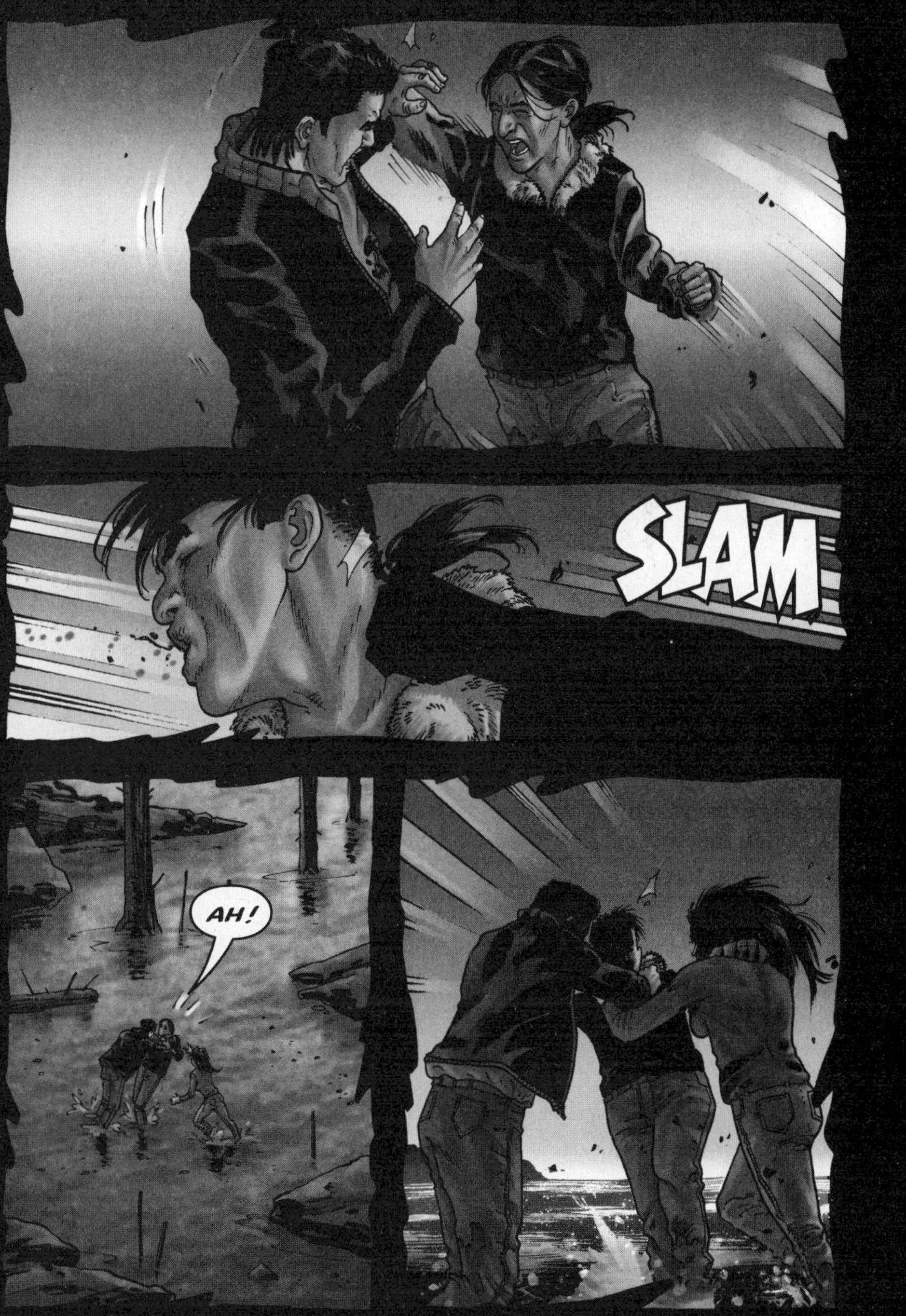
SLAM
AH!

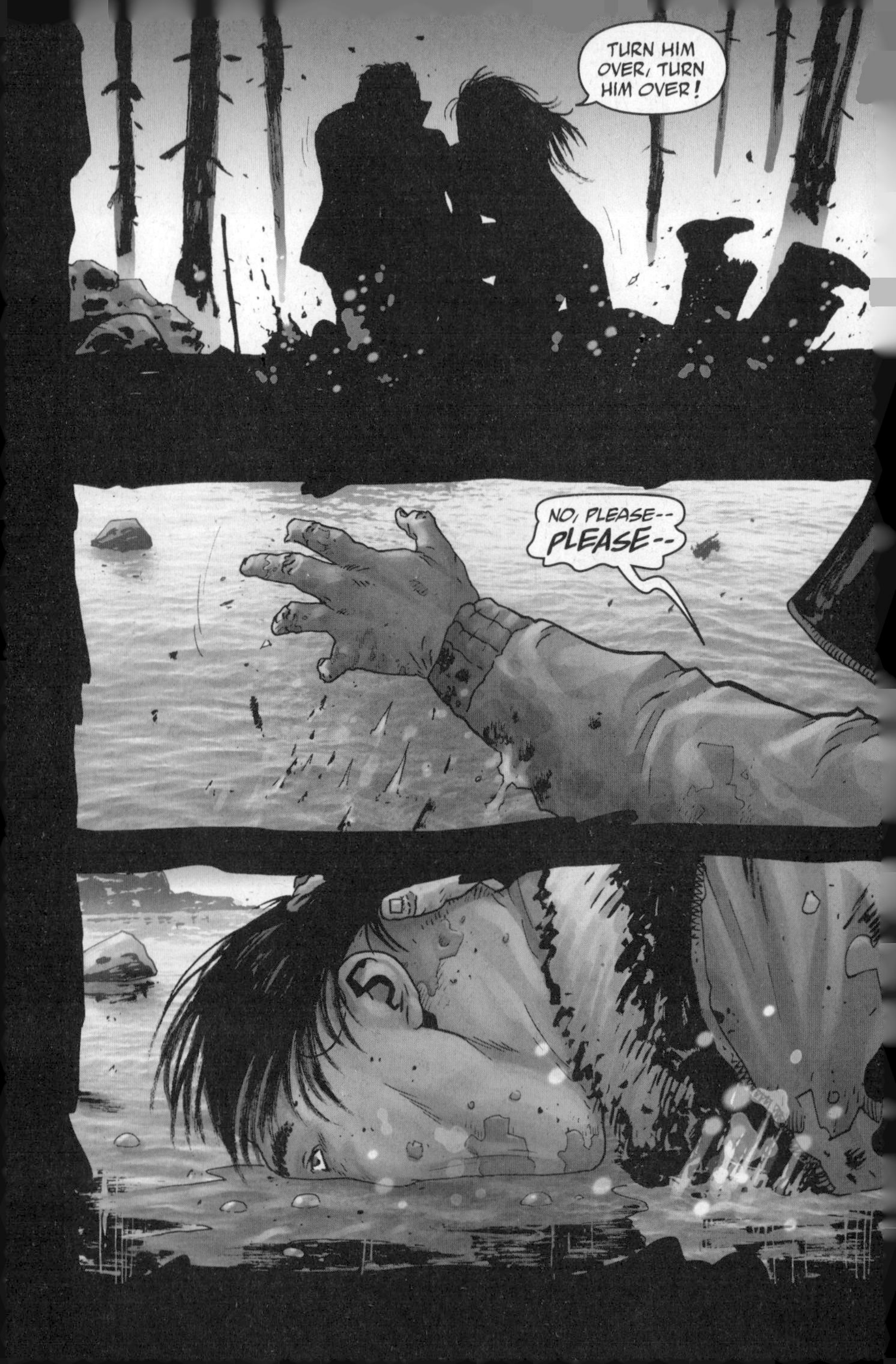
TURN HIM OVER, TURN HIM OVER!
NO, PLEASE-- PLEASE--

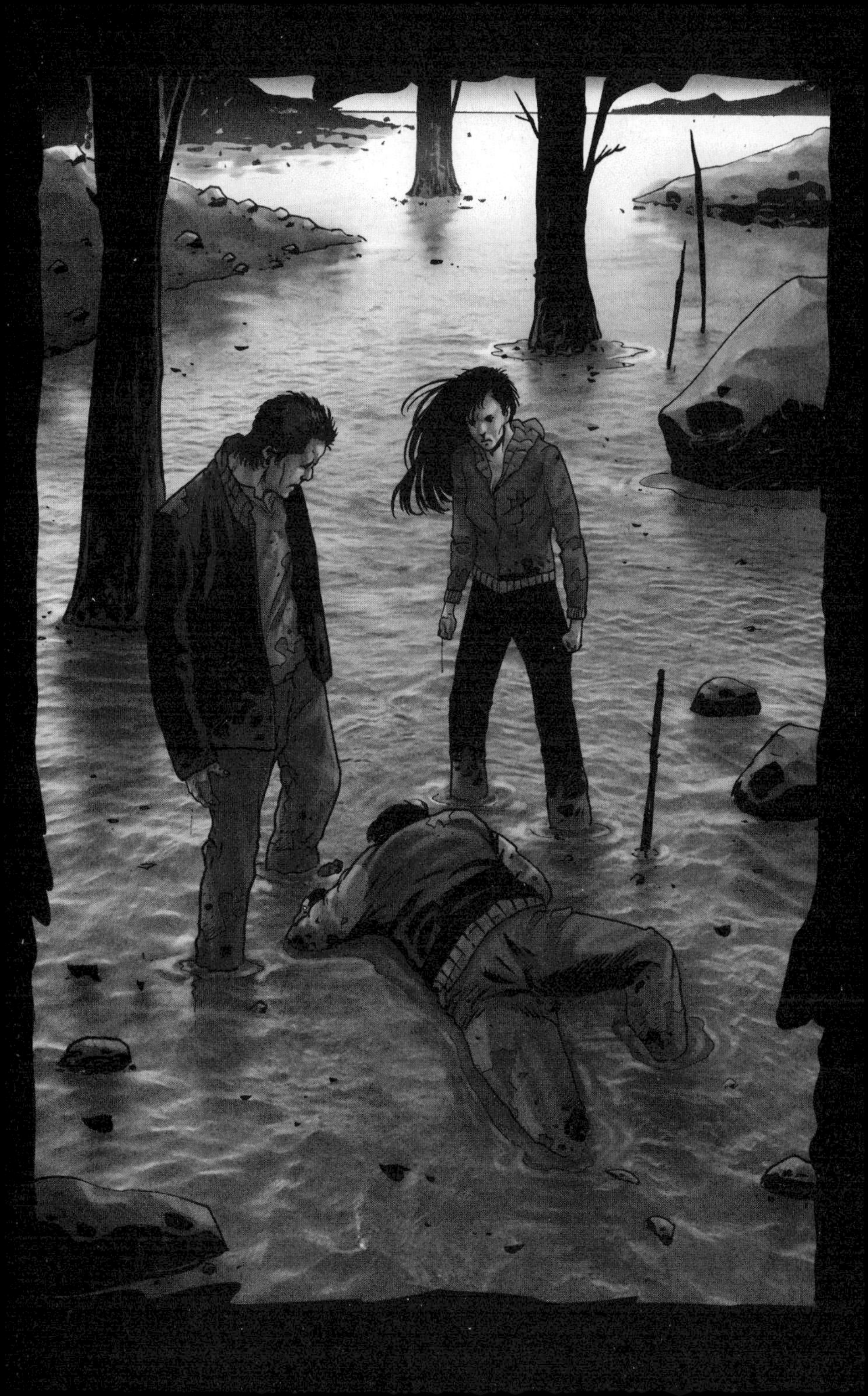

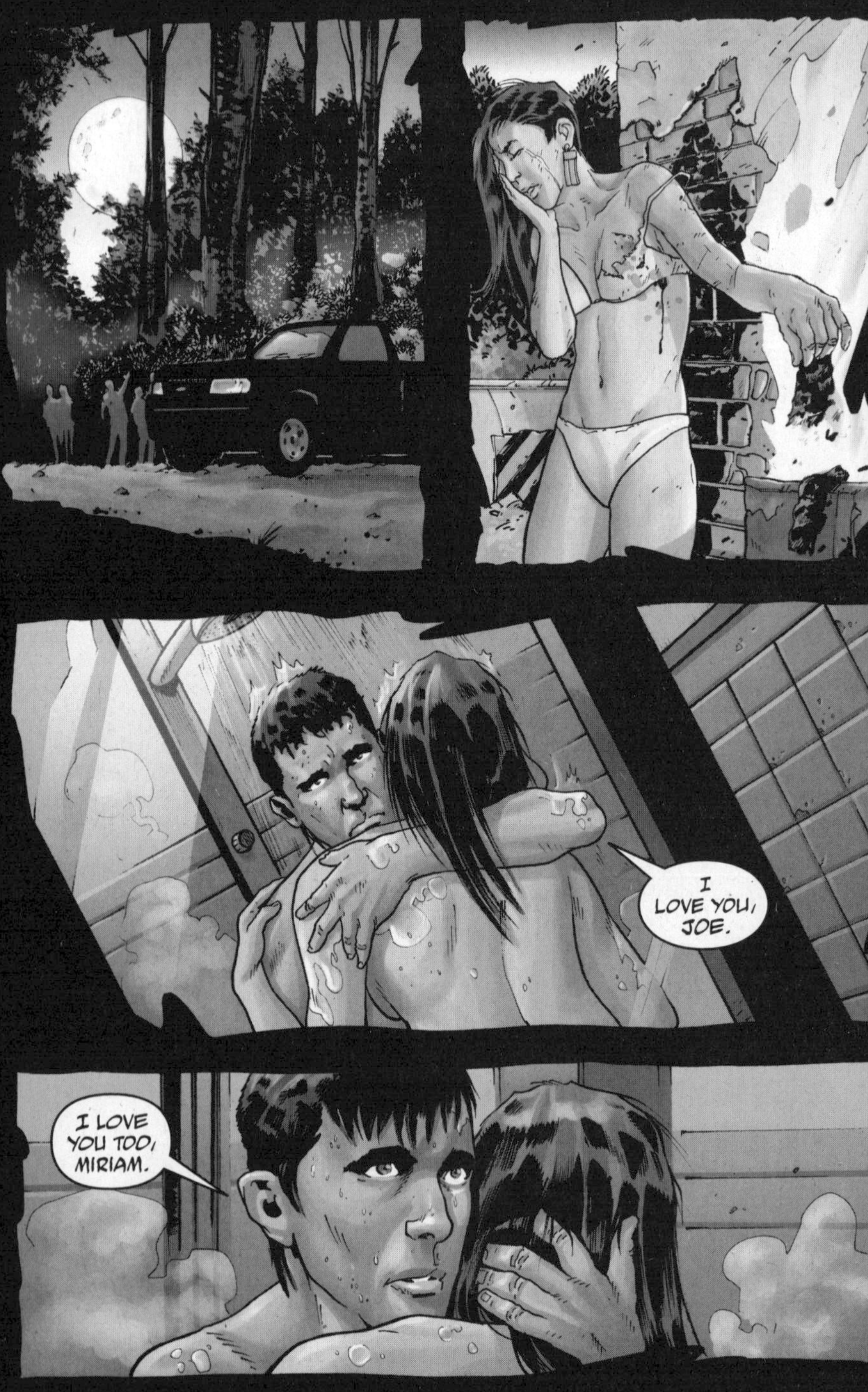
I LOVE YOU, JOE.
I LOVE YOU TOO, MIRIAM.

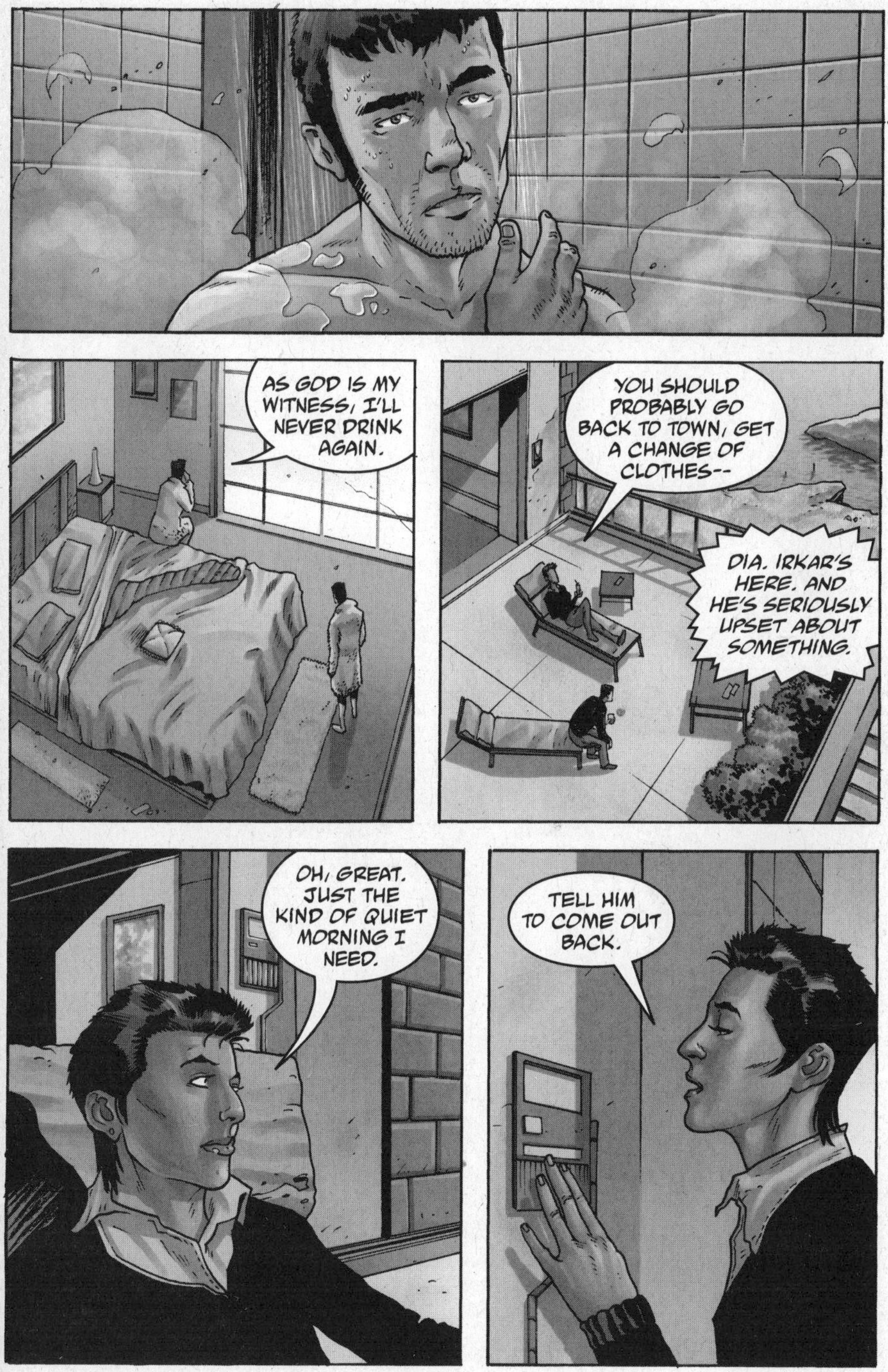
AS GOD IS MY WITNESS, I'LL NEVER DRINK AGAIN.
YOU SHOULD PROBABLY GO BACK TO TOWN, GET A CHANGE OF CLOTHES--
DIA. IRKAR'S HERE. AND HE'S SERIOUSLY UPSET ABOUT SOMETHING.
OH, GREAT. JUST THE KIND OF QUIET MORNING I NEED.
TELL HIM TO COME OUT BACK.

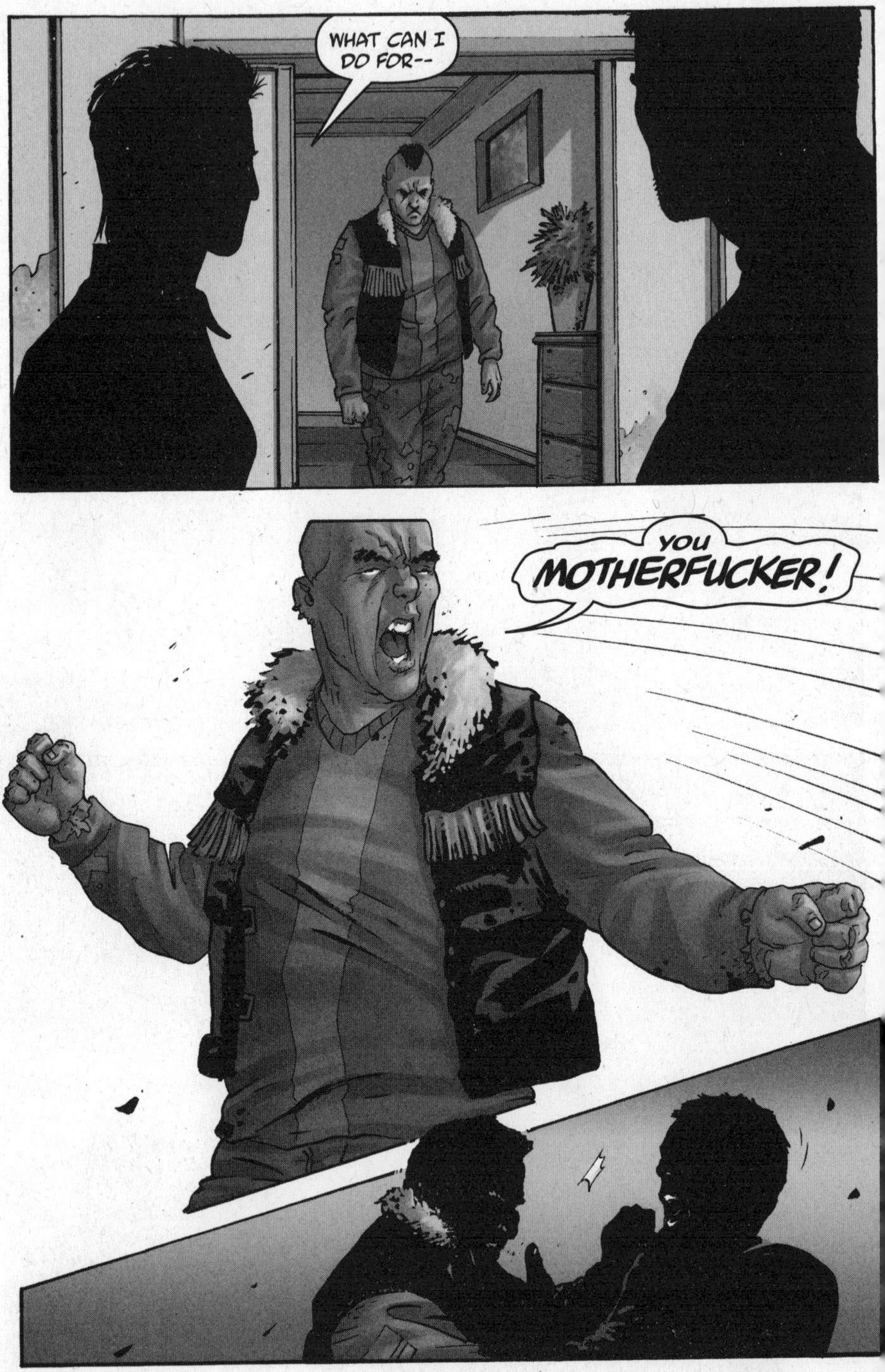
WHAT CAN I DO FOR--
YOU MOTHERFUCKER!

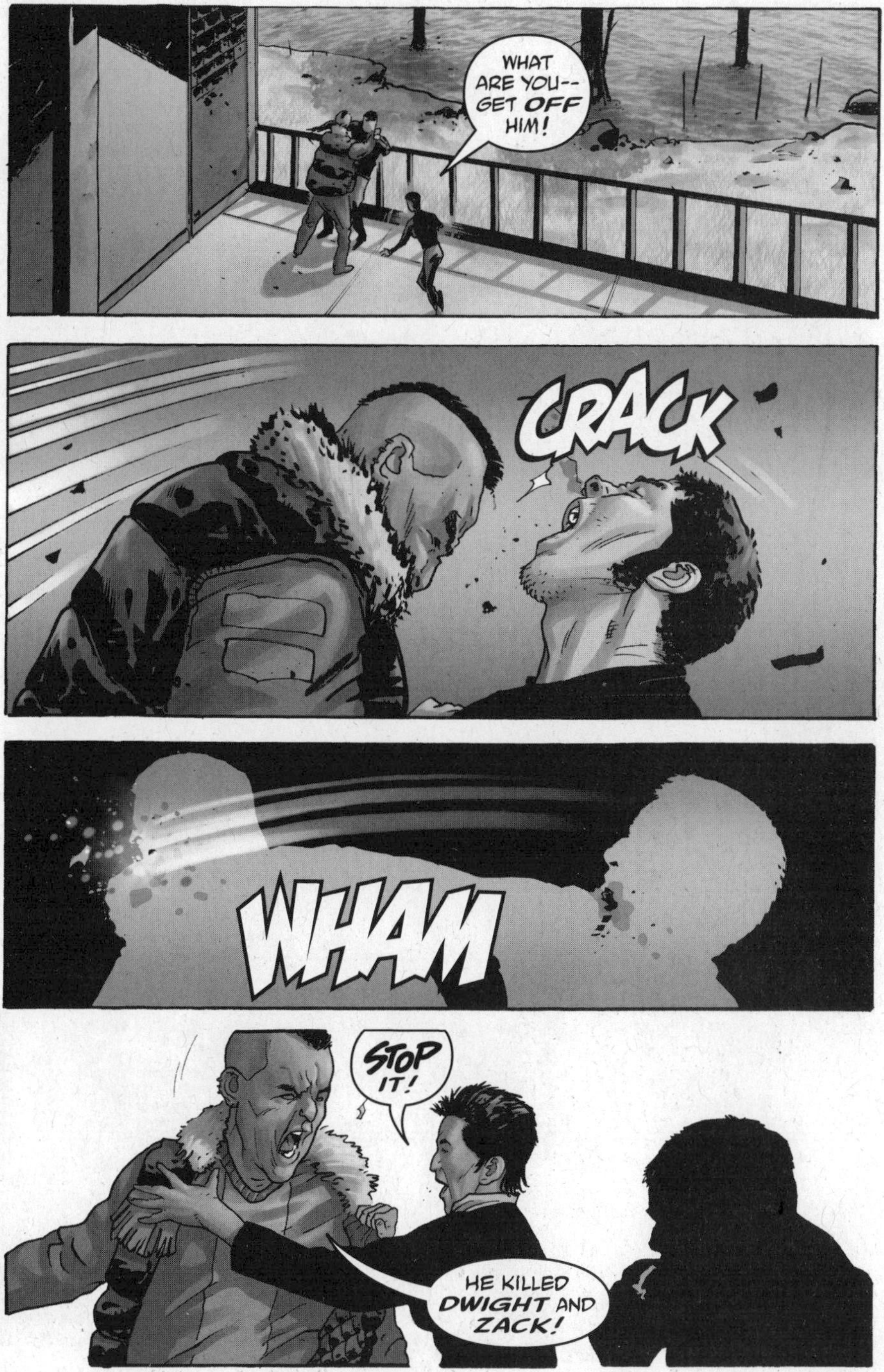
WHAT ARE YOU-- GET OFF HIM!
CRACK
WHAM
STOP IT!
HE KILLED DWIGHT AND ZACK!

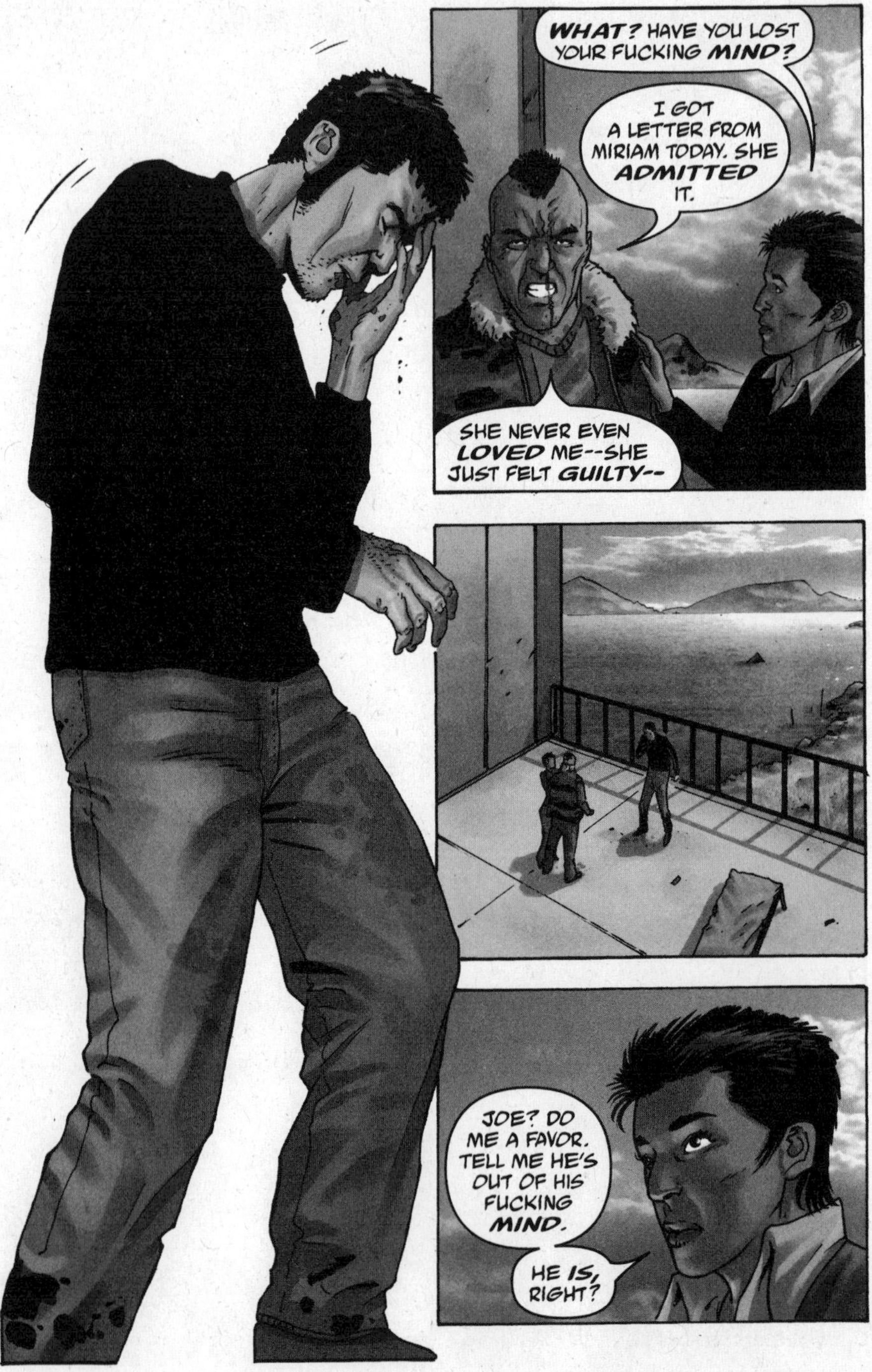
WHAT? HAVE YOU LOST YOUR FUCKING MIND?
I GOT A LETTER FROM MIRIAM TODAY. SHE ADMITTED IT.
SHE NEVER EVEN LOVED ME--SHE JUST FELT GUILTY--
JOE? DO ME A FAVOR. TELL ME HE'S OUT OF HIS FUCKING MIND.
HE IS, RIGHT?

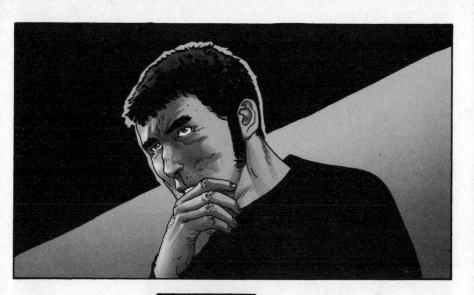

JOE?
TELL ME YOU
DIDN'T KILL MY
BROTHER.

YOU KILLED ZACK,
YOU MOTHERFUCKER.
NOW I'M GOING TO
KILL *YOU!*

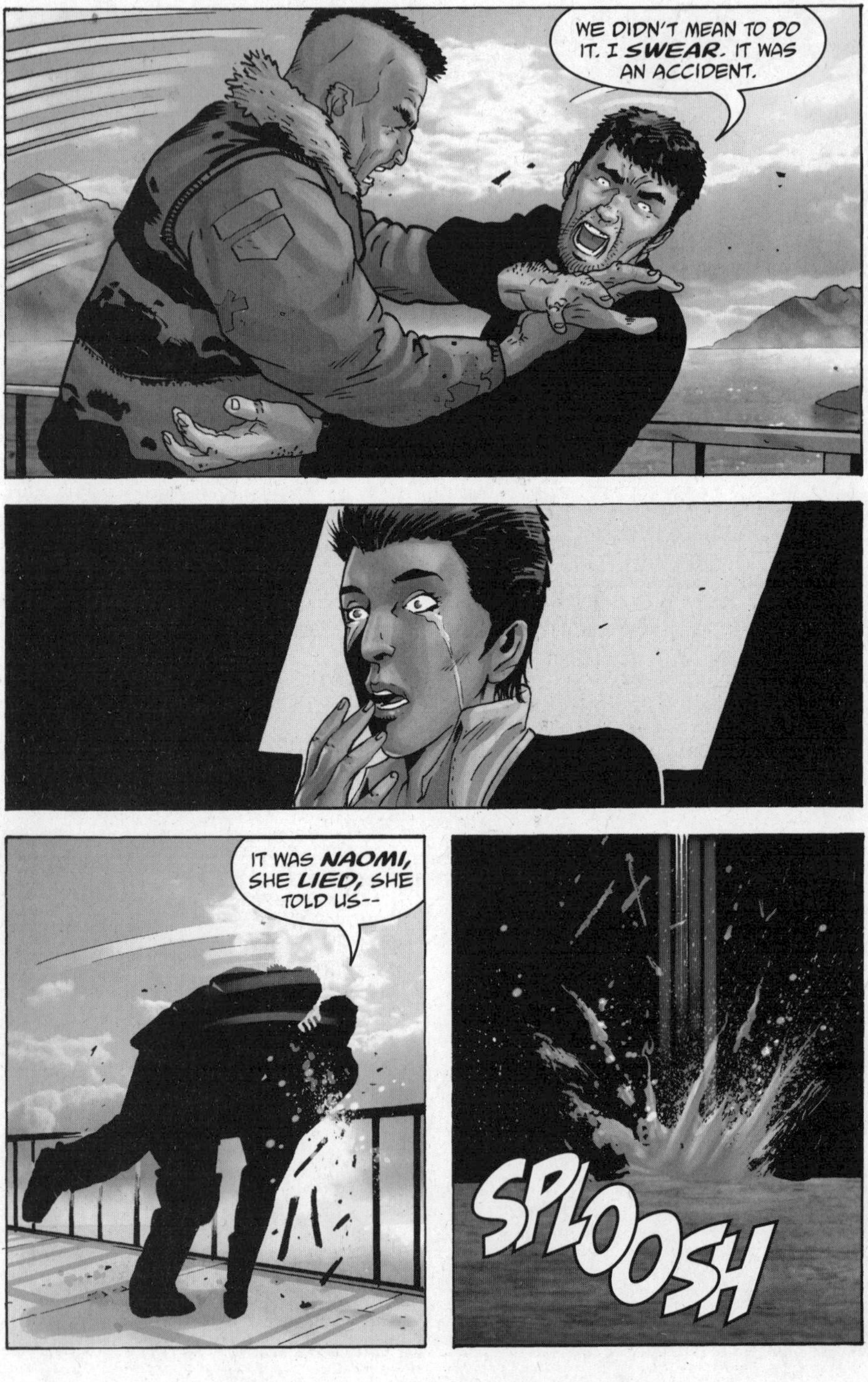
WE DIDN'T MEAN TO DO IT. I **SWEAR**. IT WAS AN ACCIDENT.
IT WAS **NAOMI**, SHE **LIED**, SHE TOLD US--
SPLOOSH

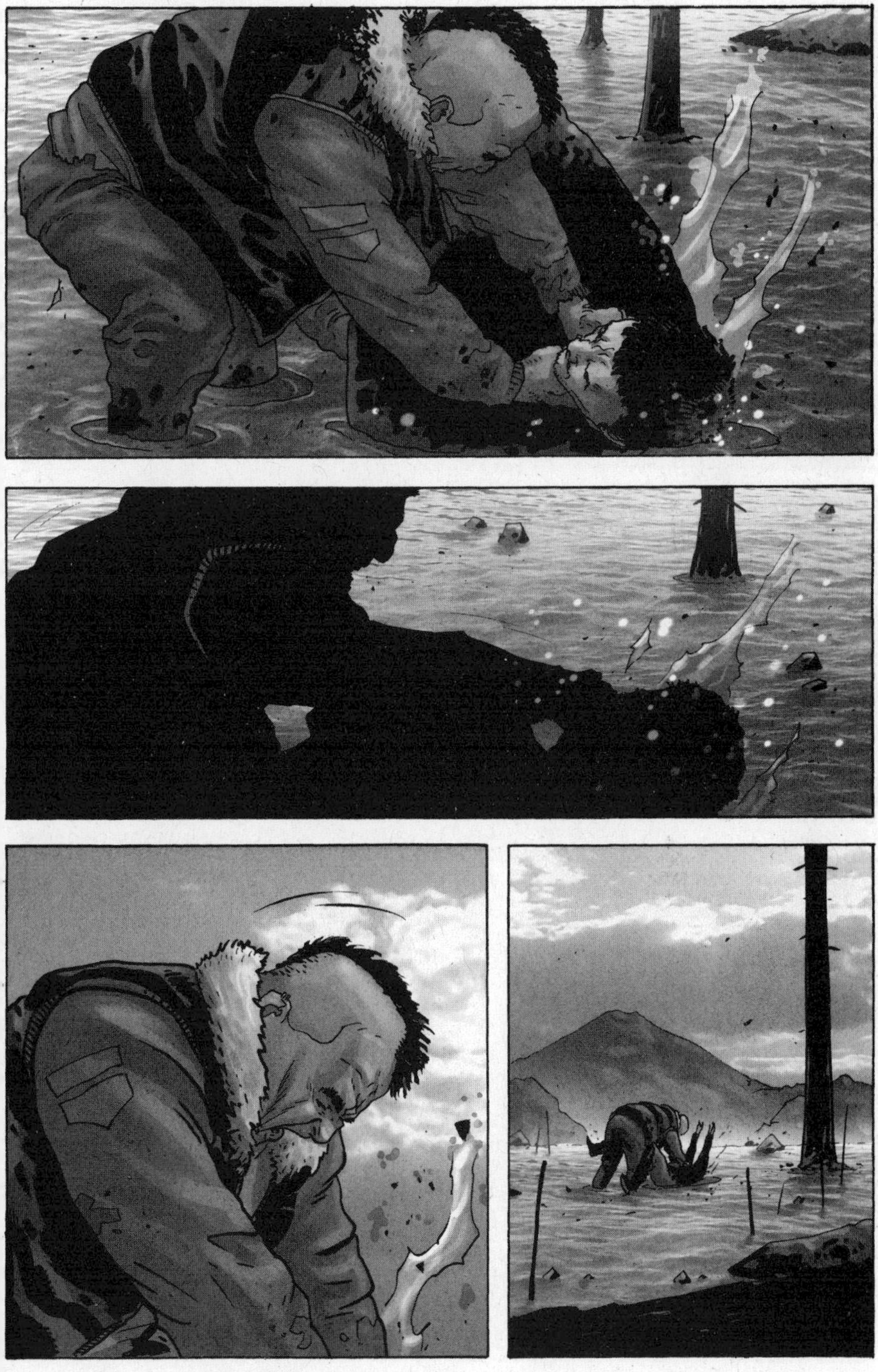

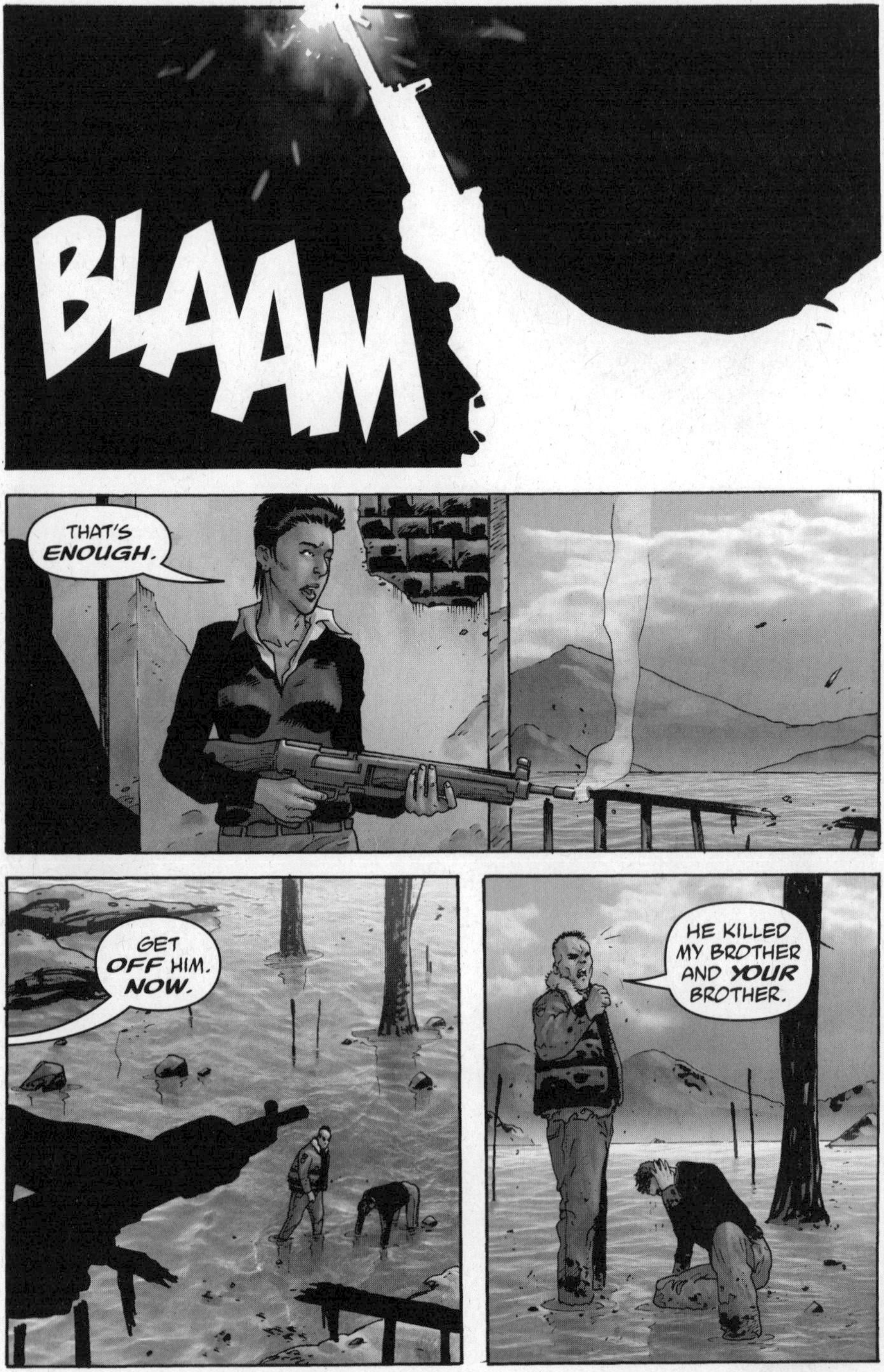
BLAAM
THAT'S ENOUGH.
GET OFF HIM. NOW.
HE KILLED MY BROTHER AND YOUR BROTHER.

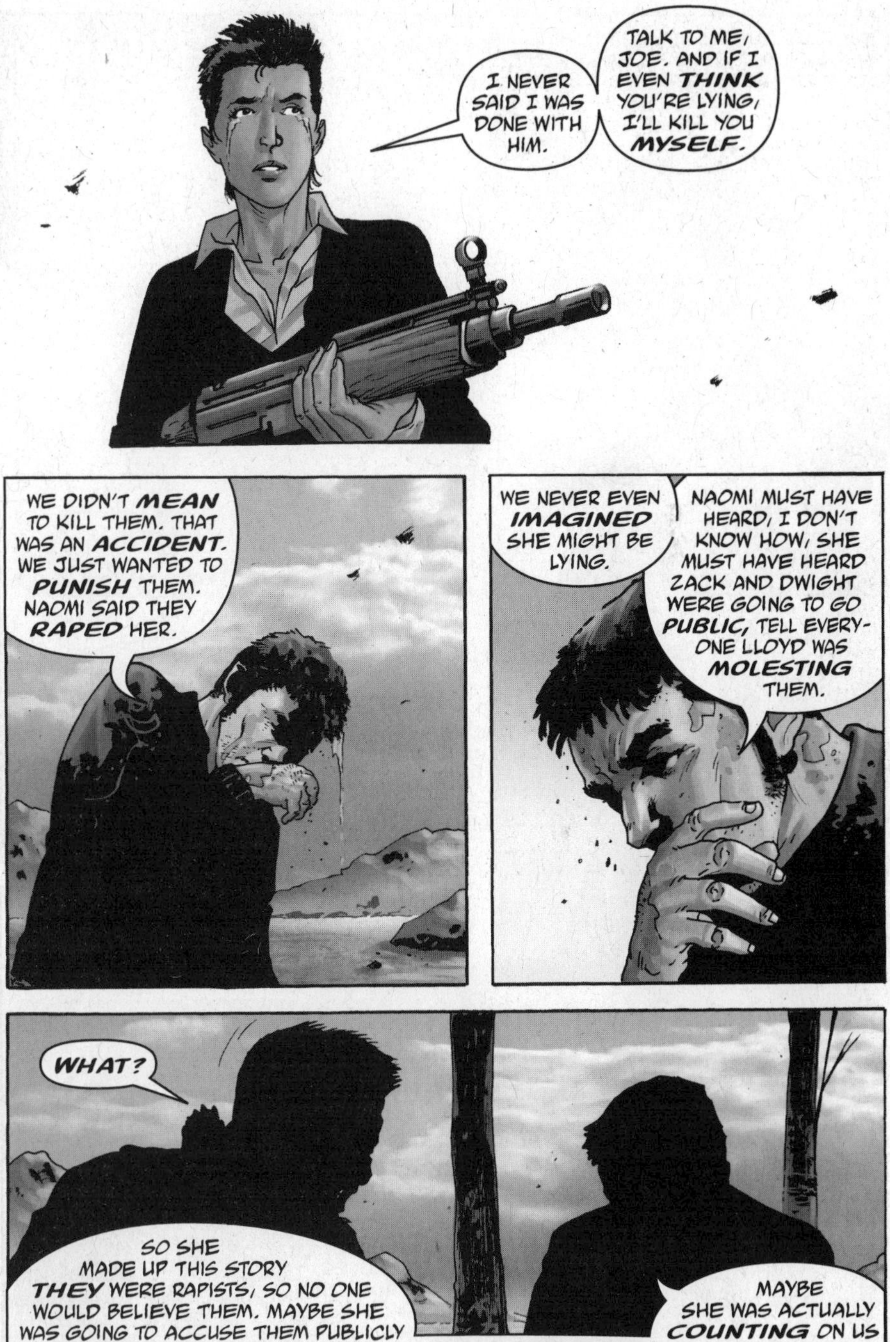
I NEVER SAID I WAS DONE WITH HIM.
TALK TO ME, JOE. AND IF I EVEN THINK YOU'RE LYING, I'LL KILL YOU MYSELF.
WE DIDN'T MEAN TO KILL THEM. THAT WAS AN ACCIDENT. WE JUST WANTED TO PUNISH THEM. NAOMI SAID THEY RAPED HER.
WE NEVER EVEN IMAGINED SHE MIGHT BE LYING.
NAOMI MUST HAVE HEARD, I DON'T KNOW HOW, SHE MUST HAVE HEARD ZACK AND DWIGHT WERE GOING TO GO PUBLIC, TELL EVERY-ONE LLOYD WAS MOLESTING THEM.
WHAT?
SO SHE MADE UP THIS STORY THEY WERE RAPISTS, SO NO ONE WOULD BELIEVE THEM. MAYBE SHE WAS GOING TO ACCUSE THEM PUBLICLY THE NEXT WEEK. I DON'T KNOW.
MAYBE SHE WAS ACTUALLY COUNTING ON US DOING WHAT WE DID.

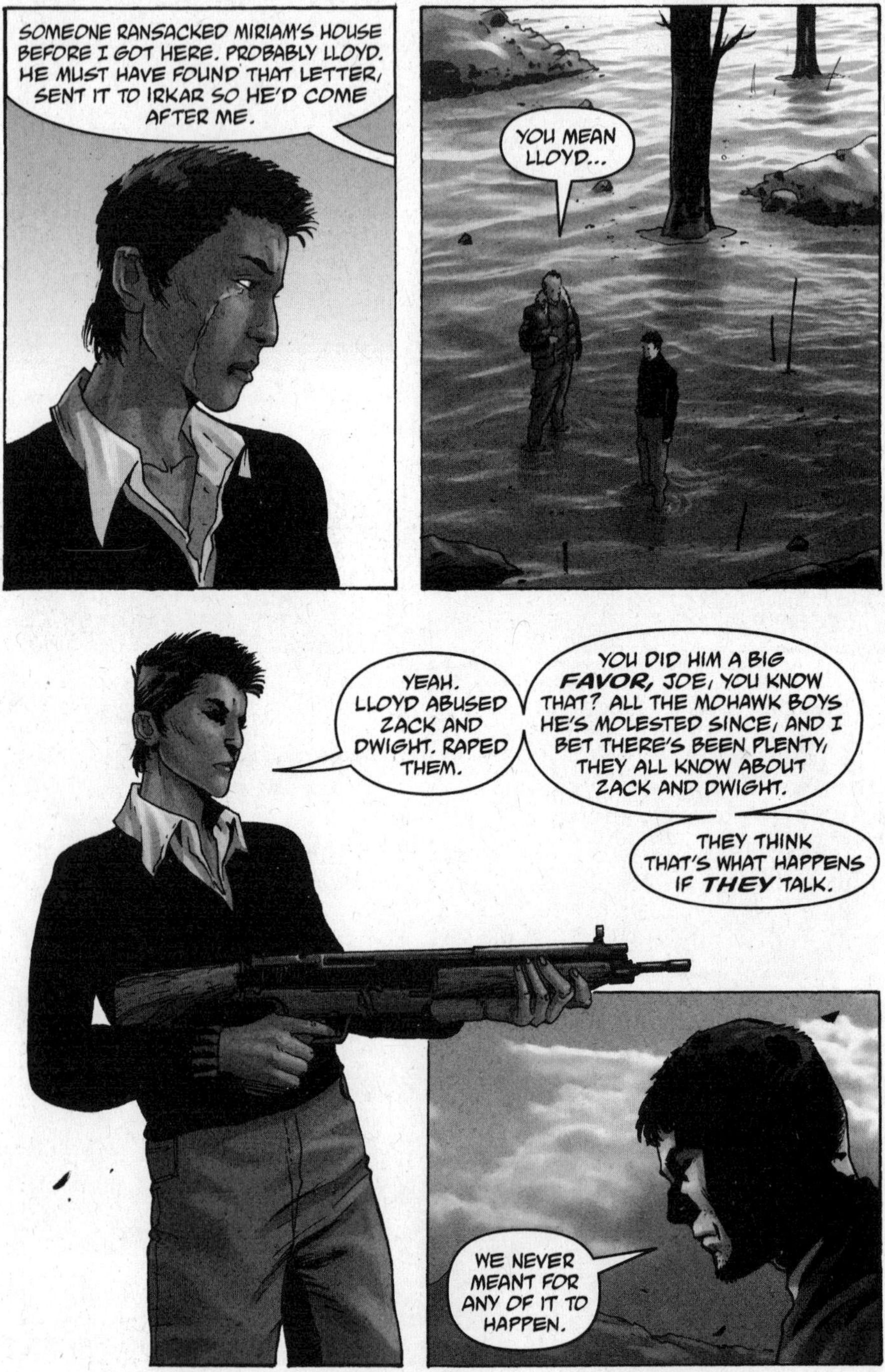
SOMEONE RANSACKED MIRIAM'S HOUSE BEFORE I GOT HERE. PROBABLY LLOYD. HE MUST HAVE FOUND THAT LETTER, SENT IT TO IRKAR SO HE'D COME AFTER ME.
YOU MEAN LLOYD...
YEAH. LLOYD ABUSED ZACK AND DWIGHT. RAPED THEM.
YOU DID HIM A BIG **FAVOR,** JOE, YOU KNOW THAT? ALL THE MOHAWK BOYS HE'S MOLESTED SINCE, AND I BET THERE'S BEEN PLENTY, THEY ALL KNOW ABOUT ZACK AND DWIGHT.
THEY THINK THAT'S WHAT HAPPENS IF **THEY** TALK.
WE NEVER MEANT FOR ANY OF IT TO HAPPEN.

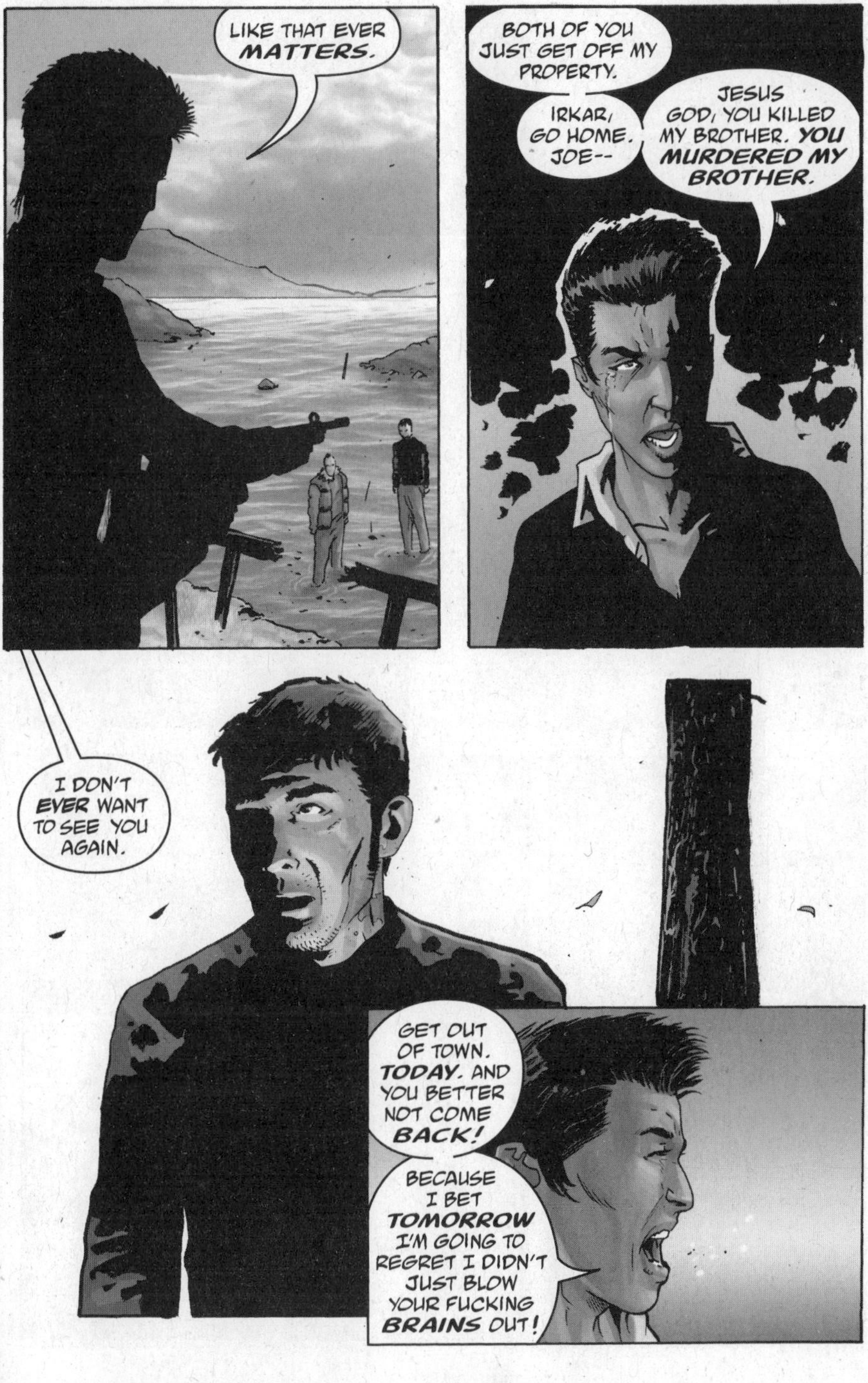
LIKE THAT EVER MATTERS.
BOTH OF YOU JUST GET OFF MY PROPERTY.
IRKAR, GO HOME. JOE--
JESUS GOD, YOU KILLED MY BROTHER. YOU MURDERED MY BROTHER.
I DON'T EVER WANT TO SEE YOU AGAIN.
GET OUT OF TOWN. TODAY. AND YOU BETTER NOT COME BACK!
BECAUSE I BET TOMORROW I'M GOING TO REGRET I DIDN'T JUST BLOW YOUR FUCKING BRAINS OUT!

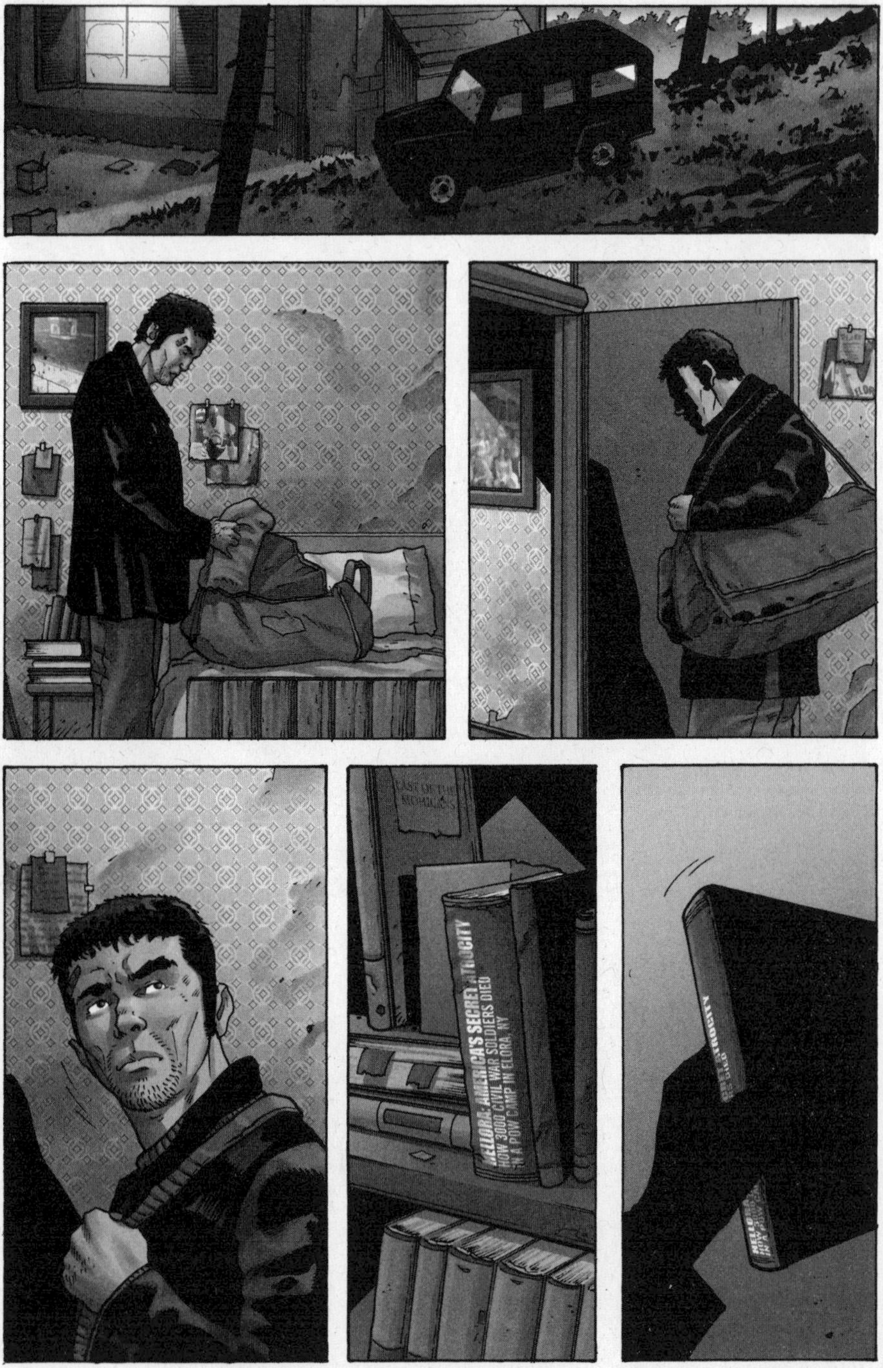
HOW 3000 CIVIL WAR SOLDIERS DIED
IN A POW CAMP IN ELORA, NY

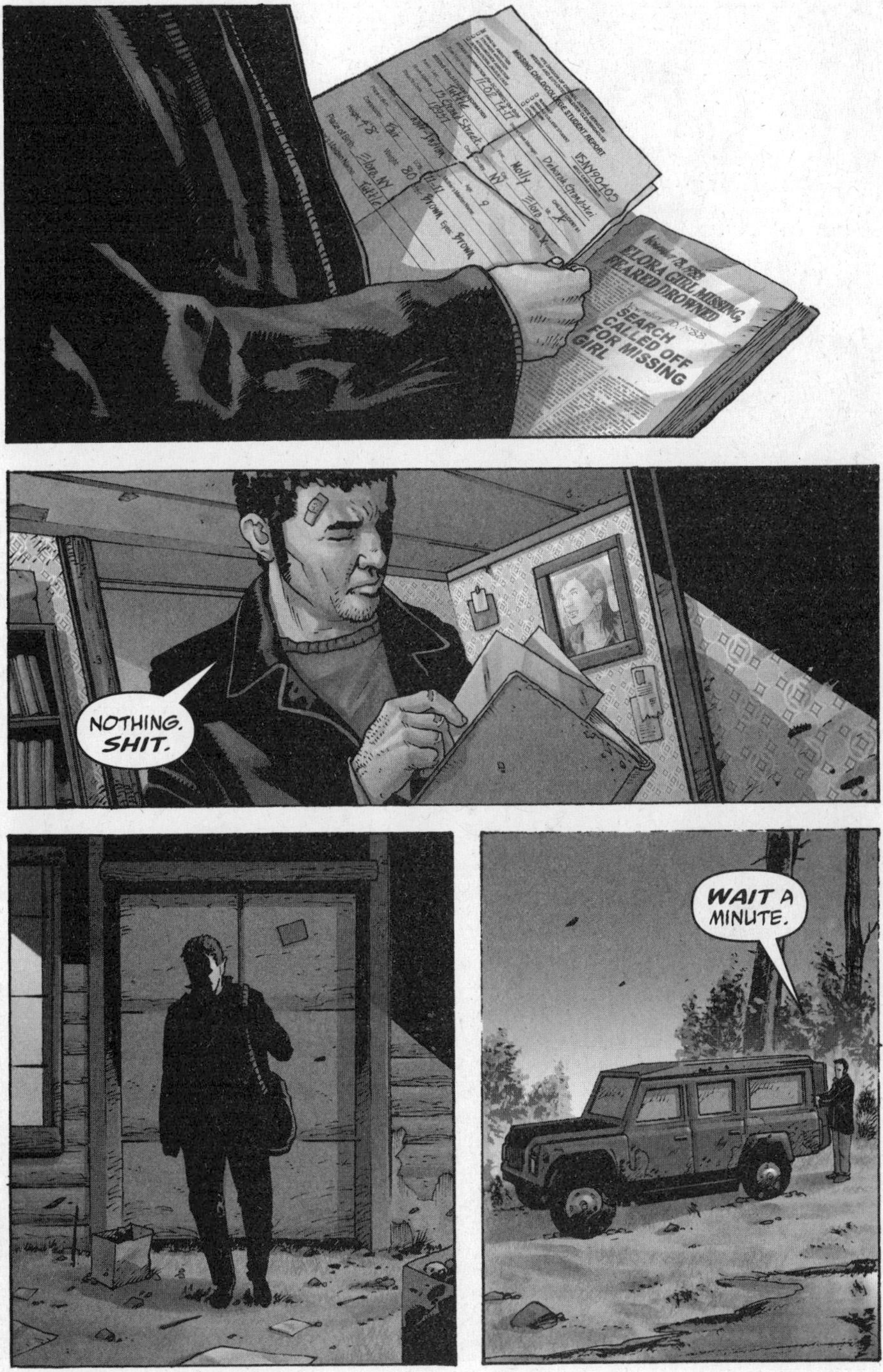
MISSING CHILD/COLLEGE STUDENT REPORT
ELORA GIRL MISSING, FEARED DROWNED
SEARCH CALLED OFF FOR MISSING GIRL
NOTHING. SHIT.
WAIT A MINUTE.

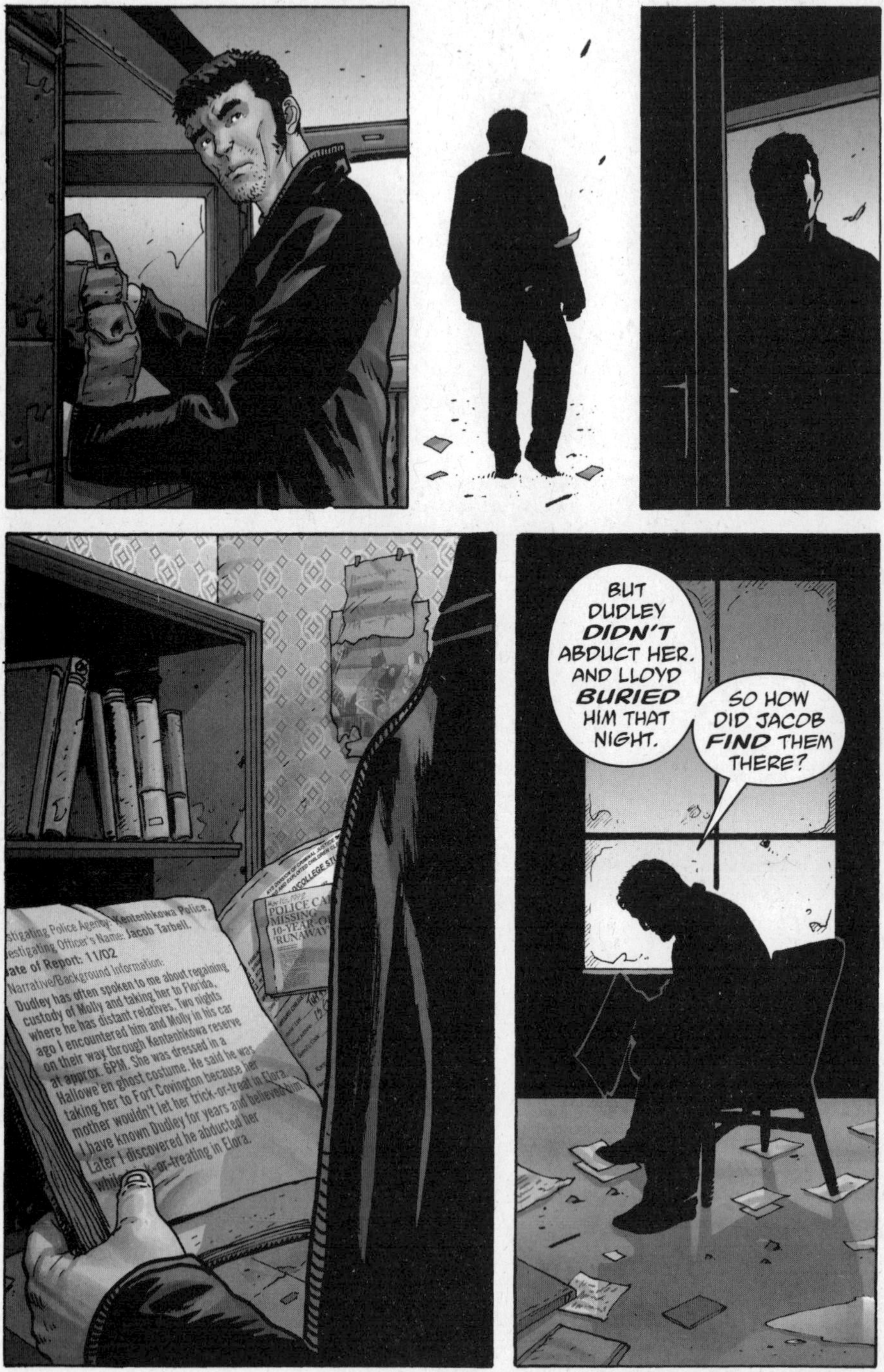
stigating Police Agency: Kentenhkowa Police.
estigating Officer's Name: Jacob Tarbell.
ate of Report: 11/02
Narrative/Background Information:
Dudley has often spoken to me about regaining custody of Molly and taking her to Florida, where he has distant relatives. Two nights ago I encountered him and Molly in his car on their way through Kentenhkowa reserve at approx. 6PM. She was dressed in a Hallowe'en ghost costume. He said he was taking her to Fort Covington because her mother wouldn't let her trick-or-treat in Elora. I have known Dudley for years and believed him. Later I discovered he abducted her
BUT DUDLEY *DIDN'T* ABDUCT HER. AND LLOYD *BURIED* HIM THAT NIGHT.
SO HOW DID JACOB *FIND* THEM THERE?

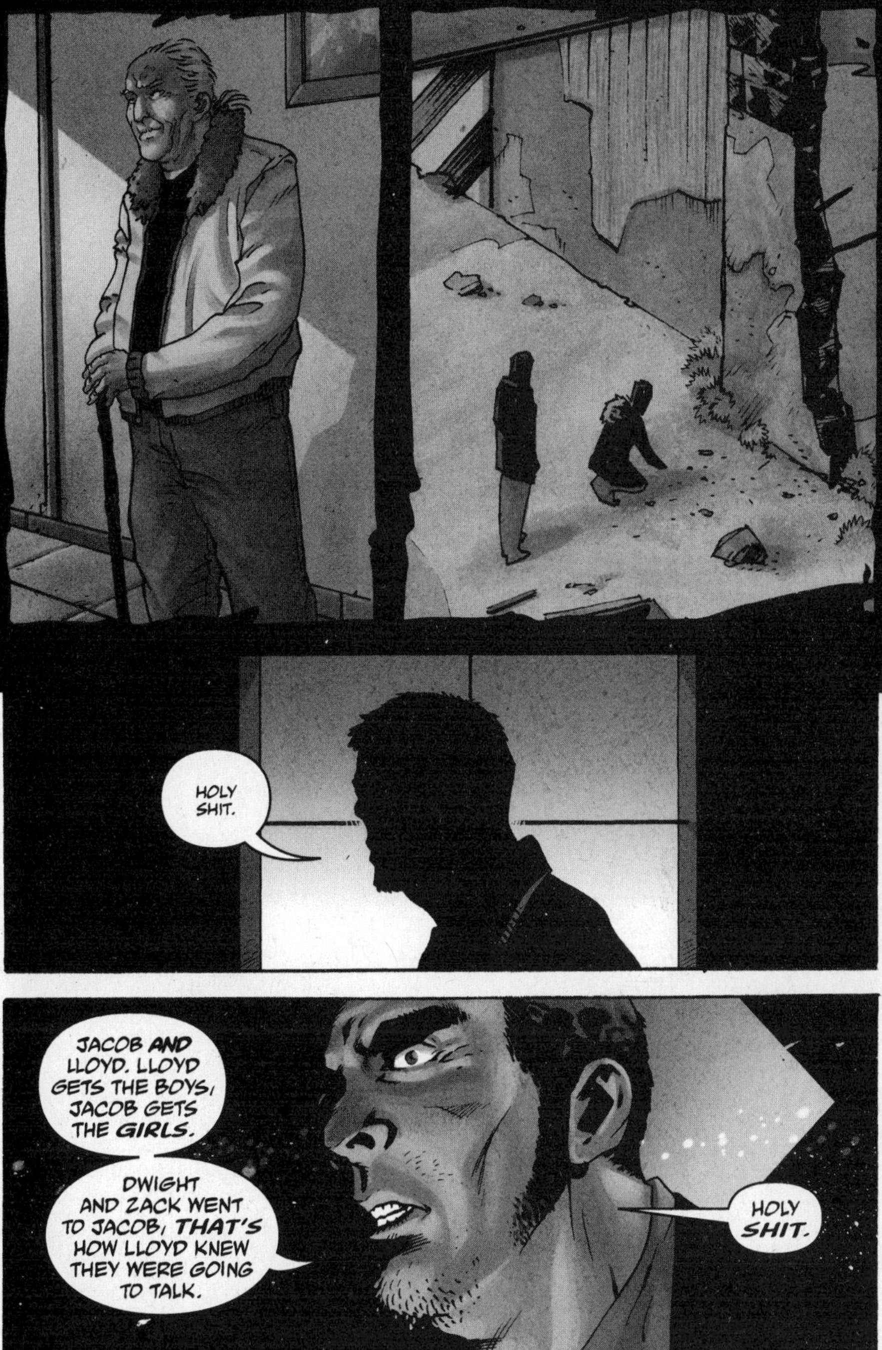
HOLY SHIT.
JACOB AND LLOYD. LLOYD GETS THE BOYS, JACOB GETS THE GIRLS.
DWIGHT AND ZACK WENT TO JACOB, THAT'S HOW LLOYD KNEW THEY WERE GOING TO TALK.
HOLY SHIT.

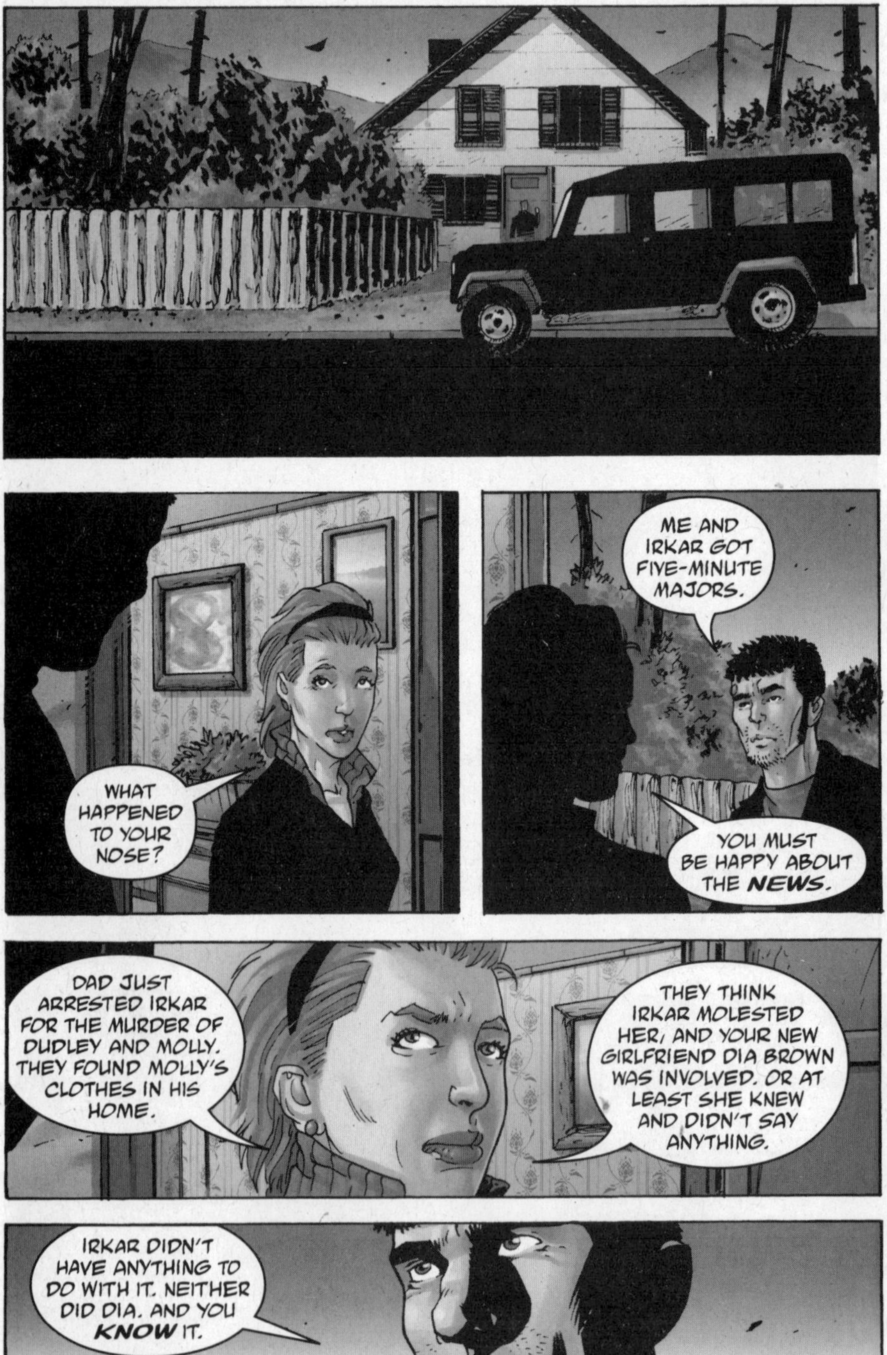
WHAT HAPPENED TO YOUR NOSE?
ME AND IRKAR GOT FIVE-MINUTE MAJORS.
YOU MUST BE HAPPY ABOUT THE NEWS.
DAD JUST ARRESTED IRKAR FOR THE MURDER OF DUDLEY AND MOLLY. THEY FOUND MOLLY'S CLOTHES IN HIS HOME.
THEY THINK IRKAR MOLESTED HER, AND YOUR NEW GIRLFRIEND DIA BROWN WAS INVOLVED. OR AT LEAST SHE KNEW AND DIDN'T SAY ANYTHING.
IRKAR DIDN'T HAVE ANYTHING TO DO WITH IT. NEITHER DID DIA. AND YOU KNOW IT.

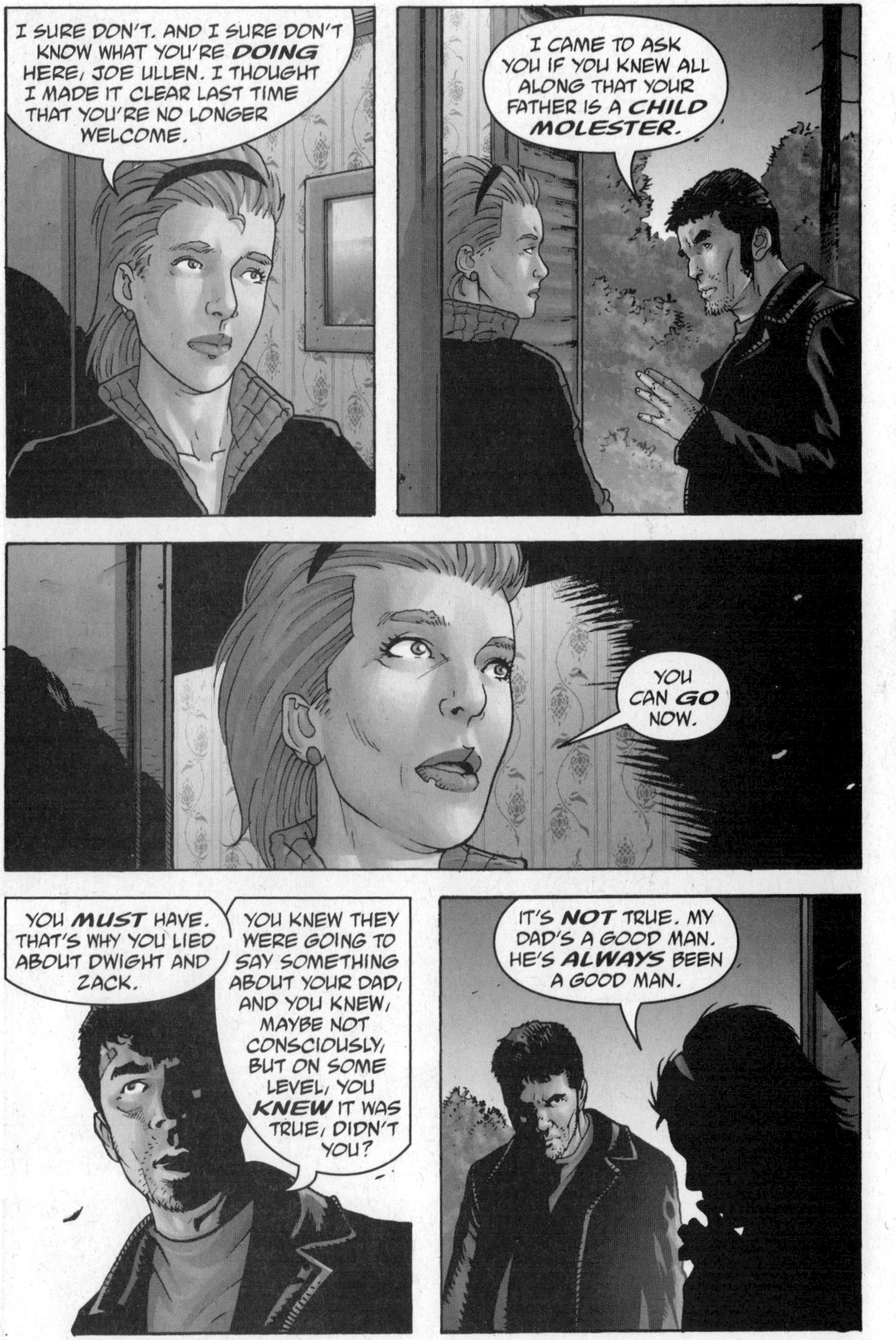
I SURE DON'T. AND I SURE DON'T KNOW WHAT YOU'RE DOING HERE, JOE ULLEN. I THOUGHT I MADE IT CLEAR LAST TIME THAT YOU'RE NO LONGER WELCOME.
I CAME TO ASK YOU IF YOU KNEW ALL ALONG THAT YOUR FATHER IS A CHILD MOLESTER.
YOU CAN GO NOW.
YOU MUST HAVE. THAT'S WHY YOU LIED ABOUT DWIGHT AND ZACK.
YOU KNEW THEY WERE GOING TO SAY SOMETHING ABOUT YOUR DAD, AND YOU KNEW, MAYBE NOT CONSCIOUSLY, BUT ON SOME LEVEL, YOU KNEW IT WAS TRUE, DIDN'T YOU?
IT'S NOT TRUE. MY DAD'S A GOOD MAN. HE'S ALWAYS BEEN A GOOD MAN.

DID YOU KNOW ABOUT HIS MAGAZINES? GAY PORNOGRAPHY?

YOU SNOOPING SON OF A *BITCH.* THINGS WERE *DIFFERENT* WHEN HE GREW UP.

WHAT ARE YOU SAYING, EVERYONE WHO OWNS A GAY MAGAZINE IS A *CHILD MOLESTER?*

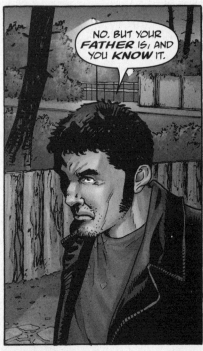

NO. BUT YOUR *FATHER* IS, AND YOU *KNOW* IT.

MY FATHER WAS HERE WITH *ME* ALL NIGHT THE NIGHT MOLLY DISAPPEARED.

I WANT YOU TO GET THE FUCK *OFF--*

THEY MUST KEEP SOME KIND OF EVIDENCE. THEY'VE GOT TO. PICTURES. *TROPHIES.*

COME ON, NAOMI. MOLLY MIGHT STILL BE *ALIVE.* WHERE WOULD THEY KEEP IT?

THEY?

WHAT DO YOU MEAN, *THEY?*

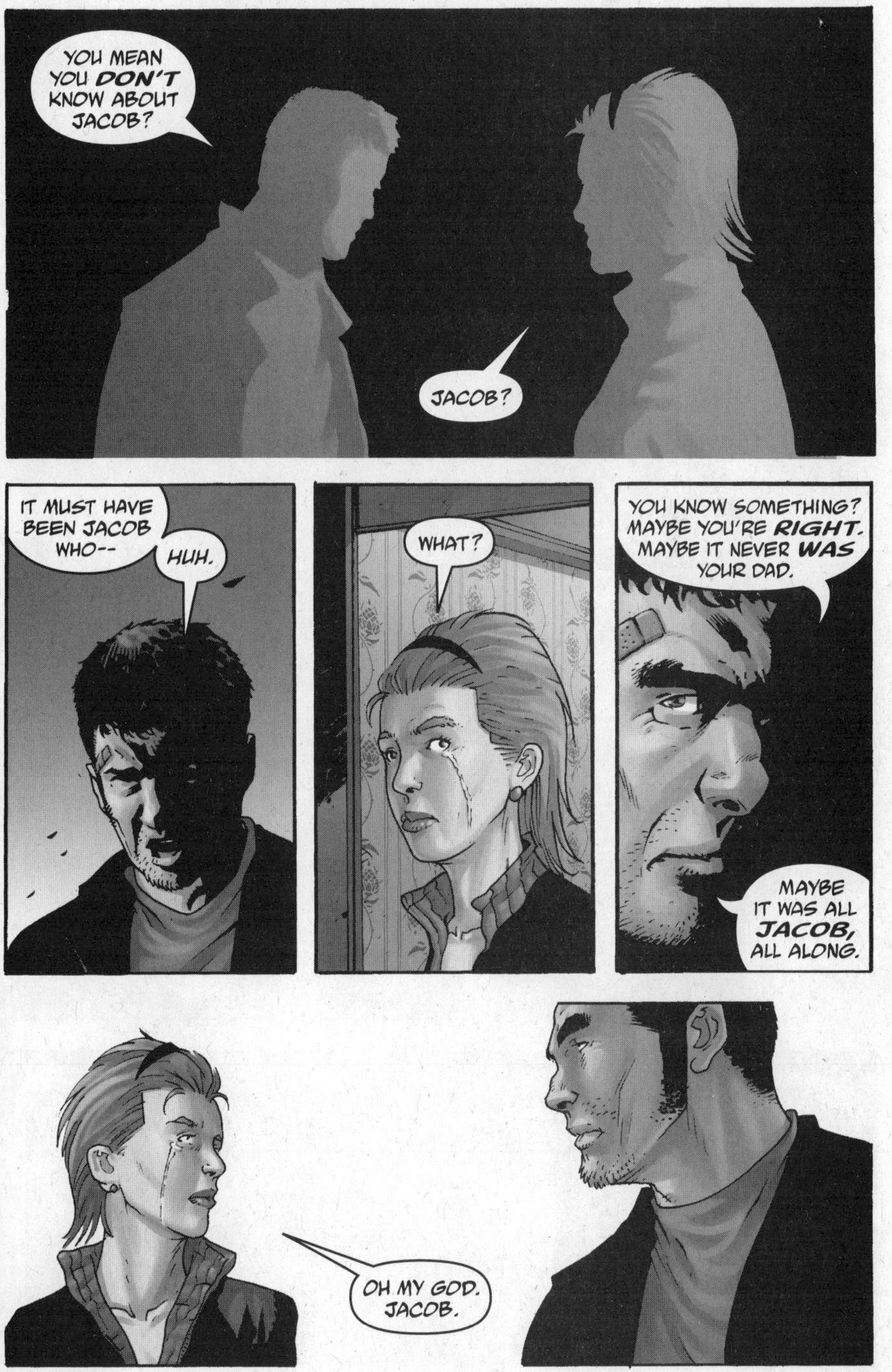
YOU MEAN YOU DON'T KNOW ABOUT JACOB?
JACOB?
IT MUST HAVE BEEN JACOB WHO--
HUH.
WHAT?
YOU KNOW SOMETHING? MAYBE YOU'RE RIGHT. MAYBE IT NEVER WAS YOUR DAD.
MAYBE IT WAS ALL JACOB, ALL ALONG.
OH MY GOD. JACOB.

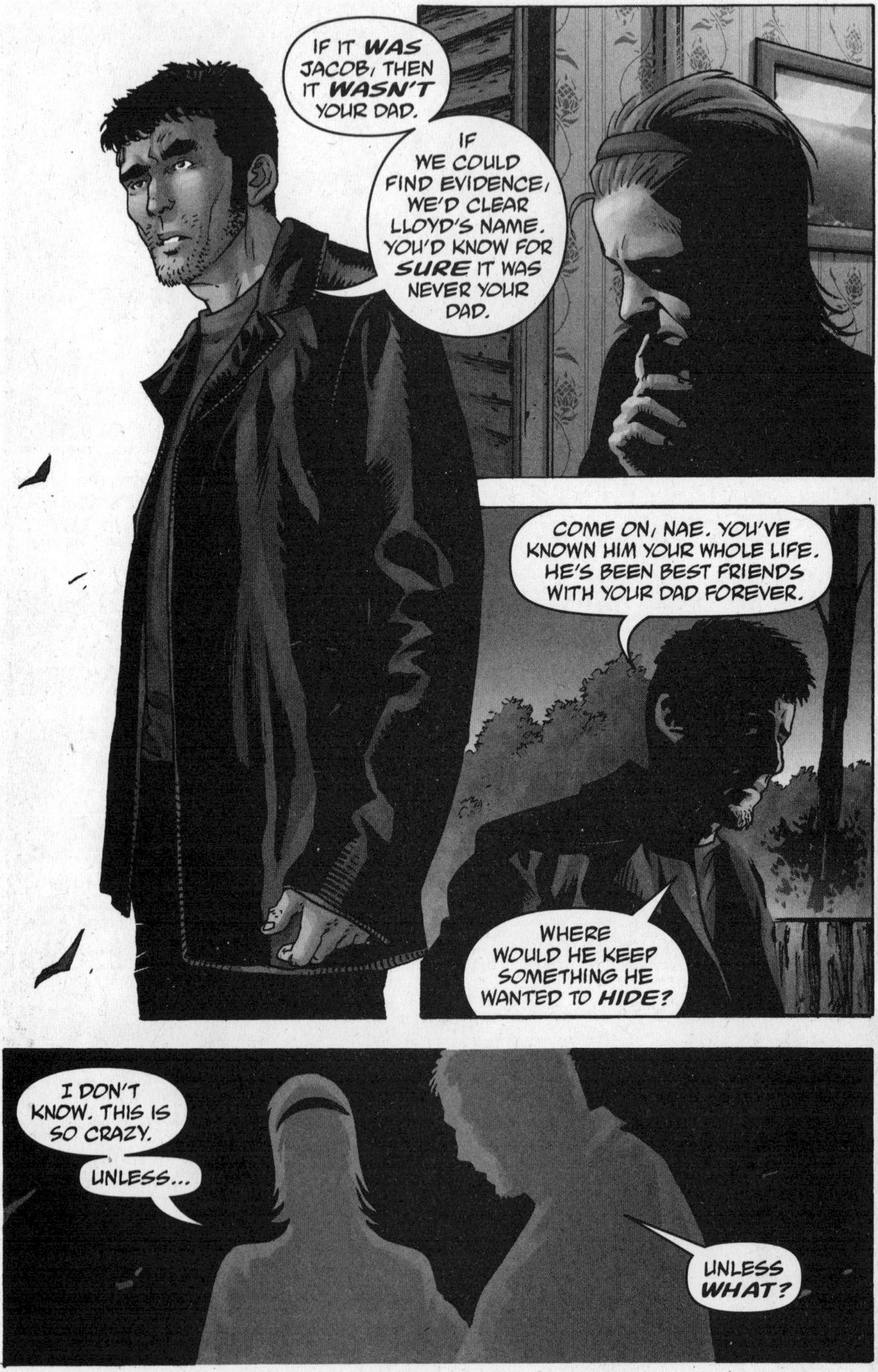
IF IT WAS JACOB, THEN IT WASN'T YOUR DAD.
IF WE COULD FIND EVIDENCE, WE'D CLEAR LLOYD'S NAME. YOU'D KNOW FOR SURE IT WAS NEVER YOUR DAD.
COME ON, NAE. YOU'VE KNOWN HIM YOUR WHOLE LIFE. HE'S BEEN BEST FRIENDS WITH YOUR DAD FOREVER.
WHERE WOULD HE KEEP SOMETHING HE WANTED TO HIDE?
I DON'T KNOW. THIS IS SO CRAZY.
UNLESS...
UNLESS WHAT?

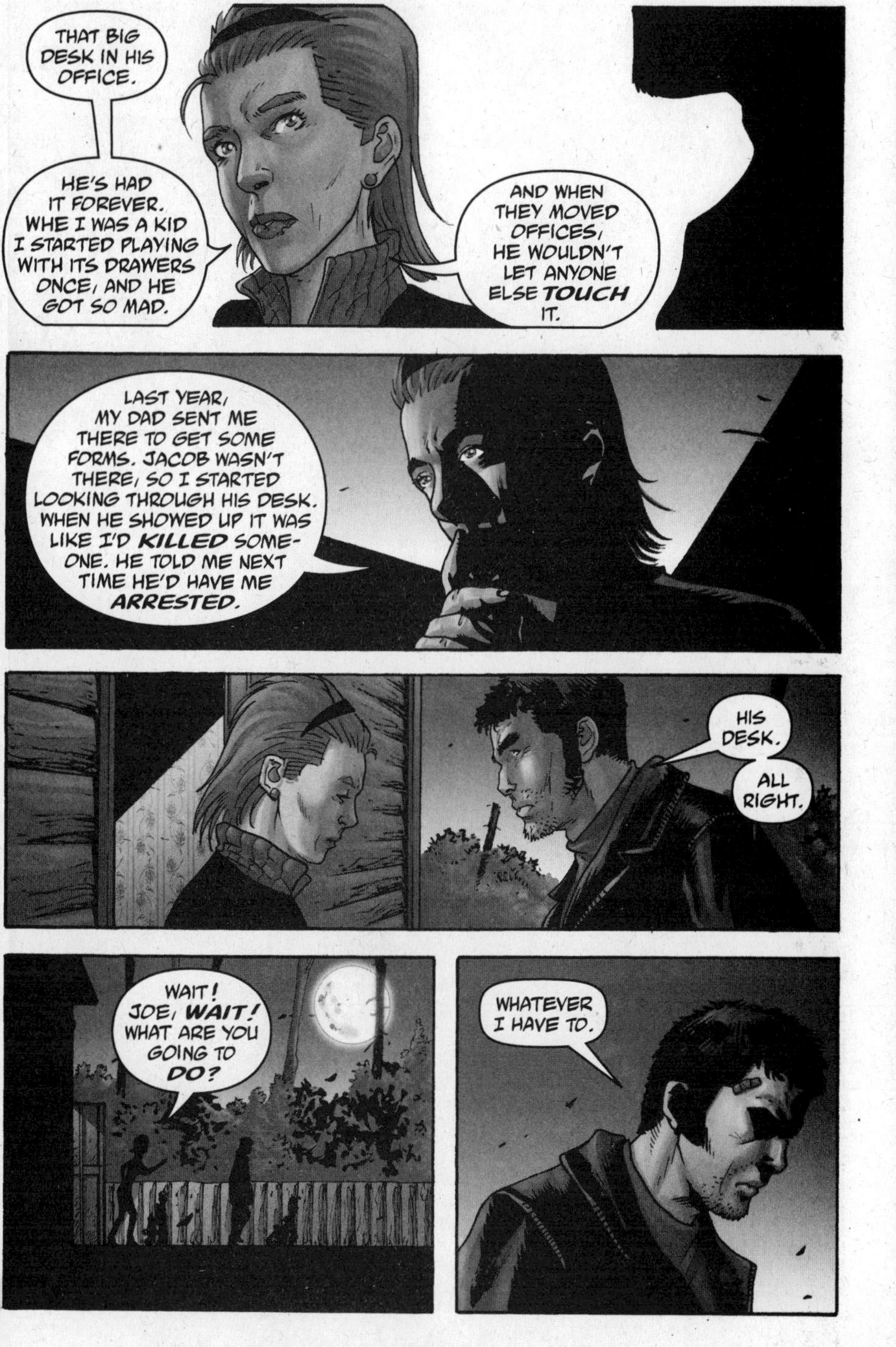
THAT BIG DESK IN HIS OFFICE.
HE'S HAD IT FOREVER. WHE I WAS A KID I STARTED PLAYING WITH ITS DRAWERS ONCE, AND HE GOT SO MAD.
AND WHEN THEY MOVED OFFICES, HE WOULDN'T LET ANYONE ELSE TOUCH IT.
LAST YEAR, MY DAD SENT ME THERE TO GET SOME FORMS. JACOB WASN'T THERE, SO I STARTED LOOKING THROUGH HIS DESK. WHEN HE SHOWED UP IT WAS LIKE I'D KILLED SOME-ONE. HE TOLD ME NEXT TIME HE'D HAVE ME ARRESTED.
HIS DESK.
ALL RIGHT.
WAIT! JOE, WAIT! WHAT ARE YOU GOING TO DO?
WHATEVER I HAVE TO.

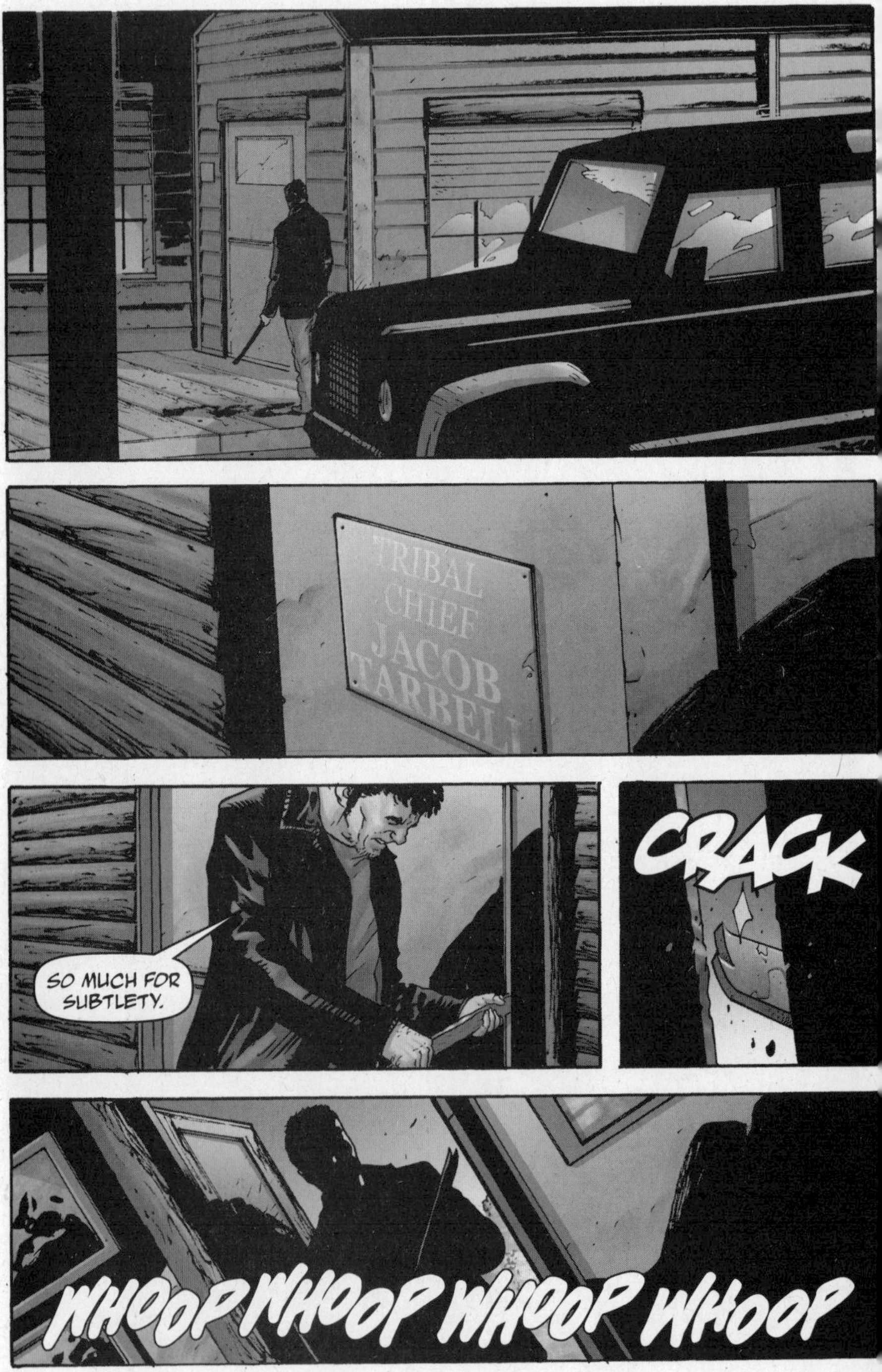

TRIBAL CHIEF JACOB TARBELL
SO MUCH FOR SUBTLETY.
CRACK
WHOOP WHOOP WHOOP WHOOP

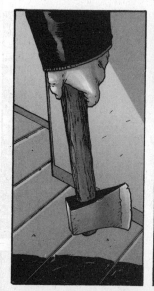

YOU WOULDN'T JUST LOCK IT IN A DRAWER, WOULD YOU, JAKE? YOU'RE A **SNEAKY** MOTHERFUCKER.

SKRAASSH

WHOOP WHOOP WHOOP

SKRAASH

WHOOP WHOOP WHOOP

FALSE BOTTOM, SECRET COMPARTMENT, **THAT'S** MORE YOUR STYLE.

GOTCHA!

WHOOP WHOOP WHOOP WHOOP

OH JESUS.

OH MY GOD.

WHOOP WHOOP WHOOP WHOOP

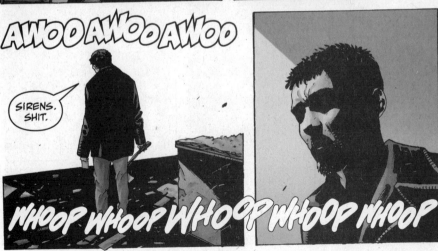

AWOO AWOO AWOO

SIRENS. SHIT.

WHOOP WHOOP WHOOP WHOOP WHOOP

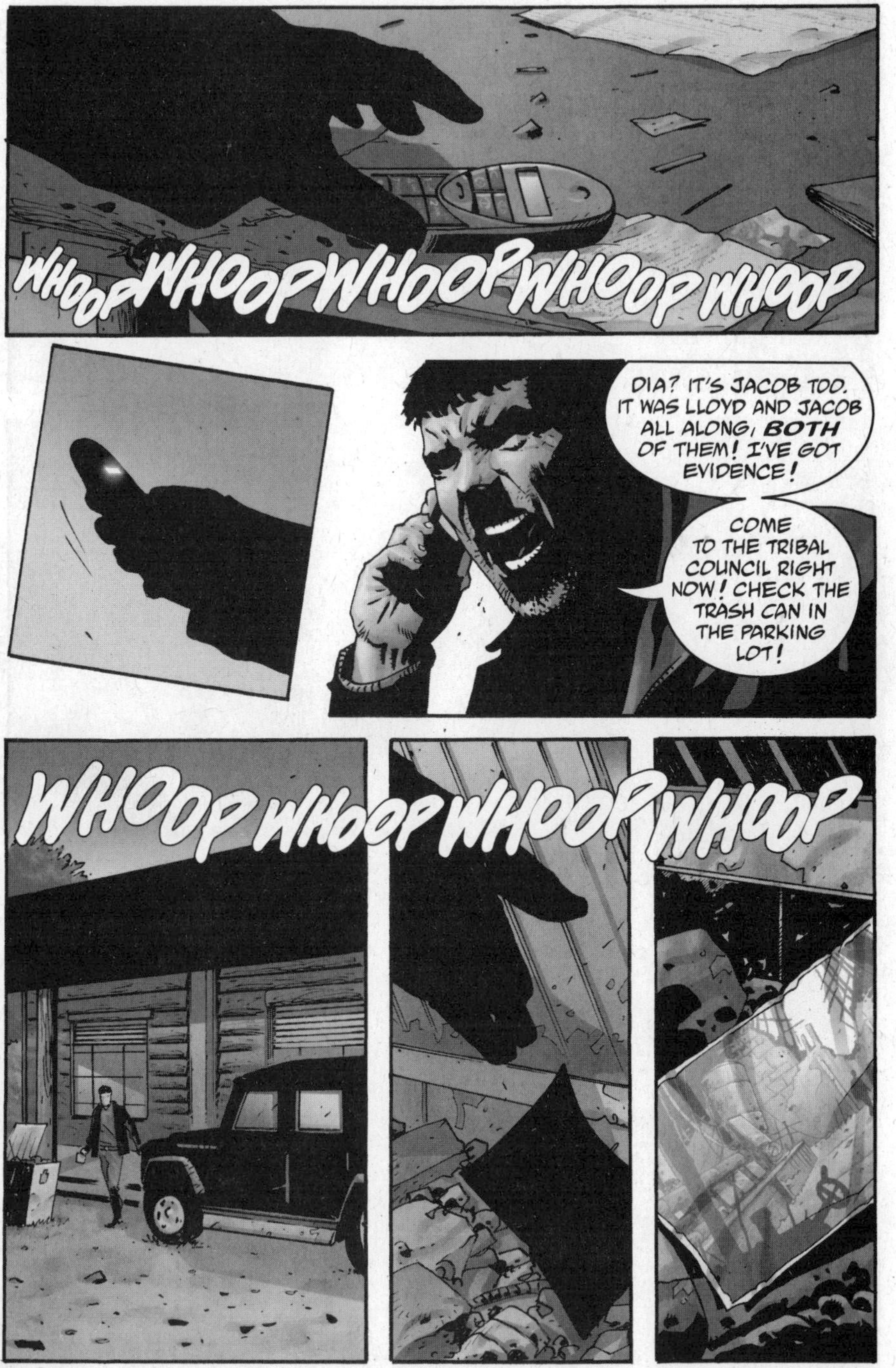
WHOOP WHOOP WHOOP WHOOP WHOOP
DIA? IT'S JACOB TOO. IT WAS LLOYD AND JACOB ALL ALONG, BOTH OF THEM! I'VE GOT EVIDENCE!
COME TO THE TRIBAL COUNCIL RIGHT NOW! CHECK THE TRASH CAN IN THE PARKING LOT!
WHOOP WHOOP WHOOP WHOOP

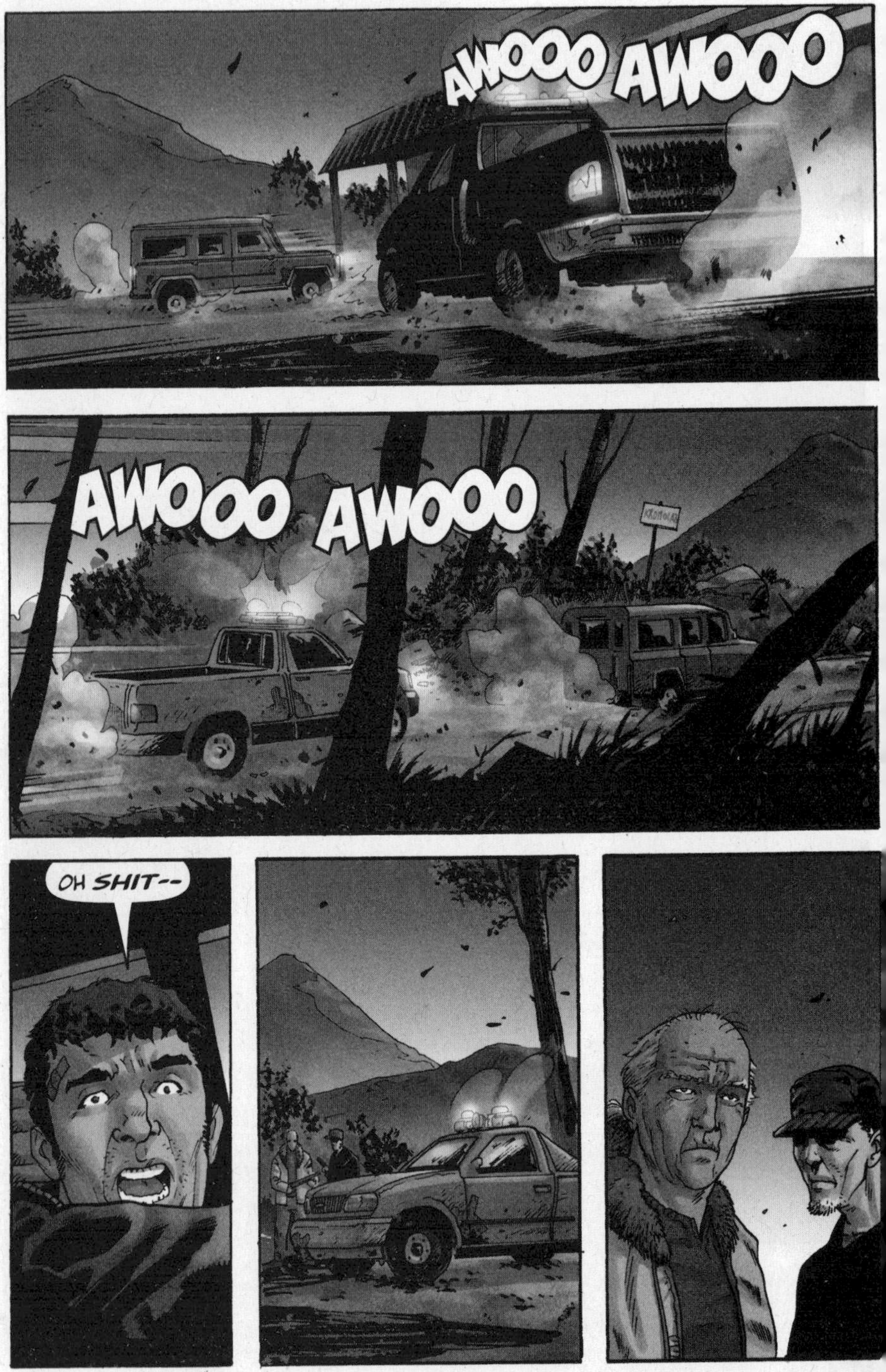
AWOOO AWOOO
AWOOO AWOOO
OH SHIT--

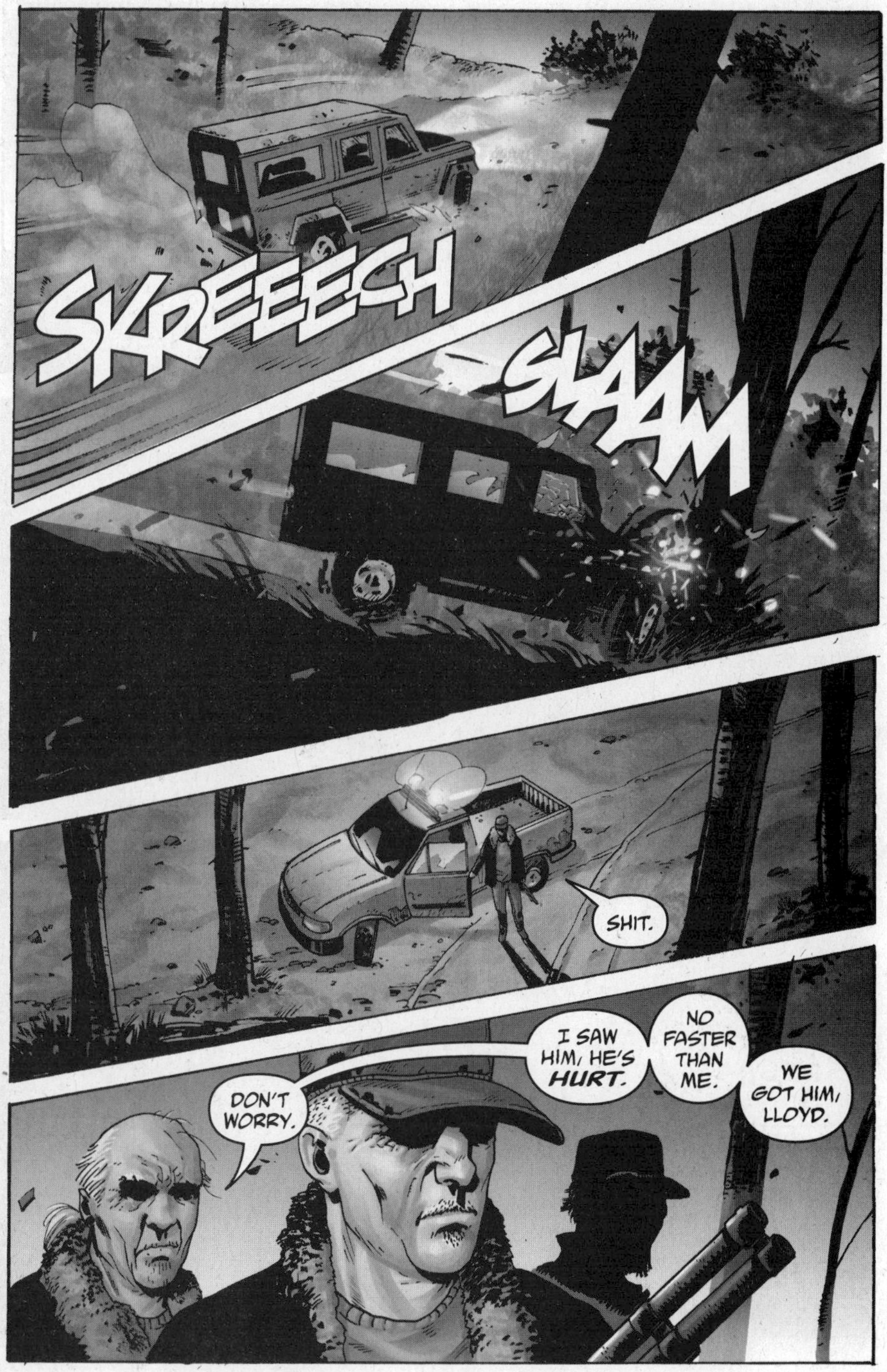
SKREEECH
SLAAM
SHIT.
DON'T WORRY.
I SAW HIM, HE'S **HURT**.
NO FASTER THAN ME.
WE GOT HIM, LLOYD.

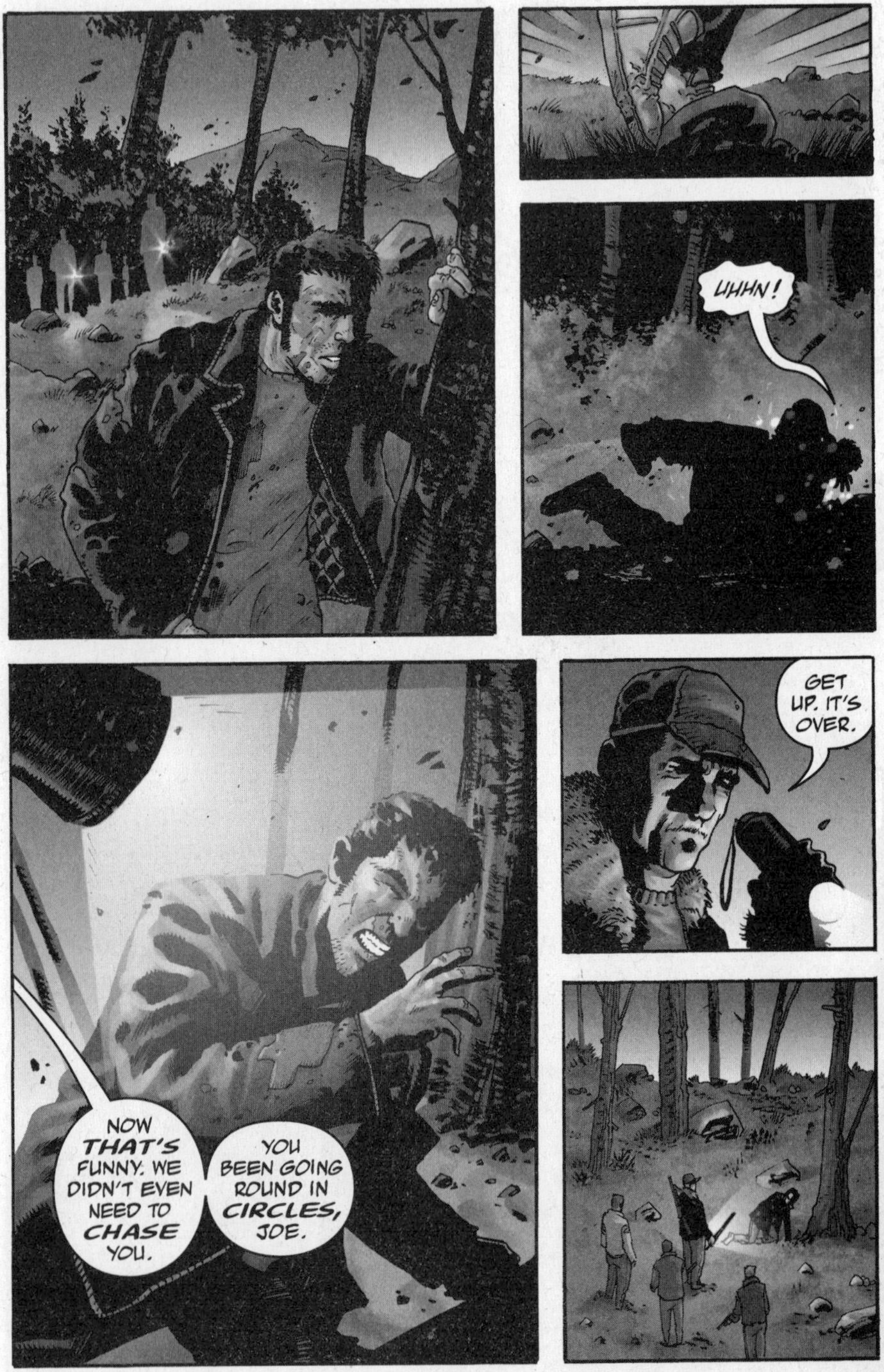
UHHN!
GET UP. IT'S OVER.
NOW THAT'S FUNNY. WE DIDN'T EVEN NEED TO CHASE YOU.
YOU BEEN GOING ROUND IN CIRCLES, JOE.

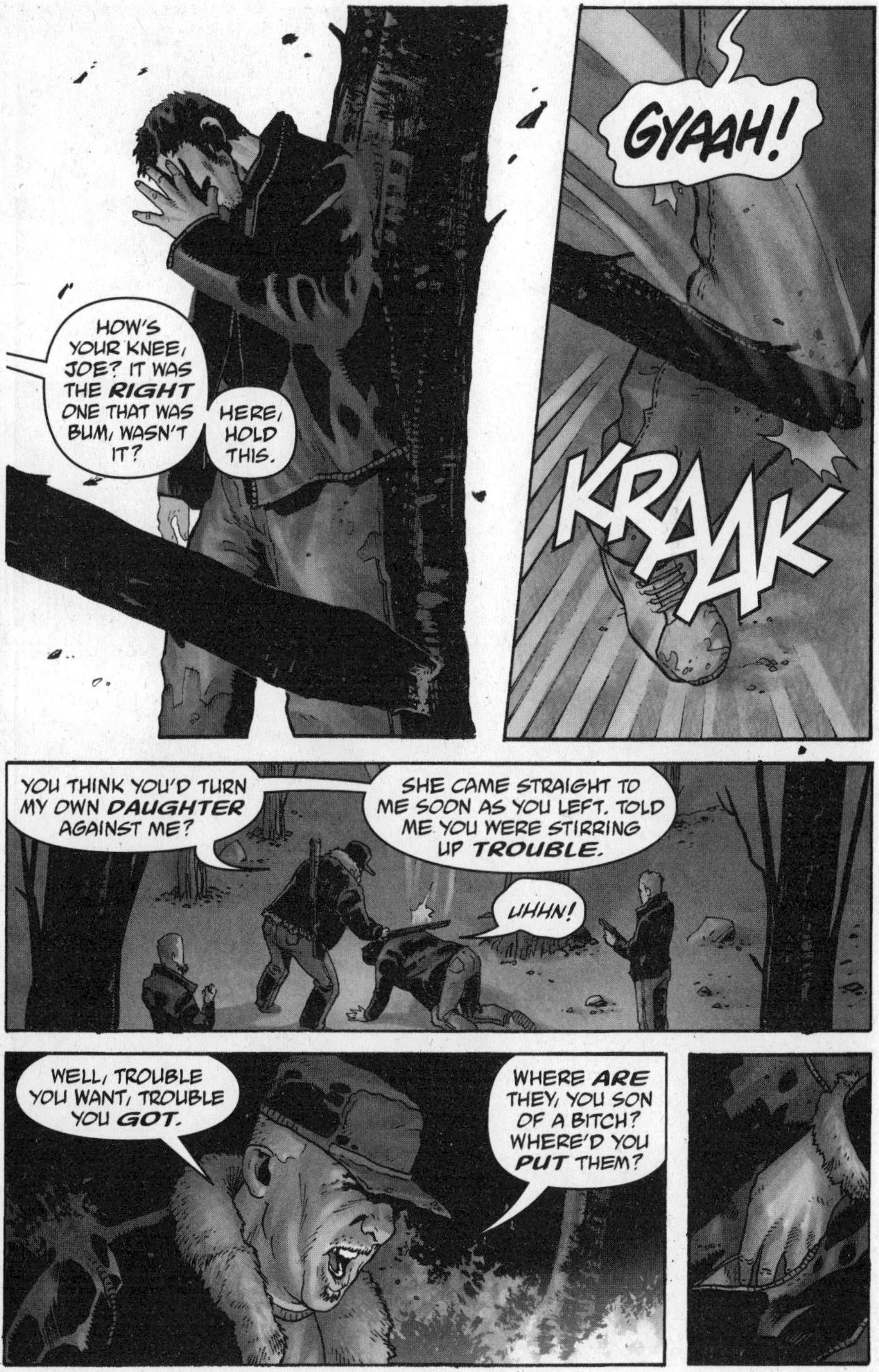
HOW'S YOUR KNEE, JOE? IT WAS THE RIGHT ONE THAT WAS BUM, WASN'T IT?
HERE, HOLD THIS.
GYAAH!
KRAAK
YOU THINK YOU'D TURN MY OWN DAUGHTER AGAINST ME?
SHE CAME STRAIGHT TO ME SOON AS YOU LEFT. TOLD ME YOU WERE STIRRING UP TROUBLE.
UHHN!
WELL, TROUBLE YOU WANT, TROUBLE YOU GOT.
WHERE ARE THEY, YOU SON OF A BITCH? WHERE'D YOU PUT THEM?

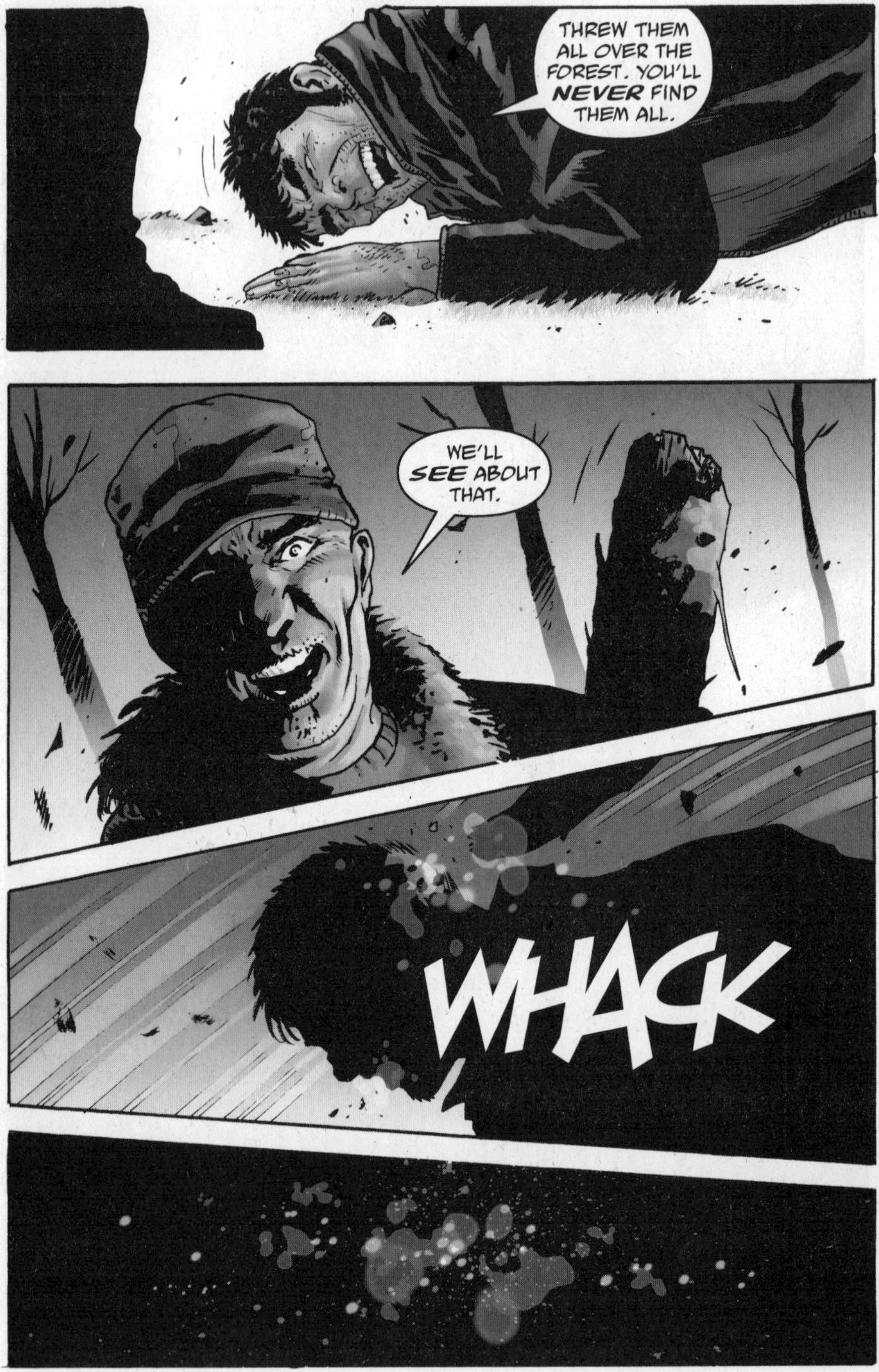

THREW THEM ALL OVER THE FOREST. YOU'LL NEVER FIND THEM ALL.
WE'LL SEE ABOUT THAT.
WHACK

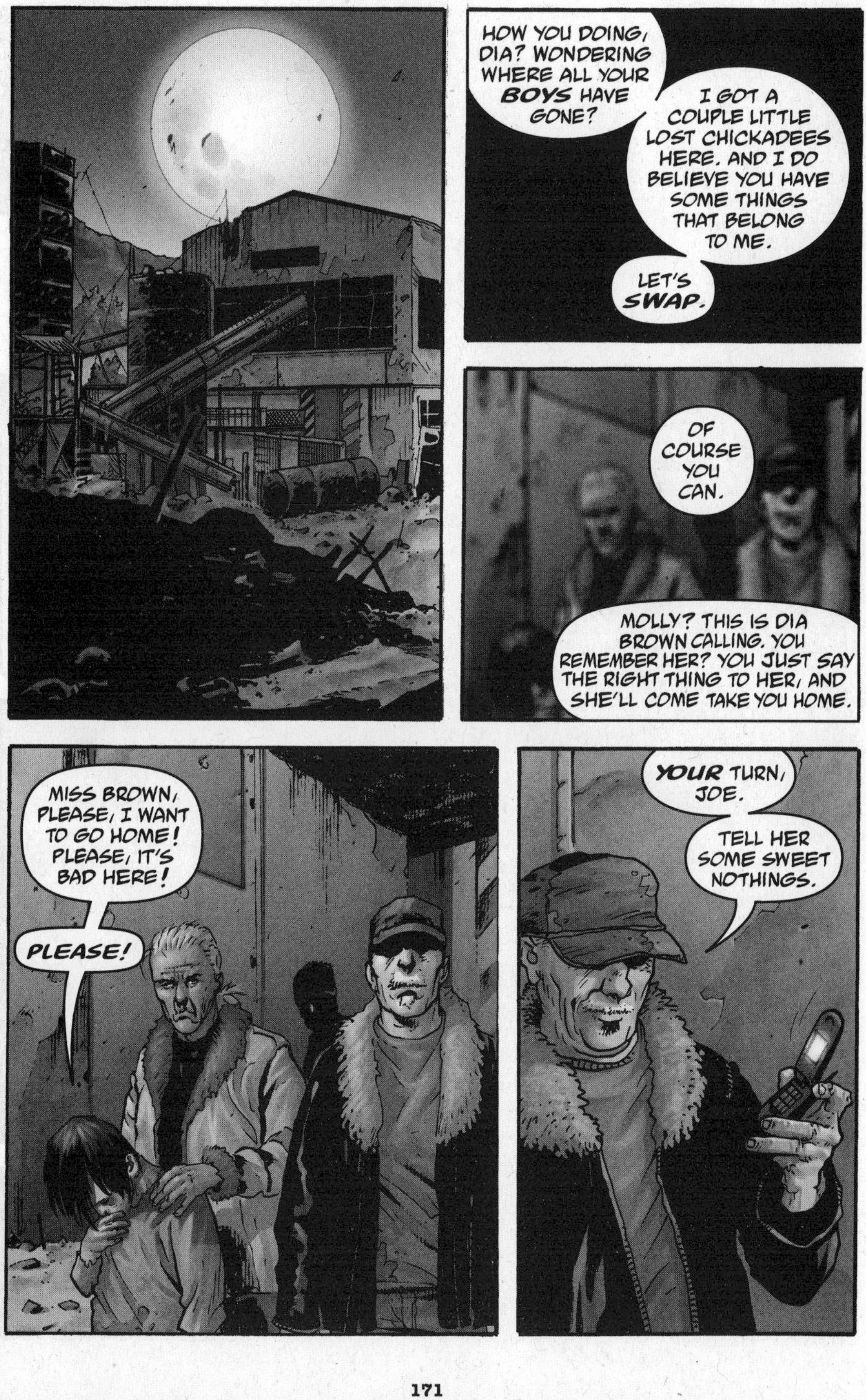
HOW YOU DOING, DIA? WONDERING WHERE ALL YOUR BOYS HAVE GONE?
I GOT A COUPLE LITTLE LOST CHICKADEES HERE. AND I DO BELIEVE YOU HAVE SOME THINGS THAT BELONG TO ME.
LET'S SWAP.
OF COURSE YOU CAN.
MOLLY? THIS IS DIA BROWN CALLING. YOU REMEMBER HER? YOU JUST SAY THE RIGHT THING TO HER, AND SHE'LL COME TAKE YOU HOME.
MISS BROWN, PLEASE, I WANT TO GO HOME! PLEASE, IT'S BAD HERE!
PLEASE!
YOUR TURN, JOE.
TELL HER SOME SWEET NOTHINGS.

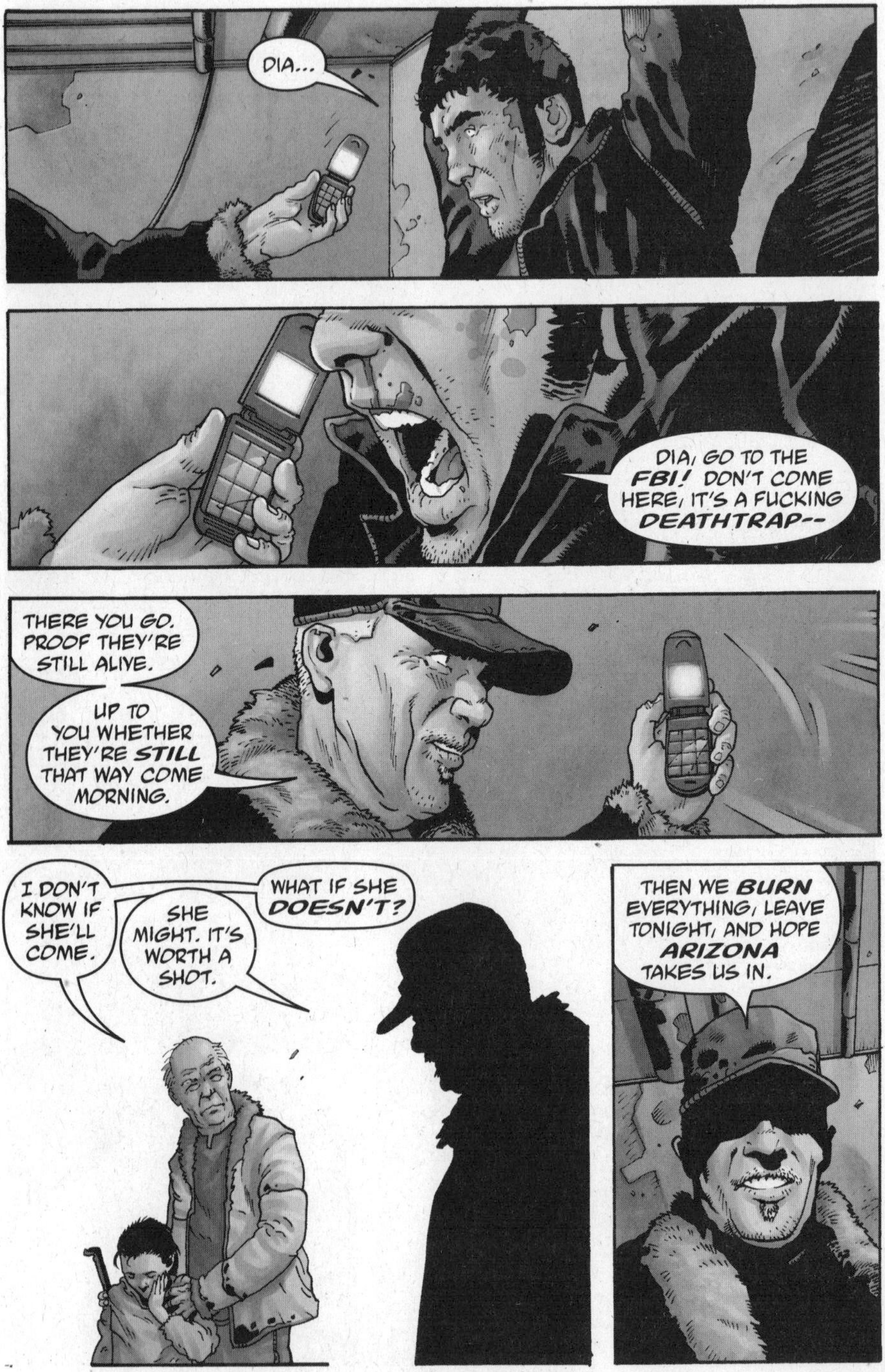
DIA...
DIA, GO TO THE FBI! DON'T COME HERE, IT'S A FUCKING DEATHTRAP--
THERE YOU GO. PROOF THEY'RE STILL ALIVE.
UP TO YOU WHETHER THEY'RE STILL THAT WAY COME MORNING.
I DON'T KNOW IF SHE'LL COME.
SHE MIGHT. IT'S WORTH A SHOT.
WHAT IF SHE DOESN'T?
THEN WE BURN EVERYTHING, LEAVE TONIGHT, AND HOPE ARIZONA TAKES US IN.

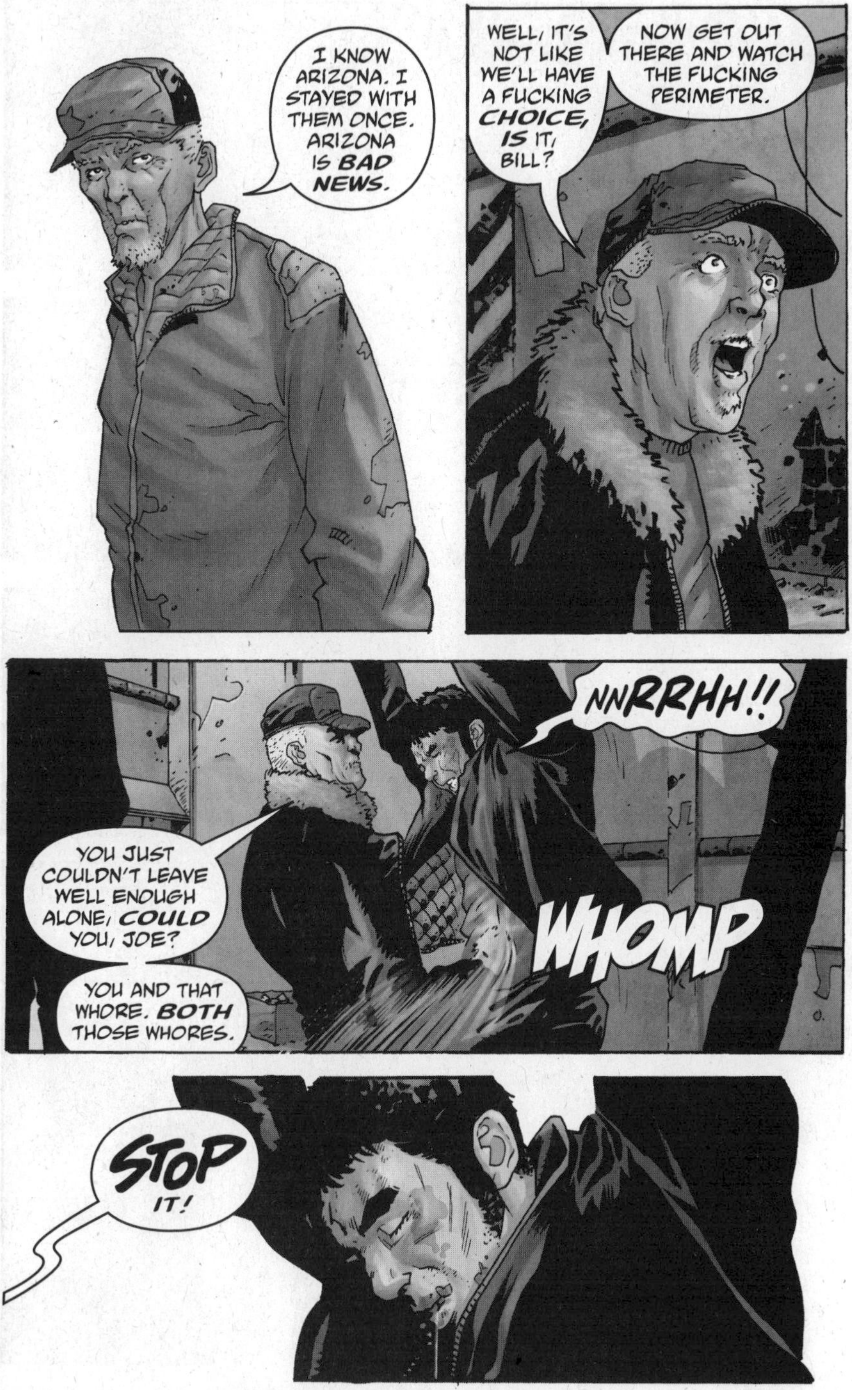
I KNOW ARIZONA. I STAYED WITH THEM ONCE. ARIZONA IS BAD NEWS.
WELL, IT'S NOT LIKE WE'LL HAVE A FUCKING CHOICE, IS IT, BILL?
NOW GET OUT THERE AND WATCH THE FUCKING PERIMETER.
NNRRHH!!
YOU JUST COULDN'T LEAVE WELL ENOUGH ALONE, COULD YOU, JOE?
YOU AND THAT WHORE. BOTH THOSE WHORES.
WHOMP
STOP IT!

DON'T HURT HIM!
YOU DON'T NEED TO HURT HIM!
SHE'LL COME. I THINK SHE'LL COME.
BET YOU'RE WISHING YOU'D JUST GONE HOME LIKE I TOLD YOU, AREN'T YOU, JOE? BET YOU'RE WISHING YOU'D NEVER GOT CURIOUS.

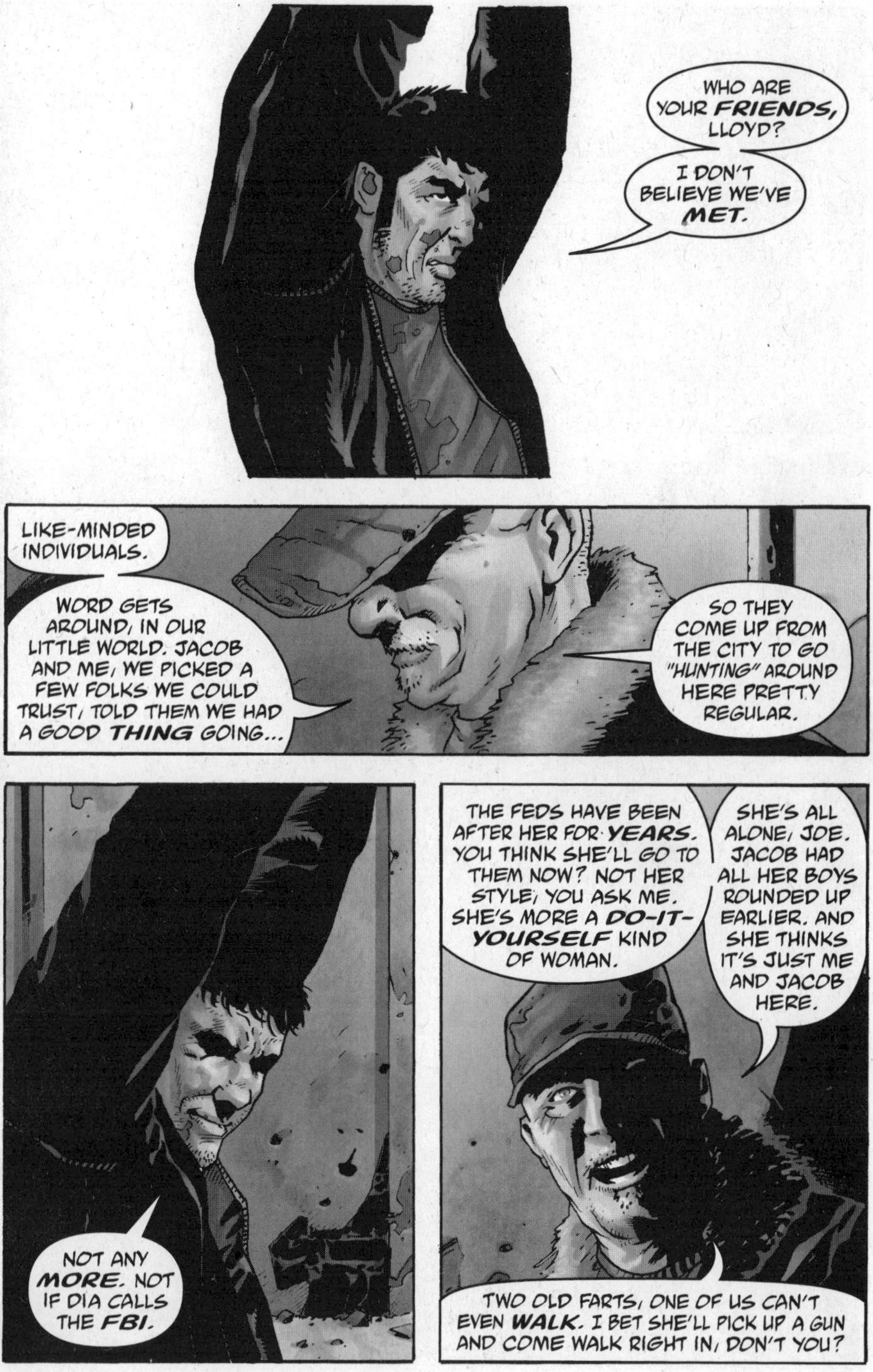
WHO ARE YOUR FRIENDS, LLOYD?
I DON'T BELIEVE WE'VE MET.
LIKE-MINDED INDIVIDUALS.
WORD GETS AROUND, IN OUR LITTLE WORLD. JACOB AND ME, WE PICKED A FEW FOLKS WE COULD TRUST, TOLD THEM WE HAD A GOOD THING GOING...
SO THEY COME UP FROM THE CITY TO GO "HUNTING" AROUND HERE PRETTY REGULAR.
NOT ANY MORE. NOT IF DIA CALLS THE FBI.
THE FEDS HAVE BEEN AFTER HER FOR YEARS. YOU THINK SHE'LL GO TO THEM NOW? NOT HER STYLE, YOU ASK ME. SHE'S MORE A DO-IT-YOURSELF KIND OF WOMAN.
SHE'S ALL ALONE, JOE. JACOB HAD ALL HER BOYS ROUNDED UP EARLIER. AND SHE THINKS IT'S JUST ME AND JACOB HERE.
TWO OLD FARTS, ONE OF US CAN'T EVEN WALK. I BET SHE'LL PICK UP A GUN AND COME WALK RIGHT IN, DON'T YOU?

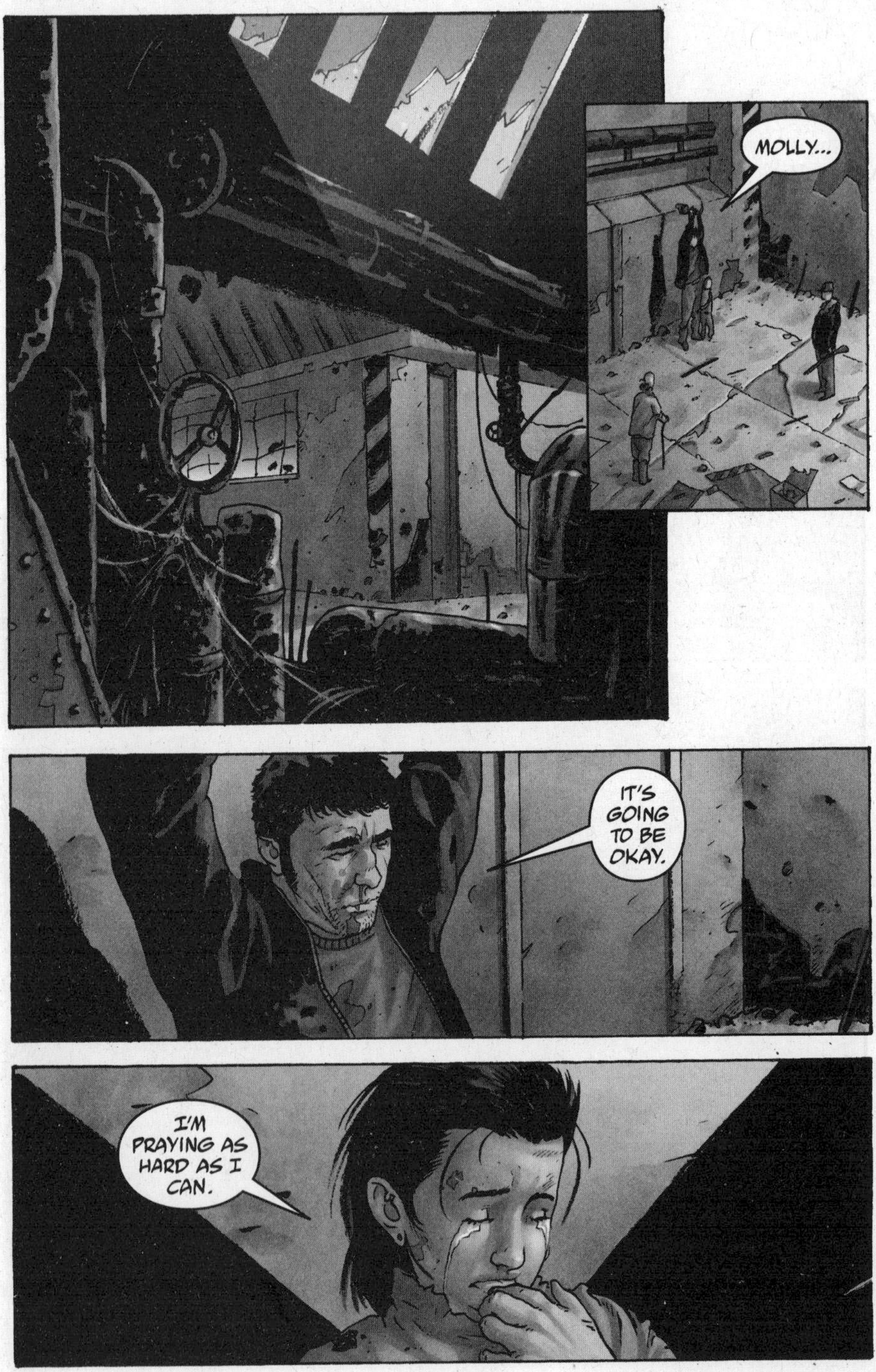
MOLLY...
IT'S GOING TO BE OKAY.
I'M PRAYING AS HARD AS I CAN.

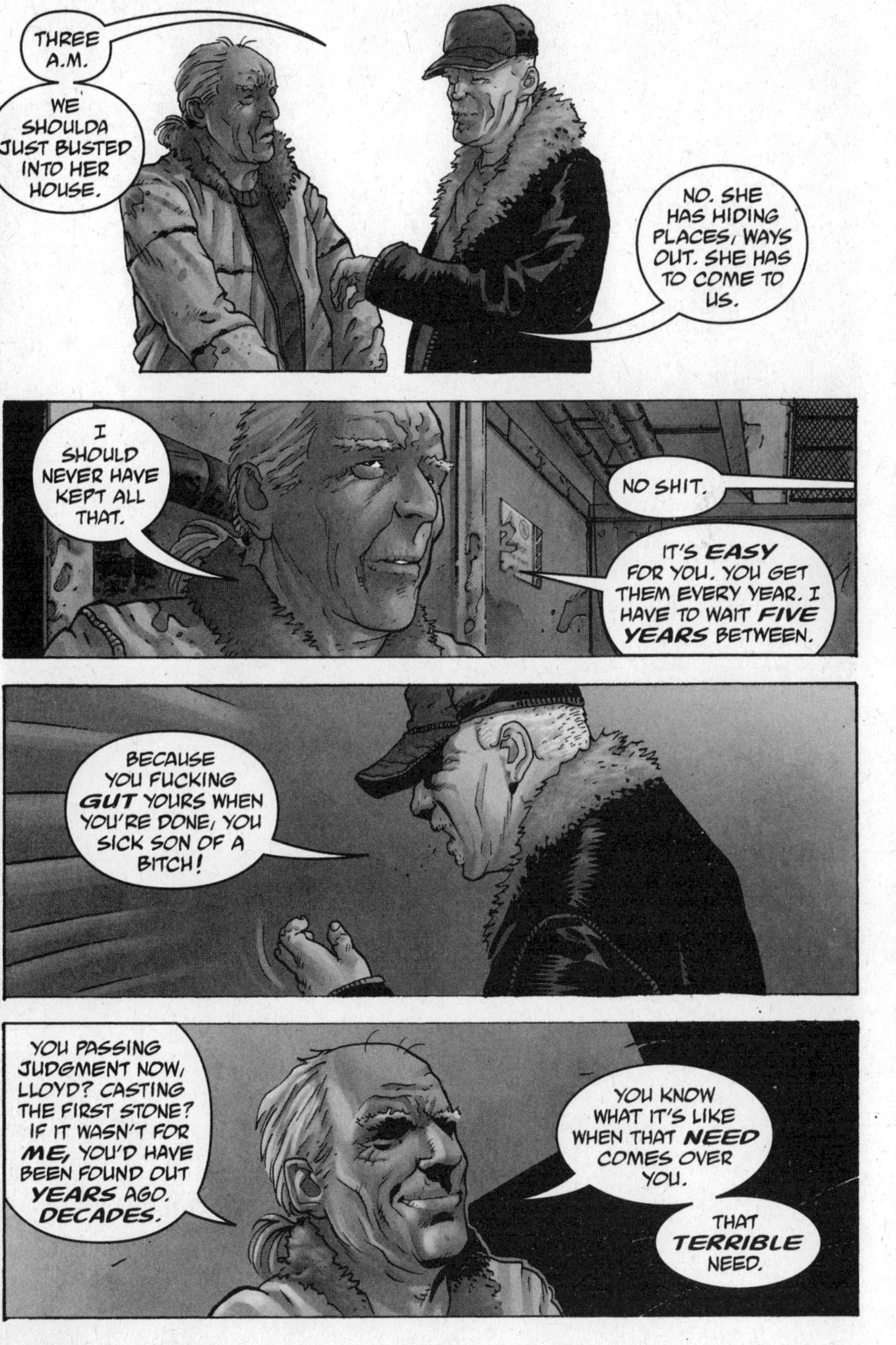
THREE A.M.
WE SHOULDA JUST BUSTED INTO HER HOUSE.
NO. SHE HAS HIDING PLACES, WAYS OUT. SHE HAS TO COME TO US.
I SHOULD NEVER HAVE KEPT ALL THAT.
NO SHIT.
IT'S EASY FOR YOU. YOU GET THEM EVERY YEAR. I HAVE TO WAIT FIVE YEARS BETWEEN.
BECAUSE YOU FUCKING GUT YOURS WHEN YOU'RE DONE, YOU SICK SON OF A BITCH!
YOU PASSING JUDGMENT NOW, LLOYD? CASTING THE FIRST STONE? IF IT WASN'T FOR ME, YOU'D HAVE BEEN FOUND OUT YEARS AGO. DECADES.
YOU KNOW WHAT IT'S LIKE WHEN THAT NEED COMES OVER YOU.
THAT TERRIBLE NEED.

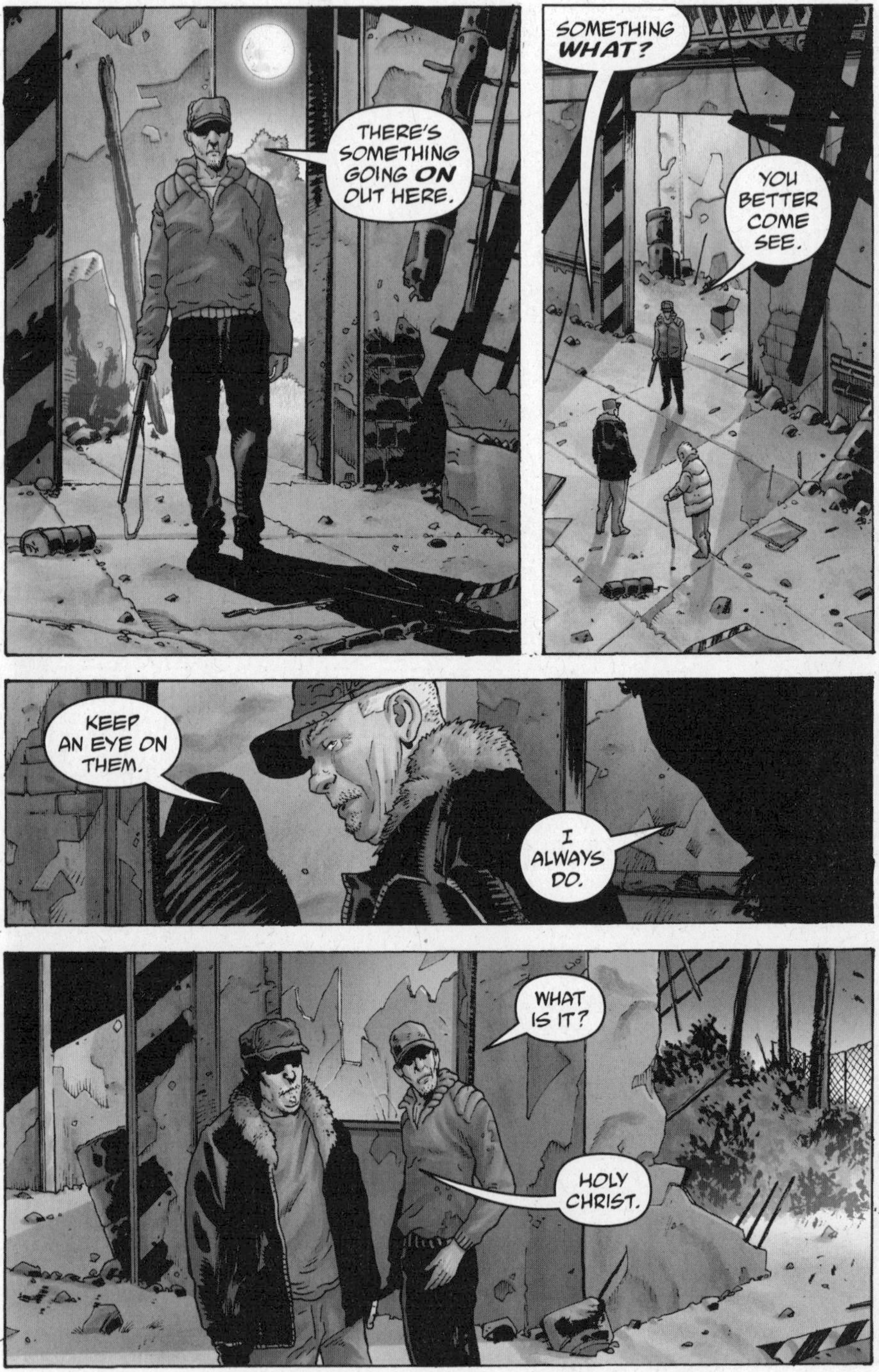
THERE'S SOMETHING GOING **ON** OUT HERE.
SOMETHING **WHAT?**
YOU BETTER COME SEE.
KEEP AN EYE ON THEM.
I ALWAYS DO.
WHAT IS IT?
HOLY CHRIST.

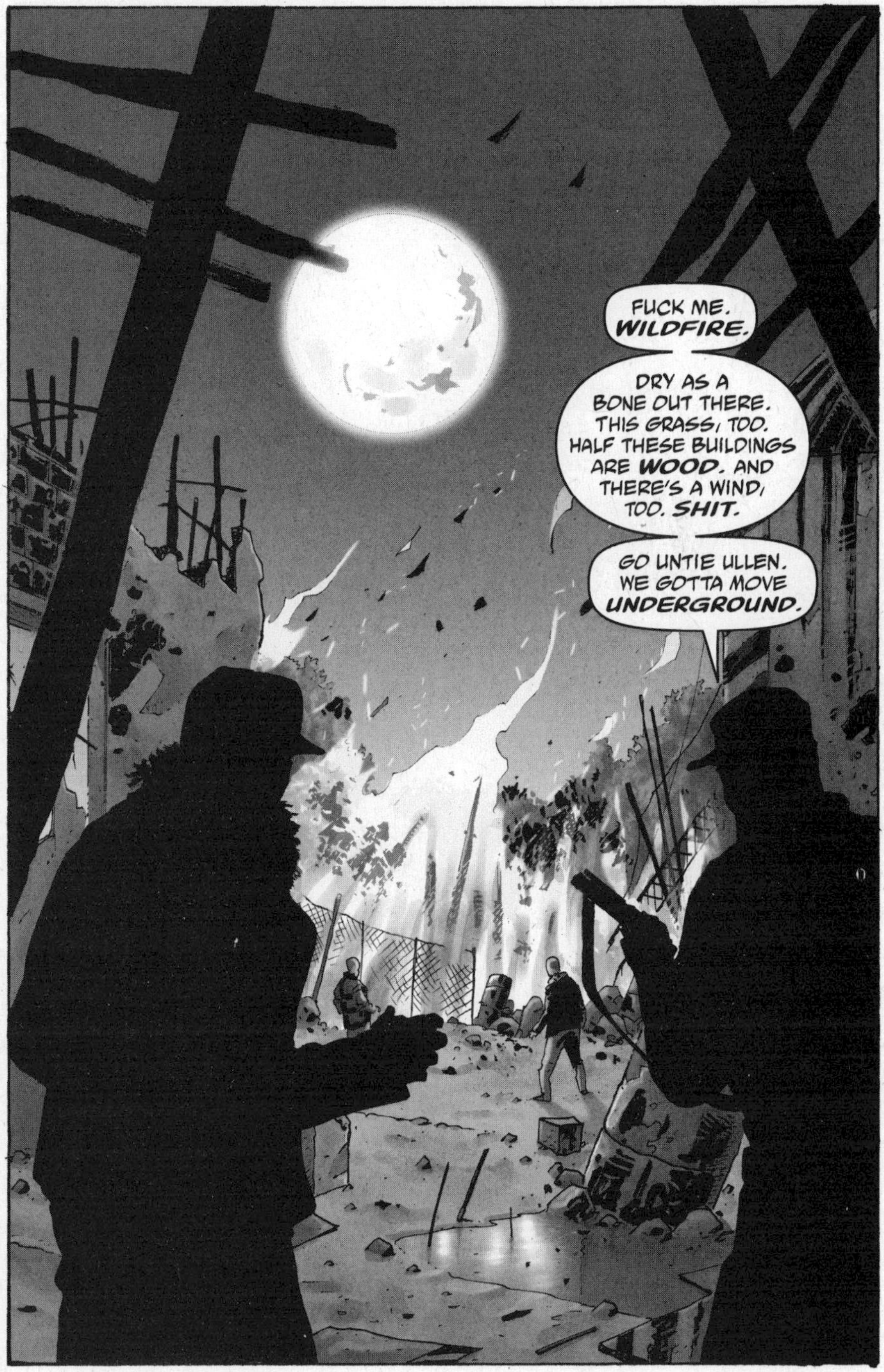
FUCK ME. WILDFIRE.
DRY AS A BONE OUT THERE. THIS GRASS, TOO. HALF THESE BUILDINGS ARE WOOD. AND THERE'S A WIND, TOO. SHIT.
GO UNTIE ULLEN. WE GOTTA MOVE UNDERGROUND.

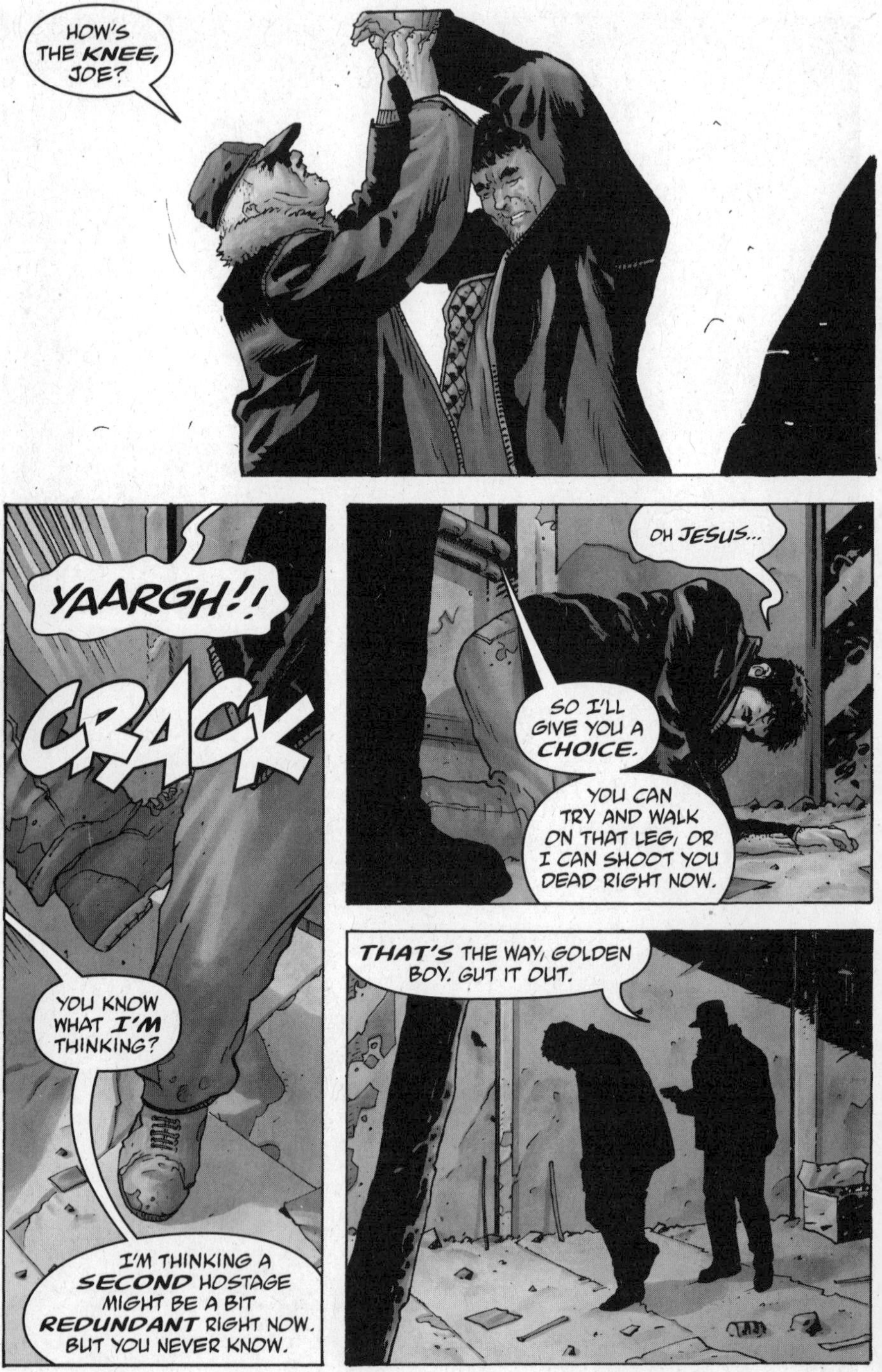
HOW'S THE KNEE, JOE?
YAARGH!!
CRACK
YOU KNOW WHAT I'M THINKING?
I'M THINKING A SECOND HOSTAGE MIGHT BE A BIT REDUNDANT RIGHT NOW. BUT YOU NEVER KNOW.
OH JESUS...
SO I'LL GIVE YOU A CHOICE.
YOU CAN TRY AND WALK ON THAT LEG, OR I CAN SHOOT YOU DEAD RIGHT NOW.
THAT'S THE WAY, GOLDEN BOY. GUT IT OUT.

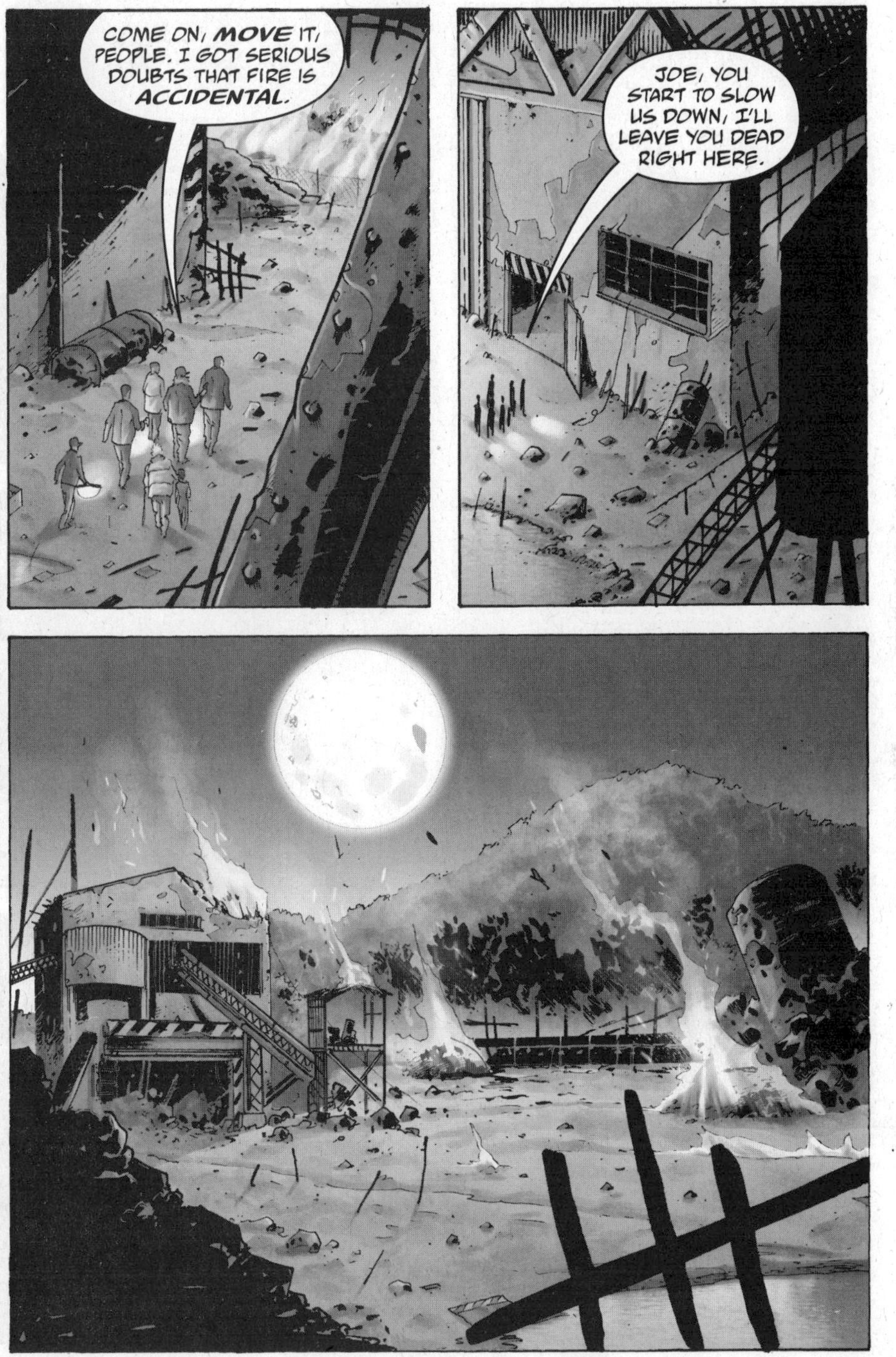
COME ON, **MOVE** IT, PEOPLE. I GOT SERIOUS DOUBTS THAT FIRE IS **ACCIDENTAL**.
JOE, YOU START TO SLOW US DOWN, I'LL LEAVE YOU DEAD RIGHT HERE.

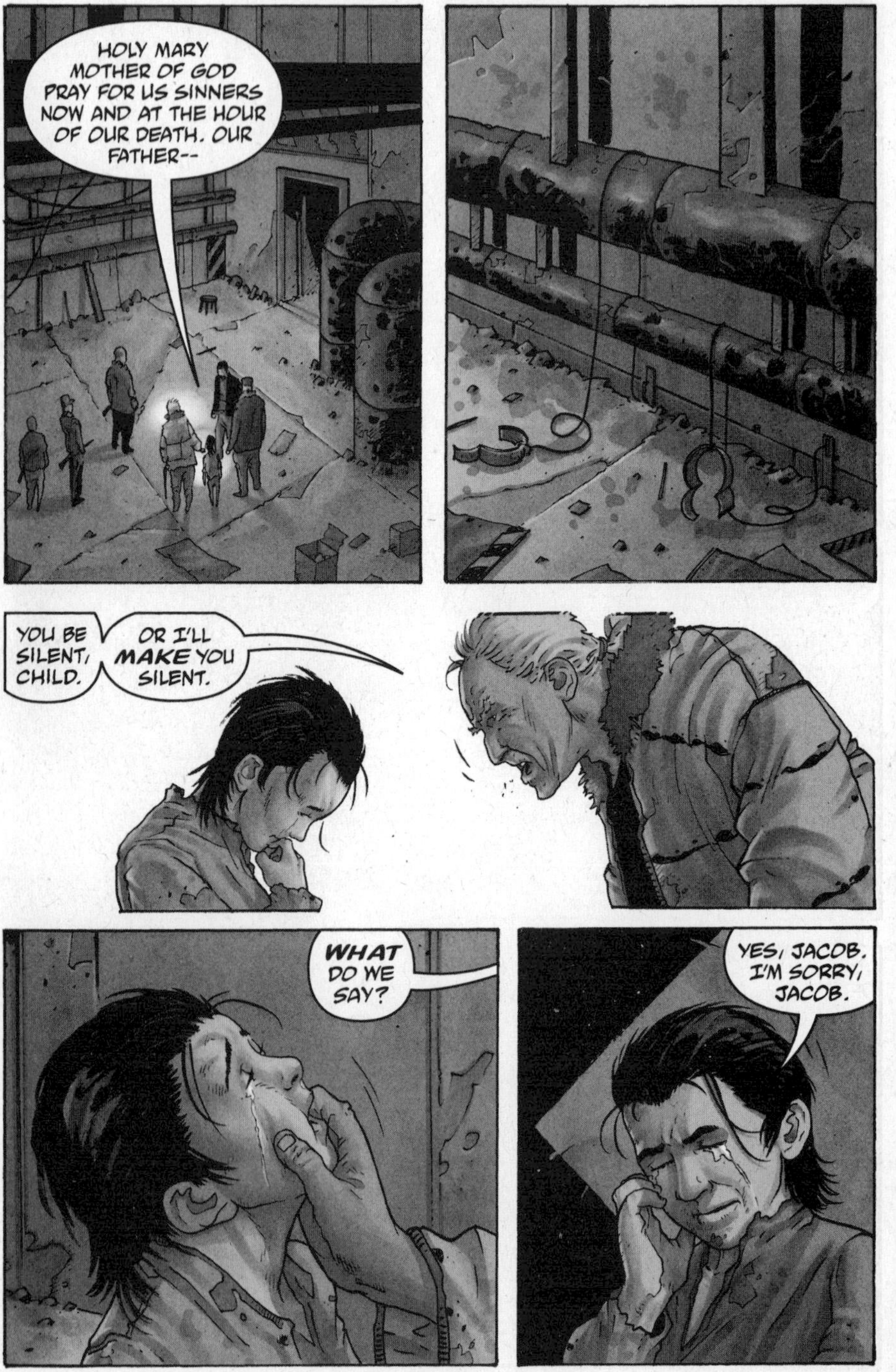
HOLY MARY MOTHER OF GOD PRAY FOR US SINNERS NOW AND AT THE HOUR OF OUR DEATH. OUR FATHER--
YOU BE SILENT, CHILD.
OR I'LL MAKE YOU SILENT.
WHAT DO WE SAY?
YES, JACOB. I'M SORRY, JACOB.

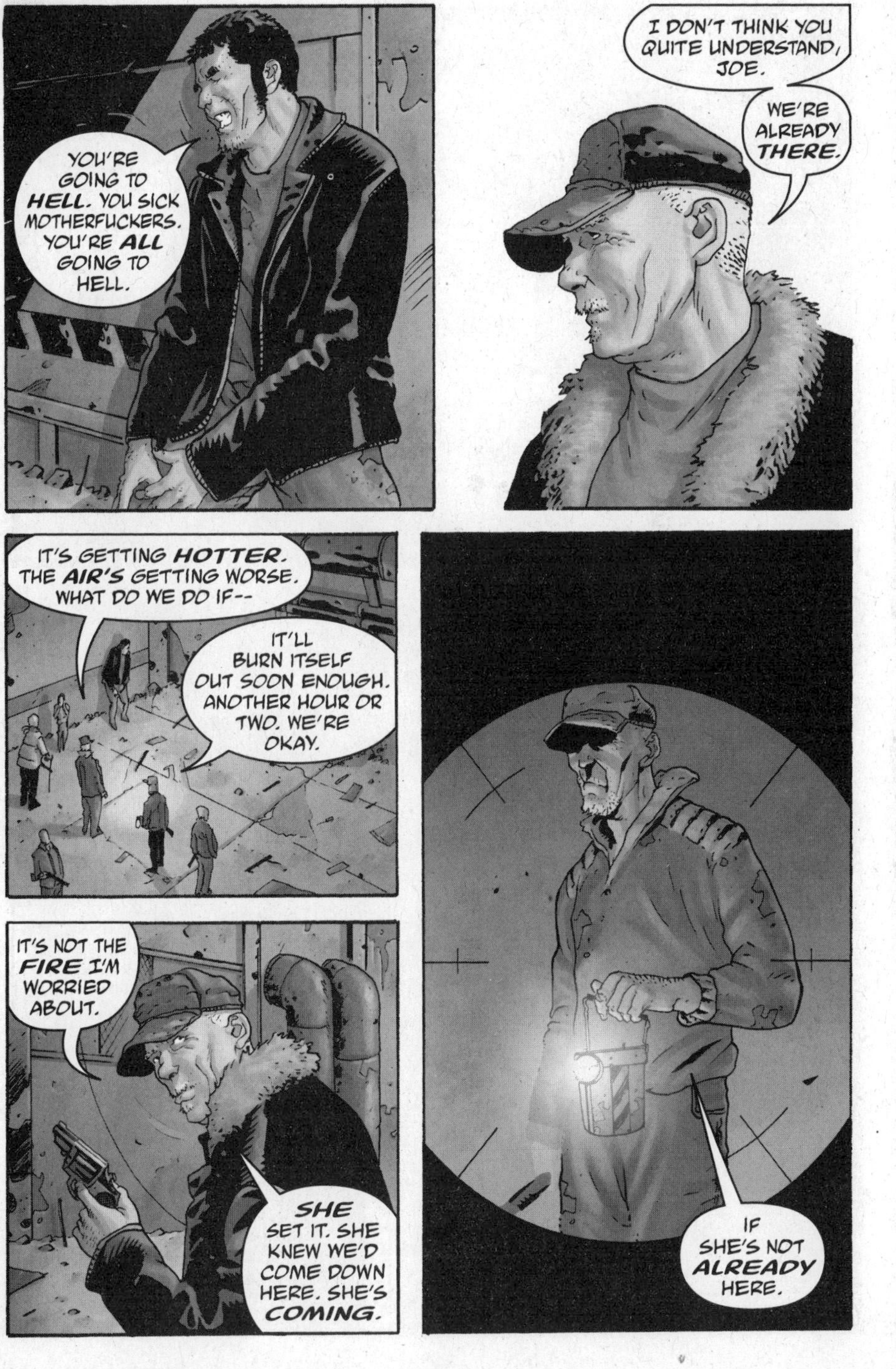
YOU'RE GOING TO HELL. YOU SICK MOTHERFUCKERS. YOU'RE ALL GOING TO HELL.
I DON'T THINK YOU QUITE UNDERSTAND, JOE.
WE'RE ALREADY THERE.
IT'S GETTING HOTTER. THE AIR'S GETTING WORSE. WHAT DO WE DO IF--
IT'LL BURN ITSELF OUT SOON ENOUGH. ANOTHER HOUR OR TWO. WE'RE OKAY.
IT'S NOT THE FIRE I'M WORRIED ABOUT.
SHE SET IT. SHE KNEW WE'D COME DOWN HERE. SHE'S COMING.
IF SHE'S NOT ALREADY HERE.

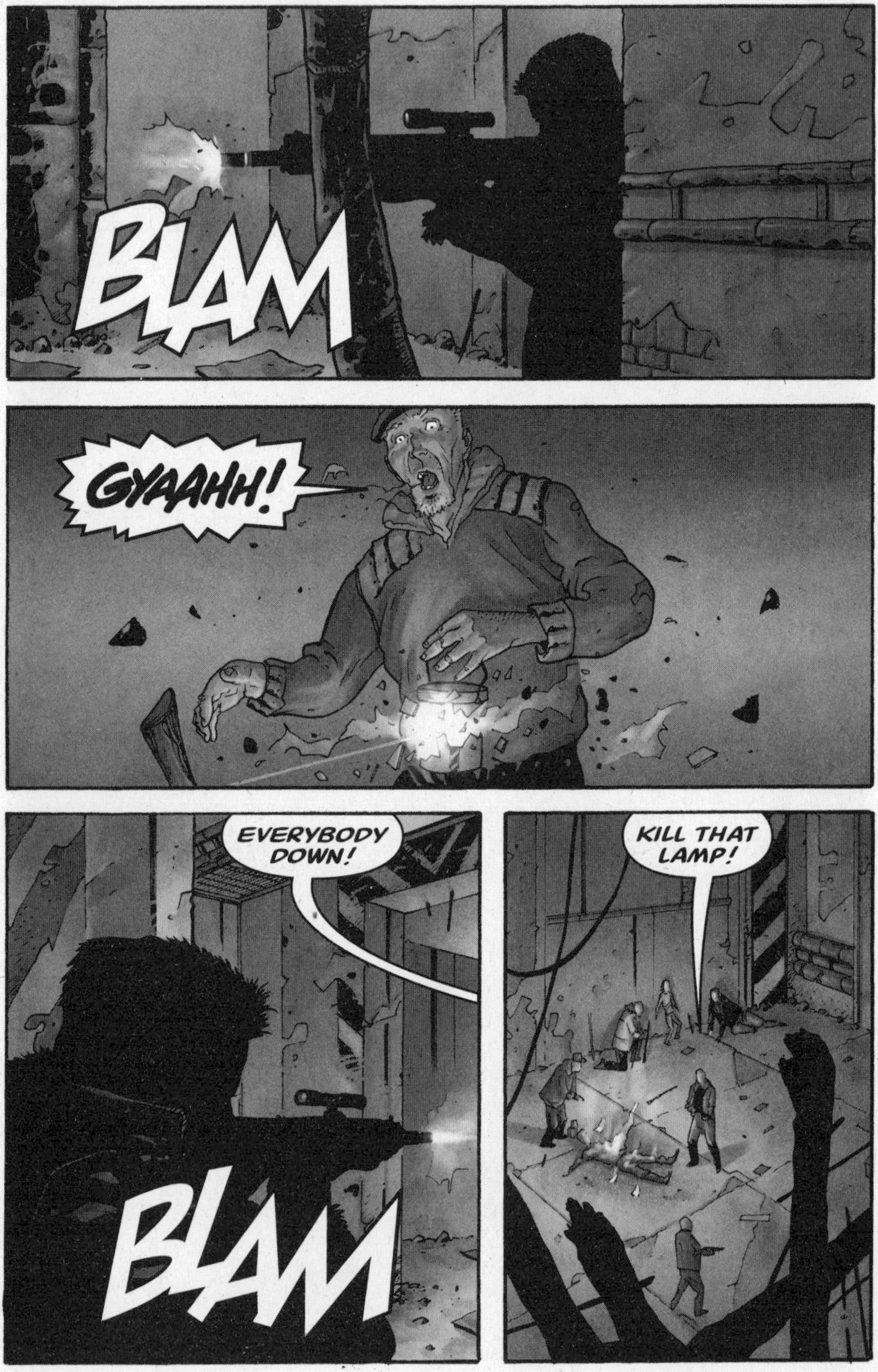
BLAM
GYAAHH!
EVERYBODY DOWN!
BLAM
KILL THAT LAMP!

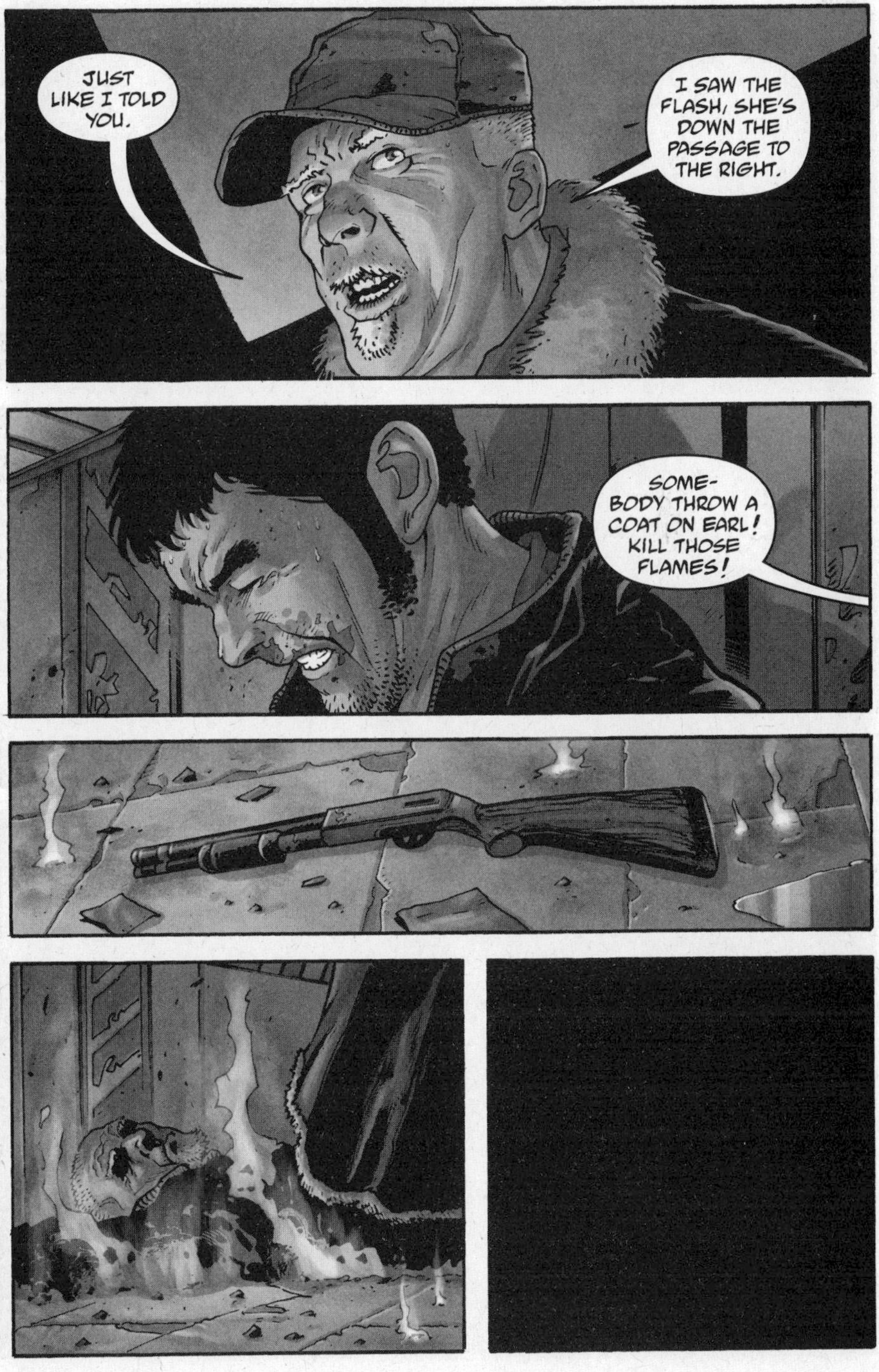
JUST LIKE I TOLD YOU.
I SAW THE FLASH, SHE'S DOWN THE PASSAGE TO THE RIGHT.
SOME-BODY THROW A COAT ON EARL! KILL THOSE FLAMES!

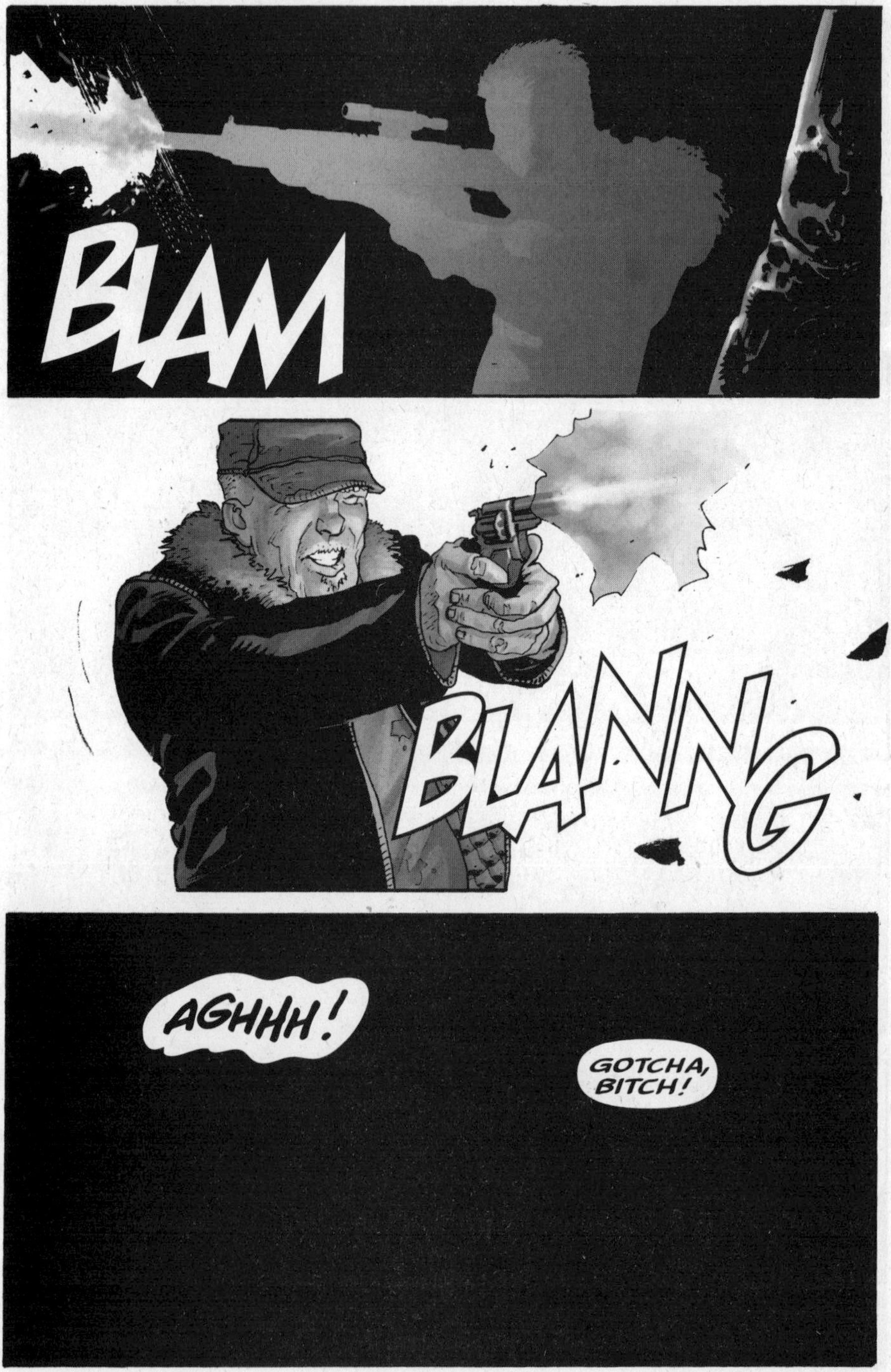
BLAM
BLANNG
AGHHH!
GOTCHA, BITCH!

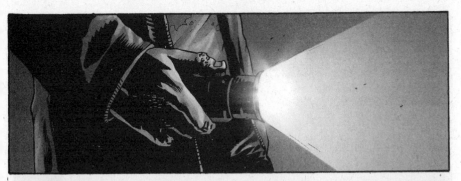

NICE TRY.

SWACK

SHE MIGHT JUST BE **WOUNDED.** DON'T GIVE HER LINE OF SIGHT.

SHE MIGHT--

EMERGENCY FIRE EXIT ONLY

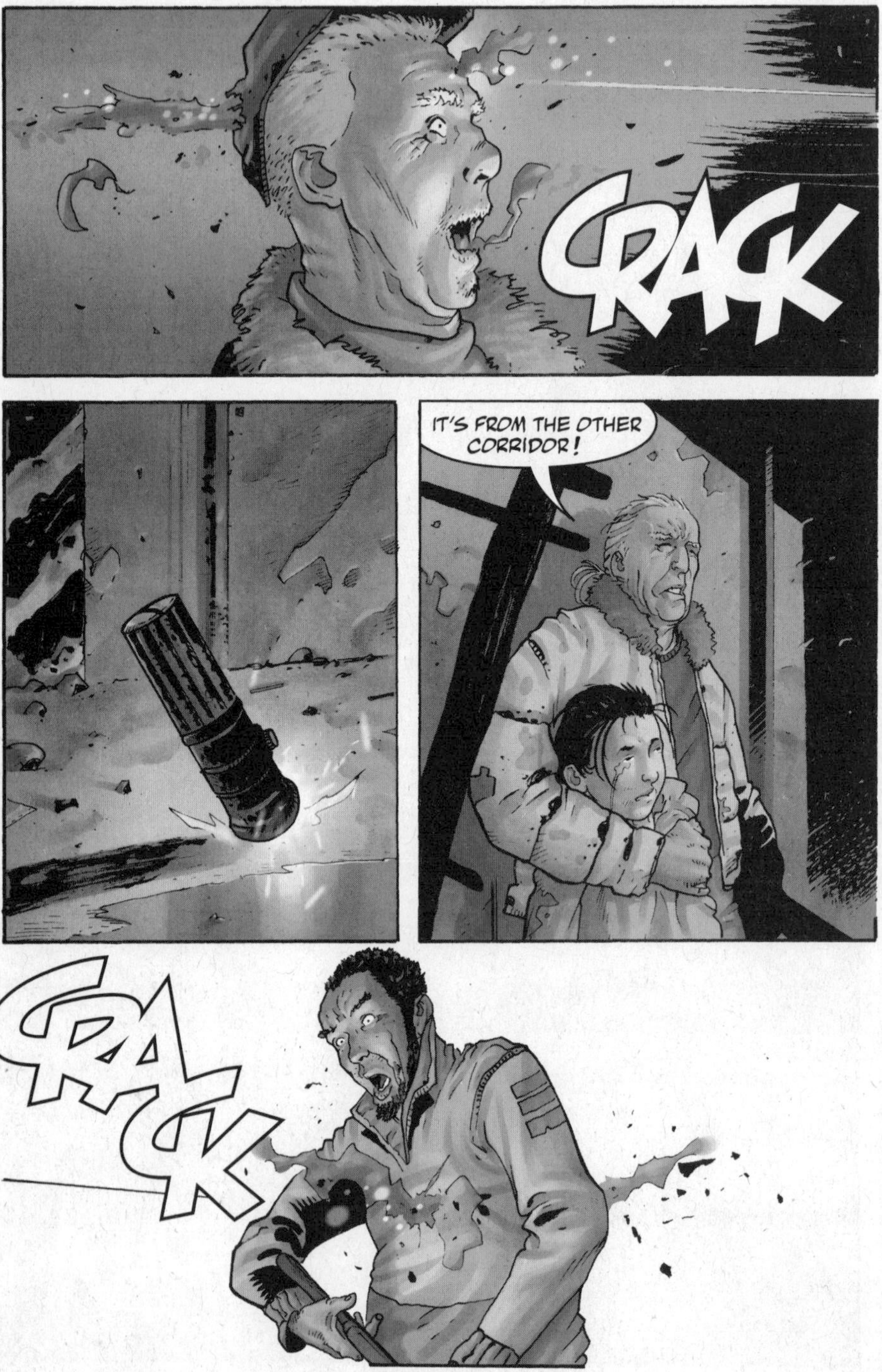
CRACK
IT'S FROM THE OTHER CORRIDOR!
CRACK

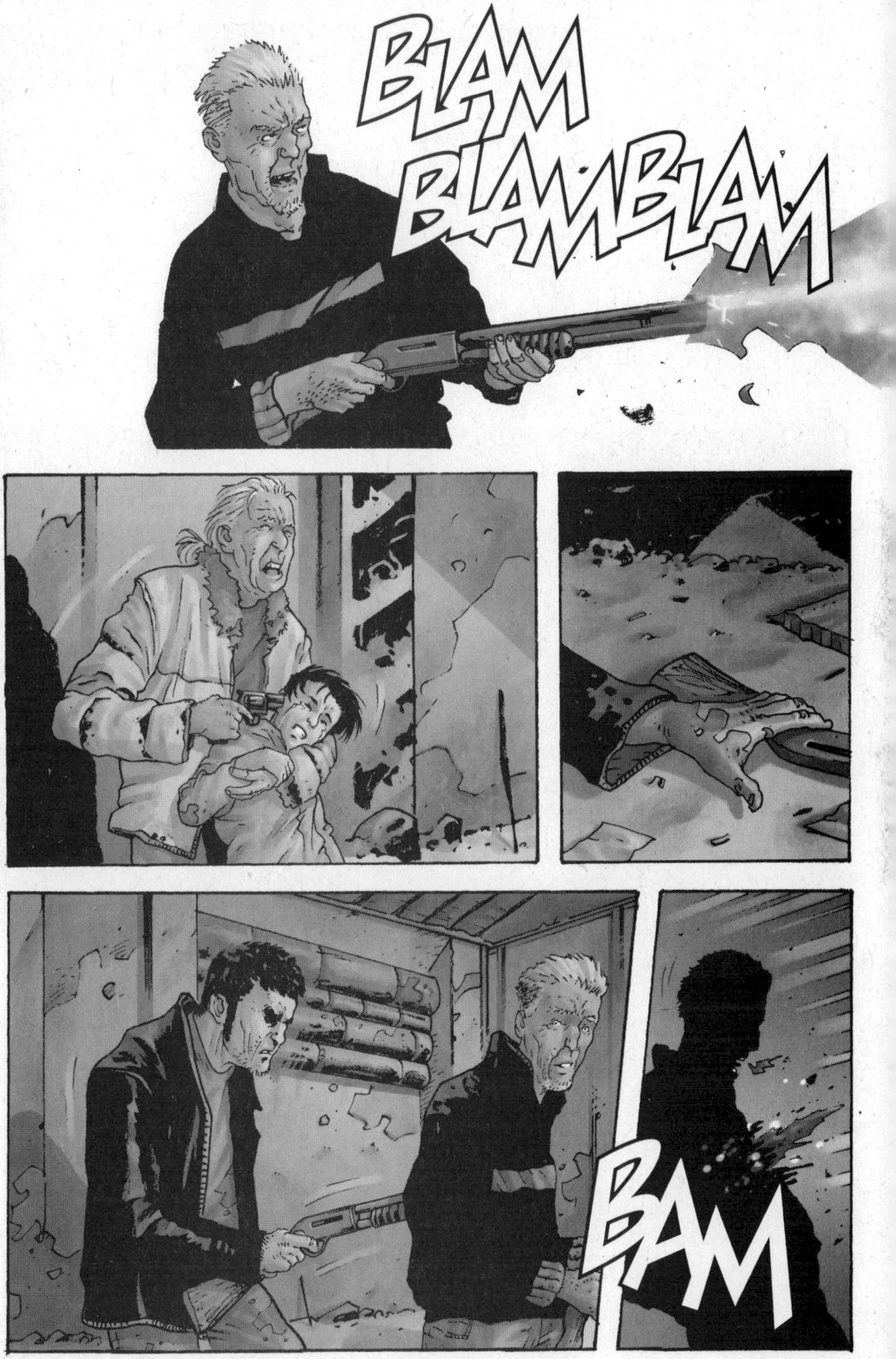
BLAM
BLAMBLAM
BAM

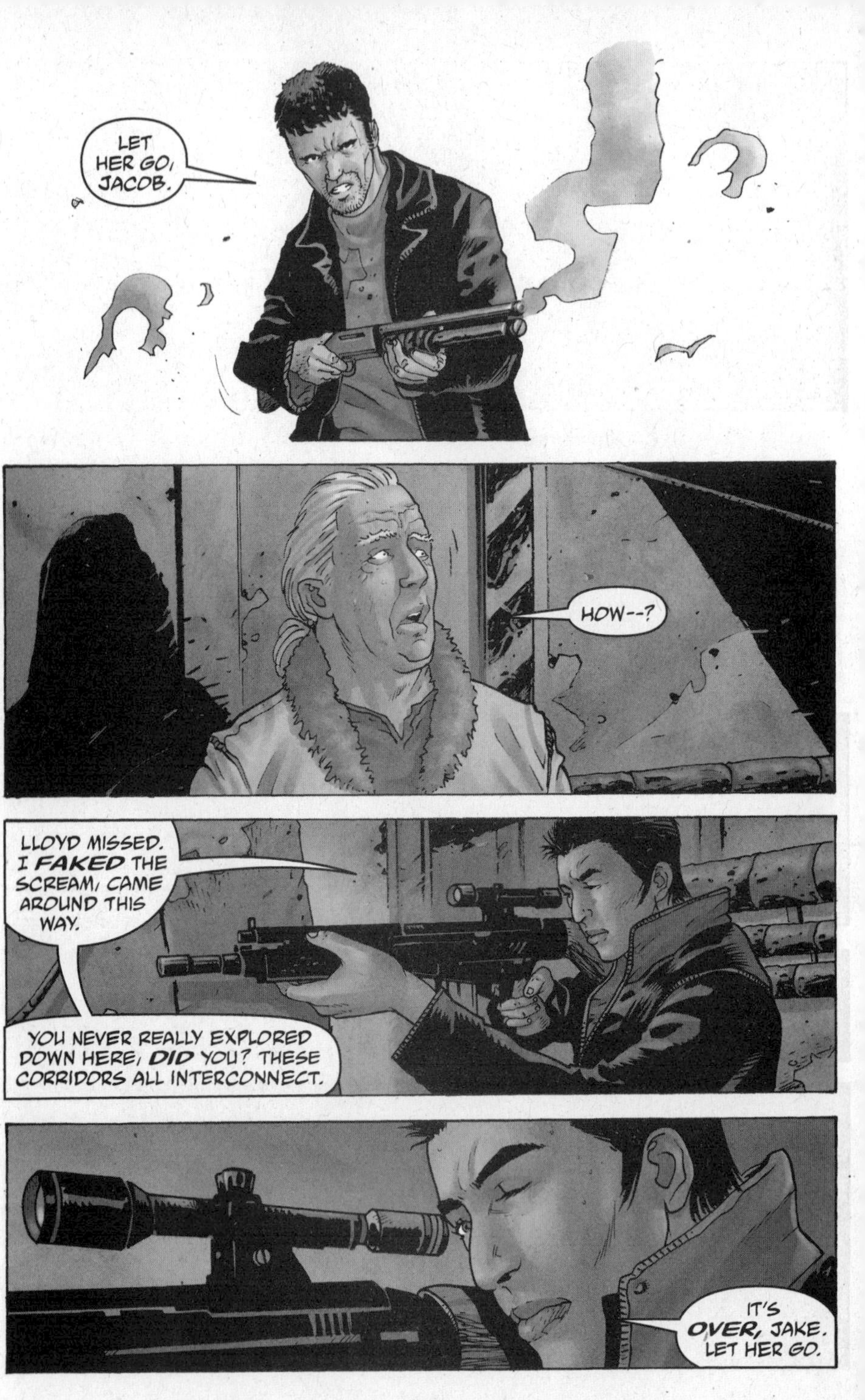
LET HER GO, JACOB.
HOW--?
LLOYD MISSED. I FAKED THE SCREAM, CAME AROUND THIS WAY.
YOU NEVER REALLY EXPLORED DOWN HERE, DID YOU? THESE CORRIDORS ALL INTERCONNECT.
IT'S OVER, JAKE. LET HER GO.

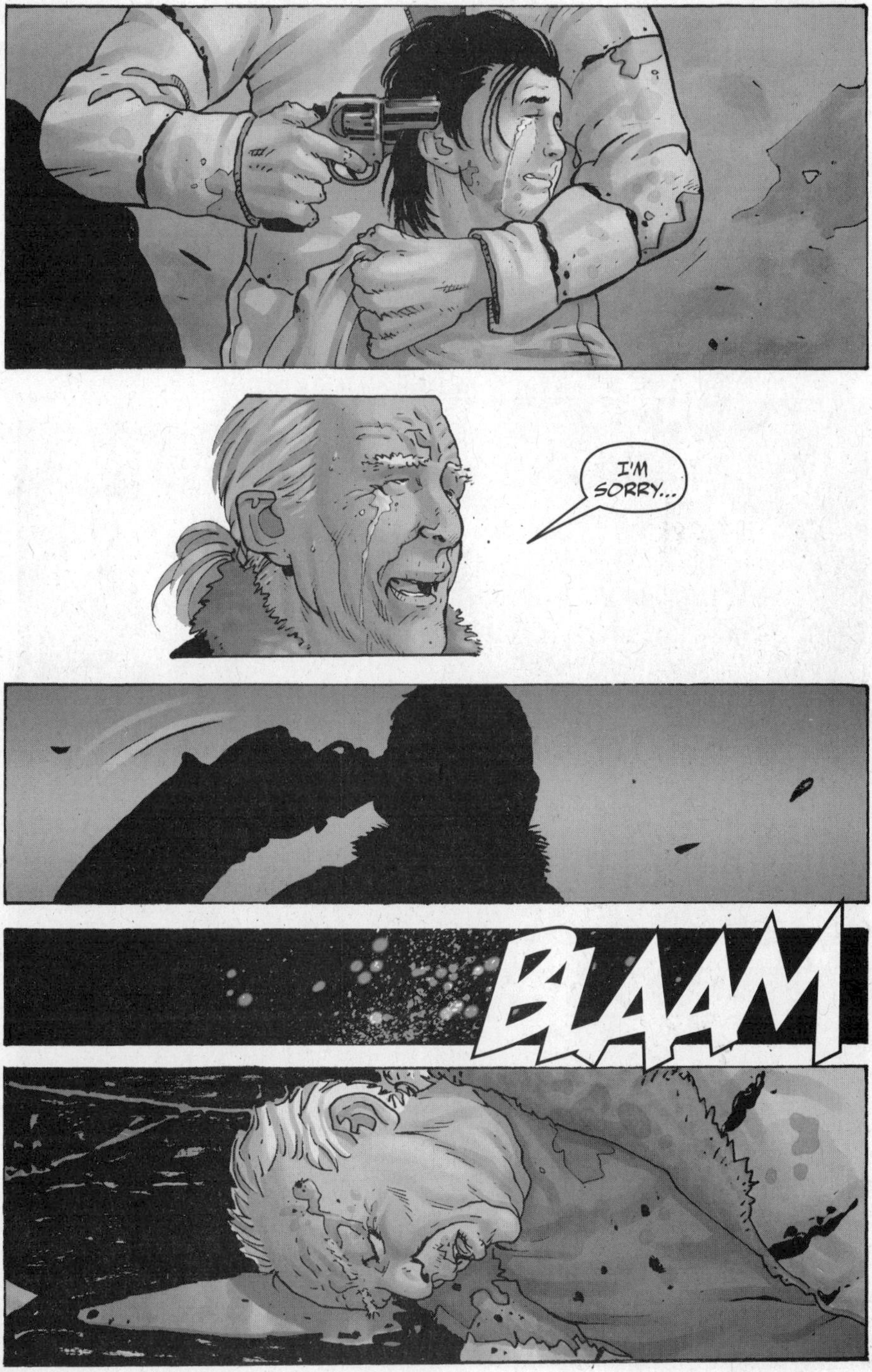
I'M SORRY...
BLAAM

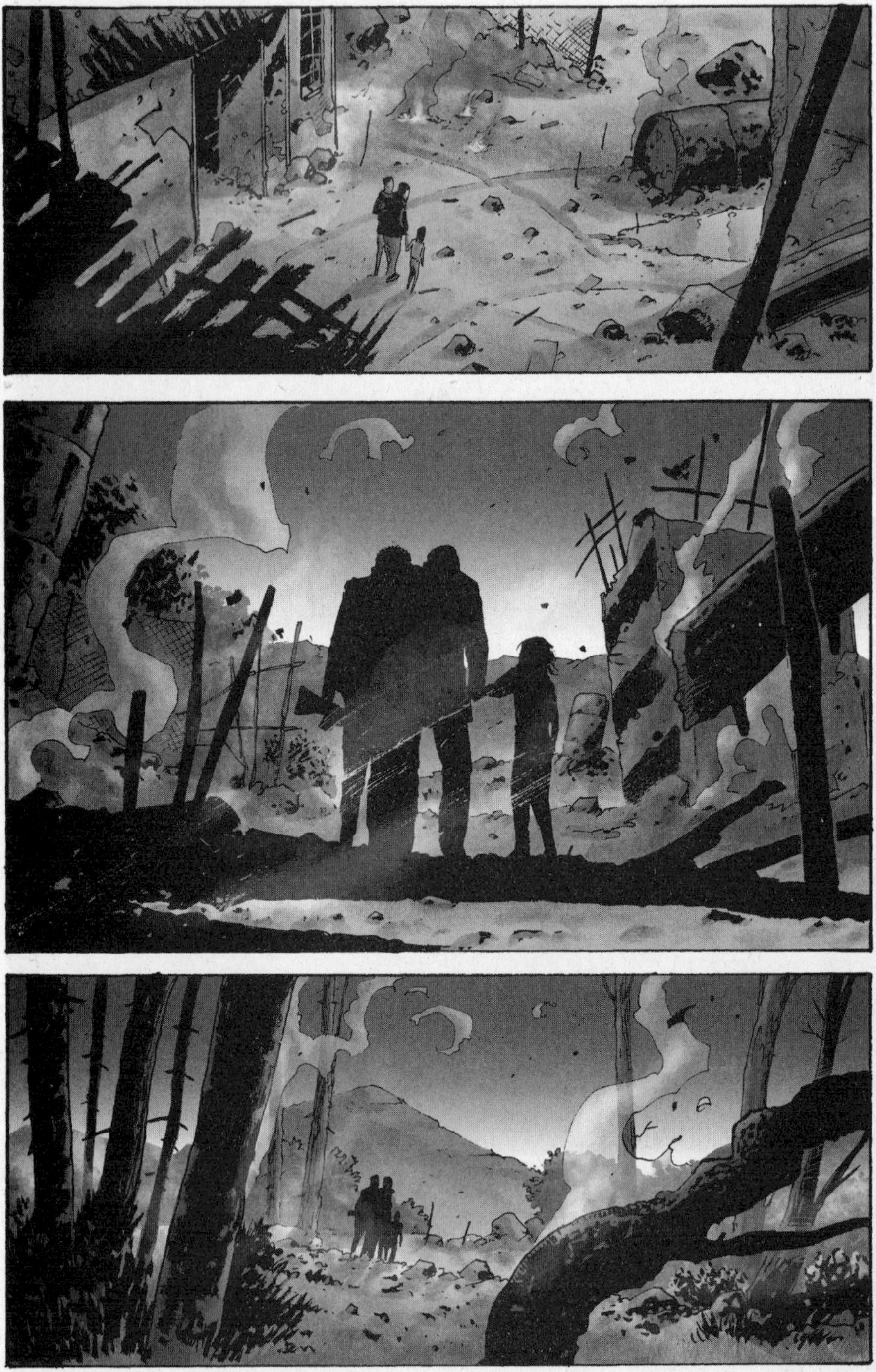

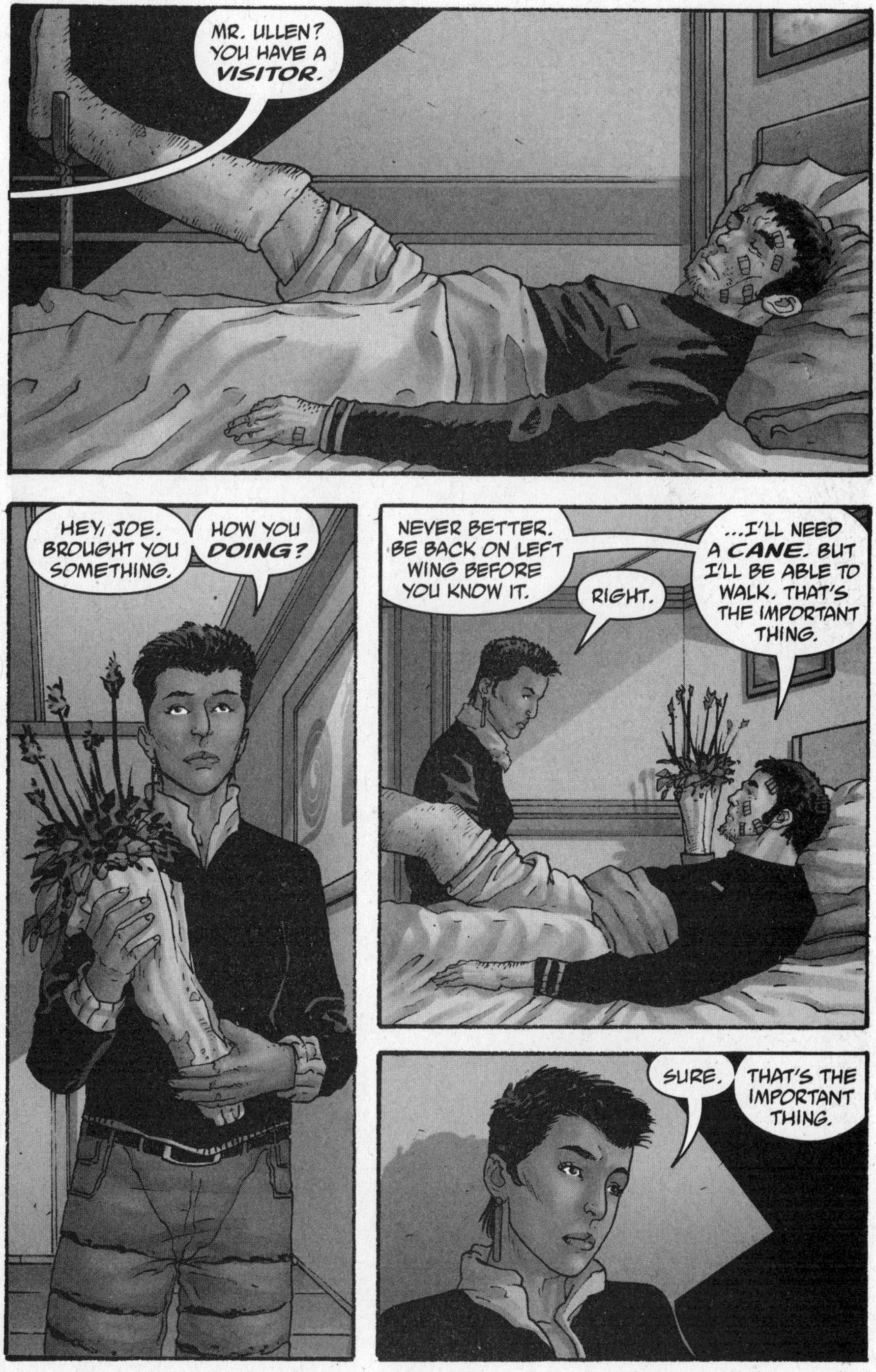
MR. ULLEN? YOU HAVE A VISITOR.
HEY, JOE. BROUGHT YOU SOMETHING.
HOW YOU DOING?
NEVER BETTER. BE BACK ON LEFT WING BEFORE YOU KNOW IT.
RIGHT.
...I'LL NEED A CANE. BUT I'LL BE ABLE TO WALK. THAT'S THE IMPORTANT THING.
SURE.
THAT'S THE IMPORTANT THING.

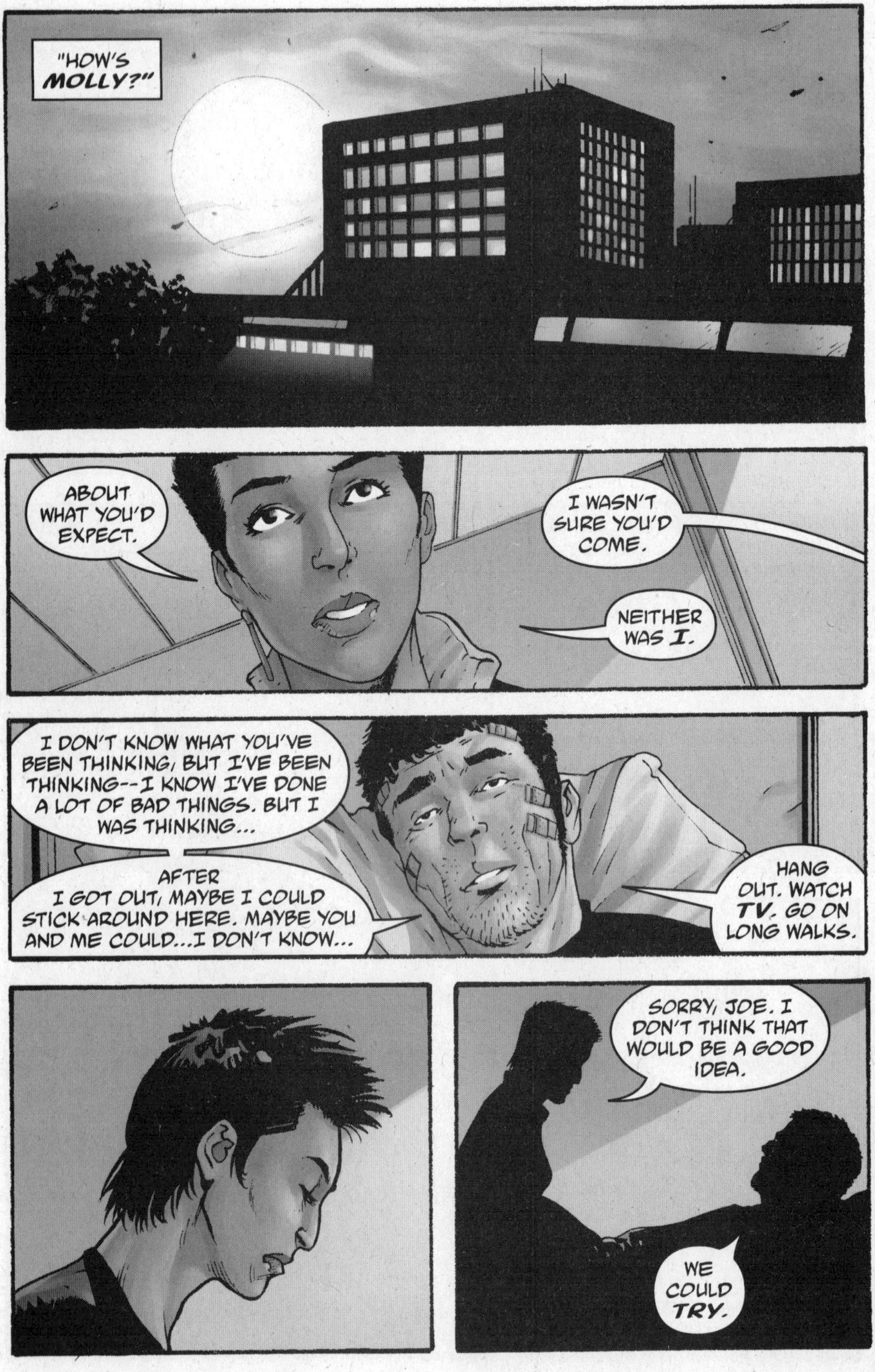
"HOW'S MOLLY?"
ABOUT WHAT YOU'D EXPECT.
I WASN'T SURE YOU'D COME.
NEITHER WAS I.
I DON'T KNOW WHAT YOU'VE BEEN THINKING, BUT I'VE BEEN THINKING--I KNOW I'VE DONE A LOT OF BAD THINGS. BUT I WAS THINKING...
AFTER I GOT OUT, MAYBE I COULD STICK AROUND HERE. MAYBE YOU AND ME COULD...I DON'T KNOW...
HANG OUT. WATCH TV. GO ON LONG WALKS.
SORRY, JOE. I DON'T THINK THAT WOULD BE A GOOD IDEA.
WE COULD TRY.

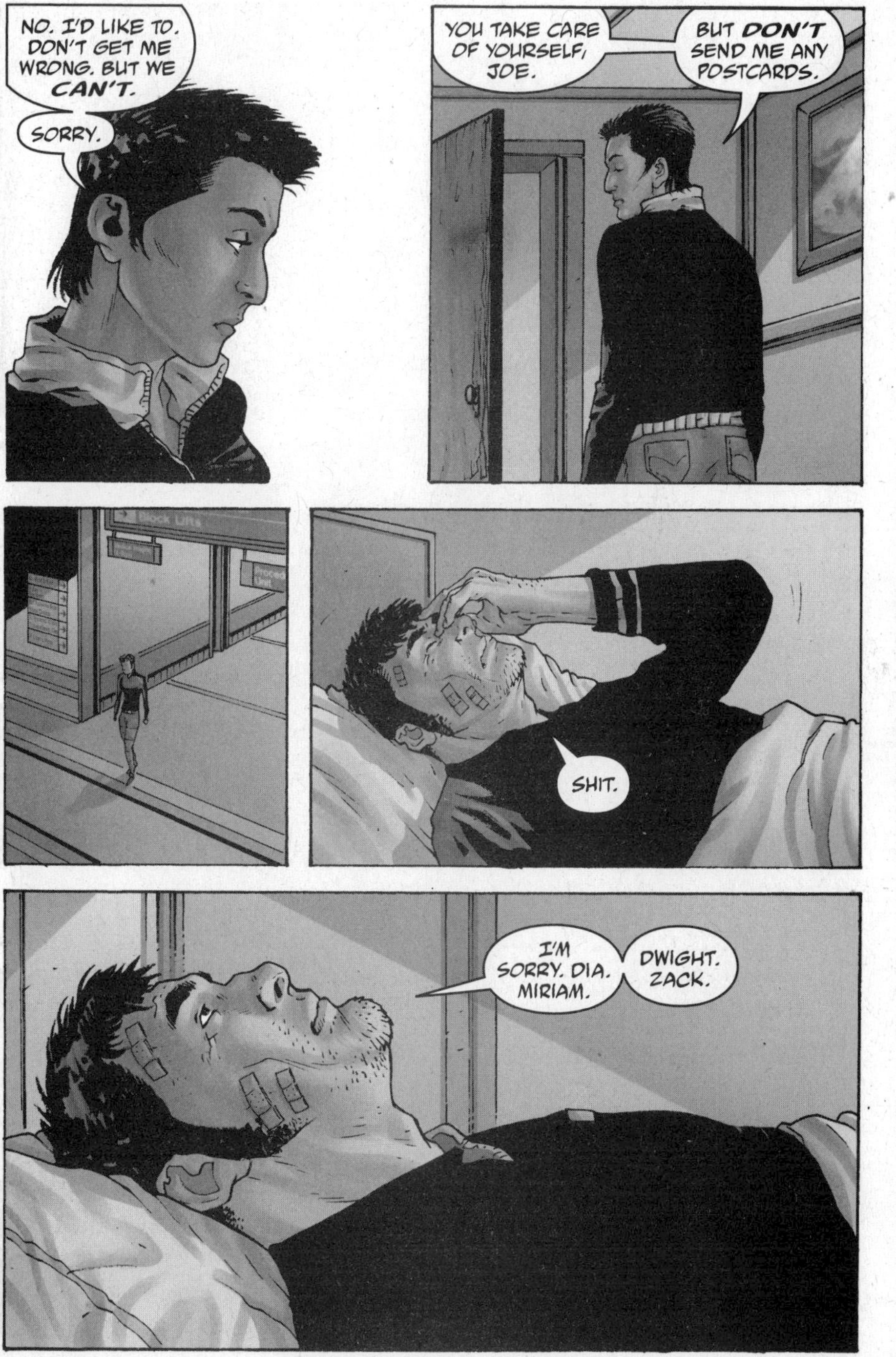
NO. I'D LIKE TO. DON'T GET ME WRONG. BUT WE CAN'T.
SORRY.
YOU TAKE CARE OF YOURSELF, JOE.
BUT DON'T SEND ME ANY POSTCARDS.
SHIT.
I'M SORRY. DIA. MIRIAM.
DWIGHT. ZACK.

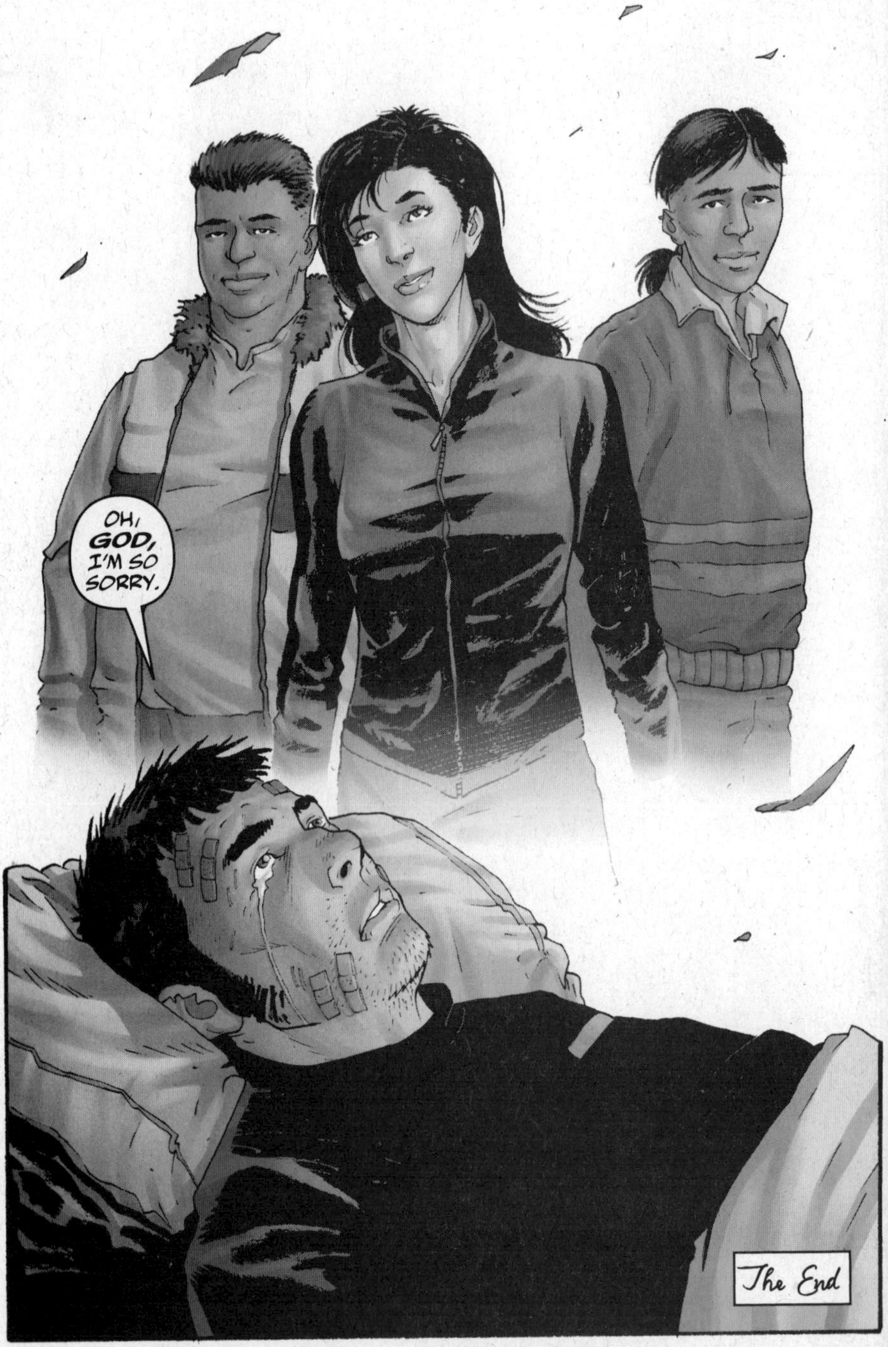
OH, GOD, I'M SO SORRY.
The End

MORE FROM VERTIGO CRIME

AVAILABLE NOW

THE CHILL

Written by **JASON STARR**
(Best-selling author of *Panic Attack* and *The Follower*)

Art by **MICK BERTILORENZI**

A modern thriller steeped in Celtic mythology –
a broken-down cop tracks a seductive killer who
possesses the supernatural power known as "the
chill." Can he stop her before her next victim
dies horribly... but with a smile on his face?

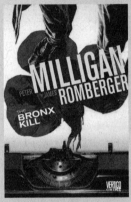

THE BRONX KILL

Written by **PETER MILLIGAN**
(GREEK STREET)

Art by **JAMES ROMBERGER**

A struggling writer is investigating his Irish cop
roots for his next novel. When he returns home
from a research trip, his wife is missing and finding
her will lead him to a dark secret buried deep in his
family's past.

AREA 10

Written by **CHRISTOS N. GAGE**
(*Law & Order: SVU*)

Art by **CHRIS SAMNEE**

When a detective – tracking a serial killer who
decapitates his victims – receives a bizarre head
injury himself, he suspects a connection between
his own fate and the killer's fascination with
Trepanation – the ancient art of skull drilling.

DON'T MISS THESE OTHER VERTIGO CRIME BOOKS

IAN RANKIN
#1 INTERNATIONALLY BEST-SELLING AUTHOR OF EXIT MUSIC
Art by WERTHER DELL'EDERA
DARK ENTRIES
A JOHN CONSTANTINE NOVEL
GRAPHIC MYSTERY

DARK ENTRIES

Occult detective John Constantine has seen his share of strange things in his career, but nothing could prepare him for the horrors of... reality television. "Haunted Mansion" is currently the hottest show on TV, but when the macabre house actually starts attacking the contestants, Constantine is hired to be the ultimate mole. Locked inside with a cast of wannabe-celebrities, his every move being monitored by a deadly figure from his past, Constantine must figure out who (or what) is pulling the strings before he gets cancelled – *permanently.*

Written by **Ian Rankin**, the Edgar-winning author of the "Inspector Rebus" series and the #1 international-bestselling author of *Exit Music.* Art by **Werther Dell'Edera.**

FILTHY RICH

Richard "Junk" Junkin has always lived on the wrong side of trouble... A former pro football star whose career was cut short by injury (and a nasty gambling problem), Junk now spends his time dreaming of what might have been, selling cars in Jersey and lusting after the boss's unbelievably spoiled, unbelievably sexy and unbelievably rich daughter, Victoria.

So when the boss asks him to be Victoria's personal bodyguard while she tears up the New York City club scene, Junk leaps at the chance. But before long, he finds that Victoria wants a lapdog and not a chaperone, someone who's going to do all of her dirty work – *all* of it – someone who wants to get filthy rich...

Written by **Brian Azzarello** – the multiple Eisner Award-winning writer of Vertigo's long-running crime series 100 BULLETS and *the New York Times* bestseller JOKER. Art by **Victor Santos.**

BRIAN AZZARELLO
NEW YORK TIMES BEST-SELLING AUTHOR OF JOKER
Art by VICTOR SANTOS
FILTHY RICH
GRAPHIC MYSTERY

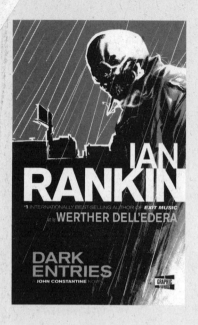

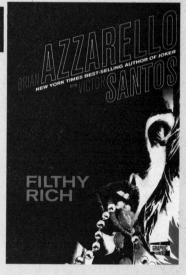